This very readable account of the founding of the College has been written by Eric Smith whose association with the College dates back to its origins in 1929. He was for many years Tutorial Fellow in History, Senior Tutor and Vice-Master, retiring in 1971. Even those not familiar with the College will find in his narrative an interest and excitement more usually associated with the novels of C. P. Snow and Anthony Trollope. The book is issued in celebration of the College's Jubilee in 1979.

ST. PETER'S
THE FOUNDING OF AN OXFORD COLLEGE

Christopher Chavasse when Master of St. Peter's
in the 1930s.

ST. PETER'S
THE FOUNDING OF AN
OXFORD COLLEGE

Eric H. F. Smith

with a foreword by

Sir Alec Cairncross
Master of St. Peter's College

COLIN SMYTHE
Gerrards Cross 1978

First published in 1978 for St. Peter's College,
Oxford, by Colin Smythe Ltd., Gerrards Cross,
Buckinghamshire

Distributed in N. America by Humanities Press Inc.,
171 First Avenue, Atlantic Highlands,
N.J. 07716, U.S.A.

British Library Cataloguing in Publication Data

Smith, Eric
St Peter's, the founding of an Oxford college.
1. St Peter's College – History.
I. Title   II. St Peter's College
378.425′74   LF741.S/

ISBN 0-901072-99-0

Printed in Great Britain
Set by Watford Typesetters Ltd. and
printed and bound by Billing & Sons Ltd.,
Guildford, Worcester and London

Contents

5

Contents

Contents

Foreword

This history of the founding of St. Peter's Hall, now St. Peter's College, has been written in retirement by Eric Smith whose association with St. Peter's dates from his appointment as a tutor in 1929 and who for many years was Tutorial Fellow in History, Senior Tutor and Vice-Master. The College is grateful to him for devoting himself to extracting from the record the remarkable story of its origins and putting it together in such a readable form. What appears here represents only the first part of his labours and is published now in celebration of the Jubilee of the College's foundation, chiefly for the benefit of present and past members. Many others, however, may find in it an interest and excitement more usually associated with the novels of C. P. Snow or Anthony Trollope.

St. Peter's started in the 1920s as a gleam in the eye of Bishop Francis James Chavasse, then in his eighties and back in Oxford after his successful efforts to launch a new cathedral in Liverpool. It was a project of the Evangelical movement in the Church of England and conceived as a kind of Low Church answer to Keble. That the project got any further, in the absence of financial support, was thanks to the energy and ingenuity of that company promoter *manqué*, the Rev. Percy Warrington. That it did not founder in the aftermath of the great slump that began in 1929, almost simultaneously with the establishment of the College, was thanks to the generosity of Lord Nuffield. Now, fifty years later, the College is firmly established on the model of other Oxford colleges, its ecclesiastical origins have been absorbed into wider traditions and there has been no recurrence of the financial crises of earlier days.

To the lay reader the drama of the story told here lies in the contest almost from the foundation of the College between the dominant figure of Christopher Chavasse, its first Master, and Percy Warrington, its financial backer. The contest between them was also between different wings of the evangelical movement, with the liberal wing in the saddle, but dependent on the fundamentalist wing for financial support. The religious differ-

9

ences and personal antipathies which came to the surface in the
deteriorating economic climate of the 1930s brought the college
near to disaster.

Viewed from this angle, the story of the founding of St. Peter's
Hall (as the College was called until it received its Charter in
1961) can be regarded as an episode in church history. It is for
this reason that space is given to matters such as the dispute over
advowsons that might be thought somewhat tangential to the
development of the Hall. But the episode was one that led on to
the rise of a new Oxford college, quite unlike anything envisaged
by the founders of the Hall, and so to a different story which it is
not the purpose of this volume to recount.

Since my own background and interest is in economics and
finance I was naturally anxious to establish how the money was
found for the building of the College. It is impossible to give any
precise answer and Eric Smith wisely avoids any attempt to do
so. Even Price Waterhouse had to give up trying to unravel the
early financial operations of Percy Warrington. As Chavasse
wrote to Lord Gisborough: 'we all know that if we studied the
balance-sheet for a hundred years we do not possess even the
material for checking (it)'. Nevertheless I have tried to make
some rough guesses at the total cost of floating the College and
the source of the funds provided. These are given below for the
benefit of those familiar with the College and interested like
myself in where the money goes. It is important to recall that
unlike more recent foundations St. Peter's started totally without
funds and enjoyed no large initial benefaction.

The Rowcroft Building (Staircases I-III) was completed in
October 1929 and cost £30,000. The Emily Morris Building
(Staircase IV) was completed a year later and cost £15,000. The
furnishing of these buildings cost a further £25,000 or so. This
gives a total of £70,000. At that stage the St. Peter's Hall Appeal
had raised not much more than £20,000, while Warrington had
borrowed £70,000 against annual payments of £7,000. Three years
later the Appeal had brought in another £10,000 but a further
£20,000 had been spent on the old Wesleyan Chapel (since
demolished), and the conversion of the building to make what
was then known as Staircase V. Hannington Hall and Linton
House were acquired for a little over £10,000, but must have
cost a good deal more to convert and furnish. There was also an
outlay of over £6,000 on St. Aldate's school as a *quid pro quo*
when the St. Peter le Bailey Schools were handed over to the
Hall. Thus the total capital cost of the entire project as it stood

in the mid-thirties was well in excess of £100,000 and probably rather more than £150,000. At the prices of fifty years later this represents about £1½m.

Where did the money come from? Interestingly enough, most of the money was raised in Appeals. By the outbreak of war these had brought in just under £100,000. Of this total Nuffield contributed £10,000 in 1934 and £12,000 in 1935, apart from anything he may have contributed earlier and apart altogether from the £50,000 which made such a decisive difference in 1936. Broadly speaking, therefore, Nuffield gave half and other donors gave the other half of what was needed to meet the capital cost of the Hall. But it was borrowed money, not donations, that allowed the project to be carried through in the first place.

Since the book deals with the founding of a college, not its subsequent history, there is little in it about the academic side of things. Undergraduates hardly appear at all in the story and even the teaching staff is kept well in the background. But those who know the college now or were members then will have no reason to complain that the focus on origins makes the narrative less engrossing. Others who are unfamiliar with the College will still enjoy an unusually dramatic case-study in the establishment of a new institution.

May 1978   ALEC CAIRNCROSS

1

On St. Peter's Day, 29 June 1932, in the early afternoon, memorials to Bishop Francis James Chavasse as Founder of St. Peter's Hall were unveiled by the Vice-Chancellor, Dr. F. Homes-Dudden of Pembroke, and dedicated by Dr. M. Linton-Smith, Bishop of Rochester, in the parish church of St. Peter-le-Bailey, Oxford. Before lunch that day the annual meeting of the Council of St. Peter's Hall had been held. At that meeting one of the Trustees of the Hall, Canon Henry Foster Pegg, had asked whether Bishop F. J. Chavasse was rightly described as Founder. It had thereupon been agreed by the Council that from the evidence of the Trust Deed itself Bishop Chavasse had been regarded as the 'Founder' of the Hall from its very inception, and Canon Foster Pegg had then no more to say.[1]

The question remains, how could a Trustee of the Hall in 1932 have been in doubt on this matter? An answer may be found by comparing two early accounts of the foundation. One is contained in the 'First Annual Report' presented to the Council by the Revd. C. M. Chavasse, and printed and circulated by authority of the Council under the cover-heading 'First Annual Report of St. Peter's House, Oxford, 1928-9'. It begins:

MY LORDS AND GENTLEMEN,

In presenting the first Annual Report of St. Peter's Hall (as we hope to call it in a few months) I would ask your leave to go back to the first conception of the project, and so place on record an authoritative history of its birth and infancy.

The Founder

It was at the Islington Conference, 18th January 1926, that Bishop Chavasse first gave public utterance to the great scheme which had gradually formed in his mind. On his retirement from Liverpool, he had settled down in his old Oxford haunts in New Inn Hall Street, and as he moved among the gardens and buildings of St. Peter-le-Bailey his sagacious eye perceived

13

how they might be rescued from their obscurity and transformed into a rich opportunity. His own words on that occasion will best describe the position as he saw it: 'In the centre of Oxford the Evangelicals hold a strategic site. The substantial stone church of St. Peter-le-Bailey, holding 500 people and built fifty-one years ago, has a parish of only 380, which is likely to grow still smaller. At present the benefice is held in plurality with the neighbouring parish of St. Ebbe. The arrangement has been a failure and ends in July. On one side the church is flanked by a good rectory house and pleasant garden, on the other by Hannington Hall, also an Evangelical trust, with a school that is no longer needed and playgrounds behind it. Here is the nucleus of a new college – with chapel, lecture room, dining hall, library, warden's house and £180 a year endowment, ready at hand, and space to erect buildings for thirty or forty men, and additional ground attainable if needed. At present the church and its surroundings are not fulfilling their mission in the City or University. If they are not put to a better use they will be pulled down and removed to another part of Oxford, or be diverted to some other purpose. Are we to let them go and lose a great opportunity? If some rich man or woman, moved by the Spirit of God, would give £50,000 or £100,000 in memory of the dead, or as a thanksgiving for the living, not only might the site be utilized for a college, but an endowment fund for a number of bursaries might be founded for ordination candidates which would reduce the yearly cost to £80.'

The Trustees

The Bishop immediately received £2,000 from three donors who desired to bring his vision into the range of practical politics. But the real response came from the 'Church of England Trust Society'. Canon Stather Hunt, the well-known Founder and Chairman of the Trust, had been informed by Bishop Knox of Bishop Chavasse's project, and immediately took up the matter with his customary enthusiasm – proving a tower of strength especially in the difficult and critical stage of the scheme's inception. The Rev. P. E. Warrington, also, a man of foresight, energy, and outstanding business capacity, vicar of Monkton Combe, Bath, Honorary Secretary and Member of the Trust, who had come very prominently before the public in connection with the remarkable success of the public schools he had founded, heard the Bishop's speech and

grasped its full significance. He had lately received a benefaction of £10,000 for the purpose of founding an Evangelical
College from Mrs. Rowcroft of Torquay, whose well-known
interest in all good works is only exceeded by her generosity.
Both gentlemen therefore waited upon Bishop Chavasse, and
then summoned their fellow trustees to meet in Oxford. The
result was that this influential Trust, with its great educational
interests, decided to stand behind the Bishop's scheme. The next
year was therefore spent in negotiating for the transfer to them
of the advowson of St. Peter-le-Bailey and of the site and
buildings surrounding the Church, including Hannington Hall;
and in the preparation of a trust deed. . . .

Then on the death of Mrs. Chavasse in July 1927, the Bishop
himself was struck down with a mortal sickness; and the enterprise which his insight and influence had inspired became his
memorial upon his death on 11th March 1928. The Trustees
had already appointed me, his son, as the first Master of the
proposed Hall. . . . On my father's death I was authorized by
the Trustees to go forward with all speed. . . . The necessary
funds were guaranteed, plans for new buildings were prepared,
and negotiations were pressed forward for the purchase of the
adjoining property to the north owned by the Wesleyan
Church. . . . The outlay thus necessitated is considerable. In all
the Trustees have pledged themselves to an expenditure of
£60,000. . . . It is a wonderful achievement, upon which both
the Trustees and the Council can congratulate themselves. But
we would all pay our tribute of admiration and gratitude to the
moving spirit, Mr. Warrington, who refused to be satisfied with
anything less than the best, who has been unwearied in overcoming difficulties and speeding the work, and who with the
highest courage has personally shouldered great responsibilities
when decisions had to be made or sudden crises threatened
the enterprise.

So much from the First Annual Report. It was presented on
St. Peter's Day, 1929, and it was clearly in the hands of the
author of a special 4-page supplement to an Evangelical newspaper, *The Record*, dated 13 December 1929. This supplement
was headed – A NEW OXFORD MOVEMENT. ST. PETER'S
HALL. A WONDERFUL BEGINNING. It gives an account
of the founding of St. Peter's which is substantially the same as
that given in the First Report, but it lays even greater emphasis
on the part played by 'the Rev. P. E. Warrington, Vicar of

Monkton Combe, Bath, Founder of Stowe and other Schools'. It mentions that when he heard Bishop Chavasse's speech at the 1926 Islington Conference it was the first and only time that he attended that Conference. 'Mr. Warrington is a man of indomitable energy, true foresight, remarkable business capacity, and wonderful organising powers. He heard the Bishop's address, and at once grasped its significance and the enormous possibilities involved. The next day he wrote to Bishop Chavasse and suggested that his Trust [sic] might render substantial assistance in launching the scheme. Some months passed by before anything was done. Then Mr. Warrington received unexpectedly a benefaction of £10,000 for the purpose of founding an Evangelical College from Mrs. Rowcroft of Torquay. He saw that a golden opportunity had presented itself to begin the carrying out of the plans outlined by Dr. Chavasse. In conjunction with Canon Stather Hunt . . . Chairman of the Martyrs Memorial and Church of England Trust, who had also been informed by Bishop Knox of the project, the great scheme was taken up with enthusiasm. Both the Canon and Mr. Warrington waited upon Bishop Chavasse, and then summoned their fellow Trustees to meet in Oxford. That meeting with the aged Bishop proved to be memorable and historic in the annals of Evangelicalism. The result was that this influential Trust . . . decided to stand behind, and subsequently to 'Father' the Bishop's scheme. The greater part of the detail work has fallen upon the Rev. C. M. Chavasse, but, as he has himself acknowledged, the moving spirit behind the whole Scheme, inspiring it, and helping it forward by his wide experience and great enthusiasm, has been the Rev. P. E. Warrington, who refused to be satisfied with anything but the best, who has been unwearied in overcoming difficulties and speeding the work, and who has, with the highest courage, personally shouldered great financial responsibilities when great decisions had to be made or sudden crises threatened the enterprise.' The supplement ended with an appeal for £16,000, urgently needed for a new block of rooms: subscriptions to be sent to the Rev. P. E. Warrington or to the editor of *The Record*.

Two days after the publication of the *Record* supplement, Canon Stather Hunt died. His successor as a Trustee of St. Peter's was Canon Henry Foster Pegg, another member of the Church of England Trust. It is not surprising that he regarded this Trust, rather than Bishop Chavasse, as the real founder of St. Peter's Hall; especially since at the first Council meeting which Canon Foster Pegg was entitled to attend, in June 1930,

16

C. M. Chavasse in his Second Annual Report included these words:

> Though no one can fully know what the death of Canon Stather Hunt must mean to the Revd. P. E. Warrington, the Hon. Secretary of the Trust Society, thus deprived of the wise counsel and unfailing inspiration of his chairman – the Council of St. Peter's will realise that it has thrown upon him a double burden of work and responsibility which would have crushed another man, and they would testify that in this (which is but one undertaking out of many) they cannot adequately express what the Hall owes to him, and to him alone, in the critical months of the past year . . . throughout these fateful decisions Mr. Warrington has been the moving spirit.

Nevertheless, Bishop F. J. Chavasse has continued to be held in honour as Founder, and the name of Percy Warrington has found no memorial in St. Peter's. When he died, in November 1961, *The Times* printed a short obituary notice, mentioning that he had been Vicar of Monkton Combe ever since 1918 and that he had played an important part in the founding of some well-known schools, but not a word was said of his connection with St. Peter's.

To understand how this happened, it is necessary to take a wider view: and first, to go back long before Bishop F. J. Chavasse returned to Oxford from Liverpool; in fact, to go back to 1870, the year in which he was first ordained. He had spent the previous four years as an undergraduate at Corpus, where his special friends had been E. A. Knox and W. Lock, both of whom were to play a part in the story of St. Peter's. During those years he had become associated with Canon Christopher, Rector of St. Aldates, and Canon Henry Linton, Rector of St. Peter-le-Bailey, then the most active of the Evangelical clergy in Oxford, and it was to a son-in-law of Linton, the Revd. W. M. Myres, Vicar of St. Paul's, Preston, that he went as a curate early in 1870.

In that same year Keble College was opened. A later Warden of Keble has written[2]: 'It was widely felt that in nineteenth century Oxford there was a need for a new college which would make all the academical and other privileges of Oxford life accessible to men of limited means and also maintain the traditional association of university education with the Church of England.' Funds were raised by a public appeal; a royal charter was granted, and in 1871 the University of Oxford recognized the College as a 'New Foundation'. The ethos of the new College was what Francis James Chavasse called 'High Church' or 'Tractarian', and not at all to his own taste. But he was fully aware of its significance, if only because his friend Walter Lock was so much attracted that he became its third Warden. The two men remained friends, and it was no accident that in his Islington speech in 1926 Chavasse specifically referred to 'the success and influence of Keble College' as 'a proof of what can be done by the exercise of faith, foresight, courage and self-sacrifice'.

In the eighteen-seventies the founding of Keble and the opening of a Tractarian theological college, St. Stephen's House, coupled with the growing influence of Father Noel at St. Barnabas's, put the Oxford Evangelicals on their mettle. Late in 1877 Francis James himself returned to Oxford, to succeed Canon Linton in 1878 as Rector of St. Peter-le-Bailey. From the start he tried to work among undergraduates as well as among his own parishioners, and his eyes were always open for new opportunities. Canon Linton had been one of the sponsors of Wycliffe Hall, founded in 1877 as an Evangelical offset to St. Stephen's House. In 1889 Francis James was invited to take charge of Wycliffe as its second Principal. This meant leaving St. Peter-le-Bailey, but he kept in touch; the new Rector, H. C. Squires, was his own brother-in-law, and Squires' successor in 1893 was another friend, the Hon. and Revd. W. Talbot Rice. Chavasse was particularly interested in the fate of New Inn Hall: Balliol had absorbed the Hall in 1887, and soon found that it had no further use for its buildings. Francis James wanted to step in. A letter from his son Christopher is relevant; it was printed in *The Record* on 27 July 1928: It may interest and inspire your readers to know that this is the second time that Bishop Chavasse has tried to utilize this central site in Oxford for Evangelical Education. Some 34 years ago, when New Inn Hall came into the market, he urged most strenuously its purchase for £10,000, that with St. Peter-le-Bailey Church and Rectory it might become the home of Wycliffe Hall, of which he was then Principal. His project was turned down, and his regretful comment always was 'The Evangelicals have not sufficient faith'.

As it was, the Corporation of Oxford was able to buy the former Principal's Lodgings of New Inn Hall, with a garden behind, and after clearing the site it built a Central School for Girls, to complement a Central School for Boys built in

Gloucester Green. But Talbot Rice and Chavasse were able to raise more than £6,000 for the purchase of the Cramer Building[3] and the area behind it, including a small chapel built by Principal Cornish in 1868. The Cramer Building was more or less gutted, and transformed into Hannington Hall; the chapel was incorporated in a primary school for St. Peter-le-Bailey parish. Chavasse went on to Liverpool in 1900 as its second Bishop, and Talbot Rice left Oxford in 1902, but they remained Trustees both of Hannington Hall and of St. Peter-le-Bailey Schools. Thus they were Trustees in 1915 (along with Bishop Knox), when Wycliffe Hall was temporarily housed in Hannington Hall, and they were still Trustees in 1928.

It is therefore fair to say that when in October 1923 Francis James Chavasse retired from Liverpool and came back to live in New Inn Hall Street, he came with conscious memories of that street as a place not for repose but for development. Already there had been changes. When he was Rector, he had lived in what is now No. 38 New Inn Hall Street. There was then no rectory, though already in October 1877 Canon Linton had bought from the Canal Company its former headquarters in New Inn Hall Street, Wyaston House, for the purpose of establishing a permanent rectory, in memory of his youngest son. But the existing tenant could not be displaced, and it was not till 1899 that Mr Talbot Rice was able to take possession of St. Peter-le-Bailey Rectory. From 1914 on the parish was held in plurality by the Rector of St. Ebbe's, Canon Stansfeld. He did not need a second house, and from that time St. Peter's Rectory was put to casual uses. So Bishop Chavasse was able to rent it for his own occupation, giving it the new name of St. Peter's House.

There is no reason to doubt Christopher Chavasse's statement that his father's 'sagacious eye' saw the possibilities of development. But one may wonder whether he would have been able to do much about it (by 1926 he was 80 years old, and very frail), had not Christopher himself been on the spot, vigorous, enterprising and full of drive. In his Second Annual Report (June 1930), after mentioning the death of Canon Stather Hunt, Christopher used these words:

> St. Peter's Hall knew him as a great Christian gentleman who was chairman of that influential educational Trust which has crowned its amazing post-war record of founding public schools by throwing its strength into Bishop Chavasse's scheme of establishing St. Peter's Hall at Oxford. My mind goes back

to the afternoon of May 4th 1927, when, on this very spot, I entered what is now our Hon. Treasurer's office, but was then Bishop Chavasse's study, and saw the white heads of the Bishop and the Canon close together in earnest talk, as they discussed for the first time the possibilities of such a Hall. That was the beginning of what you see today; and it was barely three years ago.

The white heads were in earnest talk, but the action came from Christopher Chavasse and Percy Warrington.

It may be noted that the meeting between Bishop Chavasse and Canon Stather Hunt is dated a whole year later than one would have expected from the First Report, or even from the *Record* account, which merely says that 'some months passed before anything was done'.[4] The explanation of this discrepancy seems to be that in 1928-29 all concerned had been anxious to stress the part played by the Bishop, and to high-light the Islington address: this was because the death of Francis James, in March 1928, had given the opportunity to appeal for money for St. Peter's not merely as his scheme but as his memorial. After all, the name of Bishop Chavasse meant much: Bishop Knox and he were regarded as the two great leaders of the Evangelicals, as in their opposition to the proposed new Prayer Book, and it was Bishop Chavasse whom Stanley Baldwin, as Prime Minister, in a debate on that book, described as a 'saint, if ever there were saints'. That was the special reason why in the first Trust Deed of the Hall he was called 'the Founder'. The preamble of that Deed states:

It is intended to found a Public Hall to be named St. Peter's Hall . . . to commemorate the life and teaching of the late Right Reverend Father in God Francis James Chavasse . . . formerly Bishop of Liverpool and sometime Principal of Wycliffe Hall and Rector of the Parish of St. Peter-le-Bailey . . . and in order to fulfil his earnest wish. . . .

It made sense, in the context of all that had happened since 1870.

It remains true, however, that long before the Islington address, Christopher Chavasse had had a scheme in mind and had not always presented it as solely his father's scheme. For instance, on 2 June 1925 the Bishop of Oxford, Dr. Hubert Burge, wrote to him from Cuddesdon: 'I am immensely interested in the scheme which you have thought out, and I will throw myself heartily into it when the moment for taking action comes. The question is whether we might not now go forward with the plan for dividing St. Peter-le-Bailey and St. Ebbe.'

He refers to 'your dear father', but there is no doubt that it is Christopher who is taking the initiative. Not that anything could be done immediately: it was not till 1927 that the scheme began to take definite shape. Even then there was some uncertainty about its scope. At Islington Bishop Chavasse had spoken of 'a new College', with the special purpose of helping candidates for ordination. This had produced a counter-blast: in *The Times* on 21 January 1926 appeared a letter signed by the Vice-Chancellor of Oxford University (Joseph Wells, Warden of Wadham), Francis Pember, Warden of All Souls, H. J. White, Dean of Christ Church, E. M. Walker, Pro-Provost of Queen's, Herbert Warren, President of Magdalen, and W. R. Buchanan-Riddell, Principal of Hertford. This formidable group suggested that there would be more point in raising money for the endowment of St. Edmund Hall, 'a venerable society, already devoted to this end', viz. the encouragement of men of limited means, including ordination candidates. This letter might have been expected to kill the Chavasse scheme. But Bishop Chavasse wrote back to *The Times* immediately (21 January 1926), saying that 'none would rejoice more than the promoters of the new scheme' if their proposal led to the endowment of St. Edmund Hall. But 'our contention is that there is ample room for other halls of the same kind', and he added 'the success of Keble College . . . is . . . an illustration of the generous spirit in which a great University can treat a scheme to which, at the outset, it is by no means friendly' – a good example of Bishop Chavasse's conciliatory approach. He spoke also of the restriction of the site of St. Edmund Hall (nobody then could have foreseen the way in which the Hall has overcome that restriction): here he was on less secure ground, but Dr. G. B. Allen, then Principal of St. Edmund Hall, a High Churchman, was only concerned to make it clear that he wanted no favours from the Islington Conference. He too wrote to *The Times* immediately (21 January 1926): although St. Edmund Hall was 'the first home in Oxford of the evangelical movement', it 'stood definitely on the side of the Oxford movement in the days when Dr. Liddon was the Vice-Principal', and in any case he did not want it thought that the Hall was mainly a place for ordination candidates. A week later (29 January 1926), the *Guardian* published an editorial, ending

'We much dislike the proposal to found a college specially associated with one party in the Church. Should the opposite view prevail, we hope that the experiment will not be tried upon St. Edmund Hall.' That ended the matter[5]; and of the six Heads of Houses who had brought it up, three soon showed themselves good friends to St. Peter's.

Meanwhile Christopher Chavasse was intensely busy at St. Aldates, and in preparing himself to join in the Evangelical campaign against the proposed new Prayer Book; this took up much of his time in 1926-27. But as soon as the Church of England Trust Society had definitely decided to take up the St. Peter's scheme, in the early summer of 1927, he threw himself into the work of giving precise form to what had been rather general ideas. His problem was to produce a plan which would satisfy the Trust, the University, and himself. Another quotation from his First Report is relevant:

> . . . a society is not founded in Oxford merely by great benefactions. These can only be offered to the University for its acceptance, and there are few more delicate operations than to graft a new organization on to a venerable institution. Immediately, therefore, the Church of England Trust Society had decided to father the proposed Hall, I was commissioned to approach the Vice-Chancellor, Dr. F. W. Pember, and to lay our plans before him. His response was cordial and sympathetic, and throughout the successive stages of our progress a chief asset has been the constructive criticism which he has never been too busy to place at our disposal – bringing the trained mind of a lawyer to bear upon all the details and problems of the scheme.

Chavasse here speaks of the 'proposed Hall', but when he went to see the Vice-Chancellor he was still talking of a proposed 'college'. It would seem that Dr. Pember suggested to him that the easiest way of establishing a new society was to apply for the status of a permanent private hall, a status invented in 1918 for the benefit of two Roman Catholic societies, Campion Hall and St. Benet's Hall, and also that if he wished to go ahead quickly, he might set up a hostel of non-collegiate students. Whether Dr. Pember then suggested that in due course the permanent private hall might go on to become a public hall is not clear; there was no precedent for such a transition. In any case, Chavasse, not possessing 'the trained mind of a lawyer', did

22

not at this early stage bother much about exactness of term-
inology. So, when it was decided to open a hostel, he advertised
in the press, on 16 and 23 March 1928, in the following terms:

> In pursuance of the St. Peter's College, Oxford, scheme, it
> is proposed to open a Hostel in October for Undergraduates.
> An entrance examination will be held in Oxford on Tuesday
> and Wednesday, April 23 and 24. All information will be
> supplied by the Rev. C. M. Chavasse, St. Aldates Rectory,
> Oxford.

The information sent to applicants was a duplicated sheet,
headed –

ST. PETER'S COLLEGE, OXFORD
(Founder, Bishop Chavasse)

Under a sub-heading 'BUILDINGS' it was stated:

> It is proposed to open this College in a small way in October
> 1928. At first the College will be a Hostel, and Residents will
> be matriculated by the Delegacy of Non-Collegiate Students.
> But it is hoped that within the first year they will become
> members of their own foundation, by St. Peter's College being
> given the status of a Hall.

Two months later, on 18 May 1928, the *Church of England
Newspaper*, under 'Oxford Diocesan news', recorded that 'The
Rev. C. M. Chavasse proposes to resign the rectory of St.
Aldate's, Oxford, in order to become the first Principal of the
new College of St. Peter. Mr. Chavasse will still remain Rector
of St. Peter-le-Bailey, as he has held the two livings in plurality
for the past six months or so. There is more than one opinion
in Oxford as to the advisability of establishing another College
in the University, for although at present St. Peter's will be only
a hostel, it is hoped by its founders that later on it will acquire
the status of a College.'

It is not altogether surprising that when Chavasse applied to
Dr. Kenneth Kirk, Chairman of the Delegacy of Lodgings, for
formal leave to open the hostel, he found it necessary to add
some points of explanation. On 19 April 1928 he had received
from Dr. Kirk a copy of the usual form of application to the
Delegacy for the licensing of a hostel for non-collegiate students.
It so happened that he was meeting the Martyrs Memorial

Trustees in London on that day, so that the form could be signed at once by himself as 'Principal' and by Canon D. J. Stather Hunt and Lord Gisborough as 'Members of the Council of the Church of England Trust Society'. It was then sent to Dr. Kirk with a covering letter which is worth quoting in full:

> According to your kind suggestion I am sending (with the application to open in October a Hostel at St. Peter's House, 19 New Inn Hall Street – the Rectory House of St. Peter-le-Bailey) a formal statement as to (1) the ownership of the property and (2) the composition of the Governing Body of the Hostel.
>
> 1. *Ownership:* The property is owned by the Church of England Trust Society, as Patrons of the advowson of St. Peter-le-Bailey. They appoint the Rector who is ex-officio Principal of the Hostel. The Hostel is therefore assured of permanency, for the Church Patronage Trust Society being the promoters of such Schools as Stowe, Canford and Wrekin (among others) is obviously capable of financing the Hostel.
>
> 2. *The Constitution of the Governing Body:* This has followed the general lines of that adopted for St. Edmund Hall – upon which Queen's College (as proprietors), the University, and the Hall itself, have equal representation. It is also woven round the life-work of the late Bishop Chavasse, (who was successively Rector of St. Peter-le-Bailey, Principal of Wycliffe Hall, and Bishop of Liverpool), for he promoted the scheme, and it is hoped to establish the Hostel in his memory.
>
> I should also like to bring the following before the Delegates:
>
> (1) *A Misunderstanding.*[6] I very much regret the startling headlines that appeared in the Press concerning 'the opening of a *New College* in Oxford', which must have given rise to much misapprehension. It was the prominence given by my Father's death to the notice of a benefaction for his project which was responsible for the misunderstanding. My Father's interest in this scheme was well known, and he had always spoken about 'St. Peter's College', meaning thereby a general description which in the past has designated such different foundations as Keble, Mansfield, Manchester, and the

Women's Colleges. But you yourself and also the Vice-Chancellor, have been well aware that our intention has always been to proceed on modest lines – from a Hostel to an application for a Permanent Private Hall; and that the idea of 'a College' (in the strict sense of the word) never arose and was relegated to the unknown future.

(2) *The Name.* As it is our intention to make application, almost immediately to the Vice-Chancellor for the Hostel (which I am now presuming you licence) to be given the status of a Permanent Private Hall, I should be very grateful if the Delegates would permit me to use the title of "St. Peter's Hall" from the first, and thus to avoid confusion.[7] They could at any time withdraw their permission if the Vice-Chancellor found it impossible to grant a licence for such a Hall.

Thus it will be composed as follows:

(1) *Proprietors* — The Five Trustees of the advowson of St. Peter-le-Bailey.

(2) *Education* — Two resident Masters of Art in the University of Oxford.
Two representatives nominated by the Chancellor of Liverpool University.

(3) *The Hostel* — The Principal (who is Chairman and has the casting vote).
The Principal of Wycliffe Hall.
Two members nominated by the Teaching Staff, and till this exists by the Trustees.

Thus the actual composition of the Governing Body is as follows:

Visitor
The Bishop of Liverpool
Principal
Rev. C. M. Chavasse, M.C., M.A.
Council

(1) Lord Gisborough, J.P., D.L.
Sir Charles King-Harman, K.C.M.G., LL.D.
Canon Stather Hunt
Rev. P. E. Warrington
Rev. H. B. Greene.[8]

The Patrons of St. Peter-le-Bailey and Governors of Stowe and Canford Schools

25

(2) Mr. P. S. Allen, M.A., D.Litt. (President of Corpus Christi College). Rev. E. M. Walker, M.A. (Pro-Provost of Queen's College). His Honour Judge H. C. Dowdall, B.C.L. (Chancellor of the Diocese of Liverpool). Mr. J. G. Legge, M.A. (Late Director of Education in Liverpool).

(3) Sir Charles Oman, K.B.E., D.C.L., M.P. The Principal of Wycliffe Hall, Rev. G. F. Graham Brown, M.A. The Principal of the Hostel (Chairman).

(3) *The Buildings.* The necessary alterations to St. Peter's House are being carried out in strict accordance with the instructions of Messrs. Best and Sons, the engineers employed by the Delegacy; and you yourself have most kindly given the plans your previous inspection.

(4) *Undergraduates.* These are being carefully chosen from many applicants, and have then to be approved by the Censor of Non-Collegiate Students, who has kindly undertaken to matriculate them. It is our great hope in this way to give what Collegiate Life we can to men of promise but of straitened means, for an inclusive fee of £120 or £100 per annum, and thus in some small way to advance the great desire of Dr. Wells when he laid down the office of Vice-Chancellor.

Chavasse took the trouble to send to the Vice-Chancellor, Dr. Pember, a letter (dated 24 April 1928) embodying almost verbatim the points made in his letter to Dr. Kirk under the head '(1) A Misunderstanding'. The letter ends: 'It almost seems wasting your time to repeat all this, but I should like you to have it in writing – both because of your kindness to me, and also because I am about to apply for a licence for a Hostel and shortly afterwards for a Permanent Private Hall'.

Dr. Pember replied (26 April) in a letter marked 'private and confidential', 'I was somewhat taken aback by the press headlines to which you refer, and feared that they might give rise to mis-apprehension. I have some reason to think that the matter may be mentioned by someone in Council, and possibly the suggestion made as to the desirability of getting into communication with those who are responsible for the project. [If so] would you like me to read to Council your letter of the 24th [or would you agree to an informal meeting if Council wished]?' Pember added a P.S. in his own writing: 'Of course, I well understood how misleading the Press notices were'.[9]

Chavasse jumped at the idea of consultation with Hebdomadal Council. On 2 May 1928 he heard in confidence from Dr. A. E. W. Hazel, Principal of Jesus, that 'Council has appointed a Committee (of which I am a member) which will probably take an opportunity of conferring with you'; and on 24 May he was able to go with Dr. E. M. Walker and Mr. J. G. Legge to meet the Committee. The result was satisfactory. According to Chavasse, the Committee 'gave our Governing Body the generous permission to appeal to the public for funds, when once their application was laid before you'. This sentence occurs in the letter which he wrote to the Vice-Chancellor on 2 June 1928, enclosing a formal application for the grant of a licence to open a Permanent Private Hall, 'concerning which you have most kindly allowed me to inform and consult you at all stages of the inception of the project.'

But everything was not so simple as Chavasse had hoped. For one thing, Dr. Kirk was raising difficulties. On 15 May 1928 the Bishop of Oxford, Dr. Thomas Strong, sent a private note telling Chavasse that he had heard rumours of technical complications:

'. . . please forgive my intrusion, but as some rumour did reach me, and as an extinct Vice-Chancellor, I know how much trouble arises out of these points. I thought I had better write to you as I should be extremely sorry if your start was interfered with by some technical difficulty.'

There was certainly room for misunderstanding. Chavasse believed that Kirk, a leading Anglo-Catholic, had no liking for an Evangelical scheme, but there is no reason to suppose that Kirk was being deliberately obstructive. It was rather that he profoundly distrusted what appeared to him to be Chavasse's slapdash approach. On 13 June Kirk wrote to him (referring to a talk which they had had on the previous day: 'Let me say at once that, insofar as any difference of opinion arose between us, it appears to me to have been based mainly on the fact that you have regarded the proposed "Hostel-Status" of St. Peter's House as no more than a transitional stage (perhaps of very short duration) to the status of a Permanent Private Hall; whilst I, acting for the Delegates, have had to contemplate the possibility, at all events, that the Hostel status might be a permanency for some time.'

One may reasonably guess that Kirk contemplated that possibility with equanimity. Meanwhile, he made sure that Chavasse should not take it for granted that even the licence for a hostel would be granted easily. On 12 May 1928 Kirk had asked: 'What guarantee is there that any Rector appointed by the Patrons of the advowson of St. Peter-le-Bailey will carry on the Hostel?' and on 16 May the Delegates of Lodgings stated 'that the Rectory house of an ecclesiastical benefice cannot be regarded as "established on a permanent footing" as Lodgings for undergraduates, and [they] are therefore unable at present to entertain the Council's application for a licence'. The Delegates did unbend so far as to say that once the Trustees of St. Peter's were able to buy the Rectory they would be prepared 'to give a sympathetic consideration to the application'; but when Chavasse pressed Kirk (18 May) to say whether it was safe to assume that 'sympathetic consideration' could be relied on, he received a guarded reply[10]: 'Speaking quite unofficially and in my private capacity I should be inclined to say that the words "give a sympathetic consideration" do not constitute any virtual undertaking' – unforeseen points might arise.

On 29 May Chavasse was able to write to Kirk: 'You will be glad to hear that the negotiations for the sale of St. Peter's House are now concluded, for I have heard yesterday from the Archbishop's Legal Secretary – Mr. H. T. A. Dashwood – that "the Archbishop has consented to the sale of this Rectory House to the Trustees".' But the way was not yet entirely plain. First, St. Peter's House had to be inspected by 'the Sanitary Officer of the Delegates' (Mr. G. Best, of Messrs. Best & Sons), who insisted on new plumbing in bathrooms and lavatories, and though he approved of the structural alterations that were being made to accommodate undergraduates, the rule of the Delegacy was that no licence should be issued until all structural work was finished. This was awkward, because on 31 May Chavasse's Provisional Council had authorized the issue of a printed Appeal for £150,000 for the foundation of St. Peter's Hall, and this Appeal included the statement 'It is intended to open in a preliminary way as a Hostel for the Michaelmas Term (October 1928)'. It appears that Chavasse gave Kirk a copy of the Appeal when he went to see him on 12 June, because in his letter of 13 June Kirk pointed out that the words 'subject to the consent of the University' should have been inserted. Moreover, Kirk took the matter to his Delegates, and two days later he informed Chavasse that the Delegates had decided to refuse to issue any licence for the hostel until steps had been taken to remove the implication in the Appeal that a hostel could be opened without the prior consent of the University. This was particularly annoying to Chavasse, because he had shown the draft Appeal to the Committee of Council on 24 May, and believed that it had been approved. However, he told Kirk that he would do his best to stop further circulation of the Appeal until the words 'Subject to the consent of the University' had been added,[11] and on 16 June he wrote to the Press Association, *The Times*, the *Morning Post*, the *Oxford Times* and the church newspapers making it clear that the sanction of the University was needed even for the opening of a hostel. The London papers did not regard this as anything more than an academic nicety, and as late as 20 September 1928 Kirk found it necessary to send a cutting from *The Times*, containing a photograph of Chavasse and a statement that St. Peter's would open as a hostel next month: he insisted that Chavasse should at once inform *The Times* that the opening of the hostel still depended upon a licence from the Delegates which had not yet been issued. There was a tinge of irony in the letter which Chavasse wrote on 11 October 1928: 'Dear Dr. Kirk, Thank you very much for the Licence for St. Peter's House as a Hostel, which I received this morning; and for all the trouble you have taken in helping me to secure it'.

Chavasse was not by nature a patient man; he found delays irksome, and he was always reluctant to admit their necessity. But he was learning that in Oxford at that date it was impossible to move as quickly as he wished. Originally he had even hoped that St. Peter's might open as a Hall in October 1928. His meeting with the Committee of Council had made him aware of procedural difficulties, and in his letter of 2 June he had told the Vice-Chancellor: 'I know it is impossible to ask the consent of Convocation before the Michaelmas Term'. But he was still optimistic. He explained that application was being made early because 'it was thought well to be on the safe side, and thus be assured that the Hall (if a licence were granted) could open for the Hilary Term 1928'. (Here 1928 is an obvious mistake; 1929 was intended.[12]) By October he was more cautious. The Trust Deed of St. Peter's was executed on 23 October. Two days later he told the Vice-Chancellor that he was now able to make formal application, but there is now no question of opening as a Hall before Michaelmas 1929:

Our petition is that St. Peter's hostel (already in existence) should be granted the status of a Permanent Private Hall from Michaelmas 1929. As there are only twelve undergraduates in

residence, it is unnecessary for St. Peter's to be more than a
Hostel for the remainder of the present academical year; and
it would be unwise to take the pupils from the Tutors arranged
for them by the Censor of Non-Collegiate Students, till they
have passed their first Public Examination. The Delegacy of
Non-Collegiate Students could not have been more helpful; the
Hostel is happy under their care, and we are deeply indebted
to them.

He thinks it necessary to add: *Regarding Religious Tests:* One
matter we feel should be made clear to you, in case you should
share what seems a general misunderstanding. St. Peter's whether
it is a Hostel or a Hall is not sectarian in character. Its Trust
Deed definitely states that it is for students 'of whatever religious
persuasion'.

It seems clear that at this stage Chavasse was worried about
possible difficulties within Hebdomadal Council.[13] His position
was not made easier by some of the publicity given to the Appeal.
The church newspapers, whether friendly or unfriendly, gave the
impression that the Hall would be sectarian (after all, the Appeal
stated in emphatic red type that the Hall would be 'conducted
according to the Evangelical principles of its Founder'), and
comment in secular newspapers[14] was not always so helpful inside
Oxford as outside. For instance, *The Telegraph* stated: 'The
fact that the governing body of the remarkably successful public
school of Stowe are also members of the Council of St. Peter's
should act as a reassurance, if any is needed, that this new hall
is likely to take as high a place in the University as Stowe takes
among the great public schools.' By some members of the Oxford
'Establishment', such a statement was taken as the height of
presumption; and there were the malicious who pointed out
privately that the head of this new hall was a parish parson
of no academic standing at all.[15] But there was no sign of open
hostility to St. Peter's in October 1928, and it was not till
December that Chavasse and his friends began to be worried
by rumours and hints that there might be opposition in Convocation to the decree which Hebdomadal Council proposed to submit
for approval on 29 January 1929. The terms of this decree were
'That the consent of Convocation be given —

1. To the grant by the Vice-Chancellor of a licence for the
   establishment of a permanent Private Hall.
2. To the proposal that the said permanent Private Hall be
   known as St. Peter's Hall, Oxford.

3. To the appointment by the Governing Body of the Hall of the Rev. Christopher Maude Chavasse, M.A., Trinity College, to be Master of the Hall.'

On 4 December 1928 the Council of St. Peter's met to approve the draft of the supplementary Trust Deed embodying the additions which the Vice-Chancellor had required to be made. It also had to consider how best to ensure the passing of the decree by Convocation. Dr. Walker could be relied on to put the case for St. Peter's, but it was decided also to ask Dr. Hazel to support the decree. To call in Dr. Hazel was a sound move: a brilliant, caustic speaker, enjoying controversy (one of the few academic lawyers of the time to become a K.C.), he disliked equally anything that savoured of High Church or High Tory. The fact that St. Peter's was specifically Evangelical (some people called it a 'Low Church Keble') was no disadvantage in his opinion, especially if Dr. Kirk, the most eminent of the younger Anglo-Catholics in Oxford, was suspicious of it (Chavasse maintained later, in private conversations, that at this time he had found Roman Catholics more sympathetic than the younger Anglo-Catholics). The other fact that St. Peter's was specifically intended 'to assist students of limited means' appealed strongly to Hazel's liberal views; as Vice-Principal and Bursar of Jesus College (before he became Principal) he had been one of those who made that College a place in which there was no trace of social exclusiveness.

The Council also decided on 4 December to set up a small committee (Chavasse, the Principal of Wycliffe, and Mr Legge) to ask friends to attend the meeting of Convocation and to vote in favour of the decree. The point was that in Convocation (as distinct from Congregation) all Masters of Arts, non-resident as well as resident, were in those days entitled to attend and to vote. Chavasse himself wrote to W. Talbot Rice (for Bishop Knox), to the Head Master of Eton (Cyril Alington), to the Head Master of Stowe (J. F. Roxburgh),[16] and to a number of clerical friends, such as C. J. Shebbeare, Rector of Stanhope, Co. Durham. The Principal of Wycliffe was able to call on many old members to come from their parishes and vote, and Mr Legge carried out canvassing inside Oxford. On the crucial day about thirty 'outsiders' and half a dozen relatives[17] answered the call, and most of them were given lunch before going to Convocation; an eye-witness[18] declared later that 'the place seemed to be seething with people who came up to vote'.

31

All this might be thought to verge on sharp practice, but it was then regarded as quite legitimate; just as in Congregation today, on controversial issues, there is nothing at all illegitimate in whipping up the support of members who never normally attend. Certainly there was no protest on this score in the *Oxford Magazine*, which represented opinion in the University with fair accuracy. It did however contain a protest, as will be seen later, on the tactics of the opponents of the decree in concealing the grounds for their opposition. It was because of this concealment that on 22 December 1928 it was thought advisable that Dr. P. S. Allen, Mr. J. G. Legge, Sir Charles Oman and Dr. E. M. Walker should sign a long letter to the Vice-Chancellor, which he published in the *University Gazette* of 17 January 1929 for the information of members of Convocation.

The letter made the following points:

'1. The Hall will not be denominational in character. The Trust Deeds declare that it shall be open to students of any denomination, and of the twelve at present residing in St. Peter's House, two are Nonconformists. The only stipulation is that Chapel Services shall be conducted in accordance with the principles of the present Prayer Book. There will be no compulsion on men to attend Chapel.'[19]

'2. The permanence of the Hall is assured by three facts:
(a) The site and existing buildings had been acquired, and money provided for reconditioning them and adding an additional block to accommodate about thirty. The total expenditure was estimated at £60,000.
(b) The Martyrs Memorial and Church of England Trust, who are the proprietors of Stowe, Canford, the Wrekin, Weston Birt [sic] and other schools, have not only provided[20] the great bulk of the above sum, but have also agreed that the said Trust will guarantee the permanent character of St. Peter's as a Hall, financially and otherwise.
(c) A fund was being raised to endow teaching staff; so far, £10,000 had been received.[21]

'3. Details were given of the constitution of the Council'.

'4. The Council have already secured the services of one Tutor,[22] and another has agreed to join the staff in October next. Both are Oxford men of high academic attainment in classics and history. It is proposed to add a Tutor for every twenty students who come into residence.'[23]

'5. As it is proposed to give each student three years' residence within the Hall itself,[24] the Promoters see little prospect of providing accommodation for more than 50 or 60 undergraduates at most, within the next five years.'

'6. One of the main purposes is to provide deserving men of small means with the opportunity of taking a University course. 'To this end the Trust have generously undertaken to provide several scholarships and exhibitions'[25] and the Council 'will endeavour by endowment to provide more.'

'7. It is not anticipated that the students of the Hall will permit the Council to overlook the recreative side of a University course, but efforts are already being made to provide a suitable playing-field.'

The letter ended: 'We ought perhaps to add that we quite understand that the Decree . . . simply authorizes the Vice-Chancellor to grant a licence, but does not of itself confer the licence.'[26]

The publication of this statement had an unforeseen result. It provoked a critical rejoinder from Reginald Lennard of Wadham, a medieval historian who frequently found occasion to write letters to *The Times*; on this occasion he wrote to the *Oxford Magazine* (24 January 1929). It is a good example of his controversial style. After quoting point one of the statement, he writes: 'Now I am quite certain that the last thing which either the signatories of the letter or Mr. Chavasse wishes [sic] is that there should be any ambiguity or apparent lack of frankness in the conditions under which the Hall seeks authorisation. But they have forgotten to tell us whether tutors as well as students may belong to "any denomination", and they assume that we all know what is meant by a "denomination". Will Unitarians, Christian Scientists, Moslems, Agnostics and Atheists be eligible as tutors and students . . . as they are in the case of the older colleges? If any form of test of religious or political belief is required, I shall vote against the proposal. Two things in particular trouble me. If there is to be a religious test at all, the undenominationalism of the proposed Hall seems to me far worse than a requirement that its students should be members of the Church of England . . . If the idea is to get together a body of sincere evangelical Christians, whether they are Churchmen or Nonconformists, the road is at once open to inquisitorial scrutiny of the precise shade and

33

temper of the undergraduates' convictions.' After speaking of the moral dilemma in which a poor man would be placed if he came up on a scholarship and then became a Roman Catholic or Agnostic, he went on: 'I am sorry to seem so cantankerous. But this question of St. Peter's Hall is clearly very important. I want to give my vote one way or the other. And I want to have the information that will enable me to know which way I ought to vote.'

No doubt Lennard's letter was irritating to the sponsors of St. Peter's, but even if cantankerous he was fair: he sent a copy of his letter (dated 19 January) to Chavasse, so that a reply from Chavasse (dated 21 January) could also appear in the *Magazine* on 24 January. This was helpful; for though even then the opponents of the decree had not come into the open, there were 'dark rumours' (as the *Oxford Magazine* put it) 'that the proposal is to be opposed because the new foundation is to be a denominational one' (24 January 1929). Chavasse was able to clarify the position in regard to tests. He wrote:

'I am sorry if the letter [of 22 December 1928] failed to make clear that by its Trust Deeds St. Peter's contemplates no religious tests either for students or tutors. The framing of the Universities Tests Act 1871 does allow new Foundations to impose a religious test upon their members; and the Permanent Private Halls which already exist are denominational in character. But it has always been the intention of the promoters of St. Peter's to come into line with the older Colleges and to comply with the regulations of the Tests Act. They were required to satisfy a Committee of the Hebdomadal Council upon this very point before they issued their public appeal. And, in accordance with its spirit, an adherent of Pusey House[27] is already a member of St. Peter's upon the recommendation of one of the Librarians, and Mr. Loewe[28] will testify that we were willing to receive a member of the Jewish religion.' Services in chapel would of course be Anglican; but the Universities Tests Act had specifically laid down that morning and evening prayer should be used daily in College Chapels 'according to the order of the Book of Common Prayer'; and as for the moral dilemma of poor scholars, the practice of St. Peter's would be exactly the same as everywhere else in Oxford.

It would have been equally helpful if other critics had made their views known.[29] After the decree had been passed, the *Oxford Magazine* of 31 January 1929 had a paragraph headed 'Etiquette in Convocation'. It read:

'The debate on the establishment of St. Peter's as a new permanent private hall was all that could be desired, both in the good taste of the speeches and in the clearness of argument on both sides. But it is to be hoped that its preliminaries will not be taken as a precedent. Due notice that opposition to an important proposal will be offered has on all previous occasions (but one)[30] been given at least a week previous to the time of voting, and its grounds have been at least indicated. On this occasion the post-card, stating that the decree would be opposed, reached members of Convocation not quite four days before the day of voting (and some never had it at all), and when it came, it was a bare state-ment of the fact of opposition, without any hint as to "how" or "why". It is idle to say that the details of the proposal were not known; their general outlines were familiar, and the future opponents could have had them for the asking. As it was, the promoters of the new Hall had no warning, except obscure hints in the newspapers, although it is well known that they were anxiously trying to find out what the chances of opposition were. It is the more necessary to make this protest, since it is the second time that this breach of academic courtesy has happened in this academic year.'

In fact, the Vice-Chancellor, F. W. Pember, notified Dr. E. M. Walker privately that Cyril Bailey of Balliol had just given notice of opposition. Walker sent on Dr. Pember's note to Chavasse (25 January) with the comment: 'This has just come. It looks as if the Decree was going to be opposed in the interests of the women. You had better let Hazell [sic] know at once. He may be able to find out why Bailey is opposing the Decree'. It is not clear why Dr. Walker suspected that 'the interests of the women' (i.e. the women's colleges) were involved. Certainly there was no hint of this in a personal letter received that same day by Chavasse from Cyril Bailey himself: 'After our conversation the other day I feel I ought to tell you at once that I have been very strongly urged by a number of people to speak in opposition to the St. Peter's Decree on Tuesday, and have very reluctantly consented. I need not tell you that I shall do my best to avoid giving offence and that I greatly hope that an unfortunate differ-ence of opinion, where we both feel our consciences strong, will not in any way impair our personal relations.' To this Chavasse sent an immediate reply (telephones were used remarkably little at this date in Oxford). He kept no copy, but its tone can be guessed from a letter which Cyril Bailey sent on 26 January: 'My dear Chavasse, I am very grateful to you for your most generous letter. I can assure you that I shall only do this with a heavy heart, but I have honestly wrestled the thing out in my mind and feel that I should be a coward if I did not say what was in me. But I must just liberate my soul and it is a comfort to feel that, though you naturally disagree, you and I hope others who feel with you, will not misunderstand me. Thank you again. Yours very sincerely.'

Of the actual debate in Convocation on 29 January, a fairly good account can be drawn from *The Times*, the *Oxford Magazine* and the memories of Chavasse himself. Dr. Hazel moved the decree, stressing that he spoke as one officially connected neither with St. Peter's Hall nor with the Church of England and that he supported it entirely on grounds of general University interests. He demonstrated that the objections were mere bogies; it was not true that the Hall would be controlled by an outside body, and its members, if they chose, could be as free from religious tests as any present members of the University, and more free than some.[31] On the matter of outside control, Dr. Hazel observed that Dr. Cyril Bailey, who was opposing the decree, was himself a member of the outside Council which governed Lady Margaret Hall, and asked 'why is it that what is sauce for the goose in Norham Gardens is not sauce for the gander in New Inn Hall Street?'

According to the *Oxford Magazine*, 'the opponents of the decree never attempted to answer his arguments, based as they were on the conditions of the Trust; they contented themselves with repeating that things, in their opinion, were quite otherwise, and that the new Hall would be denominational and dependent.'

Dr. Cyril Bailey declared that with great reluctance he felt compelled to oppose the decree as being against the best principles and interests of university life. Curiously, he also 'drew an eloquent picture of the new Hall as a poor men's place, which would be looked down upon because its members came from secondary schools and were not public-school men'. Cyril Bailey himself, a humane scholar in every sense, was certainly not a snob; but here he laid himself open to the *Magazine*'s query, 'Surely he must know that this kind of distinction does not count in Oxford in estimating a man's merits; or is Balliol really so full of class-consciousness?'

Dr. E. M. Walker demolished the argument that St. Peter's would somehow be 'segregated', and went on to urge with great force 'the constructive point that the scheme of the new Hall was a real and permanent contribution to the solution of one of the great problems of the day, the need of a university-educated clergy'. Mr. Weaver, however (Fellow and later President of Trinity), argued that it was unprecedented for a hostel to become a Hall so soon: Campion Hall and St. Benet's had served an 'academic apprenticeship' of some twenty-one years before being granted licences. He argued too that only three of the twelve members of the St. Peter's Council would necessarily have any connection with the University of Oxford, and he compared the new Hall with Keble to its disadvantage – an argument which struck the *Magazine* commentator as 'dangerous, when it is beyond dispute that Keble does impose tests on its members, and has an outside body of one religious complexion to control it'.

It would have been a pity if the debate had developed into, or been interpreted as, a conflict between Anglo-Catholics and Evangelicals, or between Keble and St. Peter's.[32] Luckily, Bishop Chavasse's old friend Dr. Lock, at this time a professorial canon of Christ Church but formerly Warden of Keble, prevented all danger of this by intervening with 'a few but kindly words',[33] wishing all success to the new Hall, and pointing out that 'he had learnt from long experience that a commitment to one form of religious belief acted as an educational incentive to students in the broadest sense of the word'. The gentle Dr. Lock had the last word. Dr. B. J. Kidd, Warden of Keble, was present, and would if necessary have spoken on the same side; but there was no need. Convocation voted in favour of the Decree, 260-60. The *Oxford Magazine* summed up: 'So "all's well that ends well", and Oxford's character for consistency and commonsense is to some extent retrieved.'

Immediately after the debate, Cyril Bailey took the trouble to write again to Chavasse: 'I am glad of the result for your sake, and if our protest could have the effect of suggesting certain dangers and help you in guarding against them, it won't have been in vain. I was just paralysed by Hazel's conclusion and lost my nerve, but I hope I did not say anything which could hurt.'

R. H. Lightfoot of New College also wrote: 'This is only to congratulate you with all my heart on this afternoon's debate and voting. Hazel and Walker and Lock were quite admirable, each in his own way, and it was the best level of speaking, all round, that I have heard in the Sheldonian. I appreciated Bailey's and Weaver's wish not to wound or be unfair, but they were extraordinarily unconvincing'.

But the last word comes from Hazel himself. On 30 January he wrote to Chavasse: 'I am glad if I have been of any use to

St. Peter's and I wish you "God-speed" in your work there. I think we have "lighted a candle" in Oxford which will never be put out. It may become a great Foundation if Protestant Churchmen support it as they ought. I expect you will have lots of difficulties yet, but you are over the big fence.'[34]

2

On 7 October 1929 the Vice-Chancellor granted the licence for St. Peter's to open as a Permanent Private Hall. On the following day, in his farewell oration as Vice-Chancellor, Dr. Pember gave a greeting to the new Hall: 'S. Petri Aulam, e cunabulis iam exeuntem, gratis animis et salutatione benevola excipimus, in spem habentes Universitati commodum non minimum adlaturam'. Some of those present were reminded that three years before (12 October 1926), Dr. Joseph Wells, in his farewell oration, had expressed the opinion that new colleges were needed in Oxford.[35] He had then made no explicit reference to the still inchoate proposals for St. Peter's, but in January 1929 he had been an active supporter. According to the First Report, 'he met the speakers to consult with them the night before the debate, and was prepared to speak himself if the occasion arose', and on the day after the debate he wrote to Chavasse: 'I shall not live to see its completion,[36] but I look forward with confidence to the time when St. Peter's will take its place as a *College* of the University, and I hope it will be a poor man's College'.[37]

Dr. Wells was more generous in his friendliness than Dr. A. E. J. Rawlinson (then Tutor in Theology at Christ Church, later Bishop of Derby); he had thought it necessary to write to the *Church Times* on 8 February 1929, complaining that its Oxford correspondent had referred to 'the new Evangelical College'. 'In the interests of accuracy', he wrote, 'it should be made clear, I think, that the institution in question is not a college, but a private academic hall, under the Rev. C. M. Chavasse as master'. Dr. Rawlinson's feathers might have been ruffled still more a little later on if he had read an article in the *Liverpool Post and Mercury* (23 July 1929) by the eminent architect, Professor C. H. Reilly, on the achievement of Bishop Francis James Chavasse: 'Bishop Chavasse is the William of Wykeham of our time; the builder of a cathedral and the founder of a college. Winchester and New College are today balanced by Liverpool and St. Peter's. It is magnificent. It stirs the blood'.

Unfortunately, extravagant praise was apt to stir up bad blood in Oxford. Accuracy and humility were the qualities expected there in academic newcomers.[38] This meant that Christopher Chavasse was in a position of some difficulty. As the Master of a small society, feeling its way in the University, he needed to tread gently and to conciliate;[39] as a fund-raiser, he needed to go out for maximum publicity. The two needs could be complementary, but they might prove contradictory. At this time, the most effective way of raising money seemed to be to beat the Evangelical drum; but the more successful that beating, the more tricky it would be to show that St. Peter's Hall actually was conforming to the ideas of the subscribers. For instance, a *Record* supplement of 13 December 1929, stated confidently that the forty men now in residence 'are receiving the best academical education, and are being trained in those simple truths of Evangelical faith which we all hold so dear'. This would seem the natural fulfilment of the programme put forward in the Appeal of June 1928. In the brochure of that Appeal, 'THE PURPOSE' for which St. Peter's Hall is to be established (as set forth in the Trust Deed) is defined.

'1. To promote education generally and especially to provide for students of straitened circumstances.
2. To train candidates for Holy Orders, and others who intend to labour for the Church in Missions Overseas.
3. To maintain and diffuse the Reformed Teaching of the Church of England as set forth in the Book of Common Prayer of 1662.'

The third object was underlined in black, and was followed by a paragraph in bold red type:

'St. Peter's therefore will provide three years' residence in a Hall, conducted according to the Evangelical principles of its Founder, for Undergraduates who desire to make a full use of a University course at the lowest possible cost.'

Yet the debate in Convocation had made it clear that there were to be no religious tests for undergraduates or tutors and that they need not all be Anglican. In what sense were they to be 'trained in simple truths', and in what way would the Hall be conducted according to Evangelical principles? Chavasse himself saw no difficulty here. He as Master, and anybody whom he appointed to be Chaplain, would always be Evangelicals; the chapel would play a central part in the life of the Hall, and there would always be plenty of undergraduates from staunch Evangelical homes who would set the tone of the place. Tutors too would obviously not wish to join the Hall unless they were in sympathy with its objects. Its influence would then spread. Now what Chavasse described as 'the first occasion on which St. Peter's was used for a public purpose' was when the Cheltenham Conference for Evangelical Clergy and Laity opened there on 10 April 1929. He himself presided and gave the inaugural address (the subject of the conference was 'Lambeth and Reunion'). He started: 'My dear brethren, to welcome you here at St. Peter's is like seeing a dream beginning to come true; and I hope with all my heart that this gathering is an earnest of the Evangelical influence which this place will exert increasingly throughout the whole Church. . . . It has always been the intention that St. Peter's should provide, not simply an academy for undergraduates, but a great rallying-ground for the Evangelical School. . . .' With this one may compare some words of Bishop Knox when he wrote to *The Record* on 28 November 1930, urging support for the new Appeal: 'For the plain fact is that, while Evangelicalism was simply *ignored* in Oxford for more than half-a-century in my recollection, it is now put in a position in which it cannot be ignored. It must be recognized as one of the great forces of the Church of England. We owe this change, under God, to the foresight of good Bishop Chavasse, who had seen what Keble College had done for the Tractarians, and achieved the same for us, not only by building a College, but by planting it in a most central position, and within a few hundred yards of the Martyrs' Memorial.' Again, one may quote some words used by Christopher Chavasse at the end of a sermon preached in Liverpool cathedral in October 1932: 'My task, as I see it, is simple and straightforward – namely, to establish St. Peter's as a broadcasting station in Oxford, and to found there those traditions which were taught me by my father; that so, in God's good time, his voice, though dead, may still speak to generation after generation of those who never looked upon his face.'

So far, so good. But Chavasse's address to the Evangelical Conference in 1929 had included these significant words: 'More than all, I have always prayed that St. Peter's might prove to be a great practical scheme which should reunite the scattered forces of the Evangelical party. We are here to discuss Reunion.

We need reunion in our own ranks. And the project of St. Peter's should be a great means thereto'.

The point was that in the nineteen-twenties[40] there had been a serious split in the 'Evangelical party', between 'conservatives' and 'liberals'. The ultra conservatives had taken a stand on the literal inspiration of the Bible as the word of God; they had split the Church Missionary Society on this issue and set up a rival Bible Churchmen's Missionary Society; and they had started a Bible Churchmen's theological college in Bristol.[41] The argument about a proposed new Prayer Book had temporarily united both sides in opposition to what they considered to be dangerous innovations or reversions. The part played by Christopher Chavasse in this opposition had made him acceptable to the conservatives; it also explains why the original Trust Deed (never once using the word 'Evangelical') takes for its standard of true religion 'the Book of Common Prayer annexed to the Act of Uniformity of 1662'. It was only at the last moment (5 October 1928) that the Trustees required that the words 'the 39 Articles of Religion' be added: this was not itself of crucial importance, and the Trustees would have been prepared to drop the words if Hebdomadal Council had strongly objected, but it does indicate that the Trustees were stoutly conservative. Chavasse himself was on the whole conservative, but he disliked the ultra-conservatives: among his close friends he had no hesitation in showing his opinion of what he sometimes called 'the Protestant underworld'.[42] Unfortunately his hopes for 'reunion in our own ranks' were not fulfilled.

From the very start there had been hidden tensions in the relationship between Christopher Chavasse and the Martyrs Memorial Trust. It is necessary now to go back to that start and to trace what went on behind the scenes. In the first place, it is worth while to look at the printed Report of the Trust for the year 1924-1925, of which Chavasse preserved a copy. The Report begins:

From many quarters questions are being asked – What is the Martyrs' Memorial and Church of England Trust Society? – What does it stand for? – and What is it doing?

In reply to the first two questions the Trust is a Church organisation and stands for the promotion of an Evangelical and Scriptural Protestantism in the Church of England. It was called into being about twelve years ago[43] to assist in checking Modernism, or German Rationalism, on the one hand, and Romanism on the other. Its mission is to uphold the authority of the Bible as the inspired Word of God, and to be loyal to the letter and spirit of the Book of Common Prayer.

The answer to the third question is that its policy is a definite one dealing with three branches of important and constructive work in the furtherance of Evangelical principles.

FIRST. The promotion of Public Schools for Boys and Girls.

SECOND. The assistance of Ordination Candidates, i.e., To help financially young men of known Evangelical principles with their training at the Universities and Theological Colleges who contemplate Holy Orders.

THIRD. The acquisition of Church Patronage.[44]

At this date the Trust controlled only Harrogate School for Girls and Canford School for Boys and was co-operating with the Bishop of Mombasa (Dr. Heywood) in establishing an Anglican school in Kenya. In England it had acquired the Advowsons of seventy benefices, spread over twenty dioceses. Of these seventy, eighteen had been 'secured to the Trust, either by gift or by purchase' since the publication of the previous Report. According to the published accounts, the Trust's income during the year had been about £2,500, and £2,000 had been spent on the purchase of Advowsons. All this is comparatively modest. But only a few years later, on 28 January 1929, Chavasse told the Vice-Chancellor that 'Mr. Warrington . . . authorised me to tell you that the annual Revenue of the Trust from their Schools was £300,000 per annum. This fact he says may be made public if absolutely necessary, but you will understand that he is reluctant to have it disclosed otherwise. . . .' A few months later (September 1929) Mr. Warrington publicly stated[45] that the Trust controlled nearly 200 benefices. Such rapid expansion is remarkable. But Mr. Warrington was a remarkable man.[46]

Born in 1889, he had been Vicar of Monkton Combe,[47] near Bath, since 1918. He claimed to have been the originator of the Martyrs Memorial Trust, and for all practical purposes he captured the Church of England Trust Society after the amalgamation. As Honorary Secretary and *de facto* treasurer of the Trust, he kept all possible business in his own hands, and success seemed to justify his methods. As Bishop Knox wrote to Chavasse later on (14 July 1936), 'The Secretary of the Trust was a *past master* at inspiring confidence'. As early as 1920 he had been responsible for acquiring Wrekin College (not mentioned in the Trust's

Report for 1924-25); it was he who bought Harrogate School and transferred it to the Trust; and we have his own account of the acquisition of Canford and Stowe. On 11 October 1932 he wrote to Chavasse complaining that in a sermon at Liverpool Cathedral, published in *The Record*, Chavasse had said that the Trust had 'founded' Stowe and Canford Schools. 'It is news to me', wrote Warrington, 'that the Trust founded Stowe School. It is even greater news to learn that the Trust founded Canford School. . . . The Trust had neither part nor lot in the founding of Stowe School. I, personally, called a few men together (one or two of them happened to be members of the Martyrs' Memorial Trust, namely, Lord Gisborough and Sir Charles King Harman) and I unfolded the Stowe Scheme, and my proposal received their support. It was not until a few years afterwards, when I discovered the plot of a certain Bishop[48] to oust men like Lord Gisborough and Sir Charles King Harman from the Council, that I made it a condition that when further money was advanced a new arrangement should be made whereby Stowe came more or less under the control of the Trust. . . . Not a living soul had anything to do with the founding of Canford School other than myself. I noticed in *The Times* that Lord Wimborne was advertising Canford for sale. I phoned to J. D. Wood and Co., the Agents, the same day that the announcement of the sale appeared in the paper, and the next day I visited the place. Within 48 hours, without consulting anyone, I made a definite offer to Lord Wimborne to purchase Canford Manor, and my offer was accepted. The School opened on May 14th, 1923, and then I formed a Council. Realising the possibility of the School drifting away from the Movement I put a clause in the Trust Deed making it impossible for anyone to be a member of the Governing Body who is not a member of the Trust. That, in brief, is the history of the founding of Stowe and Canford Schools. . . .'
He gave further details of the founding of Stowe to a representative of *The Bath and Wilts Chronicle and Herald* (published 6 November 1934). One afternoon in October 1922 he was told by one of his parishioners that Stowe, 'the famous home of the Dukes of Buckingham', was for sale. 'Four days later Mr. Warrington was standing in Stowe House and, within a few days, a scheme to acquire the place had been evolved.[49] Three weeks afterwards the contract was signed and the newspapers announced "Stowe saved for the nation".'
This then was the man who went with Canon Stather Hunt to talk to Bishop Chavasse and Christopher Chavasse at St. Peter's

House on 21 May 1927.[50] On the evening of the same day, having returned to Monkton Combe, Warrington wrote a letter to Bishop Chavasse which needs to be quoted in full.

> Monkton Combe Vicarage,
> BATH.
> 21st May, 1927.
> SATURDAY EVENING.

The Rt. Rev. Bishop Chavasse, D.D.,
St. Peter's Rectory,
OXFORD.

My dear Bishop,
On my way home I have been thinking much of your Scheme. I am sure it presents great possibilities and should not be difficult to carry out.

I wish to pass on to you the following proposals which I shall make to my own Trustees at their Meeting next week which I hope we may be able to hold at Oxford.

The Trust to find the Salary of the Warden, that is, £500 per annum, i.e., in addition to the stipend as Rector of St. Peter's.

The Trust to offer Scholarships, not less than four but six if possible. The Scholarships to be worth from 50 to 70 guineas. Also six Bursaries of £30 guineas each.

Hannington Hall is, in my judgment, admirably suited to make the beginning. If the Trustees of Hannington Hall would hand over the Hall to the Council we could undertake the whole cost of the necessary alterations and equipment and have the building ready for opening by the end of September.

St. Peter's Rectory. I believe you said there was some money in hand for the dilapidations. If there is not sufficient I could arrange for our Trust to find the balance to complete the dilapidations and to carry out the decorations.

The Warden. I should prefer a married man with no family. Failing finding such a person then a bachelor.

Re the £2,500 which you hold. I would suggest that an equivalent sum be raised, if possible an additional £1,000, the total amount to be invested to found the first Tutorship.

Your son informed me that he would require about £2,000 to enable him to equip his present Schools to take over the Scholars at St. Peter's. I could arrange for my Trust to find

45

this sum subject to the St. Peter-le-Bailey Schools being transferred to the Council. I am greatly impressed by the possibilities
of the Schools. In the hands of a good Architect I consider this
building could be converted into a very charming Hostel.

Canal House and Conservative Club. These should be purchased at once, that is, before the Scheme is divulged. I am
quite prepared to undertake the purchase of these immediately.

I am trying to arrange a Meeting of the Trustees at Oxford
for Thursday or Friday. I will wire you as soon as I hear from
the Chairman, Canon Stather Hunt.

> I am, My dear Bishop,
> Yours with much respect,
> (Signed) P. E. WARRINGTON.

In this letter there are several points of interest. First, Warrington
is in favour of immediate action, and he takes it for granted that
it is for him, not his Chairman, to put proposals before his Trust.
Secondly, the initial scheme is modest: the plan is to convert the
existing St. Peter-le-Bailey school into a small hostel, and there is
no suggestion of erecting a completely new range of buildings.
Thirdly, the long-term scheme is ambitious. Warrington himself is
willing to buy both the Canal House and the Conservative Club
(neither of which were then in the market). Fourthly, Warrington
is not at this stage thinking of Christopher Chavasse as the
'Warden'. Fifthly, there is no reference to the £10,000 which,
according to the First Annual Report, had already been received
by Warrington from Mrs. Rowcroft. Indeed, the First Report
gives the impression that it had been received before Bishop
Chavasse's Islington speech in 1926, and years later Warrington
himself spoke as if that had been so. Bishop Knox, in a letter to
Chavasse in 1936,[51] said: 'At what stage Mrs. Rowcroft's
£10,000 . . . came in I am not sure, but it was fairly early. It was
given to found a Theological College for men of limited means
and B.C.M.S. views. It never should have been used for St.
Peter's. . . .' It would seem most likely that Mrs. Rowcroft gave
the money early in 1927, and that it was after, not before, his
meeting with Bishop Chavasse that Warrington thought of using
the benefaction for St. Peter's. His own story, given in a letter
to Prebendary Hinde in 1938,[52] was that he had told Canon
Stather Hunt that 'for the Martyrs Memorial Trust to establish
an Evangelical Hall in Oxford would be a crowning piece of
work for the Trust, [and] that it was far more important to estab-

lish such a Hall at Oxford than to found a Theological College elsewhere. . . . The Canon was full of enthusiasm for the Scheme. He urged me to see the Donor of the £10,000 and get permission to use the money for the St. Peter's Hall project. . . .'

However that may be, there is no doubt that Stather Hunt and Warrington called a special meeting of Martyrs Memorial Trustees at St. Peter's House on 27 May 1928,[53] and obtained their approval for the scheme. In his letter to Prebendary Hinde, Warrington declared that it was at this meeting that he himself suggested to his colleagues 'that we should consider appointing Christopher Chavasse the first Master of the Hall'. He adds (and it may even be true). . . . 'As we walked away from the Rectory one of my Colleagues[54] said to me – "Warrington, you have made one mistake today, you should never have suggested young[55] Chavasse as the first Principal".'

Whatever Warrington thought of Chavasse at that time, it is certain that Chavasse had reservations in his own mind about the Martyrs Memorial Trust, and he had no desire to become entirely dependent upon it. This is evidenced by the fact that soon after the Trust had agreed to back the scheme, he made a serious attempt to find an alternative backer in W. R. Morris (later Lord Nuffield). Morris's mother was a parishioner of St. Aldates, and Chavasse knew the family well. As recently as 1925 Morris had presented a new organ to St. Aldates church, and in January 1927 Chavasse had already written to him about the St. Peter's scheme, without immediate success but without a complete rebuff. W. Hobbs (the personal secretary who for many years handled Morris's correspondence) had then replied: 'For your private information Mr. Morris asks me to let you know that he considers that the hospitals situated in the neighbourhood of his many Works have the next call on him and it is probable that he will consider these to the exclusion of other matters at present. At the same time he is, as you know, interested in the matters you mention and he will be only too pleased to confer with your Father, as you suggest, before coming to any definite decision.'

On 17 June 1927 Chavasse took the matter up. He wrote to Hobbs: 'On the 29th January you wrote me a very kind letter saying that Mr. Morris would be willing to confer with my Father, Bishop Chavasse, and myself upon the possibility of his becoming interested in the Scheme for a New College [sic] in Oxford. Affairs have moved so quickly and favourably since that date, that I venture to ask if he could grant us the promised interview. The matter has become urgent, and very much may depend upon what Mr. Morris will decide. I enclose a summary of the Scheme, and a map illustrating it. Would Mr. Morris glance through it, and see if it is worth his while going further into the matter? My Father and I could wait upon him at any time next week. . . . I should also like to bring up one of the College Solicitors [sic] . . . If Mr. Morris would care to see the possibilities of such a College with his own eyes – my Father would gladly receive him at St. Peter's House, 19 New Inn Hall Street. . . .'

The 'summary' enclosed, marked *'Private and Confidential'*, is of more than a little interest:

THE SCHEME OF ST. PETER'S COLLEGE
New-Inn-Hall Street

Ever since his return to Oxford Bishop Chavasse has been working towards the founding of a New College in Oxford. . . . The moment has arrived when the Scheme is not only possible of fulfilment, but on a larger scale than was at first anticipated.

THE NEED OF A NEW COLLEGE

1. *A New College is a necessity in Oxford.*
   All Colleges are over-full. . . .
2. *A College is sorely needed where a man may be given a University education for £100 a year.*
3. *A College is needed in Oxford* where the Chapel Services and the general Religious influence shall be on broad[56] Evangelical lines. . . .

THE PRESENT POSSIBILITIES

1. The nucleus of a site is already available. . . .
2. The Church Trust, which launched Stowe so successfully, is willing to take up the scheme, and to begin operations with £20,000. They have also offered to buy from the Corporation the City School . . . when it moves to Summertown say in three years.[57] And the Wesleyan Trust express themselves as willing to sell the land adjoining . . . so that the properties may be joined. The Church Trust will shortly launch a great appeal for this purpose.
3. It is believed that the Canal Managers would not be adverse to selling the Canal Basin – comprising 1½ acres together with a handsome house and garden, etc. – for £100,000 or perhaps more.

The College would not require all this land, but roughly the northern[58] half of it comprising the Canal House for a Warden's Lodging, and the portion adjoining. . . . The remainder could then be developed with shops, offices and the like – thus forming a source of revenue for the College, and at the same time preserving the amenities of the situation towards the station. It might also be the means of incorporating Bulwarks Lane into the College, by providing a better and alternative roadway lower down. . . .

THE OPPORTUNITY

. . . an opportunity that does not occur in a century. It is a chance of ages, to found a College of which all history should be proud, and which should at the same time open the doors of Oxford to the man of small means.

1. Would Mr. Morris most seriously consider whether he would not become co-founder with Bishop Chavasse of St. Peter's College? So many Colleges in the past have been the joint production of a powerful man and a Bishop. And there can be no worthier object at the present time.

   If so the appeal of the Church Trust would still be issued, for every College has its Benefactors.

2. The immediate necessity [sic] is the purchase of the Canal Property. Therefore in any case would Mr. Morris undertake this? It is a perfectly safe investment, as the property could revert to him if the scheme did not sufficiently develop.

   It might even be that Mr. Morris would be inclined to buy this property; give the northern [sic] portion to the College; but keep the southern [sic][59] half towards the station for his own purposes. Though regard must always be paid to the fact that if the College is to provide cheap education, the endowment must be large.

The whole document reveals the qualities of Christopher Chavasse – foresight, wide views, self-confidence, and rashness. He soon received a dash of cold water from Mr. Hobbs,[60] who apologized for giving him the impression that Mr. Morris had been more interested than he actually was: 'He now finds that as he has interested himself in so many schemes of a similar character during the past year it is impossible to add to them at the present time, and he regrets therefore that at the moment he is unable to render the assistance which is suggested by purchasing the land shown by the plan, which I now return.' There is some irony in the thought that this plan first drew the attention of W. R. Morris to the site on which he was to found Nuffield College.

A year later Chavasse still thought it worth while to send Morris a proof of the St. Peter's Appeal, but he had just undertaken to help the Radcliffe Infirmary to the tune of £78,000, and Hobbs told Chavasse[61] that until Morris knew the full cost of this help it was 'not possible for him either to subscribe or even promise subscriptions to the many other Institutions the needs of which are being constantly brought to his notice'. This was disappointing, but by now Chavasse had fully accepted the necessity of working hand in hand with the Martyrs Memorial Trust if the scheme was to get off the ground as quickly as both he and Warrington hoped. That acceptance did not preclude some jockeying for position.

Here we should go back to the First Report, already quoted. Chavasse there stated that a year had been spent in negotiating for the transfer to the Trust of the advowson of St. Peter-le-Bailey and of the site and buildings surrounding the Church, including Hannington Hall, and in the preparation of a trust deed, and that at some unspecified date before 11 March 1928 the Trustees had appointed him as the first Master. On 25 August 1927 he had visited Tunbridge Wells to talk matters over with Canon Stather Hunt, and on 22 September 1927 Warrington had also visited the Canon to discuss the scheme.[62] On the next day, 23 September, there was a meeting of the Martyrs Memorial Trustees in London,[63] and it seems probable that it was then that they made the appointment of Master. The 'Trustees of St. Peter's Hall' were created by the first Trust Deed of the Hall, and this was not signed and sealed till 23 October 1928. There can therefore be no doubt that it was the Trustees of the Church of England and Martyrs Memorial Trust who made Chavasse Master.

But the position of Rector of St. Peter-le-Bailey was a crucial part of the scheme, and Chavasse did not owe that position directly to the Trust. At the end of the year 1927 the patrons of St. Peter-le-Bailey were the Trustees of the Oxford Churches Trust, a body having no connection whatever with the Martyrs Memorial Trust. They were all friends[64] of Bishop F. J. Chavasse, and thoroughly approved of the proposals. So did Canon Stansfeld, another very old friend. Since the Bishop of Oxford, Dr. Strong, had also given his approval, there were no difficulties.

Canon Stansfeld resigned from the living of St. Peter-le-Bailey (retaining that of St. Ebbe's), and on 24 January 1928 Christopher Chavasse was instituted as Rector of St. Peter-le-Bailey, on the presentation of the patrons, Mr. J. F. W. Deacon, the Revd. H. H. Gibbon, the Revd. A. E. Hughes, Mr. M. H. F. Sutton and the Revd. L. Bradyll-Johnson. For the time being Chavasse remained Rector of St. Aldate's and continued to live in the Rectory in Pembroke Street. It was not until 23 July 1928 that the Oxford Churches Trust[65] formally transferred the patronage of St. Peter-le-Bailey to Canon Stather Hunt, Lord Gisborough, Sir Charles King Harman and the Revd. P. E. Warrington.[66] It should be noted that the Martyrs Memorial Trust did not purchase the living, though there was in fact an exchange of patronage. W. J. Pearman Smith and Sons of Walsall were solicitors to the M.M.T. at this time, and they later informed Chavasse: 'Mr. Warrington himself negotiated the exchange of the Advowson of Gislingham for that of St. Peter-le-Bailey and gave us instructions to do the legal work.'[67]

As Rector of St. Peter-le-Bailey and St. Aldate's, Chavasse was well placed to arrange for the transfer of the properties on which the scheme depended, and to negotiate with the Martyrs Memorial Trust not as a subordinate but as an equal. On 11 April 1928 the Trustees of St. Peter-le-Bailey Schools, meeting at St. Aldate's Rectory, resolved that they were willing 'to hand over the Building and playground of the said School to the Trustees of St. Peter's Hall, in consideration of the Trustees of St. Peter's Hall extending the playground of St. Aldate's Schools and effecting . . . alterations and improvements . . . in order that the School of St. Peter-le-Bailey may be transferred to the buildings of St. Aldate's School. And they empower the Rev. C. M. Chavasse to proceed with this intention'. A little earlier, on 28 March 1928, there had been a meeting in St. Aldate's Rectory of 'the Representatives of the C.M.S. and C.E.Z.M.S.[68] in Oxford', who had been closely associated in the past with Hannington Hall. At this meeting Chavasse read out extracts from the original Trust Deed of Hannington Hall,[69] from the proposed Trust Deed of St. Peter's Hall and also from the proposed Deed of Conveyance from the Trustees of Hannington Hall to those of St. Peter's Hall, and firmly stated that 'as far as he could see (and after having taken legal advice) the objects for which Hannington Hall was founded were completely and indeed even better fulfilled by its new use'. The representatives passed a resolution of approval. St. Aldate's was concerned, as well as the

C.M.S. representatives; part of the transaction was that 'the Rector and Churchwardens of St. Aldate's shall be assisted to put St. Aldate's Church Schools into such condition that parochial organisations can be carried on at the Schools thus freeing the Rectory Room 40 Pembroke Street . . . for Meetings of Under- graduates' and arrangements were 'to be made with the Rector of St. Aldate's for the holding of religious meetings of Members of the University in the Rectory Room 40 Pembroke Street'[70] – that is, members who might be deprived of the use of Hannington Hall by the transfer.

To quote again from the First Report,

> In all such arrangements the unfailing help and good will of the Rev. the Hon. W. Talbot Rice and the other Trustees of Hannington Hall and of St. Peter-le-Bailey Schools[71] must be remembered with the greatest gratitude, for it was only their enthusiastic co-operation which made the undertaking possible; especially with regard to the merging of the memorial to the martyred Bishop Hannington in the scheme for St. Peter's Hall.[72]

While all this was going on, Chavasse had been wrestling with the problem of devising a constitution for St. Peter's and embodying it in a Trust Deed – and a Trust Deed in which he himself as Rector of St. Peter-le-Bailey would be one of the contracting parties. The First Report is relevant:

> But here a difficulty presented itself. How was such a council to be formed which would satisfy the traditions of a University where religious tests had been abolished and which was rightly sensitive to any outside dictation; and yet guarantee that Evangelical character associated with the memory of its Founder, to maintain which the Trustees were expending the money of their subscribers?

In other words, how to convince the University that the Martyrs Memorial Trust would not be able to dominate the Council, while leaving the M.M.T. under the impression that it certainly would be able to dominate?

There exists a typed paper headed 'Notes on suggested Con- stitution'. It is undated[73] and unsigned, but at the end is a note in Christopher Chavasse's handwriting: 'I got this out for the benefit of the Patrons – and it is not of course for public con-

sumption – as far as the "Evangelical" part is concerned. C.M.C.'
It is worth quoting in full.

A. The Constitution is based on that of St. Edmund Hall[74]
which the University itself has suggested. Namely three
interests equally represented: —

1. *Queen's College* (who own the Hall and appoint the
   Principal). Two representatives.
2. *St. Edmund Hall itself:*
   Two representatives viz. the Principal and his nominee.
3. *Education:*
   Two representatives from the University.

St. Peter's Hall aims at the same proportion.
1. *The Patrons:* Four Representatives as Trustees.
2. *Education:* Four Representatives (Oxford and Liverpool).
3. *The College* [sic]: The Master, two appointed by the Hall,
   The Principal of Wycliffe Hall; in all, four Representatives.

B. The Constitution is also woven round the life work of
Bishop Chavasse; viz – *St. Peter-le-Bailey* (where he was
Rector), the Patrons are Trustees. *Wycliffe Hall* (where he was
Principal), the Principal is on the Council. *Liverpool* (where he
was Bishop), Liverpool University appoint Representatives.

C. But the chief merit is that Evangelical Traditions are maintained without being unduly emphasised, viz:—

1. *At the start*, the Patrons have seven Nominations out of
   twelve, viz:—

   4 Trustees
   2 Council[75]
   1 The Master of the Hall
   ──
   7

To which can be added the Principal of Wycliffe Hall whose
aim it will be that men come on to him and not Cuddesdon or
Wells. While *all* the Trustees[76] have to sign a declaration that
they approve of the objects of the Hall, viz:
'To diffuse the Reformation Teaching of the Church of
England as set forth in the Book of Common Prayer 1662.'

2. *Afterwards*
   1. It is for the Patrons to decide 'if and when' the Master and Tutors of the College [sic] shall appoint two Representatives instead of them.
   2. If they allow them to do so they have power to put on more representatives themselves.

Thus the Patrons are guarded first and last – and should not make their presence felt more than necessary in Oxford, which is very jealous of its privileges. At any rate, at the inception of the scheme, when the Trust Deed is scrutinised, this is important.

N.B. The whole tradition of the College [sic] really depends upon the Master; and if the Patrons appoint him, they must trust him.

Presumably the Patrons were satisfied by this explanation. Chavasse had been able to start collecting a provisional Council before the middle of April 1928. There was no difficulty in recruiting the Principal of Wycliffe Hall;[77] and the President of Corpus[78] and the Pro-Provost of Queen's[79] were willing to act as University representatives if Hebdomadal Council should agree to appoint. Sir Charles Oman,[80] who lived at Frewin Hall just off New Inn Hall Street, readily agreed to be nominated by the Patrons. There was a little difficulty in obtaining representatives from Liverpool University. The Vice-Chancellor, Dr. H. J. W. Hetherington, though sympathetic, was reluctant to ask his University to nominate in case the Council of St. Peter's should become a body pledged to take sides in a religious controversy.[81] However it occurred to Chavasse that the solution was to ask Lord Derby to nominate as Chancellor of Liverpool University, and this Lord Derby agreed to do. Chavasse had suggested four names,[82] and of these Lord Derby selected Mr. J. G. Legge and Judge Dowdall. This left one further place to be filled by the Patrons,[83] and they eventually nominated Lord Cushendun, an Ulster Protestant who held Cabinet office[84] under Stanley Baldwin from October 1927 to June 1929.

The first meeting of the Provisional Council took place in Oxford on 31 May 1928. Those present were Chavasse as Chairman, Dr. Allen, Judge Dowdall, Mr. Graham-Brown, Mr. Legge, Sir Charles Oman and Mr. Warrington. On the previous day[85] Warrington had thought fit to fire a warning shot. He had written to Chavasse: [86]

'I am afraid from the observations you have made with reference to the Trustees and their attitude to the Trust Deed it is clear that you do not appreciate the position from their point of view. Not only is the Church of England Trust financing the building scheme for Hannington Hall, the conversion of St. Peter-le-Bailey Schools, the building of new Schools for St. Aldate's, but it is also guaranteeing the Warden's Salary, the Tutor's Salary, and Scholarships and Exhibitions. This involves a very considerable outlay and without the assistance the Trust is giving it would have been a sheer impossibility for this movement to have made a beginning. A Trust which is doing this and finds that after undertaking the Scheme only five of its own members will be on the Board of Management of St. Peter's College [sic] is not going to release such a huge sum of money[87] from the Trust's General Fund until they have safeguarded their own position to their entire satisfaction. Their reply to your statement that 'there are other interests' is 'we are finding the money'.

In expressing the attitude of the Trustees please do not understand there is any hostility. Such is not the case. There is a very earnest desire to further the St. Peter's Hall Scheme. The Members of the Trust are men of very wide experience and if they are over anxious it is because past experience has taught them to be cautious'.

There is no doubt that at the meeting on 31 May both Chavasse and Warrington felt some anxiety. But the Minutes show no sign of this. The business was, on the face of it, straightforward. Mr. C. L. Teal[88] was appointed 'Secretary to act for the Trust' [sic], with an honorarium of £30 a year but with no duties except to summon Council meetings and to keep minutes; Mr. J. A. Cumming[89] was appointed Honorary Treasurer of the Appeal Fund; it was reported that the Revd. R. E. C. Houghton had been appointed 'an Assistant Tutor';[90] the application for licensing as a Permanent Private Hall was approved, and it was resolved to open 'in a preliminary way as a Hostel for the Michaelmas Term 1928; the draft Appeal was approved; and finally a Drafting Committee was set up to deal with the proposed Trust Deed, viz. Lord Gisborough,[91] Mr. Warrington, Canon Stather Hunt, Judge Dowdall, Mr. J. G. Legge, and Chavasse himself – Judge Dowdall to act as chairman. In this connection it was resolved that 'the Council gives general approval to the draft Trust Deed but requests the Drafting Committee to rearrange it and make its wording clearer. They would also ask the Committee to define the precise position of the Council of the Hall and of the Trustees. The former to have the general administration of the Hall, but the Trustees as undertaking the financial responsibility and the safeguarding of the Evangelical traditions of the Hall must be given the power of veto'.

Warrington was certainly responsible for the wording of this resolution, or at any rate the latter part of it, and he went away without obvious signs of discontent. But on 12 June 1928 he delivered a broadside. He sent this letter to Chavasse, marked 'private and confidential': 'I have been giving very serious thought to the correspondence I am receiving from the Trustees and their attitude to the Trust Deed which your Solicitors have drafted. . . . I view the position with grave misgiving and upon reflection I am persuaded that in the interest of the whole Scheme I ought to tell you quite candidly the attitude of my Trustees.[92] They are convinced that the Trust is being used by you as a catspaw to further the St. Peter's Scheme. They may find the money, but every precaution is being taken that they should have as little voice as possible in the control of the Hall.

With reference to the Committee which was formed last week to go into the question of the Trust Deed, you appointed over the heads of Lord Gisborough, Sir Charles King Harman and Canon Stather Hunt, Judge Dowdall to be the Chairman of that Committee. The Committee was very surprised at this action. Judge Dowdall should have come in in an advisory capacity at this juncture and not as a chairman. The Trustees regard this action as a most serious affront to the President of their Society and the Chairman of Stowe School.

The appointment of a firm of Solicitors without any reference to the Trust has greatly incensed the whole body of Trustees. The insertion of a clause in the Trust Deed forbidding the Trust to raise one penny mortgage on its own property,[93] which it will purchase entirely out of its own funds . . . has greatly added to the Trustees' indignation. . . .

All the things which I have enumerated . . . make the Trustees feel they are only required to find the money to get it going and they will be ousted from any real control of the College [sic] at the earliest opportunity. I am sorry to write you thus, but I am forced to the conclusion and it is only fair to you that you should know the attitude of the Trustees without delay and certainly before the Meeting of the Committee on Thursday next.

It is for the reasons which I have enumerated that I feel that there is every possibility of this Scheme falling to the ground.

Indeed, I should be surprised, if when it comes before the full body of Trustees on Thursday week they allow the matter to pass. From the correspondence I have received they have made it quite clear to me that they are only doing so subject to the acceptance of terms which they will lay down.'

This letter certainly worried Chavasse, but he did not treat it too seriously. On 13 June he wrote: 'My dear Warrington, your letter which I have just received caused me some anxiety, especially as I am having a difficult time with the authorities of Oxford University in obtaining a licence for the Hostel, and also seeing that I am having an interview this morning with the [Wesleyan] Trustees about the Wesleyan Schools, which will mean that I shall be able to purchase them. The difficulties really lie at this end and we must not let what I may call "domestic squabbles" handicap the greatest opportunity of this century. . . . What does give me confidence is the fact that the Evangelical interests of the Hall are adequately safeguarded, and this of course is the purpose for which the Trust was founded and why we are so glad to have this safeguard behind the whole scheme. You cannot fairly describe the Trust as being used as a "catspaw" when the Trustees have as large a representation on the Council as it is possible for the [sic] Oxford University to allow and when I have used my utmost influence to get the patronage of St. Peter-le-Bailey transferred to the Trustees and the Rectory, Hannington Hall and the Church Schools handed over to them for what economically is a ridiculous sum.

With reference to the particular points of your letter:—

Judge Dowdall was appointed Chairman of the Drafting Committee, not by me but by the Council of which you were one and you raised no objection. Lord Gisborough is a busy man, Sir Charles King Harman and Canon Stather Hunt are both ill. I am certain the Trustees will be glad to have the active interest and counsel of the late chairman of the Legal Advisory Board of the Church of England and one who is giving infinite pains and time to the drafting of the Deed and who also, from his office of Judge will safeguard impartially all interests involved.

The appointment of a firm of solicitors refers I suppose either to the drawing up of the provisional Trust Deed (which was meant to be criticized and mainly to form the basis of negotiations) or to the appointment by the Council (in which you concurred) of the Legal Secretary [sic] to the Council. In the former case the initiative was taken by my father, and rightly, as promoter of the scheme. In the latter case the Secretary must be

57

in Oxford. The prolonged delay over the transference of the Patronage of St. Peter-le-Bailey proves how impossible it would be to employ a firm of solicitors outside Oxford[94] and [sic] who were too busy with the other interests of the Trustees to give Oxford the attention which is absolutely necessary.

With regard to powers of mortgage. I am so glad that this is the matter that really causes our difference and it is unexpected by me that Trustees of property should not welcome every safeguard that is possible in this connexion. It seems to me that the purpose of a Trust Deed for the Hall is to guard against an Anglo-Catholic master on the one hand and fraudulent trustees on the other, and I am sure we can arrange this to every one's satisfaction. I must remind you that the Rectory and garden, worth at least £10,000 is being handed over to you for £4,000,[95] and that Hannington Hall, schools and playground are worth far more than the sum of money we have to expend in making the St. Aldate's Schools suitable. . . . I do feel therefore that as Rector and as Chairman of the Trustees of Hannington Hall and the schools, we are handing over this property, not so much to the Trust as their own, but in trust for the Hall.

Let me add this, that Canon Stather Hunt and Lord Gisborough have signed an application to the University to open a hostel; and that accordingly I have resigned my living[96] to take charge of this hostel and have accepted 14 residents for it. The Trust is therefore pledged both to the University and to these applicants to see them through their University course at St. Peter's for the next three years. The position with regard to a permanent private hall might be a little different. I will keep Thursday week free so that I may attend the meeting of your Trustees. . . .'

On 21 June 1928 Chavasse duly met Warrington's Trustees, and the result was a 'Memorandum of proposals agreed upon[97] after meeting between the Revd. C. M. Chavasse and the Martyrs Memorial and Church of England Trust Society':—

1. The Revd. C. M. Chavasse will sell St. Peter's Rectory to the Martyrs Memorial and Church of England Trust Society[98] (as distinct from the proposed four Trustees – nominees of the Trust Society and proposed parties to the Trust Deed who hold the advowson of St. Peter-le-Bailey).

*2. By the Trust Deed *of the Hall* the Trust Society will hand over to the Trustees of St. Peter's Hall the Rectory and Schools,[99] for the exclusive use of the Hall *and the property* *to be under their* [sic] *exclusive administration – and entitled the 'Original Property'.*

3. Any property acquired by the Trustees of the Hall apart from the Trust Society (e.g. as result of appeal) shall be for exclusive use of the Hall *and under the administration of the Governing Body of the Hall.*
    Provided always —

    (a) That the Governing Body shall have power at any time to take over the property referred to in Nos. 1 and 2 above on repaying to the Trust Society the amount expended upon it.

    (b) If the Trustees shall decide that the property should be handed over to Oxford University (for the purposes of a Public Hall) or to the Hall itself (in case the Hall decides to obtain a Charter for a College) the Trust Society undertakes to hand over the property free from incumbrances.

    If the Trustees cannot hold and themselves administer property entrusted to them by Trust Deed by the Trust Society – then let the Trust Society hold the property themselves for the Hall.

This memorandum was sent to Warrington by Chavasse, with a covering letter, of which only a draft in Chavasse's own writing has survived. Some extracts are worth quoting: —

'I send you a memorandum which I think will meet with your entire approval. . . .

. . . The Trust is in a very strong position – as even if the Governing Body were in a position to buy back the property its nominated Trustees will still (1) hold the same, (2) appoint the Master, (3) have a majority on the Council, (4) hold funds for the Hall at their discretion.

(This is in your ear – not for Oxford to know.)

. . . I feel very happy about things – as I feel there is good will on both sides, and we both understand each other's difficulties and that there is no obstruction. . . .

Cannot the Advowson business go forward without this worry about four or five Trustees? Why not four and have done with it? It may cause complications after to have five. Meanwhile the Diocesan people are getting restive and the Delegates of Lodgings are asking questions. The Trust Deed also must be settled in the next month before the Long Vacation, and my Diocesan people will not convey the Rectory till the Trust Deed is settled – as they say it must be conveyed upon the terms of the Trust Deed.'

It would seem that at this moment Chavasse had high hopes of a smooth working arrangement between himself and Warrington. A week or so later he received a cantankerous reply[100]:

'We held our Trust Meeting yesterday [28 June], when Counsel's opinion[101] was considered. . . .

. . . Canon Stather Hunt told the Council [of the M.M.T.] yesterday, that at three interviews that he had with your late Father, he was emphatic that as a condition of finding the money, the Trust would require to hold the property, and to this the Bishop agreed, and not only agreed, but assured the Canon that he warmly supported him on this point.

The question of your being let down was raised; Canon Stather Hunt assured the Trustees that he had urged and warned you that under no consideration should you resign your Benefice of St. Aldate's until the question of the Trust Deed had been finally disposed of.

. . . I do wish you had listened to me, and not allowed the question of the Trust Deed to come before the Council [of St. Peter's]. The Trust Deed is no business of the Council whatever, it is the sole concern of the Trust which is promoting the scheme.

I fear I made a very serious mistake in coming to the Council Meeting which you had at Oxford. The Trustees only the day before particularly requested me not to come.[102] I came as I was anxious not to let you down. . . .

I confess I was never more fearful of the scheme falling through, than I was at the close of the Meeting yesterday. . . .

[As to the memorandum, the terms] were not agreed, they were merely suggested after the Trustees had left.

[The clause about buying back the property] has greatly disturbed the Trustees. They are all, without a single exception, of the opinion that if funds were forthcoming, the Trust would be thrown off at the earliest opportunity.'

However, there was no real danger of the scheme falling through at this stage, and Chavasse did his best to allay Warrington's fears, and to humour his suspicious disposition. For instance, on 14 August 1928, when Warrington had complained about a particular clause in the proposed conveyance of the Rectory, Chavasse[103] wrote:

'My dear Warrington. You ought to know me well enough to be assured that my last wish would be to cause you extra trouble, for I know how busy you are . . . your lawyers have not grasped the fact that the Archbishop's legal secretary insists on some

clause being inserted with respect to the property in the eventuality of the Hall ceasing to be a Hall. It was only on this
condition that he consented to the ridiculous purchase price of
£4,000. . . . You need not be nervous in any dealings that effect
[sic] you and me – for we have the same object in view and all
will be well. The real cause for nervousness is our dealings with
the University – and hidden opposition working there. For this I
need (as you little know) your full confidence, sympathy and
encouragement; so please don't write me any more letters of the
tone of this one, and if you address me again as "Mr." I shall
counter with "Rev. and Dear Sir". . . .'

In spite of this appeal for friendly relations, Warrington's next
letter still began 'Dear Mr. Chavasse', and Chavasse gave up the
attempt to banter him: from then on it was 'Dear Mr. Warrington'. But Chavasse still tried to humour him. For instance, he
ended another exchange of letters[104] about the Rectory conveyance with the words 'A good holiday to you – you deserve it.'

It was said above that there was no real danger of the scheme
falling through at this stage. This was because on 5 July 1928
Chavasse went to London to meet Canon Stather Hunt and
Warrington, and they all three signed a memorandum, in the
presence of Mr. Pearman Smith, containing the basis of the
proposed Trust Deed. Even so, there were misunderstandings, as
late as 1 October 1928. On that date Andrew Walsh and Bartram,
Solicitors, of Oxford, wrote on behalf of Chavasse to S. Pearman
Smith and Sons, who had been responsible for producing a final
draft of the Deed:

'Mr. Chavasse expresses great surprise at the amendments that
have been made in the draft as settled by Counsel on behalf of
all parties, having regard to the Memorandum of the 5th July. . . .
Mr. Chavasse cannot understand why a draft Trust Deed, so care-
lessly amended as to be directly contrary to the principles set
out in the Memorandum . . . has been put before him, and he has
requested us to point out some of the more glaring examples of
the way the draft has been so amended. . . . Mr. Chavasse cannot
believe that this has been deliberately done, but he considers such
inadvertence inexplicable. Mr. Chavasse wishes us to clearly
point out that it was on the basis of this Memorandum that he
has contracted to sell the Rectory of St. Peter-le-Bailey to the
Trust. He cannot go back on the Memorandum and he believes
that the provisional Council at Oxford would resign in a body
if he contemplated doing so. Mr. Chavasse would also point out
that the constitution of the Council has been agreed to by the

Trust Society on two occasions at the Charing Cross Hotel in his presence, namely, on 19 April and 21 June, and that it is disconcerting to find, by the amendments in the draft Trust Deed, that the whole constitution is upset some three months later. . . .'[105]

The result was another meeting in London, on 5 October 1928, between Chavasse and the Martyrs Memorial Trustees. Differences were ironed out, and yet another Memorandum was agreed. This read:

The Principles to govern the Trust Deed of St. Peter's Hall, as decided between the Church of England Trust Society and the Revd. C. M. Chavasse, at the Charing Cross Hotel on October 5th.

1. WITH REGARD TO THE PRINCIPLES OF THE HALL the Trustees required that the words 'the 39 Articles' should be added to 'the Book of Common Prayer of 1662'. To this the Revd. C. M. Chavasse agreed, and asked that the Clause giving 'Power to vary Trusts' should be slightly amended so that 'the 39 Articles' might be subsequently omitted, if the University Authorities refused to license St. Peter's as a Public Hall, on the ground of the Test Acts of 1871.

2. WITH REGARD TO THE CONSTITUTION OF THE HALL. This should remain the same except that the Trustees should have power to add two additional members to the Council at any time, and for such time as they thought necessary.

3. WITH REGARD TO THE PROPERTY OF THE HALL. The Trustees, who are taking financial responsibility, should have absolute control (for the exclusive use of the Hall) of the site and buildings of the Hall, whether existing now or to be subsequently acquired, and which as a matter of fact they are purchasing and erecting out of their own funds. All other property should be vested in the Trustees for the exclusive use of the Hall, at the direction of the Council.

4. It should be stated at the beginning of the Trust Deed that the clear intention was 'to found a Public Hall' in 'connection with the University'.

At the next meeting of the Provisional Council, held in St. Peter's House on Monday, 8 October 1928,[106] this Memorandum was 'perused and considered and signed by the Master at the request of the Council', and on the proposition of Canon Stather Hunt, seconded by Mr. Warrington, it was resolved that a copy of the Memorandum should be set out in the Minutes of the Meeting. After this there was no more internal difficulty: the Trust Deed was signed and sealed on 23 October 1928.[107] There was a little external difficulty; Hebdomadal Council made certain stipulations, but these were satisfied in a short Supplementary Trust Deed, made on 15 January 1929. These Trust Deeds continued in force until 1948, and are therefore of some importance.

They take the form of an agreement between (A) the Patrons of St. Peter-le-Bailey Church (Stather Hunt, Gisborough, King Harman, Warrington), and (B) the Trustees of the Deed[108] (the same four persons), and (C) the Rector of St. Peter-le-Bailey (C. M. Chavasse). The preamble mentions that

. . . the Patrons are applying a sum of approximately Fifty thousand pounds or thereabouts in and about the acquisition and adaptation of premises on the west side of New Inn Hall Street and between that street and Bulwarks Lane, and that Christopher Maude Chavasse has deposited at Barclays Bank Oxford the sum of Ten thousand pounds or thereabouts collected for the purposes of the Hall and it is hoped that further moneys may be collected for those purposes.

CAP. I (The Objects and Principles) is still embodied in the Charter of St. Peter's College, and must be quoted in full: —

CAP. I.

1. The primary objects and principles for which the Hall is established are—

(*a*) To maintain and promote education religion and learning for and among students generally of whatever religious persuasion and especially to give aid to students in straitened or reduced circumstances who shall be deemed worthy thereof by the Council by way of bursaries Scholarships Exhibitions or by such other means as in the opinion of and at the absolute discretion of the Council may be most conducive to the advancement of such students and the attainment of these objects.

(*b*) To train cherish and encourage candidates for Holy Orders in the Church of England or any students or other persons intending to labour for Foreign Missions with which the Ministry of the late Bishop James Hannington was particularly identified.

(*c*) To diffuse sound information and teaching of and in Christian principles and doctrine in conformity with Holy Scripture and particularly the Protestant and Reformed teaching of the Church of England as set forth in the Book of Common Prayer annexed to the Act of Uniformity of 1662 and the 39 Articles of Religion and Ordinal as now ordinarily bound up with such Book and so that the teaching of the Hall and the conduct of the services in the said Chapel shall be in all respects in accordance with such principles.

(*d*) Generally to do all other incidental things which may be conducive to the furtherance and elucidation of such objects and principles.

CAP. II lays down that the total number of Trustees of the Hall shall not exceed eight and shall not be allowed to fall below four; and all Trustees of the Advowson of St. Peter-le-Bailey shall be appointed Trustees of the Hall. All property of the Hall, present and future, both real and personal, shall be vested in the Trustees of the Hall; but there are two important provisos: —[109]

Provided always (1) That the Trustees may if so advised direct that any property may be vested in any Statutory or Corporate Body having power to hold lands in mortmain (including the Martyrs Memorial and Church of England Trust) as custodian trustees. (2) That the Trustees shall have full and express powers of sale, mortgage, and leasing of the Trust Property or any part thereof.

CAP. III gives 'the general control of the Hall' to a Council consisting of —

(a) Not more than four of the Patrons of St. Peter-le-Bailey.[110]

(b) The Rector of St. Peter-le-Bailey 'who shall **ex officio** be Master of the Hall only so long as he shall be appointed to the Parish by the Patrons'.[111]

(c) Two representatives nominated by the Trustees of the Hall, but 'if and so soon as the Trustees shall think fit such two representatives may be nominated by the Master and Tutors of the Hall with the approval in each case of the Trustees'.

(d) Two representatives of Oxford University.[112]

(e) Two representatives of Liverpool University.[113]

(f) The Principal of Wycliffe Hall.

(g) 'The Trustees shall be at liberty if they so desire at any time and from time to time to appoint an additional Member or two additional Members of the Council for such period as they think fit.'

[The effect of these provisions is rather odd: the Trustees of the Hall are *not* **ex officio** members of the Council. But at the time there were only four Trustees and they were all members of the Council as Patrons of the living, so no anomaly then appeared.]

CAP. IV is important.

CAP. IV.

5. No person shall be competent to act as a Trustee or Member of the Council unless and until he shall have signed a declaration in writing in the following form namely: —

"I.......................................do solemnly and sincerely "declare that I approve the objects and principles for which "St. Peter's Hall Oxford is established as set out and defined "in and by the Trust Deed of the Hall dated the twenty-third "day of October One thousand nine hundred and twenty- "eight [meaning this Deed] and will use my best endeavours "in all respects to perform and observe the trusts provisions "and conditions thereof."

There is no need at this stage to go through all the other provisions of the original Trust Deed, but it should be noted that under CAP. XII the Patrons covenanted with the Trustees and also with Chavasse to make or provide certain payments, provided that they might at any time reduce or cease altogether such payments after giving six months' notice. The payments were listed in a Schedule: —

THE SECOND SCHEDULE BEFORE REFERRED TO

1. The payment to the Master of a salary of £1,000 per annum (including all emoluments derived from the Benefice) payable quarterly on the 1st January the 1st April the 1st July and the 1st October in every year.

2. The provision of a house for the Master free of rent and with such allowance for rates and taxes as may be agreed upon.

3. The provision of the salary of one Tutor subject to any endowment for such purpose as may be otherwise provided.

4. The provision of six bursaries of £30 each and such number of scholarships as the Trustees may from time to time decide.

The supplementary Trust Deed of 15 January 1929 made provision for the retirement of the Master at the age of sixty-five,[114] gave power to the Council[115] to dismiss the Master for 'misconduct, mental or physical incapacity or other grave cause', and laid down that the income and property of the Hall should be 'applied solely towards the promotion of the objects of the Hall as set forth in the Trust Deed'.[116] The final clause was a guarantee of permanency:

4. The object of the Trust Deed is to establish St. Peter's Hall on a permanent footing (subject only to its failure to fulfil its functions) and the Patrons guarantee its permanent character whether as a private Hall or a Public Hall or a College.

It should be specially noticed that it was the Patrons of the Advowson of St. Peter-le-Bailey who gave this guarantee, and nowhere in the Trust Deed was it stated that those Patrons had any legal right to give undertakings on behalf of the Martyrs Memorial Trust. For that reason, the Vice-Chancellor required further assurance. Chavasse was able to send him an extract, certified by Warrington as a true copy, from the minutes of a meeting of the Trust held on 15 January 1929: —

'RESOLVED THAT the Martyrs Memorial and Church of England Trust do guarantee the permanency of St. Peter's Hostel, i.e. in addition to providing the Master's Salary, Scholarships, Exhibitions, and the balance required for the Tutor's Salary, the Trustees hereby Guarantee that any deficit in the running expenses of the Hostel shall be paid out of the Funds of the Trust.
Further RESOLVED That the Trustees of St. Peter's Advowson be authorised to sign the Supplementary Trust Deed giving the Guarantee required by the Vice-Chancellor.'

So, when St. Peter's Hall was founded, the four Trustees of the Hall were Trustees simply because they were already Trustees of the Advowson of St. Peter-le-Bailey; and they were Trustees of the Advowson because they were already Trustees[117] of the

Martyrs Memorial and Church of England Trust Society. In fact, the Trust Society was the unity[118] which was represented by those four men in their trinity of functions; and it is not so surprising as it otherwise would be to discover that the early Trustees of St. Peter's Hall, as such, did not think it necessary to keep minutes of their own proceedings.[119] So too in letters exchanged between Warrington and Chavasse, when the word 'Trustees' occurs it is not always clear in which sense it is being used; at the time it did not appear to matter, because if there was a distinction, it was a distinction without a difference.

In the original Trust Deed, the Martyrs Memorial Trust was mentioned twice only: first, in Cap. II, already quoted, and secondly in Cap. XVII, 'Provisions for Closing the Hall'.

CAP. XVII.

36. If at any time hereafter the Hall shall in the opinion of the Council (expressed by a Resolution passed by a two-thirds majority at least at a meeting held after not less than thirty days' notice and confirmed by a similar majority at a subsequent meeting not less than thirty days later) and in the opinion of the Trustees have ceased usefully to fulfil its functions it shall be closed and after payment of all debts and liabilities properly incurred in respect of the Hall the Trust Property shall be applied (subject to satisfaction of all incumbrances thereon and including a lien for all moneys properly expended on the property) for the following purposes (*a*) the payment of a sum of Four thousand pounds to the Governors of Queen Anne's Bounty for the provision (if required) of a new Residence House for the Incumbent of St. Peter-le-Bailey Oxford or otherwise for the benefit of the said Benefice and subject thereto (*b*) sixty per cent. of the Trust Property shall be allotted to the Martyrs Memorial and Church of England Trust and the balance divided equally between (*c*) Wycliffe Hall (*d*) The Oxford Pastorate and (*e*) The Diocese of Liverpool.

This provision that sixty per cent of the Trust Property should be allotted to the Trust Society is interesting. It must be quite clear by now that whereas Bishop Francis James Chavasse was quite properly given honour as the nominal Founder of St. Peter's Hall, the actual founders were Christopher Chavasse and the Martyrs Memorial Trust jointly; and if one had to make an assessment of their contributions it would not be altogether unreasonable to maintain that, when the Hall opened in October 1929, sixty per cent of the credit might have gone to the Trust and forty per cent to Christopher Chavasse.

3

On 2 November 1929 the Council had its first meeting 'as a duly constituted Council of St. Peter's Hall'.[120] After passing resolutions of thanks to Vice-Chancellor Pember and to R. Fielding Dodd, the architect, it resolved unanimously that 'in recognition of the signal services rendered by the Martyrs Memorial and Church of England Trust Society in the inception of the Hall . . . the name of the Chairman of that Society[121] should be associated with the First Tutorship',[122] and that 'the arms of the Hon. Secretary (the Revd. P. E. Warrington)' should be emblazoned on a shield above the iron gateway leading into the quadrangle from New Inn Hall Street. At that time, it seemed likely that the south quadrangle would become known not as the 'Hannington' but as the 'Warrington' Quad. Two months later[123] Canon Stather Hunt died, and Warrington became even more dominant than before in the Martyrs Memorial Trust. Looking back to this period six years afterwards, with the advantage of hindsight, Chavasse wrote to Bishop Knox: [124]

'When the Martyrs Memorial [sic] first approached us they were differently constituted from what they were later on. They were the amalgamation of two Trusts – the Church of England Trust Society, founded by Stather Hunt, and the Martyrs Memorial Trust, with Warrington as their Secretary. While Stather Hunt was Chairman, the hope was that the decent element in the Church of England Trust would take possession. But unfortunately honest men like Sir Thomas Inskip and the late Mr. Gladstone became uneasy when Mr. Warrington ceased to produce balance sheets, and resigned. Then Canon Stather Hunt died; and we were in the soup. . . .'

But at the time Chavasse gave no outward sign of dismay. His praise of Warrington in the Second Annual Report has already been quoted, and in his Third Annual Report (1930-31) he went further: —

It has been said with truth that St. Peter's Hall is an achievement in which the work of ten years has been accomplished in less than three. This is entirely owing to the courage and munificence of our Trustees, who are representatives of the Martyrs Memorial and Church of England Trust Society; and especially to the driving force of its Honorary Secretary, the Rev. P. E. Warrington, the founder of Stowe and numerous other Schools since the War. In comparison with this great system of schools he may have regarded the establishing of St. Peter's as a relatively small though highly important enterprise. But it has meant everything to us, in Oxford, to have behind us the immense resources of this great Trust, which has been lavish in its expenditure and eager to meet every requirement suggested by the University.

This Third Report was presented to the Council on 29 June 1931. Few would have guessed that ten days earlier Chavasse had given the draft of this Report to the Tutors for their comment and on the very same day had told them that he was thinking of taking legal action against Mr. Warrington.[125] The Tutors certainly did not then know all that had been going on behind the scenes. To understand the position, it is necessary to hark back to 1928.

It has already been seen that at the end of May 1928 Mr. J. A. Cumming had been appointed Hon. Treasurer of the Appeal Fund. From the start, he had niggling financial difficulties with Mr. Warrington. On 21 June Cumming wrote to him: —

'When I met you at St. Aldate's Rectory with Mr. Chavasse, I understood you were prepared to pay initial expenses in connection with St. Peter's Hostel as a venture, provided strict accounts were sent to you . . . for sums about £25, in other words that we should work on a system of imprests. On this understanding I advanced the money to meet certain bills that could not wait. On 15 May I sent you details for £29-1-6 and reminded you on 8th inst., but so far I have had no reply from you.' A little later Cumming found it necessary to press Warrington for payment of bills for work done at St. Aldate's Schools and for the purchase by Chavasse of a second-hand piano for the Hostel, and also to remind him that 'when I saw you with Canon Stather Hunt you promised to let me have £100 for current expenses',[126] and no such sum had arrived. He found Warrington reluctant to pay. He did indeed pay the bill of £64 for St. Aldate's Schools, but rebuked Cumming for pressing:[127] 'I have to inform you that Members of the Trust have taken great exception to cheques being signed privately and they require that the Oxford business should be conducted in a proper manner and the accounts submitted to the Finance Committee. . . .' As for the piano and the promise of £100,[128] 'I know nothing whatever about the piano. . . .[129] With reference to the £100 . . . my note states that Canon Stather Hunt and myself agreed to ask the Trustees to vote that sum. . . . From the Trustees' point of view St. Peter's Hall does not exist until the Trust Deed has been settled. . . .'

This was more than Cumming could take. He wrote back: [130] 'I confess I am surprised at your letter of 25th inst. I think we should understand each other better. Having been a judge I quite understand your position as trustees. And government service has accustomed me to a more rigid system of control, check and payment, than is expected even of trustees, so I also understand your difficulties. I have had a fair amount of experience myself: when I was half my present age I was running a district in India with a revenue of nearly a million sterling. . . . I regard the Appeal Fund deposit account as Capital . . . if your trustees consider some of the expenses should come out of it, you can raise the point at the Council meeting.

. . . How do you expect me to carry on during the first term? . . . Mrs. Chavasse will run the catering on much the same lines as for her own house and must be kept in funds by me: I am particularly anxious that she should have no money difficulties to worry her in her gallant effort. . . .[131] If you have any difficulty in helping us, I must ask the Council how I am to supplement the fees in order to pay our way.'

The Provisional Council met, as has been seen on 8 October 1928. Cumming duly pointed out that income from fees would be insufficient to meet annual expenditure, and the Council authorised him to draw on the Appeal Fund up to £500 as a *loan* to meet expenditure. In addition, he was given a grant of £100 from the Appeal Fund for current expenses. That covered the immediate needs. But before the end of November bills were coming in which were not covered, and which should certainly have been paid by the Trustees. On 26 November Cumming wrote to Warrington: 'I send you a bundle of bills for furnishing St. Peter's House amounting to £747-13-3'. It was one thing to send Warrington bills: it was quite another to get them paid. On 11 February 1929 Cumming complained, 'So far as the running expenses of St. Peter's House are concerned, we have established our credit with the local tradesmen, but I fear a delay in paying the furnishing bills is affecting us injuriously.'

Meanwhile, on 4 December 1928 the Council had met again.[132]

71

This was the meeting which (as has been seen) approved the draft of the supplementary Trust Deed and made arrangements for speakers at the debate in Convocation on 29 January 1929. It also dealt with finance.[133] In particular, 'on the proposition of the Master, seconded by Mr. Allen it was resolved to appoint a Management Committee to assist the Master in managing the affairs of St. Peter's House and to report to the Council. The following were appointed members of the Committee: the Master, the Revd. G. F. Graham Brown, Mr. J. G. Legge, the Revd. P. E. Warrington'. This Committee met for the first time on 21 February 1929: Warrington could not attend. In his absence, Cumming informed the Committee that he had been caused difficulty by delay in the receipt of covenanted payments due from the Trustees, and that there was a question about the payment of the rates on No. 27 Norham Road, the Master's private house.[134] It was therefore resolved 'that the Patrons [sic] should be asked to arrange with the Financial Committee of the Church of England Trust Society for the regular settlement of [payments] on due dates, and should be further asked what their intentions are regarding the Master's rates'. Cumming also told the Committee that as his accounts had been running since March 1928 they ought now to be audited, if only to make sure that the system of accounts which he had devised was suitable and adequate. The Committee agreed, and it was suggested that Messrs. Smith & Williamson, Chartered Accountants, should be employed for this purpose.

A copy of the Management Committee's minutes was sent to Warrington; and at once the fat was in the fire. On 6 March he wrote[135] to Chavasse: 'I wish to tell you that the statement [about delay in payments] . . . cannot be regarded other than as a withering insult by members of the Martyrs Memorial and Church of England Trust. The payments on capital accounts have nothing whatever to do with the Management Committee and had I been present it would have been my duty to have told you so. The Finance Committee of the Church Trust will pay their capital accounts when it pleases them to do so and will not submit to dictation in this matter: at least, not whilst I am a Member of the Trust.[136]

The St. Peter's House Account has been Guaranteed by the Trust to the extent of £500: this should enable the Treasurer to be well in funds.[137]

. . . . I note the Management Committee considers that Messrs. Smith & Williamson . . . should be employed to audit the

Accounts. I confess that for an arrangement to be made to appoint a Firm of Accountants without any reference to the Trust which is finding the money takes my breath away. As a matter of fact I have felt for several months that the whole of the St. Peter's business should be transferred from my office to the Trustees' Accountants whom the Trustees will require to audit the portion of the accounts for which they are responsible. We cannot agree to outside Accountants having any knowledge of our affairs; that is obvious.[138] I will take this opportunity of telling you there is a good deal I do not like about the running of St. Peter's and when I meet my Colleagues at the end of this month I am going to say to them that their interests should be watched by their Auditors. . . .'

To this outburst Chavasse gave a firm but conciliatory reply: —[139]

'You really must not scent out insults where none either exist or were intended. This you would have known if you could only have been present at the Management Committee. . . .

(1) Their whole desire is to save trouble both to you (who they know are over-burdened), the Trust and ourselves. . . . We suggest that the Trustees explain the position to the Trust, and ask them to authorize the expenditure[140] yearly so that the quarterly payments can come in automatically as is generally the custom in all Societies. I think this is all helpful instead of being insulting. . . .

(2) As regards Auditors. The Accounts of St. Peter's Hall are perfectly distinct from those of the Trust and ought to be kept so. All that can be shown on a St. Peter's Balance Sheet are the generous grants made by the Trust, so there can be no more intrusion by Auditors into the affairs of the Trust than into the affairs of any donor whose name appears as giving a donation. What is quite clear is that the St. Peter's Hall Accounts have to go up before the University and that the Treasurer therefore wishes to employ Accountants now well versed in the way that College Accounts are presented. . . . It is quite useless . . . to employ any firm unacquainted with University Accounts. The Management Committee only recommended this firm to the Council and of course you are at perfect liberty to suggest another firm, though to my mind it will be much simpler to keep the St. Peter's Hall Accounts perfectly separate by employing a different firm of Auditors. We recommend this firm for a reason I think you will appreciate, not only are they versed in University Accounts, but the Auditor who would be sent to us is Mervin

[sic] Talbot Rice, the son of Talbot Rice of Onslow Square, and as his father is thrilled with the St. Peter's Hall scheme and is a Senior Trustee of both Hannington Hall and the Schools, we thought it would be excellent if we could pay him this compliment and also turn our Auditor into a Publicity Agent of the Hall. . .'.[141]

There was to be a meeting of the Council on 11 March, and Chavasse concluded his letter with a warm invitation for Warrington to come over early and to have a talk before the meeting. He received a brusque reply from Warrington's secretary, Mr. G. G. Burn: [142] Mr. Warrington 'regrets he is not sufficiently well to face the journey to Oxford on Monday. I have to inform you that the policy the Trustees will pursue will be strictly in accordance with the Covenant which has been made. Your Salary and Rent will be paid on the dates fixed in the Contract. The Bursaries and balance of Tutor's Salary will be paid at the end of the term. No alteration from this procedure will be considered. . . .'

The result was that although Cumming pointed out to the Council[143] how much more convenient it would be if Bursaries could be paid at the beginning of term, King Harman, as the only Trustee present, could only undertake 'to place the matter before' the Trust Society. As for the Auditors, King Harman insisted that the firm suggested 'should be approved by the Revd. P. E. Warrington, to ensure that there should be no inquisition into the accounts of the Church of England Trust Society'. However, the question of rates on No. 27 Norham Road was settled: it was agreed that they should be paid out of the St. Peter's House Fund and not by the Trustees.

There can be little doubt that King Harman had been primed by Warrington, who was not prepared to make any concessions.[144] On 16 May 1929 Cumming took up the matter of auditors. He wrote to Warrington: 'It is two months since the Council resolved that the accounts of St. Peter's House should be audited. You demurred to the firm suggested and rightly pointed out that, as the Trustees are finding the money, they have a right to their own audit. Since then nothing has been done.' He asked what was to happen: 'we are on a different footing from the schools run by the Trustees, each of which stands by itself and can do as the Trustees please. . . .' To this Warrington replied: [145] '. . . our Accountant is Mr. Gerald Thompson, of Westonbirt School, Tetbury, and he will audit the Accounts of St. Peter's Hall, i.e. the part which concerns the Trustees. . . .' He assured Cumming that Mr. Thompson could cope with all the requirements of the University.[146] Mr. Thompson duly arrived and did his best. Cumming's own views can be deduced from a letter which he sent to Warrington a year later:[147] '. . . I particularly wish to avoid hurting Mr. Thompson's feelings, as he is an exceedingly nice young fellow. But he cannot give the certificate that is usual for college accounts in Oxford, and has no knowledge of the requirements.'

Cumming's sense of unease was not lessened by Warrington's continued reluctance to pay bills promptly. One firm which experienced this reluctance was Capes of St. Ebbe's.[148] On 29 April 1929 Chavasse wrote to Warrington about the furnishing of the new building (Staircases I, II, and III). Five estimates had been received, and those from three Oxford firms were easily the lowest. 'Capes, from whom we ordered our first sets of furniture, are lowest of all. I should very much like to employ them for three reasons: (1) We have tested their work and find it excellent. Their Manager is a Godly man very interested in St. Peter's. . . . (2) The firm is very close to us. . . . (3) They are willing to give credit for a year. We have kept them waiting for the last lot of furniture and they have been very patient. We therefore in all justice owe something to them. . . .'[149] Warrington was not impressed, even by the thought of a Godly man's disappointment. He insisted that Messrs. Harrods should be asked to quote, and so they did. On 19 June Chavasse sent Harrods' estimate to Warrington, and recommended its acceptance: [It] 'compares favourably with the Oxford people. At the same time I believe you are right and their workmanship can be depended upon far more than a smaller firm like Capes.' In these circumstances, it is not altogether surprising that when Capes got wind that Harrods had received the order, they threatened legal action to enforce payment of their account.[150]

Chavasse himself was nearly as uneasy as Cumming, not so much at the wickedness of keeping creditors waiting for their money but at the folly of doing so if it led to bad publicity. On 7 August 1929 he appealed to Warrington, 'as a personal favour,' to 'let Miss Townsend and Miss Howson have a cheque for £156-11-0 for the Hannington window, which account has been outstanding since April 27th. . . . Seeing that Miss Howson is an old friend of mine I do not like to feel that my friendship, which was largely instrumental in securing her the work, should land her into unpleasantness. And at all costs I want to avoid adverse rumours about the financial stability of the Hall reaching Liverpool through her father the Archdeacon. I am afraid you have had lately several heavy bills to meet . . . but this sum is so small that I think it must have been overlooked.' There is no trace of a reply to this appeal, but Warrington always resented interference, or what he took to be interference. For instance, a week later[151] he sent Chavasse a copy of a letter which he had sent to the firm of Minty: 'I have received a letter from Mr. Chavasse with reference to goods supplied by you to St. Peter's House. Whilst Mr. Chavasse is the Master of St. Peter's, it must be clearly understood that he has no responsibility in this matter. The settlement of this Account rests entirely with my Trustees, and not with Mr. Chavasse. My Trustees alone decide when this matter should be dealt with. . . .'

The case of Coopers of St. Ebbe's provides even clearer evidence of Mr. Warrington's methods. On 16 September 1929 Cumming wrote to him: 'On 9 August you wrote me that the majority of the accounts I had forwarded (for furnishing St. Peter's House) had received attention. I was somewhat surprised to receive a call from the Manager of G. R. Cooper Ltd. and to learn that theirs had not been settled. He was quite reasonable, but says they must have the money this week, and I enclose his letter. Incidentally he pointed out they have lost £10 already in interest. . . .'[152] It would help us greatly if you could pay this bill this week.'

On 7 October Cumming had to write again: 'On Saturday I had a call from Mr. Swain, manager of Messrs. G. R. Cooper Ltd. . . . in spite of my letter d/16th September to you, their claim has not been paid and they have no alternative but put it in the hands of their solicitors. I ought to tell you that he added that it is common report among the tradesmen in Oxford that this is the only way they can get bills paid by the trust. . . . This is the third time I have had a similar threat in connection with bills payable by the trust. It is a new experience for me to have to wheedle tradesmen into deferring legal action to enforce their just claims, and I beg you will relieve me from this undignified position by paying Messrs. G. R. Cooper Ltd. *this week without fail*. . . .' This produced an illuminating reply from Warrington:[153] 'Thank you for your letter. A cheque has been forwarded to Messrs. Cooper. I make no apology for keeping these Firms waiting. You Oxford people should have listened to the advice I gave at the beginning and gone to Firms of repute like Harrods or Waring and Gillows. With them this sort of thing does not occur. A Trust which is having to meet the tremendous obligations we have to face must deal with Firms who will give them the most extended credit. If I had adopted "Oxford methods" this movement would have died in its infancy.'

It was really very difficult to deal with Warrington at this stage. It has already been seen that he was abnormally quick to take offence. A week or so before he preached the 'Commemoration Sermon' in St. Peter's chapel at the end of June 1929, he had written to Cumming threatening to resign from the Council immediately because in Chavasse's draft report he had been described as the Secretary, instead of the Honorary Secretary, of the Trust. 'A greater insult could not be levelled against me. . . . This is an insult I cannot lightly overlook.' There was plenty of time to insert the missing word, but Cumming thought it necessary to send a conciliatory reply: [154] 'It is a delicate matter for me to intrude in, but as the peacemakers are blessed I shall risk it. As an honorary official myself, I sympathise fully with your insistence that your position should be accurately described. But I put it to you very strongly that the whole tone of the references in the report to you absolutely negatives the possibility of any insult to you being intended. And I suggest that it is unthinkable you should contemplate resigning for what is after all a clerical error – the omission of one word! . . .' This peacemaking was so effective (for the time being) that a week later Warrington sent Cumming and his wife two tickets in case they should care to attend the opening of the new chapel at Stowe School by Prince George.

It was characteristic of Warrington to welcome big schemes and yet to boggle at trifles. In March 1929 it became necessary to do at once something which had been contemplated before, to buy from the Wesleyan Trustees the site of their school.[155] What happened can be seen from three letters from Chavasse. On 13 March he told Warrington: . . . 'I heard from a City Councillor yesterday that there is an agitation going on for the City to buy the Wesleyan property and so save themselves thousands which they would otherwise spend in building new secondary schools in North Oxford.' On 10 May he asked Warrington for a cheque for £1150 to clinch the contract for the purchase, and added: 'I am so grateful for the splendid way you come forward in these crisises [sic] and see the matter through. It is everything to know that we can rely on you.' Finally, on 23 May: 'I must first of all thank you for the way you rose to the occasion over the Wesleyan business. It was wonderful.' Yet at the same time Warrington had been outraged when Chavasse had proposed to help on work in the Rowcroft Building by spending £100 on water-proofing one of the upper floors so that plastering could be started earlier.[156] The architect approved, and the Council of 11 March had agreed; but Warrington put his foot down: [157] 'I think it is a needless waste of money. . . . The Trustees will not waste the £100, and in view of the fact that any money expended upon this work must come out of the pockets of a charitable public, we cannot be parties to the throwing away of money in this way.'[158]

Warrington had shown no such regard for the pockets of a charitable public when he had insisted that Hannington Hall should be made a show-piece: he had transformed the hall[159] by constructing a barrel-vault of plaster and a gallery of Austrian oak, matched by wall-panels of the same oak, with concealed lighting[160] of a kind not previously used in Oxford dining-halls; there was a new oak floor and a new oak staircase, and on the ground floor both the passage and the Junior Common Room were panelled with the same Austrian oak. On the very day on which Warrington refused to allow the asphalt water-proofing Chavasse had written to him: [161] 'You will, I believe, be delighted with the progress of the buildings and also with the result of Hannington Hall. I may confess that I thought at one time you had made a mistake in expending money so lavishly on the Hall, but I am absolutely converted, and now we see the result my friends tell me that you were right and that the beauty of the Hall will give great confidence and bring in more money besides making the undergraduates exceedingly proud of St. Peter's.' Again on 31 July Chavasse wrote to him: . . . 'I am of course aware that you have put St. Peter's Hall upon a new footing in popular estimation by the extraordinary beauty of Hannington Hall.' But by this time Chavasse was worried by some grandiose ideas which Warrington had conceived for improving the New Inn Hall Street frontage of St. Peter's House, possibly on the lines of a fine building in Bath;[162] he therefore continued: . . . 'I fully believe that your big ideas for the frontage of St. Peter's are true wisdom, and would produce the same good effect [as Hannington Hall].' But the immediate necessity was to get a further licence from the Delegacy of Lodgings, and . . . 'as you know, they are difficult people to deal with, and it would be folly to take risks at this eleventh hour. . . . I would therefore suggest that we do as little to the front of the house as we can, beyond making it look decent. . . .'[163] Warrington was reluctant to agree; as late as 27 August 1929 he wrote to Chavasse: 'Re

the New Front for St. Peter's House. I attach far more importance to this than to anything else. At the present time St. Peter's
has not an attractive appearance from New Inn Hall Street, and
the sooner the Hall can show buildings of dignity and character
from the main street, the better it will be for St. Peter's. . . .'

Meanwhile, the work on Block One (Staircases I, II and III)
had been going on steadily. Here too Warrington had insisted on
a rather lavish use of oak, for instance in built-in wardrobes, but
here too there were contradictions. On 6 August Chavasse was
moved to write: 'We had arranged for each study to be provided
with two arm-chairs (in addition to the writing-chair for the
desk). This is a necessity of Oxford social life. There is no room
in the University, not even at Keble or St. Edmund Hall, which
does not possess its two arm-chairs. . . . Now they inform me
from Harrods that you wish for two wooden tub writing-chairs
[instead] . . . [this] would make us the laughing-stock of the
University. . . .' Warrington replied[164] that the Trustees would
provide only one arm-chair. 'This will leave the Council to provide the other out of the General Appeal Fund. . . . Further, my
Trustees are not prepared to buy Coffee Tables for Students. I
am particularly requested to say they are astonished that they
have been asked to purchase such tables and they must protest
against using money, which has been given at great personal self-
sacrifice on the part of many people, for such a purpose!' In
another letter on the same day he declared: 'We cannot continue
this squandering of the Trust money.' No wonder Chavasse
replied as he did:[165] 'I wish you would have pity on me and realize
that sometimes I don't quite know where I am with you. You
jump on me with both feet and pour scorn on furniture which
I have procured for St. Peter's House and elsewhere, saying that
it is cheap and nasty, and quote Harrods to the same effect. And
then when I send you Harrods' estimate for articles of furniture
which they consider good and durable, you explode with indignation at the expense to which I am putting the Trustees unnecessarily. If you will have patience with me, I am sure we can work
out what is necessary, reasonable, and good. You have given us
such a marvellous building that it is a little difficult to live up to
it in the matter of furniture.'

On 6 September 1929, at Warrington's special request, *The
Record* printed verbatim a long letter which he had addressed
to the editor of the *Church Times*, answering criticism of the
Martyrs Memorial Trust made by the Anglo-Catholic vicar of
St. Bartholomew's, Brighton. The bulk of the letter consists of a

venomous attack upon Anglo-Catholics in general, but there is one passage of particular interest: 'Further, Mr. Dilworth Harrison seems very excited because we propose to spend £150,000 on the buildings and College [sic] of St. Peter's, Oxford. Mr. Harrison is again very wide of the mark. It is true that the Trust is responsible for the financing of the Memorial to the late Bishop Chavasse, and counts it an honour. . . . We propose to find not £150,000 but £250,000, and we shall need every penny of it. I hope this somewhat large sum will not shock Mr. Dilworth Harrison! ! ! !' This remarkable assertion must have shocked some of Warrington's own Trustees; it is hard to believe that if consulted they would have authorized it. Looking back now, one can detect in the letter a dangerous lack of balance which would interest a psychiatrist. But at the time nobody seems to have spotted it as a danger-signal.

There was certainly no reason why Chavasse, having read this letter, should have taken Warrington's strictures very seriously. Within a week[166] Chavasse began to take a less apologetic line. He told Warrington that he had heard from Harrods that 'most of the carpets for the sitting-rooms will not be ready till November. Though this is very annoying I am almost glad it has happened, as it vindicates me partially from the charge of fussiness which you are always bringing against me when I try to place orders several months ahead of time. . . . Harrods also say that they are daily awaiting your instructions regarding pillows and curtains. . . . Though we can do without carpets we can't do without bed-linen. . . . Rumour has come through from Harrods that only ten of the dressing-tables we ordered are to arrive at St. Peter's. . . . I am the more concerned as I had wished the bedrooms to be specially comfortable in view of Evangelical conferences held here, and of the comfort of distinguished men of the Evangelical school whom I hope we shall entertain at such gatherings. . . . [It would be a thousand pities] to put men, and distinguished visitors into rooms designed more like a cabin on board ship than ordinary bedrooms. . . .[167] I can quite understand that the expense seems staggering . . . but you seem to work miracles and I hope we do not take advantage of your wizardry. Certainly you have snubbed me often enough for being "cheap"! '

He followed this up with another letter[168] which ended: '. . . when I did not examine the estimates of the new buildings, feeling that I ought to keep out of what is a matter that the Trustees are doing most generously themselves, then I let you in for these very expensive bedroom fixtures [sic] to which I might have called your attention, if I had made myself cognizant of exactly what was purposed. I feel all points to the fact that if you could spare me more time, and we could talk over things on the spot, you might be able to trust me more, and so delegate more to me. There is one important matter concerning you personally. . . . As we shall be opening next term as a Hall with 40 men, we are hoping, each Thursday in term, to have a guest-night. . . . As you are our most important Trustee, which would, in a college, be equivalent to a Treasurer and Fellow rolled into one, it is very necessary that if possible you should dine with us at least once a term. I am very anxious to invite the Vice-Chancellor. . . . If you will let me know on which Thursday you can give us the great pleasure of dining and sleeping in Oxford, I will then issue invitations to a few of the most important people in Oxford; but I must have you at such a function.'

Warrington was not to be drawn in this way. On 23 October Chavasse tried again: . . . 'I wish . . . to press you very hard to come to us for a night on Thursday 7 November. It is our first Guest Night as a Hall'. The Vice-Chancellor had been invited, but 'the whole thing will fall flat if we cannot have you present at this Guest Night. . . . I feel very strongly that it is up to you to come if humanly possible, even as it will seem ungrateful on our part if we cannot show in some way how indebted Oxford and the Hall are to your enterprise and devotion.' Warrington's answer came at once: '. . . I do not think my presence is really necessary and for many reasons I prefer to remain behind the scenes. At the same time I greatly appreciate your very kind invitation.'

It was really very important that Warrington and Chavasse should work together with good will on both sides, if the Hall was to develop smoothly. It had been intended from an early stage that room should be made for 60 men in October 1930, 20 more than in October 1929, in order to maintain the balance of 'years',[169] and that this should be done by completing the north quadrangle in the way shown in a picture in the First Annual Report.

On 23 May 1929 Chavasse sent Warrington a memorandum, pointing out the need to take action, but found him reluctant. On 28 May Warrington said that he could not at the moment 'see how my Trustees can undertake a further liability of £15,000, but I will consider the matter very carefully and write to you again.'[170] He did write again, on 7 June: 'I am considering the question of the future building, but at the moment I cannot see

All the buildings in this picture are completed except the block on the north side, for which an appeal is now made for £15,000.

All the buildings in this picture are completed except the block on the north side, for which an appeal is now made for £15,000.

FROM THE FIRST ANNUAL REPORT

The buildings fronting on New Inn Hall Street are (from left to right) Hannington Hall, the Church of St. Peter-le-Bailey and the former Rectory ('St. Peter's House'). The Rowcroft Building consists of the three staircases at the back. The fourth, with the high arch, was never built; nor were the staircases shown on the right and extending to the west on to a site then occupied by the Wesleyan Chapel.

what can be done, other than the issue of a further Appeal. We have already committed ourselves to an expenditure of over £60,000 at St. Peter's. This is thousands more than we originally intended to spend. I am very doubtful whether the Bank will advance money for such a purpose. The difficulty I am confronted with at the moment is not so much St. Peter's, but the tremendous demands which are being made by the other Schools [sic]. Increased accommodation has to be provided at three of the Schools before September. . . . Do you think an Appeal would meet with success? I am afraid the advent of Labour[171] to power may affect seriously the kind of work we are doing. It did on the last occasion. . . .' Chavasse replied at once[172] that he thought an Appeal in 18 months' time would be feasible; meanwhile 'Mr. Dodd has supplied me with a plan which would complete the quadrangle, and provide an additional set of 21 rooms at a cost less than £14,000'. This is the plan depicted in the First Report. Two days later Chavasse declared: 'I have great hopes that it may be possible apart from the Trustees to raise the £14,000 or £15,000 necessary to complete the quadrangle.'

So far, there had been no idea of building immediately on the site of the Wesleyan school, nor had the Wesleyan Hall[173] yet been acquired, though the Trustees had contracted to buy it when it should become available. The Wesleyan school itself had been closed at least a year earlier, largely because its heating system was inadequate,[174] and the building had been used to house the children from the St. Peter-le-Bailey school when that was demolished to clear the Hannington Quadrangle. It was not until mid-July 1929 that it was certain that these children could be moved into the enlarged St. Aldate's schools for the autumn term;[175] and it was then that Chavasse began to consider further possibilities. The new block to complete the north quadrangle would not have been so attractive in fact as it looked in the picture, which had been drawn, no doubt deliberately, to give a good impression. At first sight, one might imagine that the new block would have occupied the same area as the Latner Building of 1972, but this is not so. In 1929 the northern boundary of the St. Peter's House property ran only a few feet north of the house, and was flanked by a Wesleyan burial-ground. The new block would therefore have projected much further south than the Latner Building. Chavasse had not fully envisaged the effect at first, but on 23 July he told Warrington that he had 'discovered that the block of buildings which it was proposed to erect between St. Peter's House and the Rowcroft Buildings obscure nearly

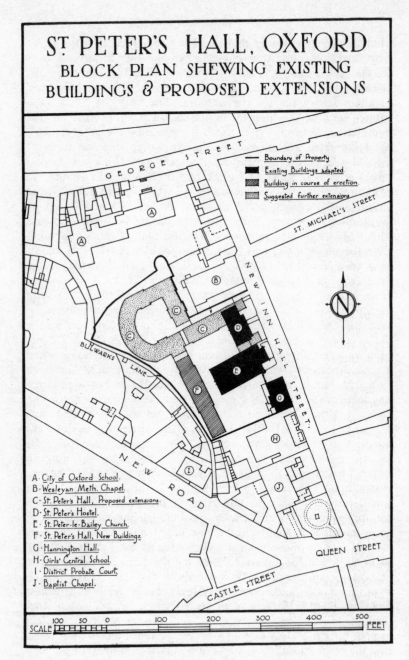

ST PETER'S HALL, OXFORD
BLOCK PLAN SHEWING EXISTING BUILDINGS & PROPOSED EXTENSIONS

GEORGE STREET

ST. MICHAEL'S STREET

NEW INN HALL STREET

BULWARKS LANE

Boundary of Property
Existing Buildings adapted.
Building in course of erection.
Suggested further extensions

N

NEW ROAD

A · City of Oxford School.
B · Wesleyan Meth. Chapel.
C · St. Peter's Hall, Proposed extensions.
D · St. Peter's Hostel.
E · St. Peter-le-Bailey Church.
F · St. Peter's Hall, New Buildings.
G · Hannington Hall.
H · Girls' Central School.
I · District Probate Court.
J · Baptist Chapel.

QUEEN STREET

CASTLE STREET

SCALE 100 50 0 100 200 300 400 500 FEET

FROM THE FIRST ANNUAL REPORT

84

half St. Peter's House, and besides spoiling the house make the entrance quad. look like a back yard.'

He said that he had therefore 'proposed to Mr. Dodd that the buildings should be erected on the waste ground at the side and back of the Rowcroft Buildings', i.e. on the site of the later Besse Staircase and the strip of garden beyond.[176] 'He absolutely agreed with me. . . . Unfortunately Sir H. Baker does not agree, as he has always had in mind a semicircular range of buildings on the west end of the Wesleyan property. We have always been against this as horrible for rooms and probably unsightly', but Dodd could not very well stand up against Sir H. Baker without Warrington's backing.[177] Baker's scheme would have entailed pulling down the Wesleyan Hall as well as the school; Dodd's new plan 'allows for further blocks of buildings where the Wesleyan Schools now stand' and would make it possible to retain the Wesleyan Hall (when acquired) as 'a handsome feature of the entrance quadrangle'.

Warrington made no immediate reply to this letter, but a few weeks later he paid a visit to Oxford and discussed the matter on the spot. On 21 August 1929 Chavasse wrote to him: 'I have been thinking very deeply regarding the suggestions you made for the future lay-out of St. Peter's Hall. . . . You seemed in a moment to have hit upon a scheme which had escaped us all, but which on further thought seems to be more suited to the curious formation of the site and to the utilization of its whole space than anything we had previously contemplated, even with the advice of Sir Herbert Baker. There were two special points you made: (1) The possibility of making a drive through the premises on the north side of St. Peter's House. . . . (2) the desirability of saving every foot of ground that was possible at the back of the site, and thus preserving an open appearance.' This would seem to indicate that it was Warrington who was responsible for the decision to keep an open space (with a view of the Castle Mound) between the Rowcroft Building and any other buildings to the north, and to start these buildings in the north-west corner of the site. But at the time he made what Chavasse politely called 'the excellent suggestion' of 'making temporary accommodation in the old Wesleyan Schools' for the extra twenty men expected in 1930. This would have cost about £7,000, and it was Dodd and Chavasse who argued that it would be more sensible to build a permanent block at once at an extra cost of about £8,000. This was the origin of Dodd's design for No. IV Staircase (Block 2).

Warrington approved the scheme:[178] '. . . I like this Elevation

very much [Dodd's design], and I think when finished, [it] will
be in every way worthy of St. Peter's. I think the New Building
[Block 1] should not be enlarged, but finished off as it is. . . .'
Then the Wesleyan Hall, when acquired, could be refaced and
kept intact.[179] The question was, where was the money to come
from? It was one thing for Warrington to talk of spending
£250,000 on the Hall, it was quite another to produce £15,000.
On 19 October 1929 he wrote to Chavasse: 'Now that the Hall
has been licensed, the time has come when we should have a
public Meeting in London and the Scheme should be properly
launched. . . . There is another matter; the finance. The Trustees
have been subsidizing St. Peter's from their various funds. Now
that all the Buildings[180] . . . are finished, we shall have to come
to an arrangement with our Insurance Company, as a portion of
the considerable sum we have spent will have to be in the form
of a mortgage which we shall take up with the Company which
holds our Sinking Fund. I am glad the new Building is finished.
It has been a very anxious year for me, as the demands of St.
Peter's have exceeded all expectations. . . .' This was really a
warning that the Martyrs Memorial Trust would not be prepared
to go ahead at once with a new building scheme; it also showed
why the Trust had insisted on having power to mortgage property.

Chavasse was not particularly happy, but there was nothing he
could do but accept the situation. He wrote back:[181] . . . 'you
have done a very hard thing, and actually staggered Oxford with
the building equipment and furniture that the Trust have
promised. I have always expected that you would have to mortgage the buildings. . . . All that the Council will need to know is
the general outline of the insurance scheme, and when the Hall
property will be unencumbered. This is immensely important, as
you will remember . . . we cannot become a public hall until
the University hold the title deeds. . . . The sooner, therefore, we
can pay off all our debts, the sooner we can take the next step
towards becoming a college, in which case all the property is
handed back to us again.'

Warrington's reply[182] threw a little more light on the financial
methods of the Trust, about which in the past he had been
secretive: '. . . the Mortgage . . . is necessary because the method
of financing the Schools which we have adopted from the beginning is to pay a fixed sum each year into a fund held by our
Insurance Company. At the end of another ten years this fund
will be adequate to release practically all our properties from

their mortgages . . . 15 years would be the maximum period of the mortgage. . . .' This disposed of the idea, for which Warrington himself had been responsible, that the Trust possessed great liquid assets, on which it would be easy to draw at any time. So it fell to the Council to decide whether it was possible to go ahead with the building of Block 2.

The Council met, as has already been seen, on 2 November 1929.[183] It instructed Mr. Dodd to prepare plans for adapting the buildings of the Wesleyan School;[184] and it agreed that certain securities[185] previously set apart for the endowment of the First Tutorship should be used as 'security for a loan against the St. Peter's Hall account' for the purpose of the new building. On 6 December 1929 the Council met again, and definitely decided to shoulder the responsibility[186] for erecting Block 2, accepting that 'the Trustees had already exceeded their liabilities'. There is ambiguity here: the Trustees referred to were the Trustees of the Martyrs Memorial Trust, but the four of those Trustees who were also Trustees of St. Peter's Hall were bound to share in the new responsibility as members of the Council, and of these four both Warrington and King Harman were present and agreed. Indeed, it is inconceivable that the Council would have made this decision if Warrington had not fully approved.

The Council proceeded to set up a 'Works and Building Committee', consisting of Chavasse, Legge, E. M. Walker and Warrington. It was taken for granted that Messrs. Parnell, who had only just finished work on Block 1, would be employed again;[187] though the Council, when it met again on 6 February 1930,[188] finding that the cost was likely to exceed £15,000, decided to put out tenders. In fact, Parnells put in the lowest tender, for £15,910, and this was accepted by the Council[189] on 24 February. It also accepted a tender for the furnishing from Messrs. T. S. Bott of Oxford. It is by no means clear whether the Council knew that as early as 19 December 1929 Warrington had himself signed an 'agreement for contract' with Parnells for digging the foundations of No. 2 Block. It was he too who signed the contract with Parnells on 28 February 1930 for erecting Block 2. The curious thing is that on both occasions the contracts were between J. S. Parnell and Son and the Martyrs Memorial and Church of England Trust Society, and Warrington signed for and on behalf of the Trust Society. This procedure had been natural enough for Block 1: the contract for that had been signed by King Harman and Warrington[190] on behalf of the Society. But one would have expected the contract for Block 2 to be between Parnells and either the Council or the Trustees of St. Peter's Hall. Another curious thing, closely connected, is that a few days[191] before the Council Meeting on 24 February Warrington instructed his assistant secretary to warn Chavasse that 'the Trustees cannot take any responsibility for the new Building if the total figure exceeds the sum of £15,000', presumably meaning the Martyrs Memorial Trustees. Chavasse must have been puzzled; he wrote back at once[192] to Warrington's secretary: 'Please reassure him that the Council fully understand that the Trustees did not even take responsibility to the extent of £15,000. They have made this matter quite clear, and Mr. Warrington will remember that the Council are undertaking the responsibility in view of the money they already have in hand, and the possibility of a loan on the £10,000 they have set aside for the endowment of tutorships. . . .'[193]

There was certainly danger of serious confusion here. It was always hard to know what Warrington was doing. For instance, on 22 January 1930 he informed Chavasse that a certain Mr. Babbs (who had some unspecified connection with the building schemes of the M.M.T.) would be bringing 'a Representative of the Ministry of Agriculture' to visit St. Peter's. 'I particularly wish you *not* to meet this Representative. My reason for asking you to keep out of his way is that he may ask you some very awkward questions, and if you are not there to be questioned by him – so much the better. It is really a case of "the least said the better". . . .' As it happened, Chavasse had already told Mr. Babbs that he would be away from St. Peter's that day, so there was no difficulty. But Chavasse must have wondered what the awkward questions would have been; and he certainly knew that Cumming had just been having trouble in getting money from the M.M.T. due under their guarantee,[194] and that a small Oxford firm, Dobson and Bing, had still not received payment of an account sent to Warrington in April 1929.[195] This sort of trouble did not diminish. On 3 March 1930 Cumming wrote to Warrington: 'On 12 December last I sent you a statement of grants due from the Trustees up to the end of last year. The only grant received was Mr. Chavasse's salary. I now send you a statement of all grants due from the Trustees up to the end of this month.[196] You will note the amount exceeds the overdraft at the bank guaranteed by the Trustees, and I should be glad if you would let me have as much as possible this month.' This had no effect at all. On 2 June 1930 Cumming had to send a further statement of 'grants due from the Trustees, both arrears

and current', asking for payment before 31 July, the end of the
Hall's financial year. Arrears amounted to £520 odd, current to
£310, no inconsiderable sum to a Hall not yet paying its way.

All Cumming received at that time was a curt note from Warrington's secretary:[197] '. . . Mr. Warrington wishes to know
whether you have made full use of the £500 overdraft at the
Bank. We shall require this information before your letter can
be laid before the Finance Committee.' This angered Cumming,
but he replied politely: [198] 'I may remind you that in my letter
d/8th January 1929 I asked you to get the bank to let St. Peter's
have an overdraft (if required) . . . this was in order to provide a
working balance (as we do not, like the colleges, insist on caution
money), and you kindly arranged for an overdraft up to £500[199]
. . . it is too early for such an infant institution to say we can
dispense with such backing. Neither Mr. Chavasse nor I contemplated that we should have to depend on the overdraft for
the terminal and quarterly grants the Trustees covenanted to
give to St. Peter's.' This was a cogent argument, but it produced
a rebuff; on 13 June Burn wrote to Cumming: 'We note that
the overdraft has not been used. The payments to be made this
quarter . . . will have to come from this overdraft.[200] Before
leaving home Mr. Warrington asked me to say that he is extremely surprised at the last sentence contained in your letter . . .
it is no concern of either yours or Mr. Chavasse's from which
source he makes the payments.'

It would have been wiser for Warrington to have omitted the
last remark: it revealed a remarkably cavalier attitude to the
use of trust funds. But this point was not taken by Cumming
at the time. In any case, he was so much encouraged[201] by a
meeting he had with Warrington a few days later that he
ventured to remind him of a debt of about £50 owed to Messrs.
Hinkins and Frewin for work done in the extension of St.
Aldate's School. This was too much. Mr. Green, Assistant
Secretary, wrote back: [202] 'The Revd. P. E. Warrington bids me
inform you that under no circumstances will the Trustees pay
any further money in connection with St. Aldate's School. They
consider they have already paid too much.'

Chavasse himself took the matter up. On 26 June he wrote to
G. G. Burn: 'With reference to Mr. Green's letter to Mr.
Cumming . . . I should be very grateful if you would recall the
following facts to Mr. Warrington's memory:—

'1. In the Deed conveying St. Peter-le-Bailey Schools and play-
    ground to the Trustees, the Trustees state they have spent

the sum of £6,000 upon the St. Aldate's Schools. This Deed
has been communicated both to the Charity Commissioners,
and to the Vice-Chancellor.

'2. Up to the present the Trustees have spent £5,000 in improvements to St. Aldate's Schools, and £600 in purchasing Carter's
Yard to enlarge the playground. . . .

'3. There would seem to be, therefore, a balance of £400 from
which this necessary work in connection with Carter's Yard
might be met.

'4. Until this work was done the City Authorities forbade any
building to be begun in connection with St. Aldate's Schools.

'When this matter comes up at our Council Meeting on
Monday it will be my duty as Chairman to produce these figures.
I am therefore anxious that Mr. Warrington shall be aware of
them, and that they shall not come to him as a surprise at the
meeting itself.'

Burn was able to point out[203] that in addition to the sum of
£5,600 there was also the additional charge of £300 for architect's
fees and that the legal charges would bring the total over £6,000.
Chavasse was not altogether convinced, but the point was not
worth further argument, and Hinkins and Frewin's bill was met
by the Council. The incident has its place, however, as part of a
series of happenings in which Chavasse and Warrington failed
to see eye to eye. For instance, back in November 1929 Warrington had sent a 'strictly private and confidential' message[204] about
Mr. Bryan Green, a brilliant young evangelist who soon afterwards became Chaplain of the Oxford Pastorate (1931-34), later
Vicar of Holy Trinity, Brompton, and finally for many years a
highly respected Rector of Birmingham. He had just been con-
ducting a successful mission to undergraduates in St. Aldate's
church. But he had managed to upset some of the Fundamental-
ists in Cambridge, including friends of Warrington, whose message to Chavasse was '. . . I hope you will keep this gentleman
out of St. Peter's Hall. Nothing could unsettle my Trustees more
than to know that he was invited to St. Peter's. . . .' Chavasse
did not reply for a fortnight,[205] because he thought it necessary
to obtain the signatures of E. W. Mowll (Rector of St. Aldate's),
H. E. H. Probyn (Vicar of St. Andrew's), Graham Brown, and
C. M. Gough (Rector of St. Ebbe's), all unimpeachable Evangelicals, to a public testimony to the credibility of Bryan Green
and his work. It ended: 'His message regarding sin and atonement was most convincing and would have delighted our Evangelical forefathers. The facts were presented on the old Biblical

lines, and the substitutionary theory of the Atonement was stated with emphasis and effect. It was indeed the old gospel presented with the old power, and with a new freshness that brought conviction.'

In fact, Chavasse was telling Warrington to check his information before making libellous statements. He had to do so again in February 1930. Then Warrington wrote a preposterous letter ('confidential') about R. F. Dodd: [206] 'Messrs Jollys of Bath have handed me a letter signed by Dodd, dated February 7th, inviting tenders for the furniture in connection with the New Block. I am astounded to read this communication. The Council did not instruct Dodd to invite tenders. [They] should have been invited by the Bursar of the College [sic]. This means that Dodd is to receive a commission on the whole of this transaction. I take the gravest possible exception to this procedure. . . . In all my experience I have never known such a procedure before. . . .' Chavasse replied: [207] 'Do you mind if I suggest that it is a little unwise, and even unkind, to jump to such rash conclusions. In the present instance you have done Mr. Dodd a grave injustice. He secured tenders for furnishing for me as an act of personal friendship and interest in the Hall, and there is no question whatever of his receiving a commission for what he has done. Moreover, it is in the recollection of both of us that you addressed him at the last Council meeting when you requested that tenders for furnishing should be obtained from Waring and Gillow, and Messrs. Jolly. He certainly took your request as addressed to him, for he took notes on the spot, and I remember seeing him write down the names of these two firms. . . .'

Warrington made no apology; he simply ignored Chavasse's rebuke, though he made no more attacks on Dodd's integrity. Then came the case of 'a young fellow named Cooper, of the B.C.M.S. College, Bristol'[208] 'He tells me', wrote Warrington,[209] 'that he and his friend Murray, are most desirous of entering St. Peter's Hall. I have known Cooper since he was a boy and I hope it may be possible for you to find places for these two lads in October. . . .' Now under Cap. IX of the Trust Deed, every member of the Council was entitled to nominate one student and to have his nominee or nominees as a student or students at the Hall, and in filling up vacancies priority was to be given to such nominees. This provision had so far remained a dead letter, and Warrington did not make a formal nomination in the terms of Cap. IX. But it is highly probable that he had it at the back of his mind, and he was not at all pleased to hear that Murray had been accepted but Cooper only put on the waiting list. On 2 May 1930 Warrington wrote to Chavasse a letter which throws light on his state of mind at the time: —

'This morning's post brings me a letter from Cooper. . . . He tells me that he has been turned down, but may be given a place if someone else falls out . . . I am not asking you to reconsider your decision: I should not dream of doing so. This letter is really to tell you that I am now considering very seriously whether in view of information given to me by Clergymen who visited St. Peter's during the Conference,[210] I can continue to remain on the Council of St. Peter's Hall. I am also considering very seriously whether I must not see Mrs. Rowcroft, and as a matter of honour, tell her that in my judgment her money is not being used for the real object for which it was given. Young men of Anglo-Catholic sympathies are given places at St. Peter's Hall, Evangelicals are refused. . . . This is the first request I have made of you since you have been the Master of St. Peter's, and it will be the last. . . . I know how to deal with men who play this game. I have told you on several occasions how greatly I regret the part I have played in the St. Peter's Scheme, and this morning I feel that I have been nothing less than an idiot to allow myself to carry the grave financial burden, and in other words, make your position possible. . . . Do not be surprised if you see from my pen an exposure of this business in the Church Papers. Perhaps it would be fair if I give you due warning that I am considering the whole position, and in all probability I shall address a communication to the Press, stating these facts. It is nothing less than a scandal that we should accept the money of Evangelical churchpeople . . . and then to find that even the man who stood behind St. Peter's to the tune of £85,000 has his one solitary nominee refused. . . .'

In a sense, this was much ado about nothing: young Cooper was put at the top of the waiting-list, and within a week or so a place was available for him. But it was certainly much ado; and Chavasse thought it necessary to take the letter seriously. On 5 May he wrote back to Warrington: '. . . the work of selecting men this year has been extraordinarily difficult . . . I have had to refuse admission to certain others recommended by persons of influence with almost as great claims upon us as yourself. But I am ready at any time to place before you a list of the candidates we have accepted, with their papers, and the reasons for accepting them, and see which you would yourself have turned down. . . .'

'As regards the charge you formulate against me of refusing admission to Evangelicals in favour of Anglo-Catholics, I must warn you that it simply will not stand the light of investigation. The facts are as follows:

1928-1929. In our first lot of men we had to take whom we could get. . . . We could have taken 20 men, I managed to secure 15, two of whom are Anglo-Catholics, and the fact that I did so helped me very materially to win the approval of Convocation to the establishment of the Hall.

1929-1930. I was able for this year to accept 25 men. . . . There was, so far as I was aware, no Anglo-Catholic among them. Sir Charles King Harman drew my attention to the fact that the father of one boy was an Anglo-Catholic clergyman in Liverpool. He was a boy I was glad to have as I wished to strengthen our claims in Liverpool.

1930-1931. . . . I should be grateful if on your next visit to Oxford you would scrutinize the list [of 20 men accepted] and pick out the Anglo-Catholics for me. I am only sorry that the pressure on our accommodation has been so great that it would not have been possible to accept any Anglo-Catholics if they had applied, for I believe that St. Peter's Hall will influence Anglo-Catholics even as Keble has exerted a tremendous influence on Evangelicals.'[211]

He continued: —

'. . . may I add two warnings? . . . our principle is that we do not accept men who are not up to profiting by an honours course at Oxford. . . . I wish to safeguard myself . . . from the charge of turning down an Evangelical candidate for Holy Orders in favour of someone else, when the real reason was that he was an intellectual dud.[212]

Then secondly, I would most earnestly request you to keep to yourself what I have said to you in utmost confidence. It would do us immeasurable harm in Oxford if the suspicion got abroad that St. Peter's refused to accept a worthy applicant because of his views.

I cannot take seriously your threat of exposure in the press. There is nothing to expose, and if there were this would be a wrong and wicked way of doing it. If I thought you were serious it would be my duty to summon an emergency meeting of the Council. . . . If you are not fully satisfied in your own mind I would suggest that I call such a Council, and that you definitely formulate your charges, when the fullest investigation will be welcomed on my part.

Personally I am a little unwilling to drag members of the Council into such a degrading business, or to expose you to the unpleasant task of bringing such charges, especially as I can say with the utmost confidence that they would be swept aside as ridiculous gossip. And yet I am desirous of clearing up matters so fully that you will repose more confidence in me and not subject me to other letters such as the one you have just written. I am, therefore, perfectly willing to attend a meeting of the Church of England Trust Society and have the whole matter thrashed out with them. I would only stipulate that I should be allowed to bring two witnesses, who, if need be, could bear independent witness to the Council, or to anyone else, that this course was taken, and that I had met the charges. . . . I would ask you to consider this proposal very seriously. . . .

As for the stories told you by anonymous clergy at the Oxford Conference, I simply do not know to what you refer. . . . As long as unknown persons divulge to you tales, of which you keep me in ignorance. I cannot do more than treat the whole matter as malicious gossip. I am certain you would do the same if you were in my place.'

It has been necessary to quote this letter at length, because it plays a significant part in the growth of serious distrust between Chavasse and Warrington. There can be no doubt that Warrington brooded over it; and the suggestion that there should be an inquest before the Martyrs Memorial Trust was taken up in the following year. But for the moment he let the matter lie, merely informing Chavasse: [213] '. . . I need not go further into the points of your letter beyond saying that now things are more established at St. Peter's I should like to retire from the Council and arrange for my place to be taken over by Mr. Greene the Vicar of Felixstowe or by General Adair: I shall make known my wishes to the Trustees[214] at the next meeting. I am quite satisfied that either of the gentlemen whom I have named would take a great deal more interest in St. Peter's than I feel able to do.'

There is no evidence that Chavasse took this threat of resignation as more than a gesture of injured pride. He made no mention of it to Sir Charles King Harman, with whom he had been having correspondence about his admissions policy. On 23 April 1930 Sir Charles had written: 'I quite see your point of view and I am inclined to agree with you. If you can lead the Anglo-Catholic youth into sound paths you will be doing a good work.

At the same time I hope that you will be careful to foster a thoroughly Protestant atmosphere in St. Peter's, and not to do or say anything that would alarm our chief supporters some of whom are rather afraid of you and whose continued support is vital. . . .' To this Chavasse had replied: [215] 'I know there are people who are afraid of me, and it must be so. All through his life my father was cast down by being suspected by those who ought to have supported him. The two vital questions at the moment are Sacramentalism and Modernism. As regards the former, the whole Church knows that I am an uncompromising Protestant; as regards the latter, I venture to send you an address on the Bible which I gave at the request of the World's Evangelical Alliance.'

Chavasse probably guessed that when Sir Charles spoke of alarming 'our chief supporters' he was referring to Mrs. Rowcroft; and when on 3 May he received Warrintgon's threat to tell tales to Mrs. Rowcroft he immediately[216] sent her a copy of the same address on the Bible which he had sent to Sir Charles. With it went what was intended to be a soothing letter: 'After all you have done in making the establishment of St. Peter's Hall possible it grieves me very often to believe that you do not consider my views on the inspiration of the Bible are sound, and that to a very large extent your great generosity has been wasted, if not abused. I hear with sorrow that you are not well, but if you are strong enough would you let some friend read to you parts of the address on the Bible which I enclose, and which I gave in the Queen's Hall, London. . . . It might, I think, reassure you, at any rate after reading it you will know exactly what I believe. . . .'

But Mrs. Rowcroft was not soothed, even by Chavasse's final sentence, 'Every Sunday in College Chapel we pray for our benefactors, as I do so I always remember you and your illness'. On 7 May she sent him a curt note: 'In a typed letter signed by you and received yesterday a very grave accusation is made against me, you must forgive me therefore for asking on what authority your assumption is formed?' There can be no doubt that Chavasse was sincere when he replied: [217] 'Your letter which reached me this morning startled and bewildered me, and I hasten to write to reassure you. I am most thankful that I kept a copy of the letter I wrote you . . . and so am able to discover exactly to what you refer, and what could possibly give rise to the belief that an accusation of any sort had been brought against you.

'I have always thought of you as a staunch conservative where the inspiration of the Bible is concerned. Forgive me for using this phrase which I dislike,[218] but do so for the sake of brevity. But it has been my impression that you shared with many a suspicion that my views on the Bible were not sound. This was partly due to the fact that in 1928 I wrote to Miss Wills of Bristol[219] hoping to interest her in St. Peter's, and though she very kindly sent me £100, she asked me about my Bible views . . . many Evangelicals were not happy about me for the same reason, and I had included you among them in my mind. Six years ago I invited Bishop Barnes[220] to lecture at St. Aldate's on "Authority", and though he said nothing to which the most conservative Evangelical could object, yet I was severely criticised for having him at all and went under a cloud as a Modernist suspect. . . .

'As for the latter part of the first paragraph in the letter I wrote you, it is perhaps badly worded and might convey the impression that someone had told me this about you. It was rather the logical conclusion I had drawn myself – namely, that if you were not happy about the Bible teaching at the Hall you had helped so materially to found, you could not be happy altogether about the way your generous benefaction had been used. This was my feeling. It was not in the slightest degree an accusation. . . . If . . . I have quite innocently blundered – please forgive me. My one desire is, if possible, to gain your confidence, and make you feel I am trying to be a faithful steward of the money you have given to God's service. . . .'

Chavasse sent Warrington[222] copies of this correspondence, saying '. . . I cannot make out what is behind it all . . . I seem to have blundered, and am so much in the dark as to how and why that I am only afraid of blundering again. . . .' There was indeed something behind it all, but at this stage neither Warrington nor Mrs. Rowcroft thought fit to explain what it was. Chavasse remained in the dark, but none the less anxious to conciliate. On 25 July 1930 he wrote to Warrington about 'The Rowcroft Inscription': 'I am rather troubled that a year has passed and the inscription which was passed at the Annual Meeting of June 29 [1929] has not yet been placed upon the Rowcroft Building. Would you be willing for me to have the inscription carved upon a stone tablet and then erected at the north end of the building? . . . At present I am a little afraid lest members of the Wills family should come to St. Peter's and not find the inscription.' Warrington's reply was a trifle grudging: [223] 'I have not overlooked this matter, but as there are three sections of the building known as "Rowcroft", and Mrs. Rowcroft's contribution only paid for one third, I think that only one section should bear this name.' The idea of putting a stone tablet at the north end of Block 1 was dropped, and the carved wood tablet which was eventually placed on No. III Staircase was conveniently ambiguous as to the meaning of the words *hoc aedificium*. But in the summer of 1930 more attention was being paid to possible names for Block 2.

4

Parnells had started to dig the foundations for Block 2 at the end of December 1929. As early as 9 January 1930 Dodd informed Chavasse that 'human remains are undoubtedly being disturbed in the excavations for the foundations of the New Building. Two complete human skulls were taken out this afternoon'. There was nothing sinister in this discovery. At a later date[224] Chavasse described the circumstances: '. . . the new Chapel [i.e. the Wesley Memorial Church] and also the old Wesleyan school and playground behind the old Chapel were both built upon the Wesleyan graveyard. When we bought the old school and play-ground and dug the foundations for our new buildings, we came across bones that must have belonged to something like thirty different bodies; and at my own expense I had these removed to a Corporation Cemetery and a small headstone erected over them. I may add that the piece of ground [between the old Chapel and the northern boundary of the St. Peter's House property] was deplorably uncared for, and suggested a rubbish-heap and not a graveyard at all. It was full of headstones dumped there when the Wesleyan School or the new Wesleyan Chapel were built . . . a forlorn, unwholesome and neglected corner which gave me an unpleasant shock every time I looked at it.' The Wesleyan Trustees were glad to sell this strip of land,[225] and its continuation to New Inn Hall Street, which was of little value to them and of great value to St. Peter's for the construction of the new roadway into the quadrangle. But this involved extra expenditure which the Trustees of St. Peter's had not at first envisaged, because the Delegates of Lodgings (i.e. Dr. Kirk) insisted on the erection of a 12ft. wall and the Wesleyans insisted that it should be built of stone. The Building Committee met on 19 May 1930 to discuss this matter. Chavasse had hoped[226] that Warrington would be present, but neither he nor King Harman could attend. Therefore, in the absence of Trustees, the Committee could only[227] 'go into the whole matter of the work that is necessary to satisfy the University . . . and to ask Messrs. Parnell to give us an estimate'. There would be incidental expenses, like the raising of the level of the north quadrangle to match that of the Hannington Hall quadrangle. Altogether, Chavasse reckoned that another £2,000 would have to be found. For most, if not all, of this the Trustees would legally be liable, because it was part of their contract of purchase that they would erect a boundary wall; but Chavasse realized that at that moment the Trustees would not be able to pay. He told Warrington that 'we have in hand some £1,400, and Mr. Cumming thinks that if the Trustees would stand behind us in this matter by making some arrangement with Parnells for deferred payment, that then the Council might reasonably hope to undertake this additional expenditure'. The matter was urgent, because the wall would take six weeks to build, 'and until it is built, and a new entrance formed, we cannot begin to lay out our quadrangles or to block up the old entrance between the Church and St. Peter's House'.

Cumming was never anxious to incur debts,[228] but he seconded Chavasse in asking Warrington[229] to help out temporarily by giving the benefit of the Trustees' credit for a few months. 'The buildings and our investments are at the disposal of the Trustees for the purpose of raising money while we have nothing we can utilise in that way, unless we tried a bill of sale on the furniture[230] and I don't think you would like that.' Warrington saw no difficulty in making arrangements with Parnells, and the way ahead seemed to be reasonably smooth. On 30 June 1930 the Council had its 'annual' meeting,[231] and all four Trustees attended. This was the first appearance of Canon Henry Foster Pegg, who had been formally appointed a Patron and Trustee on 10 April 1930.[232] Chavasse had invited him to preach[233] at a special Commemoration Service on St. Peter's Day, 29 June, but he had fractured an ankle in a car accident and had felt unable to manage more than the Council meeting. There was a large lunch[234] before the meeting, and everything went well. Probably Sir Charles King Harman had this in mind when a month later[235] he advised Chavasse: 'Be careful only about one thing and collaborate with Warrington in all that you do. In this way friction will be avoided and the harmony manifested at our recent Council Meetings will be continued.'

At the meeting Warrington had made a statement about the assistance given by the Trustees in initiating the St. Peter's scheme; they had given £20,000 and borrowed £50,000 on the security of the buildings, and insurance on four lives had been effected which would extinguish the loan in fifteen years. All this was in general terms, but it appears to have satisfied the Council at the time. Moreover Warrington did not even vote against a resolution that the Hon. Treasurer should have his accounts audited by an auditor with experience of Oxford College accounts;[236] though he had it recorded on the minutes that he had abstained from voting. Nothing at all was said about Warrington's threat to resign. The result was that on 2 July Chavasse wrote to him: '. . . I cannot thank you sufficiently for the great help you gave us at our Annual Meeting on Monday.' He might have known that it was too good to be true. Warrington chose to assume that the intention was to appoint a second auditor in addition to his nominee Mr. Thompson; and he warned Cumming[237] that 'the Trustees will not, under any circumstances, pay the Auditor; it is simply throwing good money away'. Cumming's rejoinder[238] was that in spite of the Trustees' failure to pay the deficit on the first year's working (a nice hit), 'we shall have a sufficient surplus for the second year to meet any charge an auditor is likely to make'. After pointing out that there was no question of a *second* auditor, he added: 'I am at a loss to understand your attitude in this matter. Last year Mr. Thompson said my accounts were the most accurate he had ever come across. I am sensible of defects according to Oxford standards. It is I who shall have to face all the disagreeables of a more rigorous check. . . . It is a step that would be taken by any prudent business man, and in my opinion should have been taken before.'[239] Warrington still maintained that he was[240] 'quite satisfied that Mr. Thompson has sufficient experience of Oxford College Accounts to deal with the St. Peter's paltry turnover of £10,000 a year',[241] but there was nothing he could do about it except to grumble.

He also found cause to grumble in proposals for an appeal for money. Back in October 1929[242] he had discussed the possibility of a public appeal, in which Chavasse should tackle Liverpool and the provinces and the M.M.T. should concentrate on London. Warrington suggested that Dr. Norwood, then Headmaster of Harrow, should be invited to speak at a meeting in the Mansion House,[243] and Chavasse added the names of Viscount Brentford (who had played a large part in defeating the new Prayer-Book), Archbishop Lord Davidson, Dr. Alington (Headmaster of Eton) and Dean Inge. Nothing came of these suggestions at the time. Then some time in the spring of 1930 Warrington had the idea that the new building should be named after Canon Stather Hunt and funds raised as a memorial to him. On 20 May 1930 Chavasse told him privately: 'Some weeks ago Mrs. Stather Hunt came to see me . . . she expressed herself as willing that, as you suggested, this block [No. IV Staircase] should be in memory of Canon Stather Hunt. But she also expressed a strong wish [that] appeal for funds for such a memorial should emanate from Oxford itself. I told her of course that I would be quite willing to organise such an appeal . . . but I made it clear that I must receive my instructions through you. . . . The whole suggestion is yours, and the Canon was chairman of the Church of England Trust. You may quite naturally feel, therefore, that any such appeal ought properly to come through you and the Trust Society. On the other hand, there are Mrs. Stather Hunt's views to be considered, which I gather are quite strong. . . .'

It is evident that Chavasse felt a need to mind his step, but Warrington's reply showed that he had put his foot into something unexpectedly distasteful. This reply,[244] marked 'private and confidential' in red type, began: 'As Mrs. Stather Hunt was rude to me . . . and her personal attitude to the Trust . . . is so hostile . . . I don't feel disposed to proceed with the matter. . . . [What she had done in seeing Chavasse] is nothing less than a down-right insult. I have had quite enough of this woman and I shall oppose the suggestion which I made that the new Building should be named "The Stather Hunt Block".' He claimed that Mrs. Stather Hunt had failed to 'realise that Mrs. Rowcroft gave the £10,000 to me [Warrington] and not to the Trust';[245] he seems to have been particularly anxious to have no enquiry into his management of the Trust's affairs, and to have feared that Mrs. Stather Hunt might cause trouble. That at least would appear to be the explanation of his allegation, in the same letter, that '. . . Mrs. Stather Hunt . . . has boasted to one of our Trustees that she has taken all the papers [belonging to her husband] relating to business with our Trust to the Solicitors and has gone so far as to threaten, if occasion arises, that she will use certain letters, which were confidential to the Canon, to injure our Trust. The real woman is now revealed and I am having nothing to do with her in any shape or form.'

To Chavasse, who knew Mrs. Stather Hunt well and who was a personal friend of her son, the vicar of St. Matthew's church in Oxford, it was the real Warrington who was now revealed, and not for the first time. But he sent a tactful reply: [246] 'As regards the other most difficult and delicate matter of Canon Stather Hunt's memorial . . . I fully understand your position, and thank you for the confidence you have reposed in me. . . . Don't you think that our one and only consideration must be the memory of the Canon himself, and what he was both to the Trust and to St. Peter's? . . . in sheer decency we are bound, do you not think, to do something?

The Council is making itself responsible for raising the money for the new block and will need every source and help it can find . . . an appeal issued on behalf of a memorial to the Canon will help our building fund most materially, and I for one should be very sorry indeed to lose this opportunity; we cannot really afford to do it. If, therefore, quite naturally, you wish to wash your hands of the whole matter, would you give me permission, without offence to yourself, to organize such a memorial over the names of his late curates. . . ?'

This was a clever letter: if money was to be raised, Warrington was not going to be left out. He wrote back at once: [247] 'I quite appreciate what you say about Canon Stather Hunt . . . I held him in great reverence. . . . I will give my final decision within a few days. In any case I shall insist that as I made the suggestion that we should honour the Canon's memory, my Office must carry out the Appeal. . . .' After this, it was tacitly assumed that the memorial appeal would soon be made and that it would be for the cost of the new block, to be called the Stather Hunt Building. On this assumption, Chavasse wrote to Sir Charles King Harman on 25 July 1930: '. . . on the tower of the new buildings there is a blank shield waiting for a coat of arms to be carved on it, and it would be a great convenience and saving of expense if this shield could be carved [with the Stather Hunt arms] within the next few weeks before the scaffolding is taken down.' A few days later Sir Charles paid a visit to Mrs. Stather Hunt in Tunbridge Wells, and reported to Chavasse: [248] '. . . The upshot is that she disclaims any hostility to the Martyrs Memorial Trust. . . .' Chavasse therefore had no hesitation in getting out a draft appeal in aid of a 'Canon Stather Hunt Building for St. Peter's Hall', and this he sent off to Warrington for comment and approval on 20 August 1930. In his covering letter he wrote: 'It is a matter of great thankfulness that Sir Charles King Harman's visit to Mrs. Stather Hunt was so successful that it is her express wish that the Church of England Trust should be represented on the list of signatures, and of course you and Lord Gisborough are the obvious names. . . .'

Warrington's reaction was curious.[249] Forgetting his professed reverence for the late Canon, he set about some denigration: 'The Church of England Trust Society . . . was not founded by the

late Canon – it was founded by a lady who gave all the money.
The Canon was the first chairman, but was never known to contribute to its funds. Further, the late Canon had neither part nor
lot in the educational development to which you refer. When I
purchased Wrekin College the Canon would not listen to the
suggestion, which he stigmatized as "grand but impossible".
When I founded Stowe the late Canon washed his hands of it.
When the photographs of Westonbirt House were lying on the
table the Canon asked me if I contemplated establishing a School
at Westonbirt, and both verbally and by letter urged me to do
nothing of the kind.' This may of course have been merely
another example of Warrington's prickly pride; but the attack on
Canon Stather Hunt may also have been a smokescreen to hide
the real reason for his objection to the draft, which emerges
when he protests, in the name of the Trustees, against the statement that 'Cheques should be made payable to the Hon.
Treasurer, J. A. Cumming, Esq., (Stather Hunt Memorial), St.
Peter's Hall, Oxford'. His final word was . . . 'Please do not be
too sanguine that the Trustees will endorse the appeal'.

No wonder that Chavasse expressed[250] 'surprise and distress'
and that he sent King Harman a copy of Warrington's letter.
However, he made the best of it, suggesting a revised wording
of the draft, offering solace to wounded pride,[251] and making
no bones about the destination of cheques: for Cumming to act
as treasurer was only common sense, and would save trouble all
round, but 'I have no objection in theory to a statement in the
Appeal asking that money should be sent either to St. Peter's or
to your office'. Warrington replied stiffly: [252] '. . . I made it as
clear to you as I could that our liability in connection with St.
Peter's is such that it will be necessary to use this Appeal to
secure funds for the Hall. I was warned by some of my Colleagues
when I made the suggestion that I had made a serious mistake.
I now realise I have done so.' In fact, it was Chavasse who had
made a mistake: he began to realise that he had been led up
the garden path. On 10 September 1930 he protested to Warrington: 'I am afraid I have always been under the impression that
the money for the Stather Hunt memorial was to go towards the
liability of the new building [Block 2] for which purpose it was
being asked, and in consideration of which [the] buildings were
to be called after his name. I cannot conceal that your letter was
therefore a disappointment to me as I had hoped the memorial
would help with the £15,000 liability which is more or less a
personal burden upon myself. On the other hand, I fully realise

the vast sums for which the Trustees have so generously made themselves responsible. . . . We can only be grateful at St. Peter's Hall that the money should be expended upon the Hall and not in some other direction.[253] I do not think the appeal should be sent out asking for money for building and then used for some other purpose. I suggest therefore that the appeal be slightly amended "that £21,000 is still required towards the purchase of the site and the buildings".' In that case, he agreed that Warrington's office should handle the whole appeal, but he also gave warning that he would 'keep Sir Charles King Harman informed of this new development . . . as I think it quite possible that he was under the same impression as myself.' To which Warrington's only answer[254] was 'Whilst Sir Charles King Harman has put things right with Mrs. Stather Hunt, it does not put things right with me, because I am a man who never forgets a thing of this nature. Mrs. Stather Hunt's action was mean and contemptible, and I don't care whether the Appeal goes forward or not.'

If anybody was being mean and contemptible, there is no doubt now who it was. But this letter marked the end of the attempt to link the name of Stather Hunt with Block No. 2. A memorial appeal was not issued till 1932, and then it was for another purpose. Meanwhile Cumming was still worried because the Trustees had not yet paid the deficit for 1928-29; on 11 September 1930 he sent Warrington an account showing that on 31 July the Trustees owed £517, and added: 'When I get this, we shall be prepared to dispense with the overdraft of £500. . . . The auditor points out that we should get interest on the arrears.' This no doubt confirmed Warrington's dislike of independent auditors: he wrote back: [255] '. . . I really do not understand the position at Oxford, and I shall have to ask the Trustees to please release me of all connection with the business and appoint someone else. . . . Would you please tell the Auditor from me that I regard this [the bit about interest on arrears] as an impertinent suggestion, and I shall sign no cheque for any interest.'

But something much more serious was in the offing. Within a month, Warrington was begging for immediate financial aid. What happened can be seen from a couple of letters. On 3 October 1930 Cumming wrote to him: 'Under the instructions of Mr. Chavasse as a result of his conversation with you on the telephone last night, I have sent a cheque for £1,000 . . . to Barclays Bank, Wellington, Salop. . . .[256] This leaves the Appeal Fund with insufficient [money] to meet the bills for furnishing No. 2 Block. These will come in from Oxford tradesmen at an early date, and donations to the Appeal Fund in the past five months have been much below the average. Mr. Chavasse, however, informs me you are prepared to assume liability for Bott's bill for furniture, which will amount to about £1,000. . . . We are very glad to help the Trustees in any way we can, but we fervently trust this temporary embarrassment will not in any way delay the conclusion of the purchase of the Wesleyan property, as the Vice-Chancellor will not license No. 2 Block until a copy of the conveyance of the site has been given him. Twenty men *must* go into rooms in it on the 9th inst.' On the following day Warrington acknowledged this letter: 'I am much obliged to you for sending the cheque for £1,000 to the Bank to meet Parnell's bill. . . . We shall of course accept liability for Bott's bill. . . . With reference to No. 2 Block, owing to Mr. Chavasse's very noble and generous action we shall be able to complete this matter by the 9th inst.'

The point was that Chavasse, appalled by the discovery that even the site of the new building had not yet been paid for, had been forced to save the situation by raising a loan on his own personal security. On 8 October 1930 he wrote to the Manager of the Midland Bank, Cornmarket Street, Oxford, as follows: —

'As a result of my conversation with you I wish to ask your bank to make me a loan of £6,000 for one year upon personal securities which I have deposited with you, and which amount to over this sum. Though this loan is upon my personal security it is on behalf of the Council of St. Peter's Hall in order to complete the purchase of some Wesleyan property adjoining the Hall, upon which twenty-two sets of rooms have been built, and will be occupied tomorrow evening.

'The purchase deed is already executed, and waits only this sum to complete it, and the transaction must be made forthwith in order to satisfy the requirements of Oxford University authorities that we are housing men at St. Peter's Hall on property belonging to ourselves.

'As regards the repayment of this loan: —

1. I require this loan for one year, as my Council anticipates that subscriptions to this amount will be raised during this [sic] coming twelve months. As you will see from the enclosed report our subscriptions have amounted to over £8,000 for each of the two preceding [sic] years, and they are still coming in.

2. If the flow of subscriptions dropped for any reason, I can state, in my position as chairman of the Council, that it is our intention to mortgage the new building upon the property in

105

question, and so repay this loan.

3. In the unforeseen event of either of these alternatives proving fruitless I hereby give you permission to realize my securities in payment of the loan at the latter end of October 1931. . . .'

Since Warrington accepted this as 'a very noble and generous action', it might have been expected that his relations with Chavasse would now improve. It did not work out quite like that. On 9 October 1930 Chavasse sent him a copy of his letter to the Midland Bank, and made some demands which were not at all reassuring to a man who was beginning to feel the ground shaking beneath his feet. 'I do require', wrote Chavasse, 'the assurance from you that if the new block of buildings is mortgaged by the Trustees upon the completion of the conveyance . . . the £6,000 involved . . . should be the first charge upon such a transaction. The second charge should be the releasing as far as possible of the £10,000 endowment of the first tutorship, which you will remember the Council gave permission to be hypothecated for the sole purpose of the new buildings. This of course can be discussed at our next Council meeting on 1 November, and the whole position should be greatly clarified as the Trustees produce their balance sheet at that meeting. Naturally the financial negotiations between us of the past week have made me very anxious, as I had imagined that as regards St. Peter's Hall the mortgage raised upon the Rowcroft buildings had relieved the Trustees of anxiety with regard to the great liabilities they have so generously shouldered: for the Trust Deed allows the Trustees to mortgage the property of the Hall solely for the purpose of the Hall. I can quite believe that my anxiety is only occasioned because I am in the dark, and therefore I am looking forward very eagerly to the Council meeting in three weeks time when the position will be explained.'

This amounted to a reminder to Warrington that by Cap. X of the Trust Deed —

29. The Trustees shall keep true accounts of all moneys received and expended in respect of the Hall and of the matters in respect of which such receipt and expenditure takes place and of the property for the time being vested in them and all liabilities in connection therewith and once at least in every year such accounts with a balance sheet shall be examined audited and certified by professional auditors as the Trustees shall from time to time appoint and shall be produced to the Council at their next annual meeting.

106

No such audited accounts had been produced at the annual meeting in June 1930. In Chavasse's letter there was also a hint that he wondered whether Warrington was using St. Peter's money for the benefit of the Trust Schools. There was a little more than a hint in a letter which Cumming addressed to Warrington on 10 October:

'As requested by your private secretary yesterday, I send you the following information: —

Total of bills issued this term for battels of last term and fees of this term	2838-7- 1
Total paid to 9th inst.	2055-5-10
Total outstanding	783-1- 3

I asked Mr. Burn what this information was for, and his reply was that you were preparing a statement for the bank. It is, I hope, unnecessary for me to remind you that under the trust deed none of the assets of St. Peter's Hall can be pledged for any other purpose than St. Peter's Hall, and that as far as fees are concerned it is out of the question to expect that anything can be spared for any other purpose than the running of the Hall. . . .'

To this letter Warrington replied: [257] 'Its contents occasion me most painful surprise. My Secretary asked you a question as to the income of the Hall. You immediately and for no apparent reason write me a homily. . . . It is our custom each term to notify our Bankers . . . of the total income we receive from each School and on this occasion they put on their list a note asking for information about the income of St. Peter's Hall: that is all.[258] If you knew the worry and the anxiety which St. Peter's has occasioned me perhaps you would not be surprised that I feel the bitterest of regrets that ever I allowed myself to launch this Scheme. When it was started I thought £25,000 would put it on its feet not the colossal sum that has been required. I, and not my Colleagues, have had to find the money. . . .' He added a post-script in his own writing: 'As a result of my St. Peter's experience I am today a sadder and a wiser man. P.S. As a member of the Council I am entitled to ask a question to which you should reply without comment.'

A little later[259] he sent a somewhat revealing letter to Chavasse; marked 'Strictly Confidential': 'At the Stowe Council Meeting which was held last week I was more surprised than I can express in words to hear from Bishop Kempson[260] that you had apparently discussed very freely with him the financial position of St. Peter's and what you had done in connection with the Wesleyan Schools. There was no doubt whatever from Bishop Kempson's remark made before the whole Council that you had given him an entirely erroneous view of the whole matter. It was necessary for me to tell the Bishop that you did not notify me until the Monday evening that the authorities of Oxford University would not allow the men to occupy the building until we had bought the Wesleyan property. This was the first intimation I had that such a condition would be imposed.[261] Further, I made it very clear to you all along that one cannot offer an unfinished building as security either to a Bank or an Insurance Company. When I signed the Contract to enable you to get this new building and to complete St. Peter's at once I did not anticipate the difficulties which have had to be encountered, difficulties which I may say would have crushed half a dozen men.' He did not specify what these difficulties had been, but presumably he meant the drying up of subscriptions to the Trust caused by the economic depression. At any rate he went on to tell Chavasse that through his own 'indiscretions' with reference to his attitude to B.C.M.S., St. Peter's had lost much support. 'You make no secret of the fact that as a Simeon Trustee[262] you are determined to stamp out B.C.M.S. from the parishes to which you appoint by sending strong C.M.S. men. This information has been widely circulated throughout B.C.M.S. and as a result of what you have said the Trust can get no support from this quarter for St. Peter's. . . .'

Chavasse thought it necessary to take this letter seriously, and on 30 October 1930 he sent a long reply (private and confidential): 'With regard to the matters on which you write, you must remember that I have known Bishop Kempson all my life. He was one of my father's curates at St. Peter-le-Bailey; he was a constant visitor to our home all the time he was at the King William's College,[263] and then became my father's suffragan as Bishop of Warrington. When, therefore, he called upon me when I was in great anxiety regarding the Hall and knew he was a member [sic] of Stowe School, and therefore might know more than I did about the finances of the Trust, I did discuss the matter with him as a wise old friend who could probably reassure me. . . . It is not my fault that you are unaware that the Oxford authorities would not allow the new buildings to be occupied till we owned them. Directly Dr. Pember had notified us to this effect on May 22nd, 1930, Mr. Teal informed your solicitors and has constantly reminded them of the fact. In the end he received from them the definite assurance (which we supposed was on your authority) that the money would be forthcoming early in September.

'You cannot wonder, therefore, if I became really anxious when first you asked us to send you £1,000 at a moment's notice, and then informed us that the Trust could not possibly find this promised sum for the Wesleyan property. It was at that moment that Bishop Kempson called upon me. . . .'[264] '. . . If you can bear with so long a letter you can help me greatly regarding the mortgaging of the newest block of buildings. The matter is a little involved and required the good will of the Council. The Trustees have the right to mortgage the property of the Hall (which I interpret as meaning whether the Trustees or the Council have provided the money for the buildings), but of course only for the purposes of the Hall. So far the Council have found £3,500 for the building, and raised a loan of £9,000 till the necessary subscriptions can be obtained. This accounts for £12,500 out of the £17,700 required, leaving £5,200 outstanding.' He ended by enclosing a financial statement which Cumming and he had got out for the Council, showing 'conclusively what an immense debt St. Peter's owes to the Trustees, and I am glad of the opportunity of letting the Council fully realise the fact'.

The Council met on 1 November 1930.[265] Chavasse and Warrington made statements explaining the position, and nobody chose to ask why the Trustees themselves had not yet produced accounts. It was accepted that a mortgage of at least £15,000 would be raised on Block No. 2, and that repayment of Chavasse's loan would be a first charge upon it. Nothing was said, or at any rate entered in the minutes, about the second charge being for the releasing of the £10,000 endowment for the first tutorship; Warrington had already ruled this out as impracticable.[266] In fact, it was not until 3 January 1931 that Warrington was able to report to Chavasse '. . . at last I have succeeded in getting an Insurance Company to consider a Mortgage of £17,000, at $5\frac{1}{2}\%$ . . . it must be clearly understood that the Council is liable for the Interest and Redemption, and that this will be paid out of the profits of the Hall. . . . No-one connected with the Council will ever know the difficulties I have had in connection with this matter. . . . I may add that if it were not for my personal friendship with the Lord Mayor of London the proposal would never have been looked at by any Insurance Company.' But in spite of the Lord Mayor of London's benevolence, Chavasse now viewed every proposal with caution. He wrote back:[267] '. . . the

109

proposed mortgage . . . seems to me an excellent piece of business upon which I congratulate you. . . . I have no doubt that the Council will accept the arrangement. . . . It really means that they will be responsible for the interest on the mortgage instead of upon the £10,000 securities which have been hypothecated for building this block.[268] And certainly the Appeal Fund is perfectly able to find this interest. It will involve a settlement of accounts as regards the liabilities of the Council to the Trustees, but this should present no difficulty.'

It will be noted that he said nothing directly about Warrington's suggestion that the interest would be paid from the profits of the Hall. One would not guess from this letter that only two days earlier Warrington had again asked for help in paying a pressing bill of £2,000 from Parnells, and in doing so had mentioned that 'The Trustees noted with satisfaction that there was a balance of £1,000 on last year's working.' Cumming at once sent off a cheque for £1,000 from the Appeal Fund, but pointed out that in spite of a book balance of £1,013 on the last year's working, 'the cash in hand was only £61', and no less than £517 was owed by the Trustees. This was certainly in Chavasse's mind when he continued: [269] 'As regards the arrangement of insurance to pay off the mortgage, I think the matter had better stand over until the Council can discuss it. The total liability of the Council for No. 2 Block, and the laying out of the quads., etc., is under £20,000. Of this they have already paid off £3,500, so that they are liable for less than the £17,000 raised by the mortgage. They will be in a position in a few months, when legacies come in, to pay off at least another £2,000. And they can hope with confidence to pay off the whole mortgage within, at the most, three to five years. An insurance, therefore, as far as I can see, will not help them, and may well prove to be a much more expensive way of paying off the mortgage. . . .'

This really put the cat among Warrington's pigeons. He wrote back angrily: [270] '. . . it is quite clear that you are labouring under a very serious misapprehension about the mortgage on the new building. I have been negotiating this mortgage for seven months; it has been refused by six Companies. . . . The average Mortgagees will have nothing to do with Colleges, Schools and Hospitals. . . . I wish to make it clear that the Council will either have to accept the £17,000 or nothing at all. What you propose in your letter cannot be done and no Company would consider such terms for one moment. . . . No Insurance Company will allow a mortgage unless they have some business in return and that business is a Policy for the amount of the mortgage. If you propose to interfere with the terms of the mortgage. I must tell you at once that the whole matter is off, and I must warn you that this will mean a very big smash. . . . At the last Meeting, you will remember I told the Council they would be extremely fortunate if I could get them £15,000 and I advised that once the mortgage was secured, they should hold on to it and nothing should be repaid only the annual premium. . . . Writing with a very full knowledge of this business, I should regard it as the height of folly to attempt to repay this loan. What are you going to do when the Wesleyans ask you to take over the other building if you let this loan slip through your fingers? Surely the policy to adopt is to conserve every penny in the Bank so that . . . we shall be ready, not only to purchase this property, but to proceed with erecting the final block of buildings on this site. I have negotiated the loan with that end in view; indeed I was hoping to get £20,000 for the Council which would leave them a margin to proceed with the Scheme at an early date. . . .'

If in the past Warrington had shown himself punctilious in money matters, and if he had been willing to produce accounts, Chavasse might well have accepted this letter as a convincing example of worldly wisdom,[271] even though it implied that it was a sensible practice to borrow money for one purpose and to use it for another. As it was, he simply replied:[272] 'Thank you very much for your letter of the 16th, and the very useful facts it contains, which will be fully considered at our Council Meeting on February 5th.' On 27 January 1931 G. G. Burn sent a memorandum from Warrington, for circulation to the Council (mentioning that the proposed mortgage was with the Clerical, Medical and General Company), and Chavasse took the opportunity to send to Burn, two days later, a letter which he knew very well would not please Warrington at all: '. . . Mr. Warrington might like to have the latest figures of the Council's liability[273] with regard to the new buildings. He will see that the position is most satisfactory, and that the only difficulty is regarding approximately £5,000 still outstanding. All, therefore, the Council requires is a short loan of £5,000, as I am convinced that this sum will be found in something like a year. One more point. . . . When will the balance sheet be circulated to members of the Council, so that they may be able to consider it and accept it at the meeting?'

As soon as Burn showed him this letter, Warrington wrote to Chavasse:[274] '. . . I should be very blind if I could not see your motive which is to intimate very politely that you will oppose the loan of £17,000. I also note in the statement you submit that you include the hypothecated securities of £10,000. I have told you that these cannot be released until the Trust has raised the £10,000 . . . my Trustees know that if the Loan is turned down it is the end of St. Peter's Hall: there is no way out of it. . . .' He was quite right in thinking that an effort was being made to force his hand. On 31 January he received a private letter from Chavasse[275] which ended: '. . . I think you misunderstand our gropings in the dark to discover what is the financial position of the Trustees concerning St. Peter's Hall. As I have often assured you the production of the Balance Sheet will clear the air of perplexity and misunderstandings. I am glad we have only to wait a few more days before it is in our hands.' To which Warrington replied: [276] 'I wrote to Mr. Teal to tell him that at the very last moment Thompson, the Accountant, came to me and after having had the accounts in his hands for months informed me that he felt he could not carry on with the work. This will necessitate the Trustees appointing another Accountant. My Secretary and I are preparing a statement of the Trust's position to lay before the Council on Thursday. Although this statement cannot be complete it will be such as to give the Council a good idea of our very heavy liabilities.'

The Council met in London on 5 February 1931.[277] At the end of the day one of the Tutors recorded: [278] 'Chavasse had a Council meeting in London today, and had gone prepared to *force* Warrington to produce a balance-sheet, which he had hitherto refused to do. . . . Chavasse succeeded in inducing Warrington to promise to produce a balance-sheet.' At the meeting, Warrington started by raising a hare, in connection with donations to the Appeal Fund received as a result of an appeal made by him in *The Record*.[279] On the previous day he had warned Chavasse: [280] '. . . I shall require the appointment of a Sub-Committee to examine every letter which has been received by you or the Treasurer . . . from the time of the issuing of the Trust Appeal. I shall also require the right to communicate with each Donor and ascertain whether their gift has been sent in response to the Appeal which has been appearing in the *Record* or to one of my letters. . . .[281] I am charged with . . . publishing figures in the *Record* which are not accurate. This impression is due to the fact that people have been sending donations to the Appeal Fund which have been kept at Oxford and not forwarded to the Trust.'

This remarkable sensitivity did not impress the Council, and no action was taken. Instead, the Council went on to show that it was not at all happy about the financial situation: it resolved (the Revd. P. E. Warrington dissenting) that the proposed Mortgage of No. 2 Block be adjourned until the Council had had an opportunity of examining the accounts and Balance Sheet of the Trustees after they had been duly audited. This was clearly a vote of no confidence in Percy Warrington, and he realized it. But he put the blame not on himself but on Christopher Chavasse, towards whom he was already developing a paranoid antipathy. This showed itself in carping criticism and wild accusations. For instance, at the very end of his long letter of 16 January 1931, he had added in his own handwriting: 'If our Solicitor had negotiated with the Wesleyans for this property *we know* that it would have been secured for thousands less.' Chavasse had taken him up on this 'wild and rash statement',[282] and had taken the trouble to get counter statements from Mr. Teal and from Mr. Green, the Superintendant of the Oxford Wesleyan Circuit. These he sent to Warrington on 30 January, with the comment: 'I hope that these will satisfy you . . . the Wesleyans were not anxious to sell, they knew they could obtain their price if only they waited. And as events have turned out they could have secured far more from the City of Oxford School, who would have given their eyes for this property which thank God we obtained in the nick of time.'

Again, Warrington had taken umbrage when Chavasse quite properly and with due notice had circulated to the Council Warrington's letter of 3 January about the proposed mortgage; Warrington's protest was revealing: [283] 'I am not in the habit of having my letters sent by the Headmasters of the Schools to Members of the Council without my permission, and so far as I am concerned you are in exactly the same position.' Presumably none of the Headmasters had yet had cause to stand up to Warrington.[284]

Then there was the case of Mr. Tinne. At a meeting of the Management Committee[285] on 23 October 1930, Chavasse had reported that he had appointed Mr. C. E. Tinne, Assistant Treasurer at £200 per annum, with the idea of taking over the bursarship later on at a maximum salary of £400 per annum. This was in accordance with a previous decision by the Council that Mr. Cumming should be given assistance, but Warrington at once objected: [286] '. . . It is indeed startling to find that at St. Peter's a man can be appointed Assistant Bursar without the knowledge and sanction of the Council. . . .' Chavasse had to point out[287] that under the Trust Deed it was in his power to appoint 'tutors and other officers', and the Council of 1 November 1930 ratified his action and agreed that Mr. Tinne should be appointed Bursar in 1931, at a salary of £300 x £50 to £400. But on 23 January 1931 the Management Committee met again, and Warrington found in his copy of the minutes that —

2. The Master stated that Mrs. Chavasse had ceased to super-vise the kitchen staff and catering, and that Mr. Tinne had taken charge of these duties. *It is recommended* that in respect of this extra work Mr. Tinne be given an incre-ment of £50 per annum with effect from 1st January.

3. *It is recommended* that Mrs. Chavasse be cordially thanked by the Council for the great assistance she has given for over two years in supervising not only the kitchen, but also the furnishing and equipment of the Hall.

...5. It was pointed out that the arrears of covenanted grants due from the Trustees amounted to £799-10-0 on 31st December, and that although a loan of £500 had been obtained from the bank as required by the Trustees, no further payment had been made by them as promised in Minute of Council No. 161. *The Committee desire to draw the attention of Council* to this position.

There is no doubt that Warrington resented No. 5; he called it 'an expression of ingratitude on the part of unappreciative and ungracious people'.[288] But he chose to make a major issue out of No. 2. While claiming that what he said was 'in no way a reflec-tion on Mr. Tinne', he declared that 'no-one with any knowledge of Schools and Colleges could ever call the work he has to do onerous. . . . When the late Canon Stather Hunt was drawing up the Deed I can assure you he had no intention of allowing any Bursar to be appointed without the knowledge and consent of the Trustees. If you had asked the Trustees . . . we could have found you half-a-dozen christian men who would have been very glad to accept the post in an honorary capacity. . . .' What fol-lowed is symptomatic of Warrington's state of mind: 'When I last saw you I told you that one of your students, whom [sic] I believe is being most generously helped by the Trust and other people, bought a motor-car and was flying about the country in it. I confess, when a Bishop told me of this, I was astounded beyond measure. On a previous occasion in my presence one of the students complained about the cake and intimated to the Housekeeper that it was not good enough for his highly flavoured palate, and yet this youth was at St. Peter's Hall as a result of the self-sacrificing generosity on the part of Evangelical Church-people, and not least, my Trust. . . . The object of this letter is to tell you that I am gravely apprehensive about the whole position of St. Peter's Hall. . . . I now ask myself two questions. First, can I, conscientiously, go on asking people who are denying themselves up to the hilt to give money to St. Peter's Hall, when at St. Peter's I know there is no attempt to economise? . . . In one case, there is a person who has sold flowers from her little garden to help on this work. What would she think if she knew of this? . . . My second point is this. Why should I spend my time and carry such heavy burdens as I do . . . when I know of your own attitude to the Trust, and that is to drain it of its last farthing. I have now spent a little time in considering the position and I am going to make it very plain to you that if, in view of the whole position of St. Peter's, the Council decides to incur the additional expenditure of £50 per annum, I shall not only finish with St. Peter's Hall, but I reserve to myself the absolute right to publish this letter in the *Record* and other Papers, and I shall do it without the slightest hesitation. . . . I know only too well, and have known for a long time, the resentment at St. Peter's against me, the man who has made St. Peter's possible, because he has dared to utter the word "economy". . . .'

Chavasse at once wrote a 'private and confidential' letter in his own handwriting[289] explaining that Mrs. Chavasse had had to give up her activities because she was expecting another baby, and even offering to pay the £50 to Tinne out of his own pocket, provided that not even Tinne knew about the arrangement. Warrington simply disregarded this offer,[290] repeated his previous statements, and then on 4 February wrote: '. . . I must also take this opportunity of telling you before the Meeting tomorrow that I feel I can no longer work with you, and whilst I realise what a serious crisis the severing of my connection with St. Peter's means I should be gravely lacking in self-respect if I did not take this step. I have many reasons for doing so. My chief reason can be best expressed by the words of our late Chairman, Canon Stather Hunt, who, after the interview with Chancellor Errington, in the presence of our Solicitor and myself, said: "Mr. Chavasse, I will now tell you publicly what I intended to say to you privately, you are a man who does not 'play the game' ".[291] Next, after giving a totally inaccurate version of the circumstances in which he had

signed the contract for the building of No. 2 Block, he went on:
'Whilst I have been working hard and carrying most tremendous
responsibilities . . . you have been taking the kudos, and not
making the slightest self-sacrifice in any direction, indeed from
the worldly point of view St. Peter's has been a very fine thing
for you . . . at the Council Meeting I shall state that as you
have used me as the means of getting the building, and having got
it have taken up this extraordinary attitude I must cease my work
for St. Peter's. This means that someone else will have to raise
your Salary, your Rent, etc. I need hardly say that the source
from whence this money has come, the Evangelical public, will
not be disposed to subscribe to your Salary, etc., when I have
made public my statement in the *Record* as to my reasons for
refusing to work with you any longer. In my opinion it is quite
impossible to do Christian work in this atmosphere. . . .'

In Warrington's letters at this period there is a curious mixture
of the malignant and the ridiculous. This particular letter ended
with a mysterious warning: 'There is another matter which I
shall have to deal with before the Council. It is a personal one
and a grave reflection upon myself. In connection with this I will
ask you a question before the whole Governing Body. . . .' There
is nothing in the Council minutes to elucidate this, but a clue
can be found in a letter to Chavasse in Warrington's own handwriting, dated 7 March 1931: 'This afternoon I was turning
out one of the drawers in my desk and quite by chance found
a letter written in your own hand bearing the date 18.1.29. In
that letter you say "I have often seen your 'Colt the foal of an
ass' tethered outside the Charing X Hotel". I was about to write
and tell you that after making further enquiries I am absolutely
satisfied that *you had made* this sneering reference to my car –
which you publicly denied and stigmatised as "ridiculous" etc.[292]
Now I have the documentary proof to lay before the next meeting
of the Council. Truth will out.' To this Chavasse replied at
once: 'Your letter came as a great surprise to me. But at any
rate it clears up the one thing that matters – namely that the
remark in question could not possibly have been a "sneer", but
must have been a joke which apparently we both enjoyed two
years ago – and have now forgotten. . . .' The matter was closed
by a letter from G. G. Burn:[293] 'Mr. Warrington is in bed and
I am answering his letters. He wishes me to say that he notes with
interest that his letter "came as a great surprise" to you. He
further notes your very evasive reply that "it must have been a
joke". As Mr. Warrington considers you rather an expert in the

art of evasion he is not surprised that you should thus try to pass this matter off. Mr. Warrington bids me say that as you would not dare to make such remarks against the Master [sic] of Corpus, Sir Charles King Harman, or other members of the Council you may not presume to take such liberty with him.'

But there were more serious matters at issue than sneers or jokes. Immediately after the Council Meeting of 5 February 1931 Warrington wrote to Chavasse: 'I was explaining to the Council yesterday afternoon the position with regard to Messrs. Parnells, and I said that as a result of giving the majority of our work to them in connection with Stowe, Canford and St. Peter's Hall, their overdraft is considerable. When I was referring to the payments which have to be made to the Contractors this Term you so far forgot yourself as to state definitely that the Trust was using the St. Peter's Securities for the Schools. . . . I have not a shadow of doubt that you have had this at the back of your mind all along, but our Accounts show that it is the Schools which have been paying thousands of pounds to St. Peter's. . . .' This statement, even though it contained an element of truth, would have been more convincing if it had been supported by figures, and Chavasse did not delay to say so: [294] 'I am sorry if anything I said at the Council meeting has been misunderstood by you. It must be clear to anyone that I did not and could not, make any definite statement concerning the financial methods of the Church of England Trust Society. As you know, we are entirely in the dark, and were asking questions while you very kindly elucidated the position as far as was possible without an audited balance sheet. I remember that I did ask whether the liability of St. Peter's Hall to Messrs. Parnell was included in the general liability of the Trust as a whole, or whether the account was kept absolutely distinct. It is this quite proper question that you must have misinterpreted as a definite statement. It only shows that there must be misunderstandings both on the part of the Trust and on ours until we have an audited account and balance sheet before us.'

This letter must have crossed one written by Warrington on the same day, telling Chavasse that he had already informed King Harman of his decision to give up work for St. Peter's and that he would be formally notifying the other Trustees; '. . . in view of the seriousness of the position created you may wish to meet the Trustees, but as far as I am concerned the decision is final.' Just what he meant by this is not completely clear; it would seem that he intended to remain a Trustee and to refuse to pay a penny towards the Master's salary, perhaps in the hope of forcing him to resign the Mastership. Chavasse's carefully worded reply[295] is interesting: 'I have received your letter about the Master's salary, and have forwarded a copy of it to Sir Charles King Harman, together with my own observations. Though the matter of the Master's salary is one between the Master and the Trustees, and not between you and me as individuals,[296] I would like to express to you on behalf of the Council our gratitude for your personal work in raising the necessary amount during the last three years.' On the following day Chavasse took the precaution of dropping a word into the ear of the editor of *The Record*[297] '. . . May I add in strictest confidence that if by any chance you should receive damaging letters for publication in *The Record* from Mr. Warrington either about myself, or St. Peter's – for the sake of the Hall they should not be published . . . I speak entirely in the dark, and do not really expect any such eventuality. . . .' Mr. Hogan was not altogether surprised; in another 'strictly confidential' letter he told Chavasse:[298] '. . . I had already heard of the feeling in the direction you mentioned, and of implied threats, but I could not imagine anyone being so foolish as to wish to court publicity in the matter. My interview with Mr. Graham Brown revealed the seriousness of the position, and I can assure you of my sympathy in the anxiety which must be yours at this time. . . . I feel very strongly that every effort should be made to prevent any interference with the existing management of St. Peter's, for any alteration would be disastrous not only to St. Peter's but to the whole Evangelical cause. . . .'

The position certainly was serious. On 12 February 1931 Warrington followed up his previous threats by sending a long diatribe, starting with a formal statement that at a meeting of the M.M.T. Council on the previous day he had notified his colleagues that he must bring his work for St. Peter's to an end, and finishing with a still more formal statement: 'I gave notice yesterday to the Martyrs Memorial and Church of England Trustees that a motion would be moved at the next Meeting of the Trust that the Solicitors be instructed to inform the Council of St. Peter's Hall, Oxford, that the Trustees, having lost confidence, can no longer continue to make the payments covenanted under Cap. XII and set out in the Second Schedule of the Trust Deed.' The bulk of the letter consisted of abuse and complaints, of which samples will suffice: 'I informed my Colleagues that during the past three years I have been most painfully impressed by your

insincerity . . . ; I am convinced that you have used the Trust
in general, and myself in particular, as a catspaw . . . ; I shall
never forget the fact that when St. Peter's Hall opened at the
end of the first term[299] I went into the Common Room with you,
and I found several Church Papers on the table, but not the
Record. When I asked you why . . . you replied that you had
not allowed it as you did not wish St. Peter's Hall to be
branded . . . ; you have never been able to conceal your animosity
towards the B.C.M.S. . . . We understand that from the very
outset of the Movement the policy has been to impress upon the
students not to speak of St. Peter's as an Evangelical Hall. . . .
The Rev. T. Lancaster, the Vicar of Weymouth . . . asked one
of your students . . . how that Evangelical Hall at Oxford was
getting on. The young man went out of his way to assure Mr.
Lancaster that at Oxford they did not recognise it as an Evangelical Hall . . . ; every fibre of my being rises in revolt against
such a caddish attitude. . . .'

Chavasse immediately[300] sent a copy of this letter to Sir Charles
King Harman: '. . . I know that you will understand if I make
this a purely business letter, and write to you in your official
capacity as Chairman of the Trust. But I want to assure you first
of the personal esteem with which I regard you, and my belief
in the friendly feeling with which you regard me.' He asked for
information:

'1. When is the next meeting of the Trust at which this matter
will be considered? I take it that the Trustees will refuse to
investigate these charges without hearing me. . . .

2. Am I to take it that the question of the Master's salary
is to be raised on purely personal grounds against myself. . . ?
Forgive me for asking an assurance that the Trustees are not
seeking to be rid of the liability of a covenanted payment by
making personal charges against myself their excuse for so doing.

3. With regard to these personal charges, as a well-known
administrator you will know the procedure better than myself.
Therefore, am I to take it that the only charges brought against
me, and the material for them, are contained in Mr. Warrington's
letter? You will not allow, I am confident, any charge to be
brought against me of which I have not had notice in writing at
least seven days before the meeting, together with the material
on which such a charge is based.

4. In common fairness to myself I am sure you will agree
to my request that I be allowed to bring with me two friends. . . .
I shall need them on the one hand to substantiate statements I

may make, and on the other to correct any mis-statements that may be rumoured abroad after the meeting. . . . I need not say that I make no aspersions on the good faith or honourable feeling of the Trustees, but as a public man you will know how easy it is, where a verbatim report is not made, for people either to mis-hear, or misconstrue what may be said.'

To this King Harman replied,[301] in his own handwriting: 'At the conclusion of the Meeting of the M.M. Trust on Wednesday last I left to catch a train for home and Warrington must have given the Notice, to which he refers in his letter to you, after I had gone. I have not heard anything about it from him and I cannot say when the next Meeting of the Trust will be. When that Meeting is called I shall take action in the matter and for the present I shall not act on your letter. I am not the Chairman of the Trust. The post was offered to me by the Trustees but I declined it and I am merely and temporarily presiding at the Meetings. You had better answer Warrington's letter and claim your right to be present at any Meeting at which your conduct is impugned. I could not authorize you nor do I think the Trustees would agree to any of your friends being present at such Meeting.' No letter could illustrate more clearly how much the Trust had come to be dominated by its Hon. Secretary since the death of Canon Stather Hunt; for more than a year there had been no Chairman to keep an eye on his doings.

On 17 February 1931 Chavasse accordingly sent a formal letter to Warrington, asking him to read it to the M.M. Trustees: 'I wish the Trustees to be quite certain as to my position in this matter in which there are two distinct points at issue.

1. There is the question of the salary of the Master. I am not personally interested in this matter; it is one between the Trustees as a body, and the Council of the Hall. . . .

2. With regard to the charges which occasion your resolution, I am personally concerned. I hope the Trustees will not even consider them. But if they do they will require to hear me. I shall be ready to meet them at their invitation and I hope in that case they will give me fourteen days' notice. . . .'

Chavasse sent a copy of this letter to King Harman, with a personal note:[302] '. . . You have been so kind to me that I cannot write to you entirely officially, as perhaps would be wiser till Mr. Warrington's resolution is discussed. . . .

1. I find it hard to believe that responsible members of a Trust can take Mr. Warrington's accusations seriously. If they do, I shall sweep them aside in a way that may surprise even you.

2. If these accusations fall to the ground, as they must, the Trustees will find it very difficult to find a reason to discontinue their covenanted payments. . . .

3. On the other hand, after all that has passed, unless the Trustees almost go out of their way to express their confidence in me, and their desire that I should receive my accustomed salary, I shall find it very difficult in the future to accept a penny of what will seem to me to be dirty money. After all God's work comes before salary. P.S. This is more or less for your private ear.'

To this Sir Charles replied[303] 'I am of course interested in knowing what is passing between you and Warrington. He has not yet said a word to me about his Resolution nor has he suggested any Meeting of the Trust. . . . Will you enlighten me on one point. In the event of the Trust agreeing to Warrington's Resolution what would be the result as regards St. Peter's Hall? What course would you take and what action would the Council probably take? I shall probably have to address the Trust on the matter and I should like to be able to give them some idea of the kind of catastrophe in which Warrington will invite them to take a part. I am much distressed and worried about the matter. . . . I should of course not mention to Warrington or to the Trust that I had obtained any information from you. There must also be a legal aspect of the matter which would have to be considered.'

On 23 February Chavasse gave his answer in a letter marked 'private': 'You ask me a very difficult question. . . . I cannot say what the Council would do, and seeing that the resolution concerns myself I could not seek to influence them in any direction before the Trustees made their report to them, as required in Section 18 of the Trust Deed.[304] As for myself, there is much that I should have to take into consideration. The resolution as it stands is a vote of no confidence in me by the Trustees, and it is this which concerns me personally. . . . In the event of such a resolution . . . I should feel that as Master I ought to learn whether the Council endorsed the verdict of the Trustees, and their attitude would greatly influence my future course.

'But besides being Master of the Hall I am also a Co-Founder of St. Peter's Hall with the Trustees. This is set forth on the second page of the Trust Deed, together with the fact that must weigh with me immensely, that the Hall is founded in memory of my Father. Above all things therefore, any action of mine must be guided by the following considerations. (1) My Father's memory must be preserved from any stain or dishonour. (2) I must play fair to the general Evangelical public who have rallied behind me in this venture to the extent already of £25,000,[305] and (3) to the University who granted a licence to the Hall upon my application, and agreed in Convocation to my appointment as its first Master. . . .'

King Harman found this letter useful; on 25 February he wrote: 'If and when I have to speak to [the Trustees] I know enough now to make them pause before following Warrington's lead. He has not yet said anything to me about his Resolution which is significant but I have taken care that my views on the subject should filter through to him by my conversation with others. I think it is quite possible that we shall hear nothing more about it but the matter cannot very well lie there. In the meanwhile let us let sleeping dogs lie for as long as we can.'

But Percy Warrington was never a sleeping dog; and on the previous day[306] he had sent Chavasse a rebuke for his letter of the 17th: 'With reference to your statement in which you say "With regard to the charges . . . I hope the Trustees will not even consider them". If I did not know you I should express my surprise that you should have the impertinence to make such a statement. . . . To suggest that the man who has really created your position should be ignored . . . is a piece of effrontery which I can safely leave my Colleagues to deal with.' He ended: 'After associating with you in the work for St. Peter's for three years I feel a disgusted and contemptuous person. Whatever may be the result of this difficulty I hope that it will not be necessary for me to publish the correspondence which I have addressed to you, but I reserve to myself the absolute right to publish every letter in pamphlet form and also in the press.' The bulk of the letter was a repetition of previous charges, but there was one section which made a new point: 'you may like to know that as late as last November Mrs. Rowcroft, to my very great surprise, instructed her Solicitor to address an official communication to the Trustees, and required the immediate drawing up of a covenant dealing with her gift of £10,000 which was used for St. Peter's. The terms of the Deed were written by Mrs. Rowcroft herself. We had the option of either signing the Deed or returning the £10,000.' This was the first cryptic reference to a transaction which later on proved of some importance.

Chavasse's reply[307] was short and formal: 'If the Trustees [at their next meeting] decide that they must pursue the accusations against me, and therefore wish to hear me, I am most ready to attend at their request a future meeting, provided that the usual courtesy of ample notice is given me. In the event of my being invited to such a meeting, those whom I have consulted in Oxford agree that I must request that two friends be allowed to accompany me. They would not speak unless asked to do so by the Trustees, but they would be witnesses on my behalf as to what actually transpired at such a meeting.' On the following day Chavasse sent copies of these letters to King Harman, adding a postscript: 'I have just received your most kind letter of the 25th. Of course I am most ready not only to let sleeping dogs lie but to let bygones be bygones. . . . If, as I hope with you, nothing more is heard about this resolution, I shall nevertheless try and take some opportunity of letting you know what my answer would have been to the accusations which occasioned it. As you are so good as to have confidence in me during such a difficult time as the present, I should like to show you that your confidence is not misplaced.'

On 2 March 1931 King Harman wrote to Chavasse: 'Some of the Members of the M.M. Trust have been informed that since your appointment as Rector of St. Peter-le-Bailey Church you have introduced a Cross on the Holy Table and that you have also adopted the Eastward Position in the Creed and require all the students to do the same. They have asked me to enquire from you whether this information . . . is correct. Have you seen the Article in the *Church Times*[308] of 20 February on "Religion in Oxford" wherein reference is made to the Catholic students of St. Peter's Hall?' Chavasse had no difficulty here. He thanked Sir Charles[309] for asking directly for information, and gave a detailed answer:

'1. There is no cross on the Holy Table, and indeed such an ornament would spoil our reredos with its Resurrection panel in the centre. There is a cross introduced into the carving at the top of the reredos. . . . [310] This reredos was put into the Church in memory of my Mother and its design approved by my Father before his death. I have never yet heard of even the strongest Protestant objecting to a cross being introduced into the carving of a reredos.

2. With the full approval of the P.C.C., who are a conservative body, the choir at St. Peter-le-Bailey turns to the East in the Creed. No member of the Hall is required to do this as they already sit facing east. . . . It is true that I introduced this practice, and for two reasons. (a) Because I like it, and it is recognized as carrying with it no high-church principle whatsoever.

123

My Father allowed the custom, and laid it down as the custom of Liverpool Cathedral. . . . (b) I wished as far as possible in our Chapel Service to conform to the custom of Oxford College Chapels. . . . If members of the Martyrs Memorial Trust find dangerous sacerdotal meaning in the custom of turning to the east in the Creed, which has been prevalent in Cathedrals, and even in the most Protestant College Chapels since Caroline days, I am afraid I must totally disagree with them. . . . Objection might quite as easily be taken to the fact that Churches are oriented to the east, and that there is the universal custom of burying the dead with their faces towards the dawn.

3. A friend of mine has shown me the article in the *Church Times* of February 20th – for I never read the paper myself.[311] The reference . . . must be inspired . . . from Pusey House, and refers to the two Anglo-Catholic members of St. Peter's Hall, whom you know of. . . . We have no others except these. . . .'[312]

King Harman found this explanation 'quite satisfactory'.[313] He added: 'There is a new development in this business between you and Warrington. Pearman Smith is taking a hand in it after a conversation I had with him and with Foster Pegg and they are proposing a conference about which you will I presume receive due notice. I am not taking part in it as I disapprove of the whole of Warrington's conduct and am maintaining an attitude quite aloof from all discussion with him. This, I think, is having a good effect and is leading him to think that he may be wrong. This is all to the good as there is no suggestion of a Meeting of the Martyrs Memorial Trust to consider his Resolution. So long as matters are not precipitated (and I have confidence in your good sense in this) a solution of present difficulties will not be impossible to obtain.'

There is more than a trace of wishful thinking here, and Chavasse remained alert. On 9 March 1931 he assured Sir Charles: '. . . You may take it from me that no action or letter of mine will precipitate matters in any way. I will take very good care of this.' He went on: 'Mr. Teal has reported an interview he has had with Mr. Pearman Smith at their request. Mr. Pearman Smith has suggested that Mr. Warrington and he should meet myself and Mr. Teal with the idea of coming to some agreement regarding the finances of the Hall. I have of course readily agreed to such a conference. . . . I am . . . asking Mr. Teal to let Mr. Pearman Smith know that I would gladly meet Mr. Warrington on this matter when the balance sheet has been placed in my hand, and I have been able to study it for a week. You will agree,

I think, that it is no good discussing finance until we know exactly where we are. . . .'[314]

Between Warrington and Chavasse there was for the moment an uneasy silence, each of them suspecting that the other was working against him. Chavasse thought it worth while to strengthen his own defences wherever he could. On 14 March he wrote to King Harman: 'As there are not wanting those who are quick to send you anything from the papers that they consider disparaging to St. Peter's, I think you might like to have this article written by some Oxford man, whom I do not know, and published in the *Oxford Magazine*, which is the official [sic] journal of the University. I am really pleased with it, as on the one hand it frankly admits that we are an Evangelical institution, which would naturally cause prejudice against us in Oxford; and yet, on the other hand, we have in two years won general respect, and even some kind of affection from other societies in the University. Please do not answer this letter; it is only to give you material for showing your friends that our position at Oxford is rather more difficult than they imagine, and that we are in the providence of God surmounting these difficulties.'

Again, a week later he wrote: [315] 'I am very sorry to trouble you, especially with nasty business. As you know I am keeping absolutely silent, and even trying to forget the charges Mr. Warrington not only brings against me, but constantly spreads amongst other people.

'I should, however, like you to have the facts that contradict one statement which he is always making; namely, that my one idea in trying to establish St. Peter's was to feather my own nest. As one of the Trustees who appointed me you ought to know that when I left St. Aldates I left a living worth £1,000 per annum, with a most convenient Rectory and far fewer expenses than fall upon the Master of St. Peter's Hall.

'Here my salary is the same, but my expenses are heavier, and three years I have had to be separated from my family during term time. Also I gave up a position that was settled and safe to become Principal of St. Peter's House, with the possibility (at times a doubtful one) that chiefly through my own efforts the University might agree to its becoming St. Peter's Hall. Furthermore I have just lately refused to consider a very happy and useful post which carried with it £1,600 p.a. I prefered [sic] to remain at St. Peter's despite the uncertainty, and the horrible unpleasantness, of the present position.

'I should like you to know these facts, not because I want to pose as one who has made great sacrifices, for this would not be true; but I should like you to be in a position to contradict a most unkind lie whenever you meet it. . . .'

At last, on 17 April 1931, Warrington broke the silence, not to supply financial information, but to make further attacks. He sent Chavasse copies of two 'communications'. The first was an anonymous memorandum, dated 13 April 1931, addressed to Warrington by 'THE EVANGELICAL VIGILANCE COM-MITTEE, The Boltons, Kensington'. It asked: 'Would the Rev. C. M. Chavasse please explain to the Oxford Conference of Evangelical Churchmen on what grounds he justifies the Appeal which he and the Rev. P. E. Warrington have made to the Evangelical public for funds for St. Peter's Hall . . . only a small percentage of the men are Evangelicals, and the majority of the students even go out of their way to repudiate the term "Evangelical". When we visited the Conference last year it was noted that some students had Crucifixes in their rooms whilst other rooms were decorated with lewd pictures of ballet girls. Much surprise and great disappointment was expressed on every hand. . . .' The second communication was a copy of a letter, dated 15 April 1931, sent to Warrington by an unnamed friend. This friend had visited the buildings of St. Peter's Hall, and had now sent Warrington a cheque for £1,000 for St. Peter's, in memory of his wife, because he could 'hardly imagine of [sic] any more judicious and strategic effort in the service of [Christ's] Kingdom'.

Warrington's own comment was: 'This letter is typical of the large number I receive. There is no doubt whatever that the Evangelical Public is under the impression that by giving their money to St. Peter's they are assisting young Conservative Evangelical Churchmen into the ranks of the Ministry. My friend would not give a farthing if he knew that only a mere handful of your students are Conservative Churchmen. . . . It is impossible for me to accept this £1,000.'

Warrington continued: 'I have notified Mr. Pearman Smith . . . that as soon as I feel well enough to travel to Torquay I am seeking an interview with Mrs. Rowcroft . . . I am advising Mrs. Rowcroft that the Deed of Covenant which Sir Charles King Harman and others signed as a condition of her £10,000 being used for St. Peter's has been violated and therefore the £10,000 should be refunded to her. It is the only course that honourable gentlemen could take. To accept Mrs. Rowcroft's money and despise her B.C.M.S. principles is thoroughly immoral and iniquitous. . . .'

126

This was the second time that Warrington had referred to a mysterious Covenant, but the first time that he had used the threat of forcing the repayment of Mrs. Rowcroft's £10,000. The threat, however, was so vague that Chavasse made no reference to it in his reply,[316] which was short and barbed: 'As regards the document sent by "The Evangelical Vigilance Committee", it is quite obvious that I cannot take notice of anonymous libels. . . . The matter would be very different if a member of St. Peter's Hall Council thought fit to publish its untrue allegations. Then, hateful though it would be, the Council of St. Peter's Hall would have to be made cognizant of the fact.' As to the cheque for £1,000, 'whether you accept it or not is a matter for your Trustees; but any stated reasons for refusal must not be unjustifiable allegations against the administration of St. Peter's Hall'. He added: 'I cannot myself reconcile the tenor of your letter with the appeal for St. Peter's which you insert in *The Record* of the same date. . . .'

Warrington smarted at this rejoinder. On 23 April he wrote to Chavasse: 'May I remind you that I have been ill for several weeks. I have been supremely indifferent to the Appeals in the *Record*, which, by the way, were stopped last week, as matters concerning St. Peter's have now to be brought to a serious issue. . . . I am resigning all my connection with St. Peter's Hall at the next Meeting of the Trustees. A statement is now being carefully prepared by me in consultation with my friends setting out my reasons for dissociating myself from you in the work. I believe Mr. Greene, the Vicar of Felixstowe, will be appointed to succeed me on the St. Peter's Hall Council. . . .'[317]

Chavasse did not reply till 29 April, and then his letter was very short: '. . . I deplore that you should even contemplate the possibility of resignation from your connection with St. Peter's Hall, seeing that it owes its establishment to you more than to any man. But I am afraid there is nothing I can usefully say at present.' On the same day he wrote to King Harman,[318] and found a little more to say: '. . . I do not know how far to take it seriously because he has said the same kind of thing so often before without, I think, really meaning it; at any rate nothing has come of it. It is, of course, really no concern of mine if he insists on placing his resignation in the hands of the Trustees [but] I should hear of his resignation with genuine regret, seeing that the establishment of the Hall is due to him more than any other man. But if he is serious (which I rather question) in resigning, I know I can rely on you to see that in common

127

fairness to myself the Trustees do not accept the reasons of his resignation if they are unfounded charges against myself and my administration of the Hall.'

To Sir Charles this was the last straw. On 30 April he sent two letters to Chavasse. The first, private, stated. . . . 'Things have come to such a pass that I feel I cannot usefully continue to be a member of your Council. . . . I am in such complete disagreement with recent procedure that my further presence on the Council could only lead to strife and confusion.' The other, addressed to Chavasse as 'The Chairman of the Council, St. Peter's Hall', was a formal resignation: 'In accordance with s. 8 of the St. Peter's Hall Trust Deed I am writing to tender my resignation of Member [sic] of the Council and I do so with the greatest regret. I am now 80 years of age and my medical adviser impresses upon me the necessity of withdrawing from some of the public work in which I am engaged. . . . Will you kindly express to the Members of the Council with whom I have been proud to work my grief at being no longer able to collaborate with them.'[319]

On 4 May Chavasse wrote back expressing 'grief and dismay' but full understanding. He asked leave to come and see him, in order to clear up the charges against himself and to ask for 'advice at this juncture as to any course that we could pursue to make things easier. . . . To a very great extent we are working entirely in the dark; you may be able to help us adopt the line of conduct that would send the Hall happily and safely on its way. . . .' The upshot was that on Monday, 11 May, Chavasse and Legge went over to Bedford to have lunch with Sir Charles at his home.[320] Of their discussions there is no record; but what none of them then knew was that on the previous Thursday, 7 May 1931, in the absence of both King Harman and Lord Gisborough, Warrington had induced a meeting of the Martyrs Memorial Trustees to pass the following resolutions:

RESOLVED:
THAT the Trustees of the Martyrs' Memorial and Church of England Trust Society have for a considerable time past felt uneasy about the position at St. Peter's Hall, that is, from the Conservative Evangelical position which the Hall was established to promote and which the Martyrs' Memorial and Church of England Trust Society has from its foundation laboured to further. The Trustees are satisfied that only a few of the Undergraduates at St. Peter's Hall are in sympathy with the

Conservative Evangelical principles and they have abundant evidence from their own Members and others that young men at the Hall repudiate the Evangelical position for which the Hall was established by the Trust. The Trustees deeply regret to place on record that they have lost confidence in the present Master, the Rev. C. M. Chavasse, M.A., as one who will promote the Conservative Evangelical position for which they founded St. Peter's Hall in memory of his late revered Father.
It is further Resolved:

THAT a Committee consisting of the Rev. Canon Foster Pegg, the Rev. H. B. Greene, and the Rev. T. Lancaster, together with the Trust Solicitor, Mr. Pearman Smith, be requested to interview the Rev. C. M. Chavasse, and to inform him of the Trustees' anxiety, their want of confidence, and their intense disappointment with the present position.

No notice of this meeting or of the proposed resolutions had been sent to Chavasse beforehand, nor was he informed after the meeting that they had been passed. A more devious course was followed. Since the matter was later hushed up, the story is still in some respects obscure. But a fairly clear picture emerges in a letter which Chavasse subsequently addressed[321] to Mr. Pearman Smith:

'You will remember that acting upon your request to Mr Teal, the Secretary of St. Peter's Hall Council, I attended on May 13th at Charing Cross Hotel what I was told was a friendly meeting with a deputation of the Martyrs Memorial and Church of England Trust Society, in order to talk over certain matters connected with St. Peter's Hall on which they wished to be informed. Mr. Teal accompanied me, as did also two members of the Council and Mr. J. A. Cumming, the Hon. Treasurer.[322]

'When I arrived I was informed by Lord Gisborough, the Chairman, that the deputation was in reality a sub-committee appointed by the Trust Society – "to interview" me and "to inform" me "of the Trustees' anxiety, their want of confidence, and their intense disappointment with the present position" – consequent upon a resolution passed unanimously by them on the 7th May. I had not previously seen the resolution, neither had the Trust interviewed me before accepting the allegations upon which they passed their vote of no-confidence. It was pointed out that such proceedings, to say the least, were entirely against all British tradition; and the Chairman stated that he had not been present at the meeting in question, or he would have pro-

129

tested against such action. On my part I stated that I did not
accept the resolution, but was willing to confer with the gentlemen present on the friendly basis of a deputation such as I had
been asked by you to meet.

'The result of a prolonged conversation between us was that,
on behalf of the deputation, the Chairman expressed himself
completely satisfied upon all points which had been raised –
except one. The one doubtful matter concerned a reredos which
had been erected in St. Peter-le-Bailey Church in memory of
Mrs. Chavasse with the approval of Bishop Chavasse. It was
debated whether the reredos constituted a violation of the second
commandment, in that its carved panels represented incidents
from the life of St. Peter, and so contained figures in bas-relief.
But even on this grave charge of idolatry the ideas of the
deputation appeared to be vague and divided.'

What does not emerge from this letter is that there was a
second meeting at the Charing Cross Hotel on 20 May; presumably the first meeting was adjourned for a week. On 21 May
1931 J. A. Cumming sent the following letter to Pearman Smith.

'While I recognise the efforts you made to bring about a
friendly meeting yesterday, I could not refrain from protesting
against the manner in which these charges against Mr. Chavasse
have been dealt with. Besides hearing cases in Court, I have had
to conduct many other enquiries, and you as a lawyer must be
familiar with the normal procedure in such cases. It seems to me
contrary to all British ideas of fair play: —

(1) that the Martyrs Memorial and Church of England Trust
Society should have passed the resolution of 7th May that they
had lost confidence in Mr. Chavasse on the strength of purely
ex parte statements and without giving him an opportunity of
meeting them. I must remind you that Mr. Chavasse was willing
to attend that meeting and meet such charges as he had notice
of.

(2) that Mr. Chavasse should have had no notice of this
resolution until he attended the Committee meeting of yesterday.[323]

(3) that, while Mr. Chavasse had had letters from Mr. Warrington about some of the points at issue, several points were
put to him yesterday which were entirely new to him.[324]

(4) that in many of these points the evidence on which the
charge was based was not even indicated.

We were informed yesterday that Mr. Chavasse had satis-
factorily met the charges made against him, and that the resolu-

tion could be torn up. But the original of that resolution remains on record in the minutes of the M.M. and C.E.T. Society. In view of the finding of the Committee, cannot you get the Society to delete that minute from the minute-book? I make full allowance for your difficulties, but I put this point to you strongly as a simple act of justice to Mr. Chavasse.'

No doubt Mr. Pearman Smith saw the point of this, and on 22 May King Harman wrote soothingly to Chavasse: 'I met Lord Gisborough in London yesterday and was glad to hear from him that the difficulty with Warrington is likely to be cleared up.' But Warrington was in no mood for simple acts of justice, or for taking advice from Pearman Smith. Early in May Cumming had at last received from Warrington's office a copy of the Trustees' Account, audited by a Mr. F. S. Seal, not a chartered accountant but at any rate a 'Fellow of the Corporation of Accountants'. Cumming himself found the Account puzzling, and sent it on to a discreet and friendly chartered accountant, whose name need not be mentioned.[325] In a highly confidential letter,[326] this friend stated: 'The certificate does not give me much confidence, for it leaves me with a feeling that this account has been prepared from vouchers and bill books only, and that there has not been a proper Cash book or Ledger kept by the Trustees, or even a Pass book. . . . I have no hesitation in stating that this account, in my opinion, does not comply with the requirements of Article No. 29 of the Trust Deed. . . . In view of what I have written you will no doubt realise I would not consider granting to the Trustees as a business proposition, the Deeds of No. 2 Block upon which a Mortgage may be raised and the proceeds placed at their disposal, and leaving the Council of St. Peter's Hall to pay off the Mortgage. . . .'

With this information in mind, Cumming was able to make some pertinent remarks[327] to Pearman Smith, who had asked for a copy of the Hall Accounts for 1929-30; in particular, he added a note on 'the points likely to be raised on the Trustees Capital Account as at 21 March 1931'. This note included the following statement:

'Under para. 29 of the Trust Deed, the Trustees shall keep accounts as indicated therein, have these accounts with a balance sheet certified by professional auditors every year, and produce them at the Council meeting. It is noted that no reference is made by the auditor to any account kept by the Trustees, that the account is not an annual one, and that a balance sheet is not produced. . . . It is probable that the Council will ask questions regarding the professional status of the auditor and the sufficiency of his certificate.'

This note was passed on by Pearman Smith to Warrington, and produced an explosion. On 22 May Warrington wrote to Chavasse: 'I write to inform you that my place on the Council of St. Peter's Hall will be taken by the Rev. H. B. Greene, the Vicar of Felixstowe. Would you please instruct the Solicitor to send him the notice of the next Meeting', due to be held on 28 May. Presumably Warrington reckoned that it would be easier for him to avoid awkward questions at the Council if he remained in the background as the all-important Trustee. On the following day, having had time to digest the news that the meetings between Chavasse and the Deputation had not ended in the former's disgrace, he informed Chavasse that all King Harman's recent letters had been written by himself, Warrington: '. . . Sir Charles King Harman merely signed them and forwarded your replies to me.' This was not merely a bare-faced lie, but a very stupid one: all King Harman's letters had been in his own distinctive handwriting, and if Warrington had known their contents he would hardly have wished to claim authorship. He was hitting out wildly in the dark; and so he was in another section of the same letter to Chavasse. Here he claimed to have been informed by his 'colleagues' that Mr. Teal, the Secretary to the Council, had 'stated that "money was really behind the whole business and that these things[328] were really nothing to me" . . . I do not propose to trouble the Council about this matter, but I am seeking Counsel's opinion, and if I can possibly bring an Action against Mr. Teal for libel I will do so. I will teach this young man that he cannot make these sort of statements about me with impunity.'

Then on 27 May 1931 Warrington sent off to each member of the Council four pages of foolscap, timed to reach them by first post on the morning of the Council Meeting. This document started by referring to the letter which Cumming had sent to Pearman Smith about the accounts: 'I should much like to know what Mr. Cumming, the Bursar of the Hall has to do with the Trustees Accounts. I can only conclude that this is due either to Mr. Cumming's general officiousness, of which I have had reason to complain for the past three years, or that he has prepared this Memoranda [sic] at the instigation of Mr. Chavasse. . . . Will the Council please understand that we are not fools, neither are we knaves! !

'Mr. Cumming presumes to insult the Trustees further by saying "It is probable the Council will ask questions regarding the professional status of the Auditor and the sufficiency of his Certificate. . . ." For the past three years I have endured a series of pin pricks and insults from this man. . . .

'Mr. Cumming presumes to criticise the Accounts, by what authority I know not, but of course I assume this communication is inspired. As the keeping of Accounts on a complete Double Entry System would necessitate additional work and would involve the employment of a qualified Book-Keeper, and having regard to the fact that this work has been done in an honorary capacity, the accounts have been kept as accurately as possible.'

This remarkable admission is followed by a rigmarole about Mrs. Rowcroft's gift of £10,000: '. . . on the day of receipt I paid that cheque into the General Fund of the Martyrs Memorial and Church of England Trust where it remained. Mrs. Rowcroft holds the M.M. and C.E. Trust as responsible for that £10,000, therefore it is an advance from the Martyrs Memorial Trust. . . .[329] Mrs. Rowcroft gave £6,500 to a certain institution in Somersetshire . . . the Trustees violated [the] conditions. Last year Mrs. Rowcroft instructed her Solicitors to demand back her money, and quite right too.' He goes on to refer to a statement by Judge Dowdall that the Trustees were only Trustees, and that the Council were the beneficiaries of property owned by the Hall: 'I am particularly requested to state that the M.M. and C.E. Trustees take a very different view of the position. We regard ourselves as the Founders of St. Peter's Hall and the owners of the Property.'

The document ends on an increasingly hysterical note: 'At the last Meeting of the Council Mr. Chavasse had the appalling temerity to state that "The Trustees had used for the Schools the hypothecated securities belonging to St. Peter's Hall. . . ." It will be seen in the Statement of Accounts that the hypothecated securities have been used against the large amount of Bills given under the signature of Sir Charles King Harman and myself representing the Trustees. . . . From remarks which I understand Mr. Chavasse has made it is clear to me that he is a man utterly ignorant of finance. He does not know that when a Bill bears the acceptance of Sir Charles King Harman and myself and is presented at the Bank, it is equivalent to a payment by cheque and must be honoured. . . . [We have never yet] failed to meet a Bill when presented. . . . I should indeed be blind if I had failed to see that the sustained policy of Mr. Chavasse and Mr.

Cumming has been to discredit me. . . .[330]It seems to me a most regrettable thing that the training of men for the sacred office of the Ministry of the Church of England can be in the hands of a man against whom these things may justifiably be said. I have nothing more to say and I am glad to finish.'

In fact, he found more to say. Next day he produced two more foolscap pages. But when the Council met on 28 May 1931[331] these had not yet appeared; the previous four pages were quite enough to go on with. To those members who had not seen the previous correspondence, they came as a shock: this was the great Warrington in a new guise. Lord Cushendun in Chelsea sent off a telegram to Chavasse: 'Have today received extraordinary and I think improper communication from Mr. Warrington. I suggest adjournment of its consideration today greatly regret unable attend.' On the following day Chavasse wrote to Cushendun: '. . . your telegram . . . was a great strength to me during a few tense moments at the beginning of our Council Meeting yesterday. . . . I am sure the Council pursued the right course. They did not adjourn the consideration of Mr. Warrington's communication, but they ignored its personal passages and concentrated on the material facts that dealt with the statement of accounts he had presented.' He added, with notable generosity: 'I must add, in Mr. Warrington's defence, that he has lately been extremely ill. . . . This, I think accounts for a great deal.'

The actual minutes of the Council Meeting are exceedingly discreet. They record that the Master reported that Mr. Warrington had resigned from the Council and that Mr. Greene had been appointed by the Trustees in his place; but a telegram had just been received from Mr. Greene saying that he could not fill the vacant place on the Council,[332] and the Council therefore authorized the Master to press Mr. Warrington most strongly to reconsider his decision. The only reference to the four pages of foolscap is a statement that Warrington had written that the capital account of St. Peter's Hall was kept by him in an honorary capacity, at his own expense: the Council expressed its sincere gratitude, but offered to pay for proper book-keeping. Moreover the Council decided to ask Messrs. Pearman Smith and Sons to get the Trustees' auditor to attend the annual meeting on 29 June 1931.

There is also only one indirect reference to the dealings between Chavasse and the M.M.T. 'Deputation': it is recorded that the Master reported a suggestion made by the Revd. H. B. Greene at a meeting convened by Mr. Pearman Smith on 20

May, viz. that St. Peter's Hall should take over the payment of
the annual amount previously paid by the Trustees. This particular matter is dealt with in a letter which Cumming sent to
Pearman Smith on 29 May 1931: 'You will remember that . . .
on May 20th . . . the Rev. H. B. Greene asked for my opinion
with regard to a suggestion he made, that in future the Council
of St. Peter's Hall might take on the payments covenanted by
the Trustees in Section 31 of the Trust Deed. . . . The Council
are deeply sensible of the great liabilities with regard to the
Hall which the Trustees have so generously shouldered, and have
a very strong desire to assist the Trustees by every means in
their power. . . . I am happy to say, therefore, that I was
authorised to inform you that the Council would perfectly understand if the Trustees gave notice, at the Annual Meeting on
June 29th, of their intention to cease these covenanted payments,
according to the procedure laid down in Section 31. . . .'

On the same day Chavasse wrote to Warrington a carefully
worded letter, formally notifying him that Mr. Greene had
declined appointment, and continuing: 'It is therefore my pleasant, but responsible task – as Chairman of the Council – to beg
you most earnestly on behalf of us all to reconsider your decision . . . most of all, we feel that it would be a calamity if you
were not upon the governing body of an Oxford Society which
will always be a monument of your enterprise.' This neat reminder that St. Peter's Hall was not just the 'property' of the
Martyrs Memorial Trust no doubt gave Chavasse some satisfaction, especially if before writing he had already received his copy
of the extra two pages of foolscap which Warrington had
addressed to the Council on 28 May. This document repeated
the threat to sue Mr. Teal for libel, and itself provided some
evidence that Teal did not speak without reason if indeed he
used the phrase 'Money was behind the whole business'.

Warrington states that he has had to write to Teal to complain of 'the procedure adopted in connection with the appointment of the present Accountants [Smith and Williamson] . . . I
charge Mr. Teal with deliberately suppressing the name of the
proposed Accountants from the Agenda at the instigation of Mr.
Chavasse. . . .[333] I have since discovered that Mr. Chavasse has
a personal friend who is a member of the new Firm of Accountants, and I am informed that the gentleman is a relative of the
Hon. Talbot Rice. . . .[334] . . . I have been informed that Mr.
Teal is Mr. Chavasse's private Solicitor, and a personal friend.
We think this accounts for much. [But] it is not fair to the

Martyrs Memorial Trust . . . the appointment of an impartial Firm of London Solicitors would go some way to restore the lost confidence.[335]

'. . . It may interest the Council to know that when the Trust Deed was being drawn up Mr. Chavasse took into his confidence a Dignitary of St. Paul's Cathedral about getting the Property away from the Martyrs Memorial Trust at the earliest possible moment. That gentleman reported to me what Mr. Chavasse had told him. I assured the Dignitary in question that he need have no occasion to fear, as the Martyrs Memorial Trustees were wide awake, and quite capable of dealing with the Master of St. Peter's Hall. I reported the matter to the late Canon Stather Hunt, who duly dealt with Mr. Chavasse and the Clause in the Trust Deed.[336] I think it only just[337] that the Council should know that the Martyrs Memorial Trustees are so convinced that Mr. Chavasse would like to get rid of us at the earliest opportunity that instead of making our contributions as gifts to St. Peter's Hall, which it was our full intention to do, we have been obliged as a measure of self-protection to make them as "advances" only. . . . When Mr. Chavasse's place at St. Peter's Hall is taken by a Master in whose loyalty we have the most absolute confidence, we shall be very ready to make the Hall a gift of all our contributions, and so carry out our original intention.'

It is not surprising that Chavasse was convinced that Warrington and his cronies on the Martyrs Memorial Trust were bent on forcing him out of office. Some years later[338] he wrote to Canon Foster Pegg: 'It appears to me obvious that the whole thing was a conspiracy by the Martyrs Memorial Trust to force my resignation, and so to appoint a Bible Churchman in my place.' This may well have been so; but one may also suspect that Warrington's ideal 'Master in whose loyalty we have the most absolute confidence' would be one who asked no awkward questions on matters of finance.

It appears that Warrington made no direct reply to the letter inviting him to reconsider his decision to resign from the Council, but it was taken for granted that silence meant continuance; there had been no formal resignation, and therefore there was nothing which required formal withdrawal. It appears also that nobody thought it necessary to reply to his tirade of 28 May. A sort of 'cold war' went on. There was the matter of the loan which Chavasse had undertaken. On 5 June 1931 Cumming wrote to Warrington about this: 'You will see from the Minutes of the Council Meeting of 28 May that I was authorised to repay from the Appeal Fund the loan of £5,870-5-10 . . . which Mr. Chavasse got from the Midland Bank to pay for the Wesleyan property,[339] and to deduct such payments from the amount still to be paid from the Appeal Fund to the Trustees. . . . The resolution of the Council is sufficient authority for me to act,[340] but it might be considered discourteous if I did not acquaint you with their views.' On 8 June Warrington told his secretary to inform Cumming 'that Mr. Chavasse knows perfectly well that the Trustees intended to repay him this loan out of the Mortgage they are taking up on the building. As Mr. Chavasse obstructed the Mortgage, he has himself, and himself only, to thank that it has not been repaid. . . .' Moreover, 'Mr. Warrington . . . is only prepared to sign the cheques for the Bursaries, and he will not sign any cheques for the Master's salary or rent.' Then between 18 June and 22 June 1931 there was correspondence between Cumming and Burn about a discrepancy between Warrington's statement of grants paid and Cumming's statement of grants received from the Trust; it appeared that Warrington had included as a grant *paid* a sum of £262 shown in the Hall accounts as a grant *due*.

In these circumstances, it is hardly surprising that Chavasse thought it necessary to obtain from Mr. Pearman Smith and Lord Gisborough some clarification of his position. On 22 June 1931, he sent to Pearman Smith the letter already quoted about the meeting with the M.M.T. 'Deputation'. It ended: 'As the meeting concluded in what we all agreed was a highly satisfactory manner; and as the Chairman expressed his strong view that as a result of it the Resolution of May 7th should be torn up – I think I am entitled to request that I be informed what action the Trust took upon the report of this sub-committee. Has the resolution in question been deleted from the Minute Book of the Martyrs Memorial and Church of England Trust Society, or could I be furnished with the minute that dealt with the report of the sub-committee. I should be grateful if you could let me have this information *in time for the Annual Meeting of St. Peter's Hall on Monday, June 29th* – that the incident may be closed and I hope forgotten.' Pearman Smith's answer[341] was not very convincing: 'I have heard nothing further since the meeting at the Charing Cross Hotel on May 13th [sic] when I understood the matter was to be regarded as closed and doubtless the members of the M.M. and C.E. Trust who were present so reported to their full body. I have not been informed and therefore do not know what action (if any) the Trustees took upon the

Report of the deputation but I shall be much surprised if anything further is heard of the matter.'

Chavasse at once[342] sent a copy of this 'very unsatisfactory letter' to Lord Gisborough: 'After your great kindness to me at the meeting at the Charing Cross Hotel . . . I am most reluctant to put you to any trouble or to recall the unpleasant feature of the conference; [but] . . . I think you will agree, on reading these letters, that the matter cannot end here and that I am bound, as Master of the Hall and Chairman of the Council, to have something more definite. As you were chairman of the sub-committee, may I appeal to you – as the person whom you acknowledged to have been deeply wronged – to let me know what has since transpired, and if a grave injustice has been righted?'

Lord Gisborough's reply[343] was no more satisfactory in substance, though friendly enough in style: 'I am afraid, as Chairman, I have not been able to do anything in the matter of reporting the result of our meeting to the Trust, as I have been very ill again. . . . I have written to ask for a meeting of the Trust to be called . . . in order that we may report. I do not think your account of what took place is quite accurate, as I did not say as regards the resolution that I should "have protested against it", I said I should have moved to "alter the wording". By which I meant there would have been no "pistol at your head", but rather an invitation to you to explain certain things which were causing us anxiety. . . . On our side at any rate, we have been more than justified (quite apart from your case) in being upset at the many attempts which have been made to undermine our work, and I think you ought to make allowances for that if the language used was stronger and perhaps more direct than you liked. I am sure it was not intended to hurt your feelings in any way, and that the meeting has, in fact, done much good in more ways than one.'

The upshot was that Chavasse had to face the Annual Meeting without the full assurance for which he had hoped. What very few people knew was that earlier in June he had been in consultation with Lord Cushendun. On 13 June 1931 he wrote:[344] 'I cannot thank you sufficiently for your great kindness to me last Thursday in giving me so much of your time, and also advising me in this very difficult situation. I shall also like [to thank] Lady Cushendun for so kindly entertaining us both to luncheon. . . .

As regards . . . Mr. Warrington's public allegations against me, I find myself in a difficult position. I shrink very much from being the personal cause of a first-class row which may involve the Council in unpleasantness with the Trustees. At the same time, I am deeply impressed by your advice (backed as it is with all the weight of your experience and wisdom) and, for the sake of St. Peter's, I cannot afford to let any allegation, however outrageous, go by default. I have consulted one or two of my friends in Oxford . . . and they agree with me that the best procedure would be to ask you . . . to write me a letter requesting that the Council should go into the matter of Mr. Warrington's communication to its members of May 27th. . . . This will give me the opportunity of placing myself entirely in the hands of the Council; and it may be that a Minute recording the confidence of the Council in me . . . would serve the purpose we desire, without a solicitor's letter to Mr. Warrington.'

At that moment, on his doctor's advice, Lord Cushendun was about to go to Switzerland. On 18 June he sent Chavasse a letter from Zurich,[345] explaining that illness would prevent his attending the Council: 'Had I been there, it was my intention to ask for an explanation of the letter recently received addressed to members of the Council by Mr. Warrington. I feel, however, that being at a distance, without opportunity of consultation with other members of the Council, I ought not to express any strong opinion with regard to the propriety of that letter. It was however a letter of very unusual tone, and it contained statements both of fact and of opinion which I should have supposed would have to be either substantiated or withdrawn by the writer. But as I shall not be at the Council I think I had better leave the matter without further comment, feeling sure that the Council, with all the facts within their knowledge, will do what is right in the matter.'

5

The Council met for its Annual Meeting[346] on Monday, 29 June 1931. Before lunch there was a Commemoration service in chapel,[347] and immediately after lunch there was a presentation to Cumming. The actual Meeting was something of an anticlimax, for none of the Trustees were present except Canon Foster Pegg, and the Trustees' auditor, Mr. Seal, had failed to attend, pleading pressure of business. Once again, the minutes of the Meeting were highly discreet. It was reported that Mr. Warrington had withdrawn his proffered resignation. Warm appreciation was expressed to J. A. Cumming, who was now handing over the Bursar's duties to Mr. Tinne[348] but was continuing to act as Hon. Treasurer of the Appeal Fund. It was decided to ask Mr. Seal to attend the November meeting. The Council 'considered the position of the Master, who placed himself entirely in their hands'; after a guarded reference to the meeting on 13 May between the Master and a sub-committee of the Trust, the minutes record that 'it was hoped that no further action by the Master would be necessary'.

Nobody would have guessed from these cautious phrases just what had been going on. Nor would anybody have guessed from the far less cautious language of Chavasse's Annual Report for 1930-31, which has already been quoted. This was indeed a gallant (or from Warrington's angle a crafty) attempt to paper over cracks, and it was full of calculated optimism. Perhaps the characteristic paragraph was the following:

> There is no doubt but that the Council took a risk in deciding upon the rapid development of the Hall, a risk that has even grown serious with this unforseen industrial depression. But the past year has proved not only that the risk was justified, but we shall survive it – so great is the concern for our welfare manifested throughout the whole land. Moreover both the Trustees and the Council have been influenced in their policy by the conviction that St. Peter's Hall is willed by God, and therefore must prosper. As the Trustees affirmed in

140

their appeal to the public 'This scheme . . . has been greatly blessed of God'. It is no risk confidently to expect in the future that divine blessing which we have already experienced in every phase and sphere of the Hall's creation.

It is highly probable that Chavasse meant every word of this paragraph, in entire sincerity. But it is possible that his optimism was aided by a secret assurance he had received about the stability of the Martyrs' Memorial Trust: J. G. Legge, himself a former Civil Servant in the Board of Education, had had a private talk with 'an official of the Board . . . who was deputed to go thoroughly into the Matter of Mr. Warrington's schools. . . . His testimony, I think', Chavasse had told Lord Cushendun on 13 June 1931, 'makes it quite clear that, though Mr. Warrington likes to keep us in the dark, yet his Trust is sound and St. Peter's Hall is safe.'

On the day after the Annual Meeting Chavasse wrote again to Lord Gisborough: 'I am very grateful to you for promising to raise the matter of the Resolution of May 10th [sic] at an early date with the Martyrs Memorial and Church of England Trustees. The matter is of importance, for, unless something of the sort is done, I am advised that I ought not (for the good name of the Hall) to allow to pass unnoticed all the libellous allegations which have been made against me in letters and communications. . . . I am told that unless I take some action, or the allegations are in some way withdrawn, I shall be held to have admitted them because I did not deny them. I am in a most awkward position, as the last thing I desire is a scandal which might prejudice the good name of St. Peter's, now that it is so successfully coming into public prominence. I laid my difficulty before the Council . . . yesterday, and put myself entirely in their hands. They hoped that if the Resolution of May 10th [sic] could be withdrawn or deleted my position would be safeguarded, and that there might be no need of further action. Canon Foster Pegg, who was present, most kindly promised that he would support you. . . .'

To this appeal Chavasse received no reply for a couple of months. Then, on 3 September 1931, Gisborough sent him a copy of a Resolution passed by the M.M. Trustees: [349]

RESOLVED: — 'That the Report of the Committee be accepted. The Trustees venture to hope that as a result of the interview of their Representatives with Mr. Chavasse the position of the Trustees and their difficulties may be more fully recognised and the Trustees very gladly accept Mr. Chavasse's assurance that he will do all within his power to meet them and they trust that the confidence of all the Trustees may be restored in St. Peter's Hall and its first Master Mr. Chavasse.'

[Signed personally] 'Gisborough, President,
C. of Eng. M.Mem. Trust

Gisborough explained that he had thought, wrongly, that a copy of this resolution had already been sent to Chavasse. He added: 'Enclosed speaks for itself. It may or may not be quite all you might have expected but it certainly is intended as an olive branch and I hope therefore will be accepted as such.' It was certainly not all that Chavasse had expected, but the olive branch was accepted: at the meeting of the Council[350] on 7 November 1931 'the Master read a letter he had received from Lord Gisborough enclosing a copy of a resolution passed by the Martyrs Memorial and Church of England Trust Society, which closed the matter referred to to the satisfaction of the Council.'

Meanwhile there had been the usual friction about money matters. On 9 July 1931 Cumming had reminded Warrington that 'The account year for St. Peter's Hall ends on 31st inst., and I hand over charge then. For both reasons it is especially incumbent on me to get in arrears of revenue. I have been very successful in other and larger spheres in getting in the whole of my revenue by due date, and I am loth to close my duties at St. Peter's Hall with such large arrears as are due by the Trustees for the Covenanted grants. . . . May I expect a remittance?' The Council had of course offered to take over all or part of the covenanted grants, if asked in proper form, but nothing had been said about wiping out arrears, and in any case no application had yet been made by the Trustees. No doubt Warrington had not liked one of Cumming's observations to Pearman Smith[351] in this connection: 'A sufficient reason [for an application by the Trustees for relief] would be that the Hall is probably able to meet these payments now, as of course it is understood that no reflection would be made on Mr. Chavasse.' In July Warrington still had every intention of making reflections on Mr. Chavasse: on the 15th he wrote to Cumming, 'Nothing that has been said or done during the past few months has changed my firm conviction that the man into whose pocket this money goes would leave no room in the Church of England for those B.C.M.S. supporters of our Trust who are providing his salary and his rent. . . . I am prepared to pay over the money to the Council providing I have an assurance that it will be used for another purpose. . . .' To which Cumming replied at once: 'I cannot of course enter into matters of controversy between Mr. Chavasse and you. But I may point out that of the grants overdue from the Trustees, only £475 concerns Mr. Chavasse . . . there remains £730-14-2 which I can assure you does not concern Mr. Chavasse in any way but is due under covenant for bursaries and the Tuition Fund. In this is included the £500 bank loan guaranteed by the Trustees. . . .'

Then there was the matter of money owed to Sir Herbert Baker, including an account rendered as far back as 17 December 1930. On 1 August 1931 one of Warrington's assistant secretaries, D. Lock, informed Cumming: '. . . the Trustees will not be responsible for one penny of this account. Mr. Warrington considers all the money paid to Sir Herbert Baker has been good money thrown away . . . he has done practically nothing to earn it.' Argument continued; two months later[352] Cumming still had to point out that 'it seems to me too late in the day to question the employment of Sir Herbert Baker so long after work has actually been done by him.'[353]

There was also some argument about the proposal for a Stather Hunt Memorial Appeal, for which Chavasse was still pressing. He produced a new draft towards the end of July 1931, and a month later a rough proof, but Warrington's reaction[354] was not encouraging: 'In view of the very serious falling off of the financial support given to the Trustees for St. Peter's Hall . . . I am obliged to convene a Special Meeting of the [M.M.T.] Council to consider the position. It is felt by several Members of our Trust that further appeals for the endowment of St. Peter's Hall will seriously prejudice the opportunities of the Trust for raising any money for the maintenance of the Hall, for which they are responsible. . . .' However, Warrington was now changing his tone, and realising that he would have to co-operate with Chavasse instead of trying to get rid of him.

It followed that Warrington resumed attendance at Council Meetings. On 4 September 1931 he appeared at a special meeting[355] called to receive formal notice from the Trustees that on 1 September 1931 the Revd. H. B. Greene (already a Trustee of the Hall since 11 April 1930) had been appointed a Trustee of the advowson of St. Peter-le-Bailey church, and that on the same date Brigadier-General H. R. Adair had been appointed a Trustee of St. Peter's Hall. Chavasse was on holiday in North Wales, and did not think it necessary to attend this formal meeting. If he had attended, he would probably have seen to it that the minutes were free of ambiguity. As they stood, it was not entirely clear that *both* appointments were to fill a vacancy caused by the resignation of Sir Charles King Harman: Greene was to take the vacant place as a Patron, but not as a member of the Council; Adair was to take the vacant place on the Council.[356]

Warrington was also present at the important Council Meeting[357] of 7 November 1931 which formally closed the dispute between the M.M.T. and Chavasse. The business of the meeting was largely financial. The Master reported that on the previous day, at the invitation of the Trustees,[358] he had attended a meeting in London 'to discuss the position of the Trust in reference to the Hall owing to the financial crisis in the Country. They would require the co-operation of the Council to meet all the liabilities they had undertaken on behalf of the Hall.' The Revd. P. E. Warrington 'confirmed this statement and said he wanted to make it quite clear that there was no financial crisis so far as the Trust was concerned, and that they could meet their commitments in respect of St. Peter's Hall, but that the Trustees hoped that the Council would be able to shoulder some of these responsibilities at a time of difficulty.' To ease the position of the Trustees the Master 'enquired if the Council would be willing to take over the Trustees' liability for the payments covenanted to be made under the Trust Deed as from 1 October 1931.' Since the Council had already, on 28 May 1931, offered to do this, there was not much hesitation in passing a resolution in the terms proposed by the Master, and in waiving the six months notice required to be given by the Trustees. At the same time, Warrington undertook that the arrears due from the Trustees up to 31 July and the proportion due from that date to 1 October should be paid at once; and he even promised to send a cheque for the interest due on Chavasse's loan from the Midland Bank.

The position reached was that the Council would now have to find about £800 a year extra from its own resources, but the Trustees would continue to pay £7,000 a year in interest charges and redemption insurance premiums on two mortgages; first, the original mortgage of £50,000 on Block No. 1, with the Legal and General Assurance Society, and second a new mortgage of £20,000 on Block No. 2, with the Clerical, Medical and General Life Assurance Society.[359] Warrington assured the Council that 'the Trustees considered that this redemption policy[360] was their particular liability and constituted their chief contribution to the Hall'.

'With regard to the whole question of meeting the liabilities of the mortgage on the Hall', Warrington urged the necessity of a combined appeal from the Trustees and the Council, to avoid overlapping and confusion. It was resolved that the Master, Foster Pegg, Graham Brown, Legge and Warrington should meet as a sub-committee to formulate a scheme for this combined appeal and to report back to the Council at a special Meeting[361] to be called for that purpose. So far, there was remarkable harmony. Moreover, a Trustees' Account and Balance Sheet for the three years ending 31 July 1931 was presented,[362] and Warrington had brought with him the auditor, Mr. F. S. Seal.[363] There was a cursory discussion of the accounts, but as they had arrived only that morning and the members of the Council had therefore had no opportunity of examining them, 'their acceptance was deferred to the next meeting'. On past form, one would have expected that this deferment would have led to another outburst of protest from Warrington, but nothing like this occurred. Moreover, in January 1932[364] Cumming was able to tell his chartered accountant friend that Mr. Seal had now substituted a new account and balance sheet for the Trustees. His friend was still not happy; he wrote back: [365] 'I have carefully considered your letter and the Accounts and I have had little difficulty in arriving at the conclusion that the Council ought not to accept these Accounts. . . . I entirely agree with you that the accounts should be in the name of the Trustees [of the Hall], and I am rather at a loss to understand how the M.M. Society can present these accounts. . . . It is altogether most unfortunate that these accounts have been presented in this way, for from them the Council can hardly be expected to get at the true facts covering the transactions on Revenue and Capital accounts of the Trustees. . . .'

Nevertheless, on 11 February 1932 Cumming was able to tell his friend: 'I am sure you will be interested to hear that at the last meeting of the Council[366] we were able to accept the Trustees' Balance Sheet, subject to the insertion of one other item. The original Balance Sheet has been altered in many details as suggested by us, and although we will not say that it is perfect, it represents with substantial accuracy the present position of the concern. By the time we have finished, [Mr. Seal] will have certified two different Balance Sheets to the 31st March 1931, and three different Balance Sheets to the 31st July 1931! I am very grateful to you for the assistance you have given me in dealing with this, as I should have hesitated to tackle the matter without the assurance that your opinion supported my own.'[367]

The Council had met on 4 February 1932[368] at the Charing Cross Hotel. Warrington himself had presented the revised Account and Balance Sheet, and 'in reply to questions' he had definitely stated that the sum of £25,619 shown as 'liability' to the M.M. and C.E.T. Society was a gift from that Society, that it included Mrs. Rowcroft's donation, and that it was only repayable if the Hall were closed. This statement was a considerable relief to Chavasse, especially as he was already meditating schemes for development.[369] He gave a hint of these when he told the Council that the Wesleyan Trustees were hoping to begin work on their new building[370] very shortly, and that it was therefore quite possible that the Hall would be called upon to complete the purchase of the second part of the Wesleyan property[371] sooner than had been expected. The question would obviously arise, where was the money to come from? In this connection, the Master reported that the sub-committee appointed to formulate a combined appeal for funds had met in the previous week[372] and had suggested that a 'strong letter' should be signed by the Council and sent to likely subscribers with a copy of the Third Annual Report; and Warrington promised to supply a list of 9,000 such persons. This was a 'short-term' plan; looking further ahead, the Council welcomed the news from Chavasse that he was in negotiation with the Evangelical Churchmen's Ordination Council about a scheme for a thank-offering fund in commemoration of the Fourth Centenary of the English Reformation.

So far, so good; and when the Council met again, for its Annual Meeting on 29 June 1932,[373] Chavasse was able to report that the Bishop of Worcester had convened a Conference of Evangelicals on 6 July to take the first steps towards the Fourth Centenary celebration, and that Sir Montague Barlow had become chairman of a skeleton committee to organise the thank-offering fund.[374] On the other hand, at the moment, it was hard to raise money: Cumming had to report that during the 10 months August 1931 to May 1932 donations to the old appeal had averaged only £118 a month,[375] and the new joint appeal was a flop – between 28 April and 4 June 1932, he had sent out nearly 5,000 copies of the Council's letter, and so far the response had been £14-12-0, while the cost had been about £84. A further list of 2,000 names had been received from the Trustees, but it would cost about £34 to send out appeals to these. Faced with these facts, the Council decided to abandon the joint appeal at once.

It also decided to postpone till its next meeting the question how to find the sum of £5,500 which would be needed to complete the purchase of the remainder of the Wesleyan property.[376] Meanwhile, Chavasse was authorized to have rough plans and estimates prepared; his current scheme was to convert the old Methodist chapel into a temporary Master's lodging.[377]

In all these matters Warrington was quite co-operative,[378] though he did go out of his way to modify his previous statement about the Trustees' gift of £25,000: he insisted that the minute should be amended to read – 'the Revd. P. E. Warrington stated that it was the intention of the Trustees that the sum of £25,000 shown as a liability to the M.M. and C.E.T. Society . . . should ultimately be a gift from that Society and includes Mrs. Rowcroft's donation.' At the moment there seemed to be no sinister implication in this amendment. As a matter of fact, in the previous six months Warrington had been planning the creation of another institution which would give him more satisfaction than St. Peter's Hall. First, he had the bright idea of buying a historic mansion, comparable to Stowe, as a postgraduate theological college. An appeal for £60,000 was duplicated on Monkton Combe Vicarage notepaper, marked 'STRICTLY PRIVATE AND CONFIDENTIAL' and signed by himself at the foot of a list of signatories headed by Sir Charles King Harman and the Revd. T. Lancaster. It stated: 'A residence has now been offered us by Lord Clifden. It is Wimpole Hall, a noble and stately Mansion standing in an extensive Park, situated about 9 miles from Cambridge. . . . Wimpole Hall greatly commends itself to us as being in every way suitable for the purpose we have in view.' Chavasse heard about this from a friend at Southborne, the Revd. Grantley C. Martin,[379] who had received a copy of the appeal in December 1931. Not knowing Warrington himself, Martin had written to Mr. Lancaster and to one of the other signatories, making a solemn protest. This was headed 'Seven Grave Objections from a whole-hearted Evangelical'. Three of the seven may be quoted:

'1. The scheme to accommodate 50 to 60 students seems an outrageously extravagant one.

2. Is a nobleman's magnificent mansion necessary. . . . Instead of promoting the simple life, may it not lead to "swelled head"?

7. Seeing that nearly all the great Evangelical Societies are in sore straits for lack of funds, is it RIGHT or KIND to launch a great scheme such as Wimpole Hall involves, inevitably diverting many gifts which would otherwise be given to *existing causes?*'[380]

147

On 7 January 1932 Chavasse sent on Grantley Martin's letter and his copy of the appeal to J. G. Legge, who had already heard rumours of the scheme. 'You will notice', wrote Chavasse, 'that at least five of those who signed the appeal are, to my knowledge, members of the Martyrs Memorial Trust, and were actually present at that meeting in London[381] which asked us (representing the Council of St. Peter's Hall) to help the Trust to shoulder their liabilities in connection with St. Peter's. I think this fact needs to be known, and should make us very careful in our further dealings with the Trust in this matter. . . .' Certainly no sane man could have believed that a theological college in such lavish surroundings could possibly pay its way.[382] On 4 February 1932 Chavasse was able to give Grantley Martin some reassurance: 'There is no doubt but that more theological colleges are wanted, but Mr. Graham Brown and I put it very strongly to Mr. Warrington a few days ago[383] that such theological colleges ought not to be in the middle of a ploughed field,[384] but in the centre of a University such as Durham or Bristol. . . . Mr. Warrington, I believe, agreed with us; and I am hoping that if a new theological college is started for Mr. Sydney Carter to take charge of, it will be where his undoubted gift for teaching will spread further than among the students he gathers round him in the theological college itself. . . .'[385]

In fact, Warrington had been forced to conclude that the Wimpole Hall scheme was impracticable, and he had already switched his attention to Bristol. On 22 January 1932 *The Record* and the *Church of England Newspaper* printed identical letters from Warrington, who stated: 'I have, for some time past, had under consideration the establishment of a Theological College. . . . Quite recently a mansion, in the West of England, admirably adapted for this purpose, has been offered to me.' Then on 23 February 1932 the *Bath Chronicle* announced that 'The founder of many public schools, including Stowe, Canford and Westonbirt, the Rev. P. E. Warrington . . . is now originating a Church of England Theological College for the West Country, having acquired for the purpose Stoke House, Stoke Bishop, Bristol.' Sydney Carter was to be Principal, and it was to be opened, as Clifton Theological College, on 11 May 1932.[386] On 11 March 1932 *The Record* gave a page and a half to the scheme, and appealed for support. There was no doubt that this appeal, if successful, was likely to draw away contributions from the new St. Peter's Hall appeal, and Warrington must have been quite conscious of this. But there is no reason to think that his colleagues on the Martyrs Memorial Trust approved of the Clifton scheme, even if they had supported the Wimpole Hall project. Indeed, some years later[387] Chavasse stated that it had been 'common knowledge' in 1932 that 'the B.C.M.S. members of the M.M. & C.E. Trust disapproved of a College at Clifton, which must be in opposition to the B.C.M.S. Theological College already in Bristol', and that it was his 'definite impression that Mr. Warrington claimed that Clifton Theological College was his own personal enterprise'. 'At the opening of the College it was stated that the College was a memorial to the clergyman who had made it possible for Mr. Warrington to take Holy Orders.'[388]

It would not be true to say that Warrington had lost all interest in getting money for St. Peter's; on 29 April 1932 he suggested that Chavasse should send a special appeal letter to wealthy people like Lord Wakefield, Lord Rothermere and Lord Beaverbrook.[389] The difficulty was that Chavasse never knew from what quarter a storm might blow up; and a quite unexpected storm did arise from the circulation of the Third Annual Report with the Council's appeal. A copy was sent to Warrington's old friend and colleague the Revd. T. Lancaster, who noticed the following passage:

I shall also have Sunday help which has been most generously offered me for nothing by the Rev. W. F. Scott, B.Litt., who is residing in Oxford for the next two years to read for a D.Phil. Mr. Scott was educated at Harrow and New College where he rowed in their Eight. He was ordained as Curate to Prebendary Webster of All Souls, Langham Place, and in 1913 became a Naval Chaplain in which Service he has remained ever since. His providential intervention will enable me to continue at St. Peter's the Sunday afternoon New Testament Readings started by Bishop Chavasse in Oxford half a century ago. I shall also be freed in Vacation to preach and speak on behalf of the Hall during some of the week-ends, and to welcome such gatherings as the Oxford Conference of Evangelical Churchmen which met at St. Peter's for the third time this Easter.

On 8 June 1932 Mr. Lancaster sent a serious letter[390] to Chavasse, thanking him for the Report and sending congratulations, but continuing: — 'I have read the Report carefully, and feel for your own information you should know what is common knowledge at Weymouth and Tunbridge Wells where his wife lives with her mother . . . that Mr. Scott, good man though he may be is (1) a decided Anglo-Catholic. As St. Peter's Hall has been founded on the understanding that it is to be an Evangelical College, I mention this and (2) what is more serious, and which renders his work as a clergyman well nigh impossible, is the fact that he does not live with his wife. All this is common knowledge but evidently you are unaware of it or you could not write that "the great boon of all will be to have Mr. Scott himself blowing like a sea breeze into our academical precincts, and mingling with the men". It will be good of you to help him all you can whilst he is at Oxford, but in the light of what in the interests of the work at St. Peter's I tell you, is his influence – vacillating as it has been in the most telling thing in a man's life – likely to help young men?'

This was a poisonous letter, but Chavasse could not brush it aside as he had brushed aside the Evangelical Vigilance Committee. He knew that Mr. Lancaster had informed the M.M.T. Trustees about the matter, and that those Trustees would not let it rest. A little later[391] General Adair was to describe Mr. Lancaster as 'one of the most splendid old fellows I have met for many a day – staunch, honest, learned in the scriptures, a daily *student* in the original tongues (O.T. and N.T.). . . .' What angered Chavasse was that this splendid old fellow had relied on 'common knowledge' without making further enquiries: had he done so, he might have discovered for himself that Scott's marriage had been a marriage only in name,[392] and that through no fault of Scott's. Chavasse later wrote: [393] 'The tragedy of Dr. Scott's life is that his wife is abnormal and will not live with him. There is insanity in her family.' In 1931-32 Chavasse knew about this; but everybody else at St. Peter's, senior and junior, took it for granted that Scott was a confirmed bachelor, and most of them continued to take it for granted, in spite of the meddling of Mr. Lancaster.

There was also the charge that Scott was an Anglo-Catholic. Chavasse knew perfectly well that if this were not countered, Warrington and his cronies would make the most of it, accusing him either of duplicity or of denseness in his approval of Scott. The difficulty was that in his early days Scott had indeed had Anglo-Catholic leanings. It was perhaps a good thing that Warrington never saw some of the correspondence between Scott and Chavasse. On 13 May 1931 Scott had written: 'I was terribly thrilled with what I saw of St. Peter's. I had no idea I was going to see anything so remarkable. It is a great work you are doing, and I should regard it as a privilege to help you in any way.' That was innocuous enough; but on 21 May there was another letter, a very long one. On the previous day Scott had come again

to Oxford to see Chavasse, and he now[394] took it as settled that
the Master would submit his name to the Council, and he had
no doubt that the Council would approve: '. . . my record is
particularly blameless ecclesiastically, and none of them can possibly know anything of my reputation as an A–C[sic]. In any
case you can assure them that I am more fundamentally evangelical than most people, and that modernism is the last thing
I could be accused of. . . . One does not realise the state of things
ashore in the Navy, and I clashed with the C.S.S.M.[395] seven
years ago just because I was too much out of touch with evangelical opinion ashore to realize on what dangerous ground I was
treading. I would not say the same things now as I did then just
because I know better how such statements are taken. . . . I shall
be careful to avoid causing unnecessary offence to the evangelical
extremists. Nevertheless I cannot say I am altogether charmed
at the prospect of being identified with the militant section of the
evangelical party . . . [but] I know in my heart that I am so
fundamentally evangelical that I should never work so happily as
with people of definite evangelical principles. . . .' To this
Chavasse replied:[396] . . . 'you will not find yourself at Oxford
identified with any narrow or militant section of evangelicals.'
Then on 1 October 1931, with reference to some ill-informed
criticism of Scott from somebody outside Oxford, Chavasse wrote:
'Cheer up! It is good to know of these things and to meet them.
It may give you an insight into the suspicious watchfulness that
has attended St. Peter's Hall from its start. I simply accept it
now as something to be noted, to be careful about, to be borne
with a smile, and to inspire to greater efforts in the real things
that matter.'

Chavasse decided to put Mr. Lancaster's accusations before
the Council at its Annual Meeting.[397] All that was minuted was
a request that 'the Chairman together with the Provost of the
Queen's College and Canon Foster Pegg should interview the
Honorary Chaplain, the Revd. W. F. Scott, in view of a statement made to the Trustees by the Revd. T. Lancaster'. Chavasse
proceeded to collect evidence to lay before the sub-committee,
which met on 18 October 1932 to consider the evidence and to
interview Scott. Its report was laid before the Council at its next
meeting, on 5 November 1932.[398] It is worth quoting in full: —

We examined evidence laid before us showing how Mr.
Scott was regarded by leading Evangelicals in Oxford after his
association with them during the past academic year; e.g.: —

151

(1) A letter from Bishop Graham-Brown, when he was Principal of Wycliffe Hall, dated July 4th 1932, in which he stated that when Mr. Scott lived at Wycliffe Hall during 1928, while reading for a B.Litt. degree, he found him so great a spiritual force among the men that he had asked him to take charge of an Aedes Annexae of the Hall which it was hoped would be opened. He was clear that Mr. Scott 'would never have accepted the position of Honorary Chaplain of St. Peter's had he not been able honestly to be loyal to its precepts'.

(2) A letter from the Rev. E. W. Mowll, Rector of St. Aldate's and Provost-designate of Bradford, dated July 8th 1932, in which he acknowledged the great help he had received from Mr. Scott in all the undergraduate activities which centred round St. Aldate's. He had seen a good deal of Mr. Scott, and considered him 'a real spiritual acquisition to our work on the Pastorate'.

(3) The Report of the Oxford Pastorate drawn up in July 1932, which paid a special tribute to the work of Mr. Scott – 'whose great influence with young men in all colleges, and whose brotherly co-operation with the Oxford Pastorate, the Council would gratefully recognise'.

(4) The terminal card of the 'Oxford Inter-Collegiate Christian Union' for Michaelmas 1932, in which Mr. Scott was announced as the speaker at their *first* meeting of the new Academic year. It was reported that Mr. Scott had been chosen by the leaders of the O.I.C.C.U. as their chaplain for their pre-terminal Conference held in St. Peter's Hall, on October 4, 5, 6, 1932; and had celebrated at their Evening Communion in the Hall Chapel. To this was added the fact that Mr. Scott had shown himself ready to help the Master by taking, on more than one occasion, the monthly Parochial Evening Communion of St. Peter-le-Bailey Church.

We therefore found that Mr. Scott was accepted by all the Evangelical leaders at Oxford as a fellow-worker of true Evangelical principles, and as exercising a remarkable spiritual influence among young men.

There had originally been an extra paragraph at the end of the report: — 'We afterwards had the opportunity of a long and satisfactory talk with Mr. Scott, which convinced us that he was a gentleman of unquestioned honour, who would never have offered his voluntary services so generously to St. Peter's Hall were he not – as he assured us – a true Evangelical.' When the draft report, containing this paragraph, was sent round for signature, Foster Pegg signed only on condition that the paragraph was deleted.[399] Chavasse wrote to E. M. Walker explaining this, and asking him to make a statement to the Council embodying the substance of the deleted paragraph: 'I do not feel that in fairness to Scott – whom we interviewed at some distress to himself, and who has been placed in a very unpleasant position – we ought to burke the responsibility of testifying to the impression he made upon us as a man of honour. I know he feels that a slur has been cast upon him by the suggestion that he would ever have offered his services to St. Peter's Hall for dishonest purposes.' Walker was unable to attend the Council, but he wrote a letter which was read out and referred to in the minutes: 'I think it is only fair to Mr. Scott to state in writing what I should have stated in person had I been at the meeting, viz. that I am convinced, as a result of our interview with him, that Mr. Scott is a gentleman of unquestionable honour, who would never have offered his voluntary services to St. Peter's Hall were he not – as he assured us he was – a true Evangelical.' That was the end of the matter; but it left a nasty taste in the mouth of those most closely concerned.

Meanwhile, there was the question of finance for acquiring the Wesleyan building. On 25 August 1932 Chavasse had written to Warrington: 'You will have heard from Mr. Teal[400] that the Wesleyans have given us notice that they require the balance of the money on their property by November 3rd . . . two days before the next meeting of the Council, which seems very awkward.' However, on 13 October he was able to tell Warrington[401] that '. . . a few days ago they informed me that they could not clear out of the old building till November 17; therefore the date of completion is extended to that date.' On 26 October Warrington wrote to Chavasse: 'I believe Mr. Pearman Smith has made it quite clear to Mr. Teal that it is utterly impossible for the Martyrs Memorial Trustees to provide any further capital for St. Peter's Hall at the present time. When we agreed to enter into this Contract we understood that it would be five or six years before we were asked to take over this property. . . . The question is, what can the Wesleyan Trustees do if we are unable to complete? Any arbitrary action at the present time would undoubtedly lead to the closing down of St. Peter's. There would be no way out of it.'[402] Two days later Warrington wrote a letter, marked 'private', to Cumming: 'I think I had better tell you that the Manager of the Insurance Company who does our business asked to see me last Monday with reference to St. Peter's. As the Mortgagees they strongly object to any of our funds being used for the maintenance of the Hall, and we are having to give £7,200 a year.[403] I am to have a further interview with the Manager within the course of a few weeks. If, as I have reason to believe, definite objection should be taken to the using of our funds then of course the question of the continuance of the Hall will have to be faced. Obviously our first duty is to the Schools. . . . In view of the serious industrial crisis which has overtaken the country I think it should be plain to all that every penny which is subscribed to the Appeal Fund should go to the liquidating of existing debt, and to the general maintenance of the Hall, and for nothing else until the country has passed through this grave crisis.' He enclosed a copy of this letter for Chavasse; to both he added a postscript in his own hand: 'The founding of St. Peter's Hall was undoubtedly one of the gravest mistakes we have made in connection with our Movement.'

On the same day, 28 October 1932, Warrington wrote a similar letter to Chavasse: 'Whilst all our Schools are full, and are holding their own up to the present, yet the Insurance Companies who have advanced us loans for our work, and who hold our very large Sinking Fund, feel very strongly that we have no right to use these funds for any work other than the Schools. If we did not give £7,200 to St. Peter's annually naturally the profits on the whole Movement would be much larger than they are. . . . The economic position as far as all Schools throughout the country are concerned is undoubtedly getting worse, and not better.' After all that had happened in the past, it was hard for Chavasse to know how much weight to attach to these warnings. He wrote back: [404] 'I do not know how the Council are to help with regard to the mortgage for some time to come, seeing that they still have to meet a liability of £12,000 on the new block, and at the Council Meeting we have to announce that the Trustees cannot find the £5,400 required for the Wesleyan Property.'

Chavasse did make this announcement to the Council on 5 November 1932, but he was also able to report that the Midland Bank, Oxford, were willing to lend £6,000 at 4%. It was resolved that the purchase should be completed in this way and that the title deeds of the Wesleyan building should be deposited with the Bank as security. Moreover, 'on the proposal of the Revd. P. E.

Warrington it was resolved that as the Midland Bank were prepared to give this accommodation the Hall should open an account with them in respect of the undergraduates housed in the Wesleyan Building,[405] and that the interest at least on the loan should be met by the increased revenue arising from the additional students thus added to the Hall'. This was counting chickens before they were hatched; but it showed that the idea of using the old chapel as Master's Lodgings had been dropped, and in fact Chavasse produced a plan from R. F. Dodd for converting the building into sixteen bed-sittingrooms[406] at a cost of not more than £2,500. This plan was referred to the 'Works and Building Committee',[407] which met on 13 December and decided to advise the Council to go ahead. Warrington was not there; he wrote to Chavasse on 15 December: 'I am sorry that illness prevented me coming to the Meeting. . . . My chauffeur and I have had the misfortune to be gassed by the petrol fumes from my Car, and the effects have been rather serious.'

If the Wesleyan building were to be ready for use in October 1933 there was no time to be lost. At the next meeting of the Council,[408] held in London on 9 February 1933, Chavasse was able to report not only that the purchase had been completed but that tenders had already been received for the work of conversion.[409] But he also had to report that he had received a letter from Warrington asking him to attend a meeting of the Central Finance Committee of the M.M. Trust on 17 February, with one other member of the Council, and stating that it would be desirable not to expend any money or make any decision for expenditure on the Wesleyan building until after the meeting on the 17th. This was frustrating, and General Adair felt this as much as anyone; it is clear that he, although a Trustee, did not know what was going on behind the scenes. There was nothing for it but to adjourn till 23 February.

On 10 February Chavasse wrote to tell Warrington what had happened, and added: 'I do hope that the agenda of the meeting [on 17 February] can be so arranged that we shall not be kept hanging about at the Hotel, but can interview the Finance Committee at the time appointed for us to do so.' The reply, from Warrington's assistant secretary, P. G. Green, was disturbing:[410] 'Mr. Warrington finds letter writing a very great ordeal to him these days. . . . With reference to the Meeting on Feb. 17th. Mr. Warrington does not expect to be present. I am to say that since the new Central Finance Committee has come into being Mr. Warrington does not make any arrangements in connection with these Meetings.[411] The Secretary of the Committee is Mr. Neal, the Schools Trust Accountant. . . .[412] For the past six months Mr. Warrington's health has been seriously failing, and a fortnight ago his Doctors told him that the time had come when he must give up his work and the strain of past years must not be repeated. . . . Mr. Warrington wishes me to say that if the Hall is to continue after June of the present year it is clear, from the present feeling of Members of the Trust, that a new policy will have to be evolved.' Then on 15 February, Warrington's senior secretary, Burn, wrote: 'The Central Finance Committee . . . regards the St. Peter's Hall business as extremely important, and they feel that they cannot deal with this matter unless Mr. Warrington is present. . . . [It is] quite impossible for Mr. Warrington to travel to London this week. Therefore the St. Peter's Hall matter will have to be postponed until the Committee meets in March.' This was preposterous: on the next day Chavasse was able to tell Warrington that Mr. Neal had indeed asked for a postponement, but that he seemed to know nothing about the arrangement for Chavasse's attendance; therefore Chavasse had telephoned to him and insisted on attending in spite of Warrington's absence.

Accordingly, on 17 February Chavasse and Legge went to London and met the Central Finance Committee, viz. Lord Gisborough (chairman), King Harman, Foster Pegg, Dr. A. W. Pickard-Cambridge,[413] Mr. Workman (representing the Legal and General Assurance Society), Pearman Smith and D. Neal. The Committee wanted to know whether the Council of St. Peter's could help towards meeting the £7,000 annual liability assumed by the Trust in connection with the Hall; the Trust still accepted their responsibility for this yearly sum, but they were passing through a period of great financial strain and would be grateful for any relief the Hall might be able to provide. They still thought that 'in ten years' time the situation would be quite different', but that was no comfort for the present. Chavasse and Legge could add no comfort. They put the position as it appeared to them and to the Council:

1. It had been recognised from the first that the Hall could not be run for profit. This explained the requirement of the Vice-Chancellor that the Trust should make itself responsible for any deficit on the Hall before he would licence it as a '*Permanent* Private Hall'.
2. There was at present a small yearly surplus, but this must

increasingly diminish as repairs and replacements became necessary. At present there was no sinking fund.

3. In the autumn of 1931 the Council relieved the Trust of annual covenanted payments amounting to £800. This was in order to help the Trust and pro tanto reduced the possibility of a margin of receipts over expenditure.

4. At a Meeting held on November 5th 1932 the Council had promised to try and be responsible for paying off a loan of approximately £6,000 to purchase the adjoining Wesleyan Hall which the Trustees had contracted to buy. It had been decided to expend a further £2,000 in turning the Hall in question into rooms for men, in order to produce an additional income which might in time pay off the debt of £8,000. Any surplus money therefore, the Council might obtain from its yearly revenue was already pledged to this object.

The Central Finance Committee, according to the agreed report of the proceedings, accepted these hard facts: it 'recognised that the Council of St. Peter's Hall were involved in a perfectly sound financial scheme; that for them to draw back now would be uneconomical; and that therefore they were not in a position to promise more at present. It was however pointed out that the Finance Committee would be glad to receive any sum that could be spared from time to time, even if no regular payment could be made.' This must have been a humiliating moment for Lord Gisborough and Sir Charles King Harman, who remembered the days when the 'vast financial resources' of the Trust had been taken for granted; and for Chavasse and Legge there may have been a wry satisfaction in reminding the Committee that 'the Council still owed the Trust £2,000 for the building on the Wesleyan playground', i.e. No. 4 Staircase. Chavasse 'thought it would be possible to find this sum from the Appeal Fund and from monies of St. Peter's Hall now on deposit'. He added that he had received from a friend the offer of a loan of £2,000 for the conversion of the Wesleyan building, which would release the money on deposit.

This friend was in fact C. E. Tinne. When the Council met again on 23 February 1933,[414] it gratefully accepted his offer to place securities with the Midland Bank to increase their loan from £6,000 to £8,000, and resolved that the balance owing to the Trustees on No. 2 Block should be paid as soon as possible. In view of the proceedings at the meeting on 17 February, there was no hesitation in deciding to go ahead with the conversion of the Wesleyan building, and the Master was authorised to sign the contract with Coles Brothers. It is clear that Warrington was beginning to fade into the background, and not only because he was a sick man. On 1 April 1933 Cumming wrote to him: 'I am glad to hear that you are once more able to attend to business, and I trust that you will keep well and strong so as to be able to tackle the many problems you have to deal with', and two days later Warrington replied: 'Thank you: I am well on the way to recovery and hope to do a full day's work soon.' On 22 April he got his secretary, Burn, to write to Chavasse: 'As Messrs. Parnell and Son are pressing for the payment of the St. Peter's Hall Bills which are maturing next week and the Trustees have to pay £1,600 interest to the Insurance Company, which is now due, the Revd. P. E. Warrington bids me . . . enquire whether the St. Peter's Hall Council would kindly let the Trustees have any portion of the promised £2,000.' To this Cumming replied, on 25 April; 'I send you cheque for £200 practically all that is available in the Appeal Fund. . . . Mr. Tinne is sending you £1,000 from the revenue account of St. Peter's Hall.' Burn wrote to Chavasse on the following day: '. . . The Trustees are very grateful to the Council for this assistance which is greatly appreciated in these difficult times.' The times were indeed difficult, for the Hall as well as for the Trust. In his Fifth Annual Report, 1932-33, Chavasse made the point that 'St. Peter's has felt the present economic depression almost as severely as other charitable institutions.'[415] He was referring to the need to meet some extra, unexpected, expenditure. Early in June 1933 he had discovered that there was a chance to acquire four houses in New Inn Hall Street opposite Linton House: [416] he could buy the leases of Nos. 42, 44 and 46, which had fifteen years to run before the property reverted to Brasenose College, and he could rent No. 48, for the same period. To knock these four houses into one and to produce a Master's Lodging with accommodation for undergraduates above it, was a scheme to rejoice the heart of Chavasse, who loved improvisation and adaptation. It would mean paying down about £2,250, and the alterations would cost more than £2,000. Characteristically, he decided to take the necessary action at once, without waiting for the Council.[417] As Bursar, Tinne was very much worried; as a personal friend, he responded to the challenge by depositing more securities of his own with the Midland Bank, in order to raise a further loan of £2,000, making £10,000 in all borrowed from that Bank. It was 'this fresh outlay of £10,000' which Chavasse described in the Annual Report as 'a provident, opportune and safe investment'. When the Council met for its Annual Meeting on 29 June 1933[418] it took the matter in its stride, simply recording that it 'approved the action of the Master in moving the Annexe from Beaumont Street to the property he had so acquired on behalf of the Hall.'

This meeting of the Council was unusual, in that for the first time not a single Trustee attended. In one respect it was a sad occasion, for the Master had to report that on 16 June 1933 Dr. P. S. Allen had died, after a long illness. Before that illness, he had missed only one meeting of the Council, and his advice had always been valuable. Chavasse did not exaggerate when he wrote in the 1932-33 Report: 'He was unwearied in his efforts on our behalf, and our infant Hall is orphaned of one of its staunchest friends and wisest councillors.' He had also to report to the Council that Dr. E. M. Walker, now retiring from the Provost-ship of Queen's, was going to be abroad for a year, and that the Revd. H. B. Greene had resigned his position as a Trustee. Not for the first time, there was something unfathomable in Mr. Greene's actions. Later on,[419] Chavasse heard from the Trust's solicitors that: '. . . it is a fact that Mr. Greene did send in a letter of resignation but he changed his mind and consequently as a deed of retirement (which would be necessary to make the resignation effective) was not executed he is still a Trustee.' But at the time of the Annual Meeting Chavasse had no reason to doubt the reality of the resignation, though it appears that he had been informed of it not by Greene himself but by Warrington. Finally, the Council heard that C. L. Teal was ceasing to be its Secretary, and decided to appoint in his stead Mr. R. H. Bowdler, B.C.L., J.P., an acquaintance of Cumming's, sufficiently Evangelical to be churchwarden of St. Andrew's in North Oxford.

During the summer of 1933 work went on steadily in the conversion of the Wesleyan building[420] and of the houses in New Inn Hall Street, and they were just ready for occupation in October. But before then Chavasse had received disturbing news about internal troubles in the Martyrs Memorial Trust. On 15 September 1933 Lord Gisborough and Canon Foster Pegg, as members of the 'Schools Trust Central Finance Committee' sent Chavasse a copy of a letter which was going out to the heads of all the Trust Schools: 'We beg to inform you that the Rev. P. E. Warrington has resigned all connection with the management of your School and all the other allied Schools. Arrangements are now in hand for the efficient conduct of a central office for the Schools and as soon as possible these will be advised you. In the meantime we request you to arrange for all communications regarding your School's requirements to be addressed to: The Acting Secretary, Office of the Schools Trust, Monkton Combe Vicarage, Bath. We understand that Mr. Warrington has called a Meeting for next Monday. He has no authority to do this and we shall be glad if you will not attend. We think, however, that a Meeting of Headmasters and Headmistresses is desirable . . .' and this meeting was arranged for the afternoon of 22 September 1933, at the Charing Cross Hotel. Chavasse must have attended this meeting, because in a letter dated 9 October 1933 to the Secretary of the Schools Trust he refers to 'our conversation at Charing Cross Hotel on Friday, September 22.'

There is no record of the proceedings at the meeting, and Chavasse himself was very discreet about it; but it is certain that those present were told in confidence that it had become necessary to bring in outside auditors to investigate Warrington's handling of the finances of the Trust. Everything else was quite uncertain, so far as St. Peter's was concerned. It appears that at or after the meeting, Chavasse had a word with Lord Gisborough about finding a new Trustee.[421] On 25 September he wrote to Gisborough: 'I was rather surprised when you told me on Friday that it was the Martyrs Memorial Trust, and not the Trustees of St. Peter's Hall themselves, who appointed new Trustees of St. Peter's Hall.' He quoted the Trust Deed on this point, and continued: '. . . As events are moving, St. Peter's certainly seems to be attached to the Schools Committee rather than to the Martyrs Memorial Trust. The latter, I suppose, will become more and more a patronage Trust, and the Schools Committee will assume increasingly an entity and power of its own. But certainly with our mortgages, and as an educational establishment, we are part and parcel of the Schools Trust. . . .' With this statement Lord Gisborough concurred.[422]

On the same day on which he wrote to Lord Gisborough, Chavasse also wrote to General Adair, suggesting that Dr. Pickard-Cambridge might be a suitable Trustee, and saying that Lord Gisborough approved of the suggestion. He added: 'I find I rather have to take the initiative in these matters, as naturally the Trustees are so busy with many other concerns that it is my responsibility to watch the interests of St. Peter's Hall.' He was surprised to receive the following reply, in Adair's own hand-writing, marked '*Confidential*': '. . . Now for the squall! No.

I would like to see the Revd. T. Lancaster . . . on St. Peter's Hall Council – , *not Doctor* P–C [sic]. Allow me to explain my exact feelings – as I understand it "Our Founder" (your esteemed Father) would wish St. Peter's Hall to be "labelled" and that is why it exists – *labelled* Evangelical and Protestant. It carries on its splendid young life under the shadow of the *Martyrs Memorial*. The MM [sic] members live with that as their label. When P–C was put up for the Stowe Council I went against him – I questioned his *Wisdom*. I am well aware of his *academic distinction* but you have plenty of that metal on your Council. We must keep the evangelical side of the balance the heavier. I will not vote against P–C but I will not vote for him. . . . For myself, *I thank God for* [Mr. Lancaster] . . . which I could never do for P–C. I must ask you to treat this letter as absolutely confidential. But *do* try and get Mr. Lancaster. . . . With the spirit of our Founder hovering over the Hall I want the MM members to be absolute (yes, bigotted if you like) protestant. Mr. Lancaster has real wisdom, and cares not for man's approbation. HE stands for the CAUSE.'[423]

Chavasse would hardly have agreed that his father's spirit was hovering over Mr. Lancaster; in any case, the question was academic, for the M.M.T. had other ideas. On 5 October 1933 he sent a letter[424] to Pearman Smith: 'I feel strongly that at this crisis the whole matter of the appointment of the Trustees of St. Peter's Hall, and the identity of the Trustees of St. Peter's Hall with the Patrons of St. Peter-le-Bailey Church, should be cleared up and made quite certain. The next Council Meeting of St. Peter's Hall is on Saturday, November 4th. Of course the Trustees will be present,[425] and it will be possible for them to scrutinise the Trust Deed, and also the Trust Deed of the Advowson of St. Peter-le-Bailey Church which Mr. Wykes[426] has very kindly undertaken to get from you and to have copied for our benefit. There is genuine obscurity in the matter, for if you will read through the Trust Deed you will see that according to that document the Trustees of St. Peter's Hall themselves, and not the Martyrs Memorial Trust, appoint new Trustees for the Hall.[427] A further question arises upon which the Trustees may be able to inform me, but which may require some elucidation – viz. is St. Peter's Hall connected with the Martyrs Memorial Trust or with the Schools Trust Committee? And what is the connection now between the Martyrs Memorial Trust and the Schools? It seems to me that our connection is with those who have made themselves responsible for our mortgages and are paying them

161

off; but what body is it that has done this? They are called in the Trust Deed the patrons of St. Peter-le-Bailey Church. Would it therefore be best not to consult the meeting of the Martyrs Memorial Trust on Thursday with regard to the Trustees of St. Peter's Hall, but leave it open till the matter has become clearer. . . .'

On 9 October 1933 Chavasse again wrote to Pearman Smith, pressing him to attend the Council Meeting on Saturday, 4 November, and also to get Warrington to resign from the patronage of St. Peter-le-Bailey. He said that Mr. Wykes 'tells me that it is for you to get the matter put through, but that he will give any help himself that is necessary in the matter'. On the following day Pearman Smith sent Chavasse a letter which did not entirely satisfy him: 'At the Meeting of the Martyrs Memorial and Church of England Trust on Thursday last it was decided that the Revd. R. R. Neill of Christ Church Vicarage Maids Causeway Cambridge should be appointed a Trustee of St. Peter's Hall and of the Advowson of St. Peter-le-Bailey in the place of Mr. Warrington. It is quite true that the Trustees of St. Peter's Hall are the persons by whom New Trustees have to be appointed, but you will remember that at the outset when the Hall was formed the Trustees thereof were appointed from the Martyrs Memorial Trust on the understanding that whenever new Trustees were necessary they should appoint them from the same body. The same remarks of course also apply to the Advowson of St. Peter-le-Bailey, the reason being that the Trustees of the Advowson not being able to exceed five it was thought desirable to keep the same number as Trustees of the Hall and the same persons.

'There is no direct connection between St. Peter's Hall and any of the Schools. The chain however which links them all together is the Martyrs Memorial Trust though in law each is a separate entity. There is however a direct link between the Martyrs Memorial Trust and St. Peter's Hall as the former body are responsible for payment of the interest and sinking fund premiums in respect of Mortgages amounting to £70,000.'

Chavasse replied at once: 'I have met Mr. Neill, and we have had sufficient correspondence on various matters to make us feel we know each other.[428] I take it in due course the Trustees will appoint him. It will be a relief to us to have you at our next Council Meeting to explain the whole position. . . . I had not known, for example, that the Martyrs Memorial Trust are the body responsible for the payment of interest and sinking fund premium in respect of mortgages on the Hall amounting to

162

£70,000. I had thought the Schools were responsible.[429] As you can see from the Trust Deeds, officially the Hall only knows the Trustees of the Hall; and when a man like Mr. Warrington goes, who was really the connecting link between all the manifold organisations connected with the Martyrs Memorial Trust, it is essential that we should know exactly where we are, and have everything clear and in order for the future.'

This letter crossed one despatched on the same day by Pearman Smith's firm, informing Chavasse that Pearman Smith himself would find 4 November very awkward, but that he could send his managing clerk.[430] This did not please Chavasse at all. He wrote back: [431] 'I would most earnestly press you to come even though it is at inconvenience to yourself. The whole position where St. Peter's is concerned is clouded and uncertain, and therefore very unsatisfactory. In the old days we looked to Mr. Warrington as the only man who really knew the position and as the co-ordinating factor in a complex situation. Now we do not know where we are. We have Trustees who do not seem to appoint new Trustees as the Trust Deed lays down. We have a Martyrs Memorial Trust who, you say, are responsible for our mortgages, and yet I am summoned to a Schools Committee[432] and receive letters from the same Committee on the subject of mortgages. In the past our Trustees could tell us nothing but to consult Mr. Warrington on any matter that was uncertain. I do not think they will be able to make the position any more clear at the present time. We do therefore need the help of someone like yourself who is acquainted both with the legal aspects of the situation, and also has known the affairs of St. Peter's Hall, the Martyrs Memorial Trust, and the Schools Committee from the first. It is most dangerous if an important Society in Oxford like St. Peter's Hall is uncertain about its administration, and if the members of the Council cannot give satisfying and satisfactory answers to the many questions they are being asked. I do not myself feel competent to describe the position to them as I really do not know it; and I am pretty certain that our four Trustees will look to you to help them place the situation before us. A Managing Clerk, however competent, cannot give the assistance that we need. I know of no one who can do it save yourself.'

This pressure was effective, though it was not till 24 October that Pearman Smith and Sons informed Bowdler, as secretary of the Council, that 'our Mr. Pearman Smith' hoped to be present on 4 November. Meanwhile on 14 October 1933 Lord Gisborough, in a letter marked 'private and confidential', had tried to reassure Chavasse: 'I do not think there is any need whatever for any alarm . . . we are having the closest enquiry made into the whole financial position and into the question of the organisation of the Schools, which had undoubtedly outgrown the original organisation. . . .' In spite of this reassurance, Chavasse was very much afraid that in fact the Council would be saddled with fresh responsibilities, and he was therefore increasingly anxious (as was Mr. Wykes, for the Legal and General Society) that the Council should include Trustees who were not nominees of the Martyrs Memorial Trust.[433] The crucial question was who would fill the places of Warrington and his friend Greene, if and when those places were vacant?

The Council met on 4 November 1933.[434] Pearman Smith duly attended, as Solicitor to the Trustees. The case of Mr. Greene was dealt with first. 'The Council were informed that the Rev. H. B. Greene, subsequent to the memorandum of his resignation being entered in the Minute Book at the Annual Meeting on June 29 in accordance with the provisions of Cap. XIII of the Trust Deed, had expressed a desire to withdraw his resignation. It was resolved that under the circumstances the withdrawal of his resignation could not be considered.'[435] Then came the case of Warrington. 'The Council heard with regret the notification of the resignation of the Rev. P. E. Warrington from the Trusteeship of St. Peter's Hall, and of the Advowson of St. Peter-le-Bailey.[436] They will always remember that it was his initiative, courage and persistence which gave shape to the founding of the Hall. It was ascertained that Mr. Warrington's resignation left only two Patrons[437] upon the Trust of the Advowson of St. Peter-le-Bailey Church, seeing that, by some apparent oversight, Brig. Gen. Adair was not appointed a Patron when he took Sir Charles King Harman's place as a Trustee of St. Peter's Hall.[438] It was also pointed out that according to the Trust Deed of the Advowson . . . three of the five Patrons must be Evangelicals in Holy Orders. Furthermore the Council were reminded that, by the Trust Deed of the Hall, the Patrons of St. Peter-le-Bailey Church became ex-officio Trustees of St. Peter's Hall, and four of them members of its Council. As it seemed likely that the Trustees would ask the Council to assist them in meeting their responsibilities, it was suggested to Lord Gisborough that he and Canon Foster Pegg, the surviving Patrons . . . should appoint as Patrons, in addition to Brig. Gen. Adair, the Principal of Wycliffe Hall . . . and the Master of St. Peter's Hall . . . both ex-officio members of the Council of the Hall. The meeting was adjourned until the vacancies upon the Patronage . . . had been filled, and more exact information was forthcoming regarding the financial position of the Schools Trust and of the Martyrs Memorial Trust Society.'

These minutes can be amplified from subsequent correspondence. On 6 November 1933 Chavasse wrote to Gisborough: '. . . it has become necessary, with Mr. Warrington's resignation, for someone like myself with intimate knowledge of the affairs of the Hall to take the initiative in such matters as resignations and appointment of Trustees . . . I can see that for this reason, if for no other, I should be useful as a Trustee, for I could then take Mr. Warrington's place as the co-ordinating agent on the body of Trustees. I cannot thank you sufficiently for your help and attitude at our Council Meeting. All the members of the Council came to me afterwards to express their admiration and gratification. . . .' He included a draft of a letter to Mr. Wykes about the resignation of Mr. Greene. Lord Gisborough approved this draft, but made this comment: [439] 'I trust however that if he brings pressure to bear, it will be upon any recalcitrant member himself personally, and not upon the Trustees generally. We do not need it, and I resent having a pistol pointed at me under any circumstances, but doubly so when I know I am pulling my full weight already. Why flog a willing horse? It is far more likely to make him jib than to accelerate his pace! Personally I still think that Mr. Greene is not and never has been a Trustee. . . .'

It is symptomatic of the past conduct of Trustees' business that Lord Gisborough had forgotten that Greene had ever been appointed. Chavasse wrote back[440] to confirm that Greene certainly had been appointed, and to beg Gisborough and Foster Pegg to act on the assumption that Greene had resigned and to do what the Council had suggested, viz. to appoint Adair, Taylor and Chavasse to be Patrons of the Advowson. 'The great thing', he wrote, 'is to take action on Mr. Greene's resignation before he can plead that he had formally and properly withdrawn his resignation.' This, however, was more easily said than done, for action involved Pearman Smith, and he was on his dignity. After the Council Meeting there was a slightly acrimonious correspondence. Pearman Smith had taken umbrage because Chavasse, supported by Lord Gisborough, had told the Council that he had not been notified that Mr. Greene had withdrawn his resignation; Pearman Smith's firm sent a copy of the letter of 30 September, and for all practical purposes asked for an apology.[441] Chavasse was in no mood to give any kind of apology, and maintained his ground,⁴⁴² even though he tried to soothe ruffled feelings a few days later by pointing out: '. . . the truth is that when Mr. Warrington resigned there was no machinery left through which the Trustees could either work together or keep in touch with the Council of St. Peter's Hall. He did everything himself through Mr. Burn.'

On 11 November 1933 Chavasse heard that there would be a meeting of the St. Peter's Trustees on 15 November. He very much hoped that the other Trustees would refuse to recognize Mr. Greene; he even wrote to Pearman Smith: ⁴⁴³ 'You will take notice, won't you, that when the Trustees meet on Wednesday, as far as the other Trustees are aware Mr. Greene is not a Trustee of St. Peter's Hall.' This was really too much for Pearman Smith, who was trying to straighten out a legal tangle. His record of the meeting on 15 November describes it as 'Combined Meeting of the Patrons of St. Peter-le-Bailey and of the Trustees of St. Peter's Hall held at the Offices of the Schools Trust.' It was probably the first occasion on which the Patrons and Trustees of the Hall had consciously and deliberately met as a separate body distinct from the Trustees of the Martyrs Memorial Trust; certainly it was the first meeting recorded in Pearman Smith's Minute Book.⁴⁴⁴ Lord Gisborough, Adair, Foster Pegg and Greene were present. Pearman Smith explained the situation; Greene was asked to 'define his attitude', and he dug in his heels – he intended 'to retain his Office of Trustee' and his resignation had been withdrawn. Whatever the other Trustees may have felt about it, Greene's position was legally sound. That meant that Warrington's was the only vacant place. It was decided⁴⁴⁵ that General Adair should fill it as a Patron of the Advowson, but since he was already a Trustee of the Hall there was still need for a new Trustee. The names of Chavasse and Taylor were duly considered, as the Council had requested, but it was decided to postpone action to a further meeting, to allow time for discussion.

Unfortunately, Chavasse was not informed at once of these decisions. It was not until 21 December 1933 that Pearman Smith and Sons sent him a copy of the minutes of the meeting, with an apology for delay: 'Mr. Pearman Smith gave instructions for a copy of these Minutes to be sent to you immediately after the Meeting and he will be annoyed to find his instructions were not carried out. However we can only say that the additional work thrown upon our office by reason of Mr. Warrington's resignation has been enormous.' It is not surprising that Chavasse had felt that he was being deliberately kept in the dark. He was more and more worried about the financial prospect. On 27 October 1933 he had told General Adair: '. . . from the advice which I have received from the Legal and General Insurance Society the position with regard to St. Peter's Hall is far more serious than I believe the Trustees can be aware. We of course trusted the Trustees; and in the same way, I suppose, the Trustees trusted Mr. Warrington. But the result is a fearful mess. I believe under God's grace we shall weather the storm, but there is hard and difficult work before us all.' One example of the 'fearful mess' arose from enquiries made by the Inland Revenue Department during September and October 1933 about tax deducted from mortgage payments and not passed on to that department.[446] C. E. Tinne, as Bursar, could not answer the enquiries, and on 13 November sent copies of the correspondence to Pearman Smith and Sons, who replied: [447] 'We ourselves have no actual knowledge of the payment of the interest on the two Mortgages . . . but we have no doubt that when such interest was paid tax would be deducted and it looks as if this tax has not been paid to the Revenue. Tax matters are generally speaking the concern of Accountants and it seems to us a proper course is to refer the matter to the Accountants of St. Peter's Hall.'

To Tinne, the last sentence seemed to be either stupid or evasive. He wrote back: [448] 'I am surprised to receive your letter. . . . No one in St. Peter's Hall has ever seen these mortgages. They were put through by the Trustees of St. Peter's Hall, represented by the Rev. P. E. Warrington. As he no longer occupies the position, Mr. Cumming tells me he asked you at the last Council meeting who now represented the Trustees on the financial side, and was informed by you that you did. It was for this reason I addressed you. An additional reason was that I learned from Mr. Corney[449] that the schools were assessed in Walsall. So far as we know the only connection the Schools have with Walsall is that your firm is located there. If you have reason to suppose the income tax . . . has not been paid, I must ask you what steps the Trustees are taking to pay it. . . . It places us in a most embarrassing position vis-à-vis the Income Tax authorities, if the Trustees cannot give them definite information in this matter.' No such definite information was available: Pearman Smith and Sons could only refer vaguely to Mr. Seal's accounts, state that no payments of interest had passed through their own hands, and to undertake to make enquiries.

Three weeks later, on 18 December 1933, Pearman Smith &

Sons wrote to Chavasse: 'At a Meeting of the Central Finance Committee[451] of the Schools Trust held on Friday last it was decided that a special Meeting to discuss the finances of St. Peter's Hall should be held at No. 25-27 Charles Street, Haymarket . . . at 11.45 on the morning of January 26th 1934 and we were instructed to ask you if you could attend yourself and bring with you Representatives of the Council of St. Peter's Hall to meet Representatives of the Central Finance Committee. . . .' In the circumstances, Chavasse was a little suspicious; he wrote back:[452] 'I do not see how it is possible for the Council of St. Peter's Hall to discuss the finances of the Hall with the Central Committee . . . until the Council know who the Trustees of the Hall are.' He was willing to bring members of the Council to London, 'but I want it to be clearly understood that the Council cannot and will not discuss matters of finance which concern the Trustees . . . until they know who the Trustees are and are satisfied that they are persons who possess their confidence'. The upshot was that Chavasse at last received the news that Greene was still a Trustee; and a few days later[453] he heard from Lord Gisborough that the Trustees were thinking of appointing the Principal of Wycliffe to the vacant Trusteeship, omitting Chavasse himself because he was 'the present incumbent'.[454]

The Trustees, however, were in no position to take independent decisions. On 29 December 1933 Pearman Smith informed Chavasse that the meeting called for 26 January 1934 was 'not at the instance of the Trustees . . . but at the instigation of the Representatives of the Legal and General. . . '; and the actual meeting[455] was dominated by the solicitor of that company, Mr. Wykes. The financial position was even worse than had been feared.[456] Chavasse summed it up in a report of the meeting which he prepared for the Council: —

Mr. Wykes explained that in the past the yearly sum of £7,000 due to the Assurance Societies had been found by the Schools of the Martyrs Memorial Trust, but now it could not be met by —

(1) The Trustees of the Hall, who had taken out the mortgages, but had no funds.

(2) The Martyrs Memorial Trust, who had authorised them, for the same reason.

(3) The Schools Trust, which had been constituted a separate Trust independent of the M.M.T., as their net profits were only sufficient to meet their own liabilities.

Therefore, it was necessary for St. Peter's Hall itself to become responsible for these mortgages and to meet the yearly payment of £7,000 either by raising the fees of the Hall or by obtaining money from outside sources. Now it was quite clear that the surplus income of the Hall, between £1,000 and £1,500 a year, was fully pledged to meet recent developments undertaken by the Council before they were aware of the present crisis. Raising the fees, on the existing number of undergraduates, would be quite ineffective; there were only 90 of them, and a permanent private Hall was not allowed to increase its numbers by putting men into lodgings. In any case, raising the fees to any serious extent would defeat one of the primary objects of the Hall, and would make it more difficult to appeal for money from outside; it might 'alienate public sympathy, which was now willing to contribute to a Hall for poor students'.

On these grounds, Chavasse firmly turned down the suggestion that fees should be raised; the only solution was to obtain help from outside sources. But in his view, 'it was breathing space that was essential, if the Council were to hope in any way to meet this difficult and sudden crisis'. On behalf of the Council, he asked the solicitor of the Legal and General Assurance Society to get that company 'to hold their hand for the time being'. Meanwhile, he gave an assurance that the Council would do two things:

(1) It would try and form a body of 'Friends of St. Peter's Hall', whose yearly subscriptions should at least meet the yearly payment of £2,000 on the mortgage of £20,000.

(2) It would launch a great appeal for £100,000 to culminate in 1938, to establish St. Peter's Hall in Oxford as a thank-offering in memory of the fourth Centenary of the Reformation. The first object of such an appeal would be towards paying off the £50,000 mortgage.

The meeting had taken place on a Friday. On the following Monday[457] Chavasse warned the Tutors of the Hall of the seriousness of the collapse of the M.M.T.;[458] but in telling them that the Trust had 'given up all connection' with the Hall, he went a little too far. The Trustees of the Hall had been present at the meeting on 26 January; and in their presence Chavasse had made it clear that if the M.M.T. could not meet its undertakings and if its responsibilities were now to be shouldered by the Council, then the Council must have strong representation upon the Trusteeship of the Hall, and also upon the Advowson of St. Peter-le-Bailey. Mr. Wykes entirely agreed, and the meeting ended with a request to the Trustees that they should immediately find places for the Master and the Principal of Wycliffe. The

Trustees accordingly had a meeting of their own, then and there. What happened is shown in a letter which Lord Gisborough sent to Chavasse on 1 February 1934, marked 'private and confidential': 'At our last Meeting of the M.M. Trustees [sic], we elected the Master [sic] of Wycliffe Hall a Trustee both of the Advowson and of the Hall, and in addition we appointed you a Trustee of the Hall, but as there was no vacancy as Trustee of the Advowson we could not elect you on that. We tried our best to get Mr. Greene to resign but without avail . . . he was adamant. We however got Messrs. Workman[459] and Wykes to say they would arrange an interview with him.' He added a postscript in his own handwriting: 'I am ready to resign tomorrow in your favour if that would meet the case.'[460]

On receipt of this letter Chavasse wrote two, both on 3 February. The first, to Lord Gisborough, was to ask him to make a point of attending the next Council Meeting on 8 February 1934, because he (Chavasse) was calling a meeting of the Trustees half an hour before the Council 'in order that we may have a word with Mr. Greene. . . . I am very grateful indeed for what you have done, and for your willingness to help us in our somewhat desperate, but hopeful [sic] situation. I appreciate your attitude more than I can say.' The other letter was to General Adair: 'Lord Gisborough most kindly offered to resign to make room for me on the Advowson. But if it is necessary for any resignation from the Advowson, I think you will agree . . . that it should be you who are asked to make this sacrifice, seeing that your appointment to it has been so recent.' There was no difficulty here; indeed, on the same day Adair had himself written to Chavasse: 'I intended to say to you all in open meeting that if Mr. G. [sic] persisted . . . then I would gladly resign my "advowson" claim . . . I willingly resign my trusteeship if necessary, because, really and truly, when Sir Charles K–H [sic] resigned, I *thought* I only became a *Member* of the Council – a position I am very proud of . . . I place myself absolutely in the Council's hands.'

Adair's generous attitude was in striking contrast with that of Mr. Greene, who wrote to Chavasse on 5 February 1934: 'I shall be present at the meeting of the Trustees on Thursday and I shall then decide as to whether or not I attend the Council Meeting.[461] Do please understand that I have not the slightest intention of relinquishing my position as a Trustee of St. Peter's Hall and the Advowson of St. Peter-le-Bailey Church.' In fact, Mr. Greene was ill and unable to get to London[462] on 8 February.

170

At 2.00 p.m. that day there was a meeting of 'Trustees and Patrons'. Lord Gisborough also was unable to attend, though his wishes were known. The only one of the old patrons present was Canon Foster Pegg, together with General Adair (appointed 15 November 1933) and the Principal of Wycliffe (appointed 26 January 1934). Chavasse, who had called the meeting, was the only Trustee present who was not a patron. The proceedings were simple: first Adair announced his decision to withdraw from the patronage in order to make room for Chavasse, then Foster Pegg, Adair and Taylor appointed Chavasse a patron. For good measure, it appears that Foster Pegg and Adair confirmed the appointment of Taylor as a patron; at any rate, subsequent documents give the date of his appointment as 8 February 1934, along with that of Chavasse.

At 2.30 p.m. the four were joined by Legge, and the Council Meeting was held. The first decision taken was that in view of the refusal of Mr. Greene to resign his position as Trustee, the Council should press the Trustees to increase their number to the maximum, eight; and specifically it recommended the Trustees to appoint J. G. Legge and Dr. A. W. Pickard-Cambridge.[463] It was also suggested that the Trustees should appoint Dr. Pickard-Cambridge to the Council, as an additional member[464] along with General Adair. The Trustees carried out these instructions (for that in effect was what they were) at a meeting held on 22 March 1934.[465] It was probably not realized at the time how inconvenient it would be to have so many Trustees, all of whose signatures would be required for every change in investments or transfer of property.

The rest of the business at the Council Meeting on 8 February 1934 was mainly financial. The Master made his report on the meeting with the Central Finance Committee of the Schools Trust, and he was authorised to go ahead with the proposals to create a body of 'Friends of St. Peter's Hall' and to launch an appeal for a 'Thankoffering to establish St. Peter's Hall in Oxford' in connection with the Reformation Fifth Centenary celebration. To enable him to devote more time to money-raising, he was voted £60 a year from the Appeal Fund, for the next two years, towards the payment of a curate.[466] Next, it was resolved to instruct the Trustees to sell stock amounting to about £8,000[467] and to use the proceeds for current needs. Finally, it was resolved that the balance sheet of the Trustees, drawn up by Price Waterhouse, should be presented by the Trustees at the next meeting of the Council. This would give time for further investigation.

The position was certainly formidable. The total liabilities of the Council now amounted to £90,000; £50,000 on the Rowcroft Building, £20,000 on Staircase IV, £20,000 on the Wesleyan Building and the New Inn Hall Street houses. So much was clear; but much was still unclear. On 1 February 1934 Cumming had addressed a series of questions to Pearman Smith, which showed how much Warrington had kept in his own hands: —

'(1) Who is authorised to receive money and grant receipts on behalf of the Trustees and to operate on their bank account?

(2) At what bank and branch is the Trustees' account kept and by what name is it designated?

(3) In whose names are the following investments of the Council [£4,954 3½% Conversion Loan, £3,728 5% Conversion Loan] registered or inscribed, and are they registered or inscribed?[468]

(4) The Trustees were authorised to hypothecate these and other securities to the bank to raise funds for the construction of No. 2 Block. May I take it that the bank has no further lien on our investments than the amount shown in the balance sheet, viz. £3,250. . . ?'

Pearman Smith replied on the following day: '. . . you will doubtless realise that in none of the matters mentioned were we consulted as Solicitors and therefore we have no first hand information. (1) I think in the circumstances that you must consider no one other than the Trustees themselves is authorised to receive money. . . . (2) I understand that the Bank Account of the Trustees is at Barclays Bank Wellington Salop and it is designated Martyrs Memorial and Church of England Trust "Oxford Account". I do not think it has been operated upon since the resignation of Mr. Warrington. . . . (4) I am not prepared to say definitely, but I believe the Bank has no further lien on the investments. . . .' However, on 19 February 1934 Pearman Smith sent Cumming a further letter: 'You will understand that neither I myself nor my Firm were consulted by the M.M.C.E. Trust or by the Trustees of St. Peter's Hall with reference to their Banking arrangements. . . . I am now informed by their Solicitors [those of Barclays Bank Wellington] that the Bank claim that they are entitled to hold these securities as against the general overdraft of the M.M.C.E. Trust. I further gather from a letter which Messrs. Robbins Olivey and Lake the Trust's Solicitors have written to the Bank's Solicitors that Messrs. Robbins Olivey and

Lake accept the Bank's claim in this respect. . . .[469] I believe that arrangements have been come to between the M.M. Trust and the Bank whereby the whole of their overdraft is to be paid off by instalments. . . .'

This information confirmed Cumming's previous fears. On 23 February he wrote to Pearman Smith: 'It was a shock to learn from your letter . . . that the bank claim that they are entitled to hold all our securities against the general overdraft of the M.M.T. In spite of the acquiescence of Messrs. Robbins Olivey and Lake in this claim, we consider that the Trustees had no authority to pledge them for the M.M.T. either under their general powers under the Trust Deed or under the special power given by the resolution of the Council [of 2 November 1929].' The result of Cumming's insistence was that on 2 March 1934 he was able to attend a meeting in London between Mr. Robbins,[470] Mr. Edge, solicitor to Barclays Bank Wellington, and Mr. G. Hawley, a junior partner of Pearman Smith; and on 6 March Hawley was able to inform him that the Martyrs Memorial Trust 'have now passed the necessary resolution which will enable the Bank to release the St. Peter's Hall securities.'

So far, so good. But Cumming had also been engaged in discussions with Mr. K. H. Adams, an accountant who had been appointed Secretary of the Schools Trust. Both sides were concerned with what might be called the legacy of Percy Warrington.[471] First, there was the trivial but annoying matter of the three-year old bill from Sir Herbert Baker; secondly, more important, the matter of the income-tax deducted but not accounted for by Warrington. On 20 February 1934 Adams wrote to Cumming: 'If the Inspector at Oxford is unwilling to agree to dealing with the tax on the lines we are going to suggest, I am afraid the position will arise in which we may have to refer the Inspector of Taxes to the Trustees of St. Peter's Hall. I sincerely hope that, under the circumstances, and having regard to the embarrassing position [in] which we all find ourselves at the present moment, that [sic] he will not contemplate action in this connection.' With another of his favourite references to Lord Curzon's belief in the time-saving value of interviews,[472] Cumming persuaded Adams to join him in Oxford on 6 March for a talk with the Inspector of Taxes. It would seem that the Inspector did not press for immediate payment,[473] but on 24 March 1934 Adams wrote to Cumming: 'In view of the unsatisfactory result of the meeting held on the previous afternoon, it was decided [on 23 March] that the Central Finance Committee could not recommend payment of Sir Herbert Baker's fees, Income Tax, premiums or interest until such time as the position was clarified.'

The meeting referred to, on 22 March, had been between representatives of the Martyrs Memorial Trust, the Schools Trust, the insurance companies and the Trustees of St. Peter's Hall; it is not clear who else attended, but Chavasse, Taylor and Cumming certainly did.[474] On 8 March 1934 Pearman Smith had informed Chavasse that the Legal and General had certain proposals to make: 'Mr. Workman and Mr. Wykes regard the matter as urgent, and it is suggested that assuming the Trustees of St. Peter's Hall approve the proposal, the matter might be completed on Thursday 22nd inst.' What happened can be seen from subsequent correspondence. On 23 March 1934 Cumming sent a lengthy personal letter to Mervyn Talbot Rice: 'With Mr. Chavasse's approval[475] I am writing to ask if you can help us in a rather critical situation. As we all expected would happen sooner or later Mr. Warrington retired last year from all connection with St. Peter's Hall, Martyrs Trust, etc. And of course he left a mess behind him. The Schools Trust has been formed to take over all their schools at the instance of the Legal and General who have a large financial interest in the whole concern. Our Trustees haven't a cent and the Martyrs Memorial Trust are practically bankrupt. The result is that we have to face the two mortgages our Trustees contracted – £50,000 to the Legal and General (charged also on the schools) and £20,000 to the Clerical and Medical on No. 2 Block alone. We think we can manage the latter, but the former is a stiff proposition.

'The Legal and General have been very reasonable and have told us they will do all they can to help us, but they say the Schools cannot afford to meet the annual charge, which is as follows —

Interest at 6% p.a.	3,000-00-0
Premiums on 5 endowment policies of £10,000 for redemption in 20 years	2,035-11-0
	5,035-11-0

a total of £100,711 in 20 years (if no death occurs)[476] of which £60,000 is interest.

'To ease the situation the Legal and General advised that the Trustees should take the surrender value of the premiums already paid and take out a sinking fund policy of £785-7-6 for 35 years.

For £7,128-18-7 paid in premiums they offer £5,040 as surrender value. The sinking fund policy works out as follows —

Sinking fund	£27,488-2-6
Interest	105,000-0-0
	132,488-2-6

The Trustees met yesterday, and their lawyer tried to rush through the documents,[477] but Mr. Chavasse who is now a Trustee objected mainly on two grounds:

(1) that in the circumstances the surrender value was inadequate.

(2) that the interest is crushing and in view of the fall of the rate of interest owing to the conversion of War Loan from 5% to $3\frac{1}{2}$% excessive.

'At a later meeting of the Martyrs Memorial Trust, Mr. Chavasse, Mr. Taylor (Principal of Wycliffe Hall and a Trustee) and Mr. Neill (Secretary of the Martyrs Memorial Trust) were authorised to see the Legal and General and endeavour to secure better terms, and it is hoped a meeting will be arranged for 2.30 p.m. on Tuesday, 27th inst. at the Legal and General Office in Fleet Street. Could you possibly be present at that Conference?

'I have helped as far as I can and we have already met the Legal and General and other interested parties. But my knowledge of endowment policies, sinking funds, current rates of interest is more theoretical than practical. I have a very high opinion of Mr. Workman (Manager of the L. and G.) but these clergymen cannot meet him on the same plane. They must have the advice of someone who is quite au fait with the business aspect of the points at issue. I have discussed the matter with Mr. Chavasse, and he agrees that you are the best adviser they could possibly have. I can come up and supply all the facts and figures, but I do hope you can come and help us in the struggle for terms. . . .'

As it happened, Talbot Rice was unable to attend the meeting, but two hours before it took place he had met Cumming, together with an 'insurance friend', and had had a long talk. Talbot Rice refers to this long talk in a private letter to Chavasse, dated 29 March 1934, and gives it as his 'preliminary impression' that the Legal and General was 'trying to get its full oz. of flesh out of you all.' This idea had already been in the mind of Lord Gisborough, who had sent a private letter to Chavasse on 26 March: 'I think you ought to know that at our last Central Finance Committee Mr. Wykes remarked that he understood we were under the impression they did not mean business and Mr. Workman added that he could not wait much longer and that if we did not accept their terms he would ask his Directors to foreclose and sell the place, and Dr. Pickard-Cambridge then assured them there would be no difficulty in selling it as he said the existing leases of Boarding Houses were falling in, and would not be renewed except on much higher terms and that consequently all the Colleges who had not got their own Boarding Houses were on the look out for them and would snap up a place like St. Peter's greedily. The whole thing was so palpably a bluff that I made up my mind to write and tell you about it, in case they try it on you. The more I think of your proposals the more just and fair they appear to me, but I doubt if we shall get them to give way. *But do not be bluffed* by them.' To this warning Chavasse replied[478] 'I remember that Dr. Pickard-Cambridge made very much the same statement at our first meeting with the Legal and General last Autumn; and I do not know at all whether he is right or not. . . .'[479] In fact, there is no reason whatever to suppose that he was right:, there was no acute shortage of lodging-houses in Oxford until much later. In any case, it was clearly in the interest of the insurance companies to keep St. Peter's Hall intact as a going concern.

It has already been mentioned that when the Trustees met on 22 March 1934 they had appointed Pickard-Cambridge and Legge to be Trustees. On 27 March Pickard-Cambridge wrote to Chavasse: '. . . I shall be glad to serve . . . I ascertained on Friday last that my joining you would have the good will of the Legal and General representatives on the Central Finance Committee; and if I can be helpful in any way I shall be glad. Your father's memory is a thing which I value, and the Hall has already made good in everything except finance – and that is no fault of the Hall.' This gave Chavasse the chance to say this to him about the Legal and General: [480] 'I know we have their goodwill, but having embarked upon what must be to them a bad investment I wish they would nurse us rather than treat us as a strict business proposition. Anyway they have got Easter to think over it, and I shall hope for better terms. . . .'

There is no record of the meeting which had taken place on the afternoon of 27 March, but it was certainly not entirely unsatisfactory. Chavasse seems to have given an account of it to Talbot Rice,[481] who replied on 3 April 1934: 'I am delighted to hear that you have won the first round with the Company and have got the mortgage interest reduced to a more equitable rate, namely 5% for 3 years in place of 6%. I am still awaiting the Deed under which other parties were brought in as guarantors of the interest and premium payments.[482] This seems to me to be a very important point, because if the Insurance Company were only prepared to grant a loan on such guarantees now that such guarantors have failed it is, in my opinion, a strong point in your argument to submit that it is they, the Company, who should suffer the loss in the meantime and not the Trustees. The Company, in effect, made a bad business deal, and I am still of the opinion that you should stick it out and pay only what you reasonably anticipate you can pay. . . .'

Chavasse and Cumming went to see Mr. Workman and Mr. Wykes at the Fleet Street office on 12 April 1934, after having a preliminary talk with Talbot Rice which helped to strengthen Chavasse's hand. The result was fairly satisfactory, as can be seen from the terms of the provisional agreement then reached between Chavasse and Workman:

1. That the interest on the Mortgage shall be 5%.

2. That the £5,000 surrender value of the policies taken out with the Legal & General shall be used to reduce the Mortgage to £45,000.

3. That the Legal & General Assurance Society will receive at any time any sum for the reduction of the Mortgage; but that the Hall shall find on an average £1,000 per annum for this purpose.

4. This involves a payment of £3,250 for the first year, decreasing by £50 each year for 45 years. If more than £1,000 is found in any year the interest will be further decreased to a proportionate extent.

5. The Schools Trust can give no help for at least 2 years, but they are still pledged to give what help they can, and may do so hereafter.

6. The Council as well as the Trustees of the Hall to become parties to this agreement, which involves no personal liability.

6

The financial outlook for St. Peter's was still very gloomy, and before putting the provisional agreement with the Legal and General to the Council, Chavasse thought it worth while to have yet another approach made to William Morris, now Lord Nuffield. He had regularly sent Morris copies of the Annual Report.[483] In September 1930 he had sent him a copy of the sermon he was preaching in St. Aldates church at the unveiling of a screen which the congregation had installed to complement the organ previously given by Morris. In November 1930 he made a serious approach:[484] 'I have always believed that when the right time came you would wish to identify yourself and your philanthropy with St. Peter's Hall. . . . The future is hopeful and I had not meant to approach you so soon. I have always remembered your kind promise to grant an interview to my Father and myself regarding St. Peter's when you had discharged your intended benefaction to the [Radcliffe Infirmary]; and I am only sorry that you and my Father never met.' He went on to explain the need for a Master's house and to point out that Canal House 'is the obvious one for the Master of the Hall, and the whole of the Canal property is tentatively in the market. . . .[485] My only hope is that if you could see with your own eyes the possibilities of the Hall and its unique site, you would even now identify yourself with its establishment, or at any rate be willing to put some proposition before us. I ask, therefore, not for promises, but simply that you should inspect St. Peter's and investigate its possibilities on the spot. Though I must warn you that these possibilities are so unique that no one can view them without becoming an enthusiast. I could arrange for such a visit to be short and quite private. . . .'

Not even a short and private visit could be arranged. On 27 November Hobbs told Chavasse that 'Sir William has today had an opportunity of reading your letter. . . . This, in conjunction with the many that he has received of exactly similar nature since the publication of his recent gift to the Orthopaedic Hospital,[486] convinces him that the way of the would-be philanthropist is even harder than he had previously supposed. The pleasure obtained from giving assistance to a needy and praiseworthy cause is apt to be neutralized by the number of denials which must inevitably result. During the past few years, he has given a great deal of consideration and study to the whole subject of charitable and philanthropic donations, and, as a result, he is convinced that money so given can best be expended in directions in which it offers prospects of benefitting [sic] the greatest numbers of the community, with preference, always, for his own work-people. It is this conviction that has induced him to regard the need of the hospitals as unequalled. . . . He thinks it best that he should give you this full explanation of his position, and he is confident that it will enable you to appreciate what his feelings are.'

No doubt a similar letter went to many other applicants for help: the style and language were those of Hobbs, but the sentiments were certainly those of Morris himself. Chavasse regretfully[487] told Hobbs that he fully understood, but seized the chance to send a copy of the life of Francis James Chavasse[488] as a Christmas present for Sir William. However, there was clearly nothing to be gained by direct appeals for money, and Chavasse bided his time. Luckily, he went on visiting his former parishioner, Emily Morris, and when she died, on 8 January 1934, at the age of 84, it was Chavasse who took her funeral service. It was this renewal of personal contact with William Morris, now Lord Nuffield, which emboldened Chavasse[489] to make one more attempt. This time the approach was indirect: J. G. Legge, now a Trustee of the Hall, managed to carry it out.[490] The result was that on 27 April 1934 Lord Nuffield gave Chavasse a cheque for £10,000.[491] He was overjoyed: on the following day he sent the news to all members of the Council, with the remark, 'I believe that in the future it will be seen that this gift occasioned the saving of the Hall.'

Many letters of congratulation came in. One was a personal note from W. J. Pearman Smith;[492] 'Heartiest congratulations to you upon Lord Nuffield's handsome gift to St. Peter's Hall. Coming as it does it is a positive "God-send" and what is very important it will give *you* fresh courage.' It certainly gave Chavasse courage to make a new arrangement with the Legal and General, which was set out in a letter from Mr. Workman dated 9 May 1934.[493] In order to give effect to this provisional agreement, Chavasse thought it best to summon an emergency meeting of the Trustees and the Council for 2.15 p.m. on 11 May 1934.[494]

179

There was some initial confusion: Chavasse had called the meeting and took the chair, but Lord Gisborough objected on the ground that he was chairman of the Trustees and when present had always presided over their meetings; in fact, he did not see how a meeting of the Trustees and Council could be held jointly. Here he was technically correct; but Chavasse got over the difficulty by ruling that what was first being held was a meeting of the Council, at which the Trustees were invited to be present 'in order to facilitate the transaction of business'. Then, when the business in which both Trustees and Council were interested was concluded, the meeting continued as one for Trustees alone, under the chairmanship of Lord Gisborough. Afterwards, Pearman Smith drafted minutes of the whole meeting, for the Trustees' minute book, as a meeting of the Trustees, omitting items which concerned the Council only, while Bowdler produced minutes of the meeting as a joint meeting of Trustees and Council. This was confusing; but having a joint meeting in the circumstances was sensible and saved time, and the precedent was followed in September 1934.

The business on 11 May was important. First, 'the Council received with the greatest thankfulness the Master's announcement that Lord Nuffield had given him a cheque for £10,000', and 'requested the Master to convey to Lord Nuffield their deep gratitude for this munificent benefaction which they believed would prove to be the turning point at a critical time of financial anxiety; and also their satisfaction in knowing that he would allow one of the buildings of the Hall[495] to be named after and to commemorate the late Mrs. Emily Ann Morris, his Lordship's Mother'. The point was that the £10,000 had made it possible to pay off the £20,000 mortgage on 'Block 2'; the other £10,000 was to be found by using up the balance in the Appeal Fund, by selling investments[496] and by obtaining the surrender value of the endowment policies from the two insurance companies previously taken out by the Martyrs Memorial Trustees.[497] This was all covered by the revised agreement with Mr. Workman, which was now formally ratified by the Trustees and Council. The effect was that the Clerical, Medical and General Society, once they had been paid off in full, would disappear from the picture, and the title-deeds of Block 2 would be deposited with the Legal and General. Furthermore, the Trustees and Council agreed to mortgage the Wesleyan building also to that company as additional security for the £50,000 loan. Under the new arrangement, the Legal and General had made substantial concessions: the rate of interest was reduced from 6% first to 5% and then to 4½%, and the period of repayment was extended to 50 years. The Council was to find on an average £1,000 a year for reduction of the mortgage; if it could find more (e.g. on receipt of gifts or legacies), so much the better. At the worst, the Council would have to pay, in interest and capital repayment, £3,500 for the first year and thereafter a sum decreasing by at least £50 a year for 50 years. In the circumstances, the arrangement could be called generous; and at its meeting on 29 June 1934 the Council[498] acknowledged it, resolving that 'The Governing Body of St. Peter's Hall desire to place on record their high appreciation of the consideration, courtesy and helpfulness shown to them by the General Manager, Solicitor and Directors of the Legal and General Assurance Society. . . . They believe that largely through their co-operation and goodwill the Hall has been saved in the recent crisis, and that the mortgage will be redeemed in due course.'

The Council had expressed the hope on 11 May that Mr. Wykes would undertake the necessary negotiations with the Clerical, Medical and General Society; this was a little too much to expect, but he did promise Cumming to give Pearman Smith,[499] if he required it, 'every assistance . . . to bring influence to bear upon the Clerical, Medical and General in order to incline them to receive full payment immediately and not wait for six months' notice'. On 31 May 1934 the General Manager of the C.M.G. Society, Mr. A. H. Rowell, was able to tell Pearman Smith that his Directors 'will be prepared to accept repayment of the £20,000 on three months' notice or with three months' interest in lieu of notice'. At this stage Chavasse was hoping to pay off this mortgage immediately, and was not happy at having to give even three months' notice; but his hopes were soon dashed. On 8 June Pearman Smith informed him: 'I have now heard from Mr. Wykes that he and Mr. Workman both consider that the intimation given us by the Clerical Medical and General Office in their letter of 31 May is the absolute limit of concession as regards Notice that can be obtained, and such letter was the result of an interview by Mr. Workman with the General Manager of the C.G.M. Office.' Four days later Pearman Smith reported that definite arrangements had been made to repay the mortgage on 31 August 1934, and this was what Chavasse told the Council on 29 June.

There were, however, some complications. The Legal and General Society were unwilling to pay the surrender value of their life policies until the Deed of Further Security had been signed, and this caused delay. It did not help matters that just at this time there was friction between Chavasse and Pearman Smith. On 28 July Pearman Smith sent Chavasse a copy of the draft Deed, which he had received from Mr. Wykes 'for my approval on your behalf. I think it well to enclose a copy of the draft as submitted as there are one or two observations I wish to make upon it. . . .' He went on to suggest a 'joint meeting of the Council and Trustees some time in August for the purpose of signing the deed'. On 30 July Chavasse replied: 'I am sorry you have been bothered with the matter. Some time ago Mr. Wykes had informed me that the Legal and General Assurance Society would require the Council as well as the Trustees to become partners to the Trust Deed [sic]; and therefore the Council, at their Annual Meeting on June 29, arranged for the solicitor in Oxford, whom they were employing for other work, to represent them with the Legal and General. . . . I have notified Mr. Wykes that Mr. Chilton is representing the Governing Body of St. Peter's Hall in this matter.' It was perfectly true that the Council had then resolved, since it would be necessary to have legal assistance in connection with the revision of the Trust Deed, and also in connection with the Agreement with the Legal and General, now being prepared by Mr. Wykes, that 'Mr. C. Alan Chilton, of the firm of Messrs. Markby Stewart and Wadesons, be appointed to represent the Council in these matters.' But it was a little disingenuous to call Chilton a 'Solicitor in Oxford'; certainly he acted for the Diocese of Oxford, whose office was at 88 St. Aldates, and visited that office at regular intervals, but his normal place of business was in Bishopsgate, London, as Pearman Smith could very easily ascertain.

On 2 August 1934 Pearman Smith told Chavasse what he thought of this treatment: 'I have to thank you for your letter of the 30th Ultimo and in view of what took place at the Meeting of the Council and the Trustees held on May 11th at which I was present I must express surprise at its contents. It was definitely understood at that Meeting that I was to be considered as Solicitor for the Council for the time being, and particularly in connection with this matter and you Yourself [sic] stressed my exceptional knowledge of the business. Mr. Wykes also knew this, which is why he sent me the draft Deed . . . for approval. I think if only merely [sic] as a matter of courtesy the moment the Council decided to appoint a Solicitor to represent them generally I should have been notified. There has been ample opportunity for I have been in constant communication with you and as late as the 26th Ultimo you wrote me a letter dealing with points on this very matter. However I now understand that my firm represent the Trustees and that Mr. Chilton represents the Council. . . .'

It is highly probable that Chavasse had intended no discourtesy, but he had never really been on close terms with Pearman Smith,[500] and he now made no special effort to conciliate him: [501] 'I was in error in not asking the Secretary of St. Peter's Hall Council to let you know that the Council had decided . . . to employ Mr. Chilton. . . . So far all the negotiations with the Legal and General Assurance Society regarding this new agreement had been conducted personally between Mr. Wykes and myself, with no legal representation on behalf of the Council of St. Peter's Hall. I had therefore imagined that Mr. Wykes would send me direct the draft of the agreement, when I should have passed it on to the solicitor chosen for this purpose by the Council at their Annual Meeting.' Pearman Smith had no option but to accept the situation, and to get in touch with Chilton.[502] He was still thinking that a joint meeting of Trustees and Council would be needed, but no such meeting could be arranged during August.[503] The question was, how to raise the money to pay off the Clerical and Medical on 31 August. On 13 August Pearman Smith warned Cumming: 'I will of course do my very utmost with the Clerical etc. Solicitors, but I am afraid you must not assume they will readily consent to receive their principal in two parts with merely adding interest to the part outstanding until actual payment.' However, when Cumming proposed to borrow the necessary sum from Chavasse's bank,[504] Pearman Smith told him to hold his hand,[505] and on 18 August was able 'to report that I have succeeded in inducing the Clerical Medical and General Life Assurance Society through their Solicitors to agree to postpone payment of the £5,040 until it has been received from the Legal and General, so there is no need for you to send a further banker's draft.' The affair hung over till 16 October 1934, when Pearman Smith and Sons informed Cumming: 'We have heard from Messrs. Markby Stewart and Wadesons this morning that they have completed the repayment of the Clerical and Medical Mortgage for £20,000 and also (with the exception of the signature of Sir R. W. Livingstone) the Deed of Further Security with the Legal and General Assurance Society.' It is hard to see that Chavasse had gained anything by bringing Chilton into this particular matter; he had merely lost some goodwill on Pearman Smith's part and had incurred extra legal charges.

Meanwhile the financial implications of the decline and fall of Percy Warrington continued to be unravelled. On 28 May 1934 the Oxford Inspector of Taxes had sent the secretary of the Schools Trust[506] a computation of the amount of income-tax owing for the past three years; Adams sent a copy to Cumming, with a note that in October 1933 Stowe School had paid £1,500, less tax £375, interest at 6% on the £50,000 mortgage. On 13 June 1934 Cumming had replied: 'Your letter is the first intimation that we have had that Stowe School paid interest and premiums to the Legal and General. . . . I take it that there is no question of our being asked to meet the liabilities detailed in your letter. With our present commitments we could not even if we admitted our liability.' On 29 June[507] Adams referred to the new arrangements between St. Peter's and the Legal and General: 'I understand that the Legal and General have made extremely heavy sacrifices in your favour. . . . Under these circumstances it was decided [by the Central Finance Committee on 27 June] that this tax liability must be a matter for the Trustees of the Hall to deal with.' It has already been seen that this news came as a sharp surprise to Cumming.[508] On 9 July Adams wrote to him again: 'I am sorry that you feel shocked that the Governing Body of St. Peter's Hall may be called upon to meet this liability, and yet from many points of view as between two injured parties I do not feel that it is entirely unreasonable. From my own point of view I feel it very much that I am unlikely to obtain from St. Peter's Hall the very large amounts which my Schools have lent it, and you will appreciate that were it possible to obtain this sum today my task would be a much easier one. . . . With regard to the item "Amounts owing to the Schools totalling £18,310-14-8", this definitely represents expenditure made by the Schools, the benefit of which has been obtained by St. Peter's Hall. . . . I do not think there is any intention to ask you to pay any portion of this sum, at any rate for some considerable time. . . .'

The last two sentences quoted refer to the Trustees' Balance Sheet up to 31 October 1933, drawn up by Price Waterhouse and Co. At the Council Meeting on 29 June 1934 Dr. Pickard-Cambridge, attending for the first time, had pointed out that this Balance Sheet needed to be brought up to date, and the whole position carefully discussed before there could be agreement about final figures. The Council thereupon appointed a small committee to interview representatives of the Schools Trust. The interview took place on 13 July 1934, at the Millbank offices of the Schools Trust. Chavasse, Legge, Cumming and Bowdler represented the Council;[509] K. H. Adams and Mr. Wykes represented the Schools Trust, and Mr. Robbins attended as Solicitor for the Martyrs Memorial Trust. The report of the proceedings, signed by Chavasse and Wykes, and presented to the Council on 26 September 1934, needs to be quoted in full: —

(1) Mr. Wykes and Mr. Robbins informed the Sub-Committee that the Martyrs Memorial Trust, as such, had never possessed the power to pledge the revenues of the Schools they had founded for the establishment of St. Peter's Hall. The Governing Bodies of the various Schools on which there was a majority of Trustees of the Martyrs Memorial Trust did have the power to apply the revenues of the Schools for such objects as the founding of a College in Oxford; and in this way the annual payments on the mortgages on St. Peter's Hall had become an obligation of the Schools. The Schools however could no longer undertake this obligation.

(2) As regards the £16,000 found by the Schools up to October 31st 1933; and the £2,000 found subsequently by Stowe School to pay interest to the Legal & General Assurance Society, the Sub-Committee were assured that the Schools Trust would never seek to lay claim to the recovery of these amounts; though they might ask for a donation from the Hall if it ever found itself in a really prosperous condition and the Schools were needing money.

(3) As regards the £3,000 arrears of income tax upon interest paid in respect of the mortgages on the Hall and Sir H. Baker's bill, the Schools Trust stated emphatically that they were not in a position to find this money, and the Sub-Committee on hearing particulars agreed that this was the case. It was pointed out that the Income Tax authorities had promised to show every consideration to St. Peter's Hall, and were willing to receive payment by instalments. Mr. Wykes, also, promised the Hon. Treasurer that if by reason of having to find the first instalment of this arrear of income tax, the Appeal Fund could not find, the first year, the whole of the £1,000 annual repayment of the £50,000 mortgage, the Legal and General Assurance

185

Society would favourably consider an application for reduction of the payment.

So ended the curious association between St. Peter's Hall and the Schools Trust. A few months later it was announced in *The Times* that the schools had been reorganized as 'Allied Schools', and that Dr. Cyril Norwood,[510] late Headmaster of Harrow and now President of St. John's College, Oxford, had become president of their central Board of Finance. The only remaining connection with the Martyrs Memorial Trust was the presence on all the Governing Bodies of the Secretary of the Trust, the Revd. R. R. Neill. *The Times* made no mention of the Revd. P. E. Warrington, but that did not deter him from seizing the chance to give an 'exclusive interview' to a reporter of the *Bath and Wilts Chronicle and Herald*; on 6 November 1934 that paper printed a long article headed 'Monkton Combe Vicar's Achievements – Romance of a Vision Which Materialised – Huge Sums Involved'. No reader would have guessed that Warrington himself was under a cloud.[511]

On the whole, Chavasse had reason to be satisfied. In his Annual Report for 1933-34 he had given the Council, and the public, a highly dramatic account of the crisis 'that at one time threatened our very existence'. At the end of the Annual Meeting there was one item of business not on the agenda: Judge Dowdall moved a vote of congratulation to the Master 'on the dauntless faith and tireless energy and skill with which he had navigated St. Peter's Hall alike through fog and storm and narrow waters. Everyone felt complete confidence so long as he was at the helm.' It is recorded in the minutes that 'The Resolution was carried with cordial unanimity'; there can be no doubt that it was justified. There can be no doubt either that Chavasse himself believed that the worst was already over.[512]

There was indeed some risk that Chavasse, always buoyant, might become over-confident. At the joint meeting on 11 May 1934 he had persuaded the Trustees to appoint Talbot Rice to audit their accounts for the future, as well as those of the Council, and another resolution had been passed of some importance: 'In view of the fact that it had become necessary for the Council to assume greater responsibilities for the financial liabilities of the Hall, it was resolved that a sub-committee of the Trustees and Council . . . be appointed to consider the question of the revision of the Trust Deed of St. Peter's Hall.' This sub-committee consisted of Chavasse, Dowdall, Legge, Taylor and

Walker; not one of the Martyrs Memorial members was included.[513] This of course was intentional; the chief object of revising the Trust Deed was to eliminate the Martyrs Memorial Trust. This too was why, when Chavasse and Taylor had become patrons of St. Peter-le-Bailey, they had insisted on joining Lord Gisborough and Foster Pegg to make up the four representatives of the patrons on the Council, to the exclusion of Mr. Greene. Since he had been a patron since September 1931, and since both Chavasse and Taylor were already ex officio members of the Council, this could be regarded as sharp practice, though perfectly legal. Chavasse must have been conscious of this when he thought it necessary on 21 March 1934, to defend his position in a letter to Pearman Smith: 'The Trust Deed lays down that four of the Trustees of the Advowson . . . shall be members of the Council. I want it to be quite clear that this obligation has been fulfilled with the presence on the Council of Lord Gisborough, Canon Foster Pegg, the Principal of Wycliffe and myself. I would contest the contention that because the Principal of Wycliffe and myself are also members of the Council through other clauses in the Trust Deed that therefore this obligation is not fulfilled as regards the Trustees of the Advowson of the Church.' To which Pearman Smith and Sons replied, two days later: '. . . we should have thought it was a matter for the Patronage Trustees to have decided who were to be their representatives on the Council. No doubt it will be mentioned at their next meeting.' Chavasse had the last word; writing to Pearman Smith on 24 March 1934 he declared: 'Mr. Greene had never been appointed a member of the St. Peter's Hall Council, therefore when Mr. Taylor and myself were appointed on the Patronage of the Church there was no need to bring up the matter of representation of Trustees upon the Council, as both he and I were already members of the Council. . . .' That is to say, Lord Gisborough, Canon Foster Pegg and Mr. Greene had been presented with a *fait accompli*. It was not worth fighting about, but the matter was not forgotten by Gisborough, Greene or Pearman Smith. It is not surprising, in these circumstances, that at the Annual Meeting on 29 June 1934 Chavasse suggested to the Council that C. A. Chilton rather than Pearman Smith should be asked to act for it in the revision of the Trust Deed.[514]

When the Council next met, on 26 September 1934,[515] Chilton himself attended, and was able to report that he had met the Sub-Committee and that he was now preparing a draft of a Supplementary Trust Deed under which the Council would become the governing body and the Trustees would be custodian Trustees. This meeting had been called by Chavasse as a 'Special Meeting of the Council and Trustees', to deal mainly with the negotiations that had been going on with the insurance companies and the Schools Trust. Talbot Rice was also present for a discussion of the Trustees' Balance Sheet, which was to be the basis of the account which he had the task of preparing. He pointed out that the sum of £18,000 referred to would not be shown as a debit provided a letter was received signed by the Chairman of the Schools Trust confirming the arrangement with Mr. Wykes; and as regards the further sum of £4,193 shown under M.M.T. he suggested that the solicitors of the M.M.T. should be asked to obtain a statement, signed by the Chairman of the Trust, that they would not seek to recover this sum.[516]

Now it should be noted that none of the M.M.T. members had attended this meeting. On 13 September K. H. Adams had suggested to Cumming that the Council should meet at Thames House, because a meeting of the Martyrs Memorial Trust had already been called for the 26th; and when Cumming told him[517] that 'Mr. Chavasse does not consider it necessary or desirable that our Council should meet in London', Adams replied: [518] '. . . I was requested to make this suggestion to you by the Secretary of the Martyrs Memorial Trust, who considers your meeting to be one of importance from the point of view of the M.M.T., and was anxious that as many members of the Trust as possible who are on the St. Peter's Hall Council should attend.' One odd thing is that Lord Gisborough maintained that he had heard of this Council Meeting only indirectly and at the last moment, although Chavasse declared that his Secretary was sure that she had sent him notice; and when Gisborough did receive his copy of the agenda, there was no reference to its being a joint meeting of Trustees and Council. There is no reason at all to think that there had been any attempt to keep Lord Gisborough in the dark; but from this time he and his close associate Pearman Smith became noticeably less co-operative.

Towards the end of October Chavasse sent out notices for another joint meeting of Council and Trustees on 3 November 1934. He received a rebuff from Lord Gisborough,[519] who explained that he could not attend on that day, and continued: 'I also notice that you are calling a meeting of the Trustees for the same day. Surely this is a mistake? I believe I am still Chairman of the Trustees, and in that capacity I think it is usual for me to call the meetings, and as it is not convenient for me to

attend on Nov. 3 I am arranging a meeting for Dec. 11th. I must
ask you therefore to delete all items relating to Trustees business
from your agenda paper. . . .'

This drew an immediate reply from Chavasse: [520] 'Forgive me
if I ought to have written to you before describing the meeting of
the Governing Body on November 3rd . . . as a con-joint meeting
of the Trustees and the Council. As a matter of fact the presence of the Trustees at the Autumn Meeting of the Governing
Body is a matter of routine and has been our usual practice from
the first. According to the Trust Deed of the Hall the Trustees
are bound to present an Annual Statement of Accounts to the
Council; and this has always been supposed to take place at the
Autumn Meeting after their Accounts had been closed on July
31st. Last year no balance sheet was presented, and this year at
the request of the Trustees Mr. Talbot Rice is producing a
financial statement showing the financial transactions of the
Trustees from the beginning to October 20th 1934. He is coming
in person to explain it. But before the Council can receive it,
the Trustees have formally to accept it. There are financial
decisions the Council have to make which depend on this
Trustees' statement of accounts: and these cannot wait till after
December 11th. . . . Of the 11 members of the Council of the
Hall (Lord Cushendun,[521] the 12th, being dead) 7 are Trustees;
and as busy men it would be hard to ask them, when they are
met together, to defer transacting business for another month.
Meanwhile, after the extraordinary and embarrassing delay there
has been in the presentation of the Trustees Accounts, and the
unsatisfactory character of these accounts,[522] the Council will be
very upset if they are again held up, and even with the Trustees'
Balance Sheet before them, can yet take no action upon it;
because the Trustees (who are present) are prevented from
accepting it. I do hope I have said enough to show you that any
informal action on my part was due not to discourtesy to you
but to my taking for granted that the Trustees, in that they were
presenting the Balance Sheet, will be attending the meeting on
November 3rd as a matter of ordinary routine. And I do plead
with you not to hold up this very important business which the
Council must transact, when at last we see our way to placing the
finances of the Hall upon an established basis.'

Lord Gisborough would not budge. On 30 October he replied:
'Thank you for yours of the 27th inst. I would gladly have
acceded to your request to hold the meeting of the Trustees the
same day as the Council meeting, but I do not see how it is

feasible. One of the items on your agenda is the presentation of accounts by the Trustees. How is it possible with the Chairman absent, and before any of the Trustees have had an opportunity of seeing the Accounts or of checking them? Another item is the appointment of a new Trustee [sic] to take the place of the late Lord Cushendun. It seems rather hasty to be choosing his successor before he is cold in his grave. . . .'

This reply crossed another letter from Chavasse, written on the same day. It contained some important news: 'I must follow up Saturday's letter by another, as I am now at liberty to divulge a suggestion regarding the vacancy on the Governing Body caused by the death of Lord Cushendun. Some of the Oxford members of the Council felt that we ought, if possible, to secure another Peer of the Realm in order to create confidence in the Hall in the world outside Oxford. I therefore very tentatively approached Lord Nuffield,[523] who, as you know, has given the Hall a benefaction of £10,000. Today I have received a most kind letter from him allowing me to submit his name to the Trustees of the Hall as willing to fill the post.[524] I know you will agree that with our present anxiety regarding the finances of the Hall, and loaded as we are with a debt of £60,000, there is no appointment which could be more helpful at the present time. Also, as regards the Evangelical traditions to be maintained at St. Peter's, I know Lord Nuffield is in sympathy with us in this matter. His sister-in-law[525] was one of the most devoted members of my congregation at St. Aldate's, and Lady Nuffield frequently worships with her at St. Aldate's. Lord Nuffield himself gave me an organ for St. Aldate's when I was Rector, and asks me to see him when he is ill or whenever he needs the ministrations of a clergyman. For example, during this past year I buried his mother, Mrs. Morris; and married his niece at St. Peter-le-Bailey Church. It would be a tragedy to keep him waiting and not to welcome immediately his willingness to take a personal interest in us. As you are not able to be present at the meeting on Saturday, November 3, could you let me have a line which I could read to your fellow Trustees expressing your approval of their appointing Lord Nuffield in place of Lord Cushendun on the Governing Body of St. Peter's Hall? I think it may be that this great piece of good fortune may eventually save the Hall.'

On the following day, 31 October 1934, Chavasse replied to Gisborough's letter of the 30th. He reminded him that Cushendun had not been a Trustee and explained that five of the Trustees would be present on 3 November: '. . . I simply do not know how

we can request a busy man like Dr. Pickard-Cambridge, who is
making a special journey from Sheffield to be with us, to come
to London on Dec. 11th to transact business that is already prepared for November 3rd. As regards the other matter of the
Balance Sheet . . . the old Trustees, as a matter of fact, have in
effect already done so [checked it]. You will remember that in
January last Price Waterhouse & Co. presented a Balance Sheet
dated 31 October 1933, which early in this October the old
Trustees (i.e. Canon Foster Pegg, General Adair, Mr. Greene
and yourself) agreed should "form the basis upon which the
accounts of St. Peter's Hall should be built up for the subsequent
period, as there were no other figures available". The Trustees
asked Mr. Talbot Rice to produce a Balance Sheet up to October
20 1934 based on the Price Waterhouse figures agreed to by the
old Trustees, and which they have had ample opportunity of
checking for the last nine months; and any alteration in his
figures he is coming (at great inconvenience to himself) to explain
to the Trustees. We all know that if we studied the Balance Sheet
for a hundred years we do not possess even the material for
checking the Balance Sheet setting forth the Trustees' account –
for example, even you could not help us regarding the £2,000 that
Price Waterhouse has shown as being owed to the Hall by Mr.
Warrington. And in effect, at the meeting on Saturday the four
new Trustees (Dr. Pickard-Cambridge, Mr. J. G. Legge, the
Principal of Wycliffe Hall and myself) will be asked to accept as
a basis for the future finances of the Hall figures already agreed
to early this October by the old Trustees, and which none of us
are able to check. . . .'

Lord Gisborough never liked being bullied;[526] he wrote back
at once:[527] 'I am very sorry if any inconvenience has been caused,
but you must not blame me for that. You, having selected your
own date, called a meeting of a body of which you were not
chairman without even asking the real chairman whether it suited
him or not. . . . I specially chose December 11 because I knew
[Pickard-Cambridge] would be in London attending a meeting of
the Stowe Council, of which he is Chairman, that morning. I also
propose to ask permission to retire myself as soon as a suitable
successor can be found. . . .'[528]

Moreover, on the previous day[529] Pearman Smith and Sons, on
Lord Gisborough's instructions, had sent a formal letter to each
of the Trustees: 'We understand that the Trustees of the Hall
have received Notice from the Honorary Secretary of the Council
of a joint Meeting of the Council and Trustees for the 3rd prox.

Lord Gisborough finds that it will not be possible for him to be present on the 3rd prox., and he has accordingly asked us to write to the Trustees informing them that so far as a meeting of the Trustees is concerned this will have to stand over until a later date and we understand that his Lordship's suggestion is a meeting of the Trustees shall be called for 11th December. Part of the business for the Trustees will be to receive and consider the Trustees Accounts from the commencement up to the present date prepared by the Trustees' Accountants and a further matter for the Trustees will be to appoint a representative on the Council in the place of the late Lord Cushendun. His Lordship has therefore asked us to write and let you know that the Meeting on the 3rd prox. will be a Council Meeting only and that consequently the business we have referred to will stand over until the Trustees Meeting to be held at a later date.'

This was disconcerting, to say the least. Chavasse's first reaction was to challenge Lord Gisborough's authority to take such action. On 1 November 1934 he informed Pearman Smith that he had received his letter 'with some astonishment'; he went on 'on one occasion at a Council Meeting, and in letters to me, Lord Gisborough has claimed to be the Chairman of the Trustees of St. Peter's Hall. Can you please furnish me with any Minute or other authority by which Lord Gisborough was appointed to this office,[530] as the question is sure to be raised at the meeting on Saturday, November 3rd.' At the same time he also wrote to Gisborough himself: 'My dear Lord Gisborough. On one occasion I remember you thought (until reassured) that I had gone behind your back in some transaction. I therefore enclose a copy of a letter I have sent to Mr. Pearman Smith, and if it should turn out that you have never legally been appointed Chairman of the Trustees of St. Peter's Hall I shall be honoured to propose your election as Chairman when the Trustees meet on November 3rd. I am sure you will agree in the critical state of the Hall we must proceed according to strict regularity.'

No doubt, knowing that the Trustees had not kept minutes at all in their early days, Chavasse thought that by this move he had put himself in a strong position and that Gisborough's caveat could be ignored. But on the following day, 2 November, he decided to change his ground, and to avoid a conflict. He wrote to Lord Gisborough: 'I think the way is clear for the Trustees' business to be executed at a meeting on Dec. 11th, called by yourself, without hanging up the work of the Council on Nov. 3rd.

'(1) The Council (which will include a majority of the Trustees) can accept the balance sheet . . . subject to its acceptance by the Trustees on Dec. 11th.

(2) . . . the Council can . . . ask the Trustees to make the nomination [of Lord Nuffield] at their meeting on Dec. 11. I can then communicate this fact to Lord Nuffield who is expecting to hear from me next week.

(3) If I find that you have never been formerly [sic –? formally] appointed Chairman of the Trustees of St. Peter's Hall, I will get the Trustees present at the meeting on Nov. 3 to appoint you to this position, and thus regularise absolutely the summoning of the Trustees to a meeting on Dec. 11.

'On personal grounds I was grieved to hear of your intended resignation from the Trusteeship of the Hall, as I have greatly valued your help and encouragement from the beginning of our enterprise. It has meant a great deal to me to be able to rely upon your judgement and help at many a critical time. . . .'

Gisborough accepted this letter with good grace. On 3 November he replied: 'To be honest I cannot now recall the circumstances under which I became chairman so cannot say whether it was entered in the minutes or not. All I know is that I was put into the chair and have acted in that capacity ever since without challenge until now. It is very kind of you to offer to propose me, if it proves necessary, but I would not press it for one moment if I thought there was any desire to elect anyone else, and in any case it can only be for a very short time as I am giving up all my School and Hall work by degrees as I cannot stand the strain.'

So the meeting on 3 November 1934 was recorded as a meeting of Council only.[531] Two days later Chavasse told Gisborough what had happened: 'As far as Pearman Smith can inform us there are no Minutes of Trustees' Meetings before November of last year 1933. But the Trustees present at our Council Meeting on Saturday wished me to let you know that they fully recognise your position as Chairman of the Trustees of St. Peter's Hall – so much so, that they felt there was no need to pass any resolution to this effect. Six of the Trustees were present, and they have booked Dec. 11th. . . . As it turned out, we could not in any case have put through, for the acceptance of the Trustees, the Balance Sheet. . . . Mr. Talbot Rice . . . explained the Balance Sheet he had prepared. . . . But all he asked was that the Council should approve the form in which it was drawn up, when he would have a final Balance Sheet prepared to submit to the

Trustees on Dec. 11th. . . . If it would save you any trouble, on the receipt of a postcard from you I will send out notices in your name to the eight Trustees calling them to a meeting on Dec. 11th. . . .'[532]

These tactics were successful, from Chavasse's point of view. On 12 December 1934 he wrote to Foster Pegg, General Adair, Greene, Pickard-Cambridge and Taylor: 'At a meeting of the Trustees of St. Peter's Hall held yesterday at the Carlton Club, Lord Gisborough informed the Trustees that at his advanced age of 79 he could no longer make the long journey to Oxford or London . . . and wished therefore to resign when the Trustees agreed upon a Chairman to take his place. Several Trustees intimated to me that they would like Mr. J. G. Legge to occupy this position, and in a talk which I had with Lord Gisborough after the meeting he authorised me to write to all the Trustees asking whether this was their will. . . .' A week later[533] Chavasse informed Lord Gisborough that Adair, Pickard-Cambridge and Taylor had agreed to Legge's becoming chairman, and continued: 'I have not heard from Canon Foster Pegg, but you will remember that he told us that he also approved, when you were kindly giving us tea at the Carlton Club. . . . Mr. Greene has not answered my letter, but we could count him out. And of course I thoroughly approve of my very good and dear friend Mr. Legge holding such a position. . . . With your departure one chapter of the history of the Hall closes. It has ended on a tragic note, but at the same time it is a chapter of great achievement. . . .' On Christmas Eve Gisborough thanked Chavasse for his 'far too kindly worded letter'. He had had bad attacks of cardiac asthma: 'I doubt whether I shall be allowed to travel as far as London again . . . I realise what a heavy burden of debt I have helped to place on your shoulders. . . . I certainly did my best in what was a rather difficult position as I had to try and serve two masters! I am glad to think my successor will be in a freer atmosphere.'

Chavasse himself had no doubt that a free atmosphere would only be attained when all association with the Martyrs Memorial Trust had been dispelled. To that end he hoped to make a clean sweep of the original Trustees. Immediately after the meeting of the Trustees at the Carlton Club, he wrote[534] to Foster Pegg: 'I had no opportunity of catching you alone and asking whether, in view of Lord Gisborough's resignation, you did not feel that the right moment had come when you should put into effect your own resignation from the Trusteeship of St. Peter's Hall, which

you were intending to effect in the near future. I know of your
eagerness to be quit of the Martyrs Memorial Trust and all the
tangle connected with it; and as far as St. Peter's Hall is concerned, the right opening has arrived when you can do so feeling
that you have stayed by the ship during the crisis and are leaving
it when circumstances have changed.' On the same day he wrote
to the Revd. H. B. Greene: '. . . may I make one more appeal to
you to help us at St. Peter's Hall by resigning from the Trusteeship of the Hall. . . . The total result is that, as you will see from
the Balance Sheet, the Hall's liabilities over its assets are nearly
£10,000; and if the Hall collapsed the Trustees would be personally liable for this amount. . . . You can understand that I am
weighed down with anxiety, and only ask to be given a fair chance
of rescuing a project which is to me more important than any
other consideration in life. May I therefore appeal to your most
generous and Christian feelings to help us in the way you can by
resigning and thus making room for a man who can pull his full
weight in tackling our difficulties. It would give me real hope if
you could do this; and it would be the best Christmas present I
shall receive this year.' Finally, on 9 January 1935, he wrote to
General Adair: 'The time has therefore come for me to ask if
you will now put into effect your intention of resigning from the
Trusteeship, but *not* from the Governing Body of St. Peter's
Hall.'

The response to these letters was disappointing. Foster Pegg,
certainly, was ready to oblige,[535] and on 17 January 1935 Chavasse
showed his satisfaction: 'When all is over and our difficulties
settled, I shall hope to propose to the Council that you be co-
opted upon the Governing Body.[536] We have worked so long
together on behalf of the Hall that I am sure they would wish
to retain your services; and I was touched and pleased that you
expressed your wish to remain one of our company. . . .' But
General Adair was not quite so helpful; on 11 January he wrote
to Chavasse: '. . . We have a Martyrs Memorial Meeting on
Friday 18th and we shall, I hope, consider the point as regards
myself and them and the Trusteeship – so I must say no more
now. I am not clear as to how far I am morally bound – as
having been nominated by them to succeed Sir Charles K–H. I
do not think I am quite a free agent . . . I do not wish to make
any trouble but I want to do the right thing.'

Chavasse revealed disappointment, and some annoyance, when
he wrote back to Adair: [537] 'I expect you are quite right to consult the Martyrs Memorial Trust, and that it is the honourable

thing for you to do; though you will not expect me to agree that
the Martyrs Memorial Trust, after the way that they have treated
us, have any connection with the Hall save to make our difficult
path as easy as possible. . . . I think your experience in the past
will have shown you that it is the Council that is the important
body with influence in connection with the Hall. As regards the
Trusteeship of the Hall, which is simply a matter of guarding the
financial concerns of the Hall, my strong feeling is that the
Martyrs Memorial Trust have nothing whatever to do with it;
and I should resent very warmly indeed any interference on their
part, after their conduct in the past.

1. In the first place, the M.M.T. itself has contributed practically nothing to the finances of the Hall. As a Trustee you will
be familiar with the last Trustees' Balance Sheet, and can check
the following items: —

(a) The Schools Trust have found £18,000 for the Hall. This
was the result of Mr. Warrington's enterprise and I am still
grateful to him. The M.M.T. cannot take any credit for Mr.
Warrington's schools.

(b) Mrs. Rowcroft has given £10,000 to the Hall. This Mr.
Warrington always affirmed was entrusted to him personally, and
not to the M.M.T. If the Trust dissent from this, they should
have done so when Mr. Warrington was in power, and not agreed
with him.

(c) The M.M.T. has found £4,000 in some way or other
through donations for the Hall. But on the other hand, they have
allowed Mr. Warrington to go off with £2,000 of money belonging
to the Hall; and also they failed to pay £3,500 arrears of interest
to the Clerical Medical and General and the Legal and General
Assurance Societies, which the Hall itself now has to find. The
net result is that we have to thank the M.M.T. Society for a
debt of £1,000, and this could never have occurred if they had
done their duty as Trustees of a Trust.

2. So much for the past . . . as, as far as the M.M.T. was concerned, the whole Hall would have been sold up a year ago, you
can understand that I will tolerate no intrusion on their part at
the present moment. As I said in my first letter, I personally
(and so do the rest of the Council) welcome your presence on the
Council to help us keep the Hall Evangelical in character. . . .
As a Councillor of the Hall, you will have all that you or the
M.M.T. Society really desire. . . . When therefore you consult
the M.M.T., will you very kindly state the case as it appears in
Oxford? The Trust Deed makes it quite plain that they have no

legal rights whatsoever. By their conduct during the past as regards finance, and their abandoning St. Peter's Hall to its fate in January 1934, they have forfeited any moral right they may think they possessed. Will you ask what any single one of them has done during the past year to save St. Peter's Hall?'

General Adair was considerably embarrassed. On 19 January he replied: 'I laid the matter before our Chairman, Sir Charles King Harman, and Committee, yesterday – and, one and all, opposed my resignation, and I feel I should follow their ruling. . . . I feel sure that you perceive how awkward it is for me to pursue the subject under the circumstances. . . .' Chavasse assured him[538] that he fully understood and sympathised, but in fact he was decidedly anoyed, if only because he had already told Foster Pegg that Adair was definitely resigning; now he had to explain to Foster Pegg[539] that as yet there was nothing definite about it. However, there was something else of greater importance in the offing, which concerned Chavasse and all the Trustees.

The Revd. H. B. Greene had not responded to Chavasse's suggestion that a resignation would be a good Christmas present. It was not till 31 December 1934 that he sent any reply. Then he wrote: 'I am sorry not to have written sooner, but you will realise that in such an important matter I cannot act without consulting Mrs. Rowcroft, with whom I with others entered into a Covenant when she gave £10,000 for the founding of the Hall. It is quite possible she will communicate with you through her lawyer. . . .' This was an obscure answer; but Chavasse interpreted it as favourable. On 3 January 1935 he wrote to Greene: 'I am grateful for your letter of Dec. 31, and for the fact that you are willing to contemplate resigning your Trusteeship of St. Peter's Hall.' He went on to suggest coming to Felixstowe for a talk, and gave a list of possible dates. To this Greene replied immediately:[540] 'I quite fail to understand how you could read into my letter to you dated Dec. 31st any contemplation on my part to resign the Trusteeship . . . no useful purpose would be served by an interview. Our last meeting made me realise how difficult it was to have anything in the way of a helpful talk. You told me that if I did not then and there resign you would look on anything I said as "hot breath" and I would be a "continual thorn in your side". I can assure you that it is no pleasure to remain a Trustee. I only do so from a very deep sense of responsibility.'

Meanwhile there was the matter of the mysterious Rowcroft Covenant. Presumably Chavasse had not forgotten that Greene had previously mentioned such a covenant, in his letter of 5

197

February 1934: 'Mrs. Rowcroft's gift was made for the establishment of a Theological College to propagate the principles of the B.C.M.S. Not for a Hall at Oxford. She constantly expressed her dissatisfaction at the use made of her gift of £10,000, though she afterwards agreed to the Hall. I am one of the signatories to the covenant between Mrs. Rowcroft and the Trustees of the M.M. Trust dated Nov. 22, 1930.'[541] Chavasse now took the matter up with Robbins, Olivey and Lake, who had succeeded Pearman Smith and Sons as solicitors to the Martyrs Memorial Trust. On 3 January 1935 he wrote to Mr. W. J. Robbins: 'I had a letter the other day from the Rev. H. B. Greene . . . in which he mentioned a covenant between Mrs. Rowcroft on the one hand and himself and others on the other regarding the £10,000 which Mrs. Rowcroft gave to St. Peter's Hall. I have heard rumours of such a covenant; and, if it exists, it must have been made between members of the Martyrs Memorial Trust Society and Mrs. Rowcroft. As such a document vitally concerns St. Peter's Hall, we wish to know its precise contents. . . . I think you will agree that as a Trustee of St. Peter's Hall and Chairman of the Council of the Hall, I have a right to full knowledge of such a covenant if one exists.' Mr. Robbins replied at once[542] that 'a Deed was entered into with Mrs. Rowcroft providing that the Advowsons purchased with her money should be given to men in sympathy with the B.C.M.S.', but it was not until 15 January that he was able to send Chavasse a copy of the deed.

It was a Deed of Covenant (nearly all the signatures were witnessed by W. J. Pearman Smith) made on 22 November 1930 between Mrs. Rowcroft and the Trustees of the Martyrs Memorial and Church of England Trust, viz. Mrs. K. H. Leach (widow, of Tunbridge Wells), Canon Foster Pegg, Mrs. F. W. Walter (widow, of Bath), Lord Gisborough, Percy Warrington, H. B. Greene, the Revd. R. Middleton (a vicar in Rugby), H. Pavitt, Esq. (of Brighton), R. Heath, Esq., J.P., D.L. (of Stoke on Trent) and Sir Charles King Harman.

WHEREAS the Donor at various times has made gifts of certain sums of money to the Trustees amounting in the aggregate to the sum of £35,400 for the purpose of acquiring the several advowsons mentioned and referred to in the Schedule hereto and has also given to the Trustees the sum of £10,000 for the purpose of establishing a Hall within the University of Oxford known as St. Peter's Hall and the further sum of

£15,000 for the benefit of or for the purposes of the Jersey Ladies College and the further sum of £9,500 for the benefit of or for the purposes of Felixstowe Ladies School AND WHEREAS the Donor made such gifts on the condition that the Trustees should enter into the covenants hereinafter contained NOW THIS DEED WITNESSETH that the Trustees hereby covenant with the Donor as follows: —

1. The Trustees will present or cause to be presented to the said Advowsons mentioned or referred to in the Schedule hereto only such Clergymen who subscribe to the scriptural basis of a Society known as the Bible Churchmen's Missionary Society and who do not subscribe to any other Society having a scriptural basis other than the present Scriptural basis of the Bible Churchmen's Missionary Society and will only present or cause to be presented to the said Advowsons such Clerygmen as shall hold the views of the Bible Churchmen's Missionary Society and be believers in the teachers of the plain truths and doctrines of the Bible as taught in the Church of England in the past and free from the new and questionable Modernist Teachings and from Anglo Catholic teachings and the teachings of the Roman Catholic Church.

2. The religious teaching given at the Jersey Ladies College and at Felixstowe Ladies School and at any other School under the direct control of the Martyrs Memorial and Church of England Trust shall be in accordance with the scriptural basis of the Society known as the Bible Churchmen's Missionary Society and shall be free from the new and questionable Modernist teachings and from Anglo Catholic teachings and the teachings of the Roman Catholic Church.

IN WITNESS whereof the said parties hereto have hereunto set their hands and seals the day and year first before written.

THE SCHEDULE before referred to
(Viz. 70 livings)

....

57. The Advowson of St. Peter-le-Bailey Oxford in the Diocese of Oxford.

....

It should be noted that the Deed was prefaced by a 'preamble' in which —

The Trustees record their grateful thanks to Mrs. Rowcroft for her munificent Gift to the Trust for the purchase of Advowsons. They readily accede to the condition laid down by Mrs. Rowcroft that to all Benefices acquired, a Schedule of which is appended herewith, they will appoint only Clergymen who subscribe to the Scriptural basis of the Bible Churchmen's Missionary Society.

Chavasse's first reaction on reading this document can be judged from the letter which he dashed off to Mr. Robbins: [543] 'This Covenant was executed on November 22, 1930. In the following May . . . the M.M.T. passed a Resolution of no confidence in me as Master of the Hall, which they followed up with an interview with me . . . at which they brought fantastic charges against me. Lord Gisborough, who was chairman of that meeting, sub-sequently wrote to me to say that the Minute recording this Resolution had been expunged from the records of the Society.[544] It is clear that there must be a connection between the two, and that having covenanted with Mrs. Rowcroft to appoint an adherent of B.C.M.S. as Master of St. Peter's Hall and Rector of St. Peter-le-Bailey . . . they attempted to force my resignation. Though I was not acquainted with the fact at the meeting, Mr. Warrington sent down Mr. Burn to take a transcript of all that passed, which action again points to the same conclusion. It is necessary now for me to obtain a copy of this transcript in order to have evidence which cannot be contradicted of the kind of man that would be appointed to St. Peter's Hall and the Rectory of St. Peter-le-Bailey if the signatories to the Covenant with Mrs. Rowcroft had had the opportunity of carrying it into effect. . . .'

It appears that Mr. Robbins made no answer to this letter. There is no particular reason why he should have had a copy of the transcript, even if Chavasse was right in thinking that he had 'all papers connected with the Martyrs' Memorial Trust'; and even if he had a copy, as solicitor to the M.M.T. he might well see no reason to disclose it without instructions from his clients. In any case, Chavasse made no further attempt to obtain it, probably because he found other matters of more immediate concern. He had written to Robbins on 17 January 1935. On the same day he had also written to Pearman Smith, telling him that 'There has come into my hands a Covenant drawn up between Mrs. Rowcroft and certain members of the M.M. Trust, among whom were those who held the patronage of St. Peter-le-

Bailey Church. . . . This raises a difficult question with regard to Mr. Greene, who remains the only Patron of St. Peter-le-Bailey who signed the Covenant.' Chavasse was assuming that Lord Gisborough and Foster Pegg had now resigned from the patronage. But on 25 January Pearman Smith wrote: 'I have received a letter from Lord Gisborough that his resignation is only to extend to his position as a Trustee of the Hall and his membership of the Council.' This came as a shock to Chavasse: he replied at once[545] 'I hope you have pointed out to him that by the terms of the Trust Deed of the Hall – for the drafting of which you were yourself so largely responsible, and to which Lord Gisborough himself was a contracting party – a Patron of St. Peter-le-Bailey Church is an ex officio Trustee. . . .' It was no comfort to Chavasse to be informed: [546] 'We have not lost sight of Cl. 2 of the Trust Deed to which you refer, but whilst we agree it was no doubt intended that the then Patrons of the Advowson should remain Trustees of the Hall so long as they were such Patrons yet we cannot see anything in the Clause which would prevent such a Patron who with the consent of his co-Trustees retires from his Trusteeship of the Hall remaining a Trustee of the Advowson and that is of course the position of Lord Gisborough.' Moreover on the same day he received a letter from Lord Gisborough himself: [547] 'Needless to say I do not want to make things more difficult than they are already, but I have been acting at the request of those who are responsible for [sic – ? to] the donors of the moneys with which the living was bought. . . .[548] I am communicating with the Martyrs Memorial Trust and will write you again as soon as I hear from them. I am afraid it is impossible for me to give you an answer until I hear from them.'

This letter, on top of the correspondence with General Adair, made it clear to Chavasse that the Martyrs Memorial Trust had no intention whatever of giving up all connection with St. Peter's Hall. Now it happened that on 30 January, the very day after Lord Gisborough's letter had arrived, there was a meeting of the Sub-Committee appointed by the Council on 11 May 1934 to revise the Trust Deed of the Hall. There were present Chavasse, Dowdall, Legge and Taylor, together with Cumming, Bowdler and C. A. Chilton.[549] Chavasse was armed with copies of the Rowcroft Covenant, and was delighted to find that Judge Dowdall, Bowdler and Chilton took the matter very seriously. It was decided to submit an interim report to the Council, concluding as follows: —

The Committee felt it was useless to proceed with the revision of the Trust Deed until this matter had been cleared up. It was therefore unanimously resolved, on the proposal of Judge Dowdall, 'that the Council of St. Peter's Hall take Counsel's opinion as to whether the signing of this Covenant by a Patron of St. Peter-le-Bailey or a Trustee of St. Peter's Hall does not constitute obvious and certain grounds for his removal by a Court of Chancery, as flagrantly transgressing his obligations under the Trust Deeds of the Church and the Hall'.

In order that no time might be wasted, Judge Dowdall further requested Mr. Chilton privately to consult Chancellor H. B. Vaisey, K.C. (an authority on Chancery law) on the matter; and to report to the Council at their meeting on Saturday, February 16.

On the following day, 31 January 1935, Chavasse sent Pearman Smith a copy of this interim report, with some significant remarks: 'I shall withhold distributing copies of the report to the Council till the last moment; and shall hope that instead I can report to the Council on February 16 the resignations of Lord Gisborough, Canon Foster Pegg, and Mr. Greene, both from the Advowson of St. Peter-le-Bailey and the Trusteeship of St. Peter's Hall. Unless these deeds of resignation, duly executed, are in my hands by Feb. 16 . . . the Council will be informed of this Covenant, and will certainly take action. In the view of Judge Dowdall (Chancellor of the Diocese of Liverpool), Mr. Bowdler, B.C.L., and Mr. Chilton (Chancellor of the Diocese of Oxford), the Covenant flagrantly trangresses both the Advowson Deed of the Church,[550] and the Trust Deed of the Hall. Some members of the Committee believe that good service would be rendered to the Church if the terms of the Covenant became public. . . . Personally I am unwilling that St. Peter's Hall should be the occasion of such a scandal. But we are all quite determined to apply to the Court to secure the removal of any Trustee who has signed this Covenant and does not resign forthwith.'

A copy of this letter and of the Committee's report was sent on the same day to each of the three Trustees concerned, with a covering letter from Chavasse. To Greene he wrote curtly: 'The two enclosures will explain themselves, and I am hoping that the Council of St. Peter's Hall may be spared the necessity of taking further action, by receiving your resignation from the Patronage of St. Peter-le-Bailey Church and the Trusteeship of St. Peter's Hall before Feb. 16.' To Foster Pegg he wrote a little less curtly:

'The indignation of the Sub-Committee . . . was even greater than I had foreseen; and it was impressed upon us by the three lawyers who were present that the Council of St. Peter's Hall might get into trouble if they condoned the action of the signatories of the Covenant and did not take the necessary steps to remove them from their Trusts. I am very desirous of saving you all I can. . . . If I receive all three resignations in time, I can keep the official knowledge of the Covenant out of the Minutes of the Council.' To Lord Gisborough he wrote as if more in sorrow than in anger: 'When you read the two enclosures you will see why I was so worried when I learned from Mr. Pearman Smith that you were not resigning from the Patronage of St. Peter-le-Bailey. . . . I had hoped above all things that by your resignation your name would have been kept out of the disclosure. That is why I wrote so urgently to you on Saturday, without mentioning this Covenant as I did not want to seem to threaten.[551] Now, however, the matter is out of my hands; and the lawyers . . . impressed us with the fact that we might get into trouble by condoning the betrayal of Trusts if we did not take necessary action. But they asked me to write to you and express their urgent wish to keep you out of it if possible. . . . I cannot tell you how sorry I am that your connection with St. Peter's Hall should end in this way. . . .'

The reaction of the Trustees was not quite what Chavasse had hoped. Foster Pegg appears to have made no written reply, though he may have telephoned. Lord Gisborough wrote on 2 February 1935:[552] 'I am afraid the position is not quite so simple as it seems, first because if, as you suggest, I have put myself in the wrong in any way the fact of my resigning now would not absolve me from the responsibility for the past, and under the circumstances I think it would be cowardly of me to resign at the present juncture, and leave my colleagues in the lurch. But surely the suggested action of the Council is unnecessarily severe, and seems to be dictated more by the desire to get rid of M.M.T. influence by hook, or by crook, than as an act of self-defence. It seems to me that this result, which appeared to be slowly, but surely coming by natural evolution, could be obtained without such drastic treatment. Personally I was not aware that I had ever been a party to any covenant containing such a narrow minded condition as you say is the case. If it is so, and I am making enquiries, it cannot have been explained to me at the time, and I must have signed under a misapprehension.[553] However I am entirely in the dark as to the nature and purport of the Covenant in question and until I get a copy of it must hold my hand. Legal documents are so deliberately wrapped up in such ridiculous language that they are wholly incomprehensible to the ordinary lay mind, and one is entirely dependant [sic] upon one's advising solicitors for their meaning.[554] I am afraid that the last sentence in your letter to Messrs. Pearman Smith of 31st inst. rather complicates the matter, as it undoubtedly savours of the nature of a threat and I never allow myself to be influenced by threats whatever the costs may be. . . .'

Mr. Greene was even more outspoken: [555] 'Any desire I may have entertained of resigning from the patronage of St. Peter-le-Bailey, Oxford, and the Trusteeship of St. Peter's Hall, is rendered impossible by your threat and latest communication. Such a step would entail acquiescence in your monstrous insinuations of dishonour and wrong doing on the part of the Trustees you are trying to dislodge, and also on the part of Mrs. Rowcroft. By all means fulfil your threats and thereby let the public see C. M. Chavasse trying to cling to the £10,000 by which St. Peter's Hall came into being, while seeking at the same time to evade the conditions imposed by the Donor, and accepted by the original Trustees of the Hall in a legally executed document. Never mind the Courts. I am neither afraid of them nor concerned with them. Public opinion (which is usually just) will require that if you repudiate the terms of the contract, the least you can do is to fulfil the moral duty of returning the £10,000 with *full interest* to the Trustees, who will hand it back to the Donor.'

Chavasse made no reply to this letter. To Lord Gisborough, however, he had written on 4 February in a conciliatory tone: 'Thank you for your letter. If you will allow me to say so, I appreciate more than I can say its kindly, sincere and high-minded spirit. I only write to say that, as I tried to make clear in my letter to you, there is no suggestion of a threat where you are concerned. My one desire, and that also of the Sub-Committee . . . was to save you being involved in an unpleasant business. My letter to Pearman Smith was strongly worded in an attempt to try and make Mr. Greene see reason. You know how difficult he is. And if he forces us to proceed to extreme measures, we do not wish either you or Canon Foster Pegg to be mixed up with it. Canon Foster Pegg, even when I showed him[556] the document of Nov. 22, 1930, could not believe that he had put his hand to it. . . . I agree that it is quite inconceivable that either you or Canon Foster Pegg could have bound yourselves to so narrow a choice. . . . But the only way to put this right is for anyone who has signed this document to resign from the Patronage of the Advowson . . . [Pearman Smith] witnessed your signature, so he must know all about it. And when you see it, you will appreciate the real concern and friendliness that has prompted my letters to you.'

Lord Gisborough seems to have accepted that no threat to him had been intended, but he stood his ground. On 25 February 1935 he wrote to Chavasse confirming that he wished to resign from the Council and from his Trusteeship of the Hall 'whilst at the same time retaining my position as a Patron of the living, which I am advised I can do. I am sorry I cannot see eye to eye with you with reference to the Covenant. . . . I have not yet seen the Covenant in question, and have no recollection of having signed such a clause, or I think I should have refused to agree to it, although after all it is only making sure that the person appointed shall be an unequivocal Evangelical. Even so I think perhaps it is too narrow-minded and would be better left out. But surely this could be done by tactful negotiations with the donor of the £10,000 with which the living was bought.[557] If this failed then I think would be the time for considering stronger measures. I cannot believe that any fair and just Court would be so grossly unfair and tyrannical as to "remove" Patrons from their office with all the scandal that would naturally follow such treatment merely because we had agreed to carry out the wishes of the donor, especially when they realise it was done under a mis-apprehension, and that we are anxious to have the offending clause annulled.'

As a matter of fact, Chavasse himself was not entirely averse from the idea of 'tactful negotiations' with Mrs. Rowcroft. Back in the autumn of 1933 he seems to have had at any rate a faint hope that the downfall of Percy Warrington might lead to a closer relationship with her. On 2 November in that year she thanked him for a letter, and went on: 'I am so very sorry for you for I know how much your Bible Classes have been appreci-ated and how you must have worked in building up so fine a College [sic]. It is all too sad and heartrending. I am in almost constant communication with my lawyers about the [M.M.] Trust, having sunk in one way or another about 80,000 [sic] – I feel I ought to take proceedings against the finance committee of the Trust, it may end in this, I do not yet know, it is too sad that money given for God's work should be squandered and such wickedness allowed to go on. I certainly cannot add more

money to my big lump sum and have yet to find what remains!'
In May 1934 Chavasse heard that Mrs. Rowcroft had been
seriously ill, and proposed to visit her, but she told him that she
was too ill to see him; and on New Year's Day 1935 she mentioned that she had had a slight stroke.

A few weeks later[558] she was able to write him a long letter:
'As I have heard (whether rightly or wrongly) that in connection
with St. Peter's Hall you are forming a new Trust, may I ask if
you will kindly let me know by whom my stipulation as regards
B.C.M.S. will be safeguarded, I gave my £10,000 to Mr. Warrington for the College on his *pledge*, all my sympathies go with the
sound Bible basis of above society, for I regret to say I have
been unable to find any settled basis held by many other Societies,
if your dear Father were alive now I think he would agree with
me, not so long ago a missionary belonging to a certain Society
told me it was dreadful what some of her fellow missionaries
were teaching the poor heathen, for you know in these sad days
how Modernism and Spiritualism and man made-ism has crept
into our beloved Church,[559] I know you are teaching the Bible
Truth so please do not think I refer to you in above. I am very
glad you are keeping the College afloat, I have been so abomin-
ably treated by the M.M. Trust but I won't go into that!'

To this, Chavasse thought it worth while to send a long
reply:[560] 'Your kindly and rather sorrowful letter touched me.
We have both suffered much from the misconduct of the Martyrs
Memorial Trust Society. The Governing Body of St. Peter's Hall
does not, and could not, contemplate the forming of a new Trust
Deed. The original Trust Deed of October 23, 1928, must by
law stand and safeguard the objects for which the Hall was
founded for all time. We are only revising certain administrative
clauses in the Deed,[561] such as the power the Trustees now possess
of mortgaging the property of the Hall without the consent of the
Governing Body – a power which the Trustees appointed by the
Martyrs Memorial Trust Society actually exercised in connection
with a building erected with funds provided by the Governing
Body itself.

'By the Trust Deed of the Hall (according to the provisions of
which your most generous benefaction of £10,000 was received
and devoted towards the £30,000 required for the erection of the
"Rowcroft Building") the object of St. Peter's Hall was declared
to be to perpetuate the life and *teaching* of my father Bishop
Chavasse. Now my Father was a staunch supporter of the C.M.S.
As you will know, he did all in his power to prevent the B.C.M.S.

split. When it occurred he circularised all subscribers of the
C.M.S. in Oxford begging them not to desert the old society. . . .
I saw for the first time on January 16th of this year the Covenant
signed by the Patrons of St. Peter-le-Bailey Church on November
22, 1930 (i.e. two years after the execution of the Trust Deed of
the Hall) whereby they pledged themselves only to appoint a
B.C.M.S. clergyman to the living, and never a C.M.S. clergyman.
You will see by what I have quoted of my Father's views that
the terms of that Covenant are not merely valueless but actually
trangresses [sic] the Trust Deed of the Hall. . . . This, I am
afraid, may cause you pain, but it is kindest to be quite honest
about it; and I believe that you are inclined to trust me and to
expect straight dealing from my friends and myself at Oxford.
You believed in my Father, and I thank you with all my heart for
your expression of trust in me in your letter and your confidence
that I do teach Bible truth. . . . I should like you to know that
when I asked if I might visit you during the Christmas vacation
it was not to discuss this unfortunate Covenant, about which I did
not then know, save by vague rumour. It was to ask if you
could help us in our struggle to save the Hall. . . . May I plead
with you to trust us, and to be of good courage. By God's grace
you will yet thank him that there are Rowcroft Buildings in St.
Peter's Hall, Oxford.'

Unfortunately, Mrs. Rowcroft was not moved by this appeal,
and made no reply. It was not till the end of October 1935 that
Chavasse thought it worth while to make another approach.
Meanwhile, other developments had taken place. The Council
had met on 16 February,[562] and received 'with the greatest satisfaction' the news (which of course was not news to those present)
that the Trustees had on 11 December 1934 appointed Lord
Nuffield to be a member of the Council.[563] Legge, as Chairman of
the Trustees, reported that they had approved the Trustees'
Balance Sheet, and the Council now formally accepted it.
Chavasse made a formal announcement that Lord Gisborough
and Canon Foster Pegg had resigned as Trustees[564] but not yet
as Patrons. On the financial side, authority was given to pay off
£1,000 of the mortgage to the Legal and General, but as it
was reported that the Midland Bank was prepared to advance
£50,000 at bank rate, minimum 4% maximum 5%,[565] it was
resolved to ask the Legal and General Society whether they would
be willing to reduce the mortgage interest to 4%. The most
important item on the agenda, however, was the interim Report
of the Sub-Committee on the Trust Deed. C. A. Chilton was

present, and reported the views of Chancellor H. B. Vaisey, K.C., with the result that —

(1) The Master and Mr. Chilton were authorised to consult Mr. Vaisey (in accordance with his own request) and to obtain from him an opinion as to the correct procedure in order to have the [Rowcroft] Covenant pronounced null and void and to remove from the trusteeship of the Advowson any patron who had signed the Covenant.

(2) When such an opinion had been obtained, the Master was requested to summon a special meeting of the Council with a view to taking any action that might be necessary.

It should be explained that on 8 February 1935 Chilton had told Chavasse: 'I had a long talk with Mr. Vaisey yesterday afternoon, and he pointed out that this matter bristles with legal difficulties. Mr. Vaisey doubted whether there was any trust of the Advowson[566] unless a trust was created by the deed of covenant of 22 November 1930. . . . Mr. Vaisey argues that until the execution of [that] deed . . . the Trustees for the time being were merely the legal owners of the Advowson, and as such could at any time declare a binding trust of it. . . . Mr. Vaisey, however, thought that there was another way of attacking the deed of covenant (which he stigmatized as "disgusting") because to his mind the document, when studied carefully, meant nothing and bound nobody. . . . You will see, therefore, that in Mr. Vaisey's opinion the case is not so clear as we hoped. He is of opinion, however, that Chancery proceedings could be taken to have it declared that the deed . . . is so vague as to be of no effect. . . .'

Three days later Mr. Vaisey put his opinion into writing: —

'1. I am of opinion that the Deed of Covenant of 22 November 1930 is wholly inoperative [because vague and uncertain].

2. It is difficult to see how any Patron could have properly entered into this Deed of Covenant. If any Patron now regards himself as being in any way bound by its terms, it would be desirable to have the question of its effect (if any) determined by the Court.

3. I am not at all satisfied as to the present legal ownership of this Advowson. The Deed of 20 April 1864[567] created no valid *trust*, seeing that it merely obliged the grantees[568] to perform the duty incident to the ownership of every advowson, and it is in almost precisely the same terms as the deed in reference to which this principle was established by the Court of Appeal in the case of Re Church Patronage Trust, 1904, 2 Ch.

643. If there was no trust, the purported appointments of new Trustees and consequent vesting declarations must be inoperative, but while the materials before me are sufficient to show that the position is one of great doubt and difficulty, they are not sufficient to enable me to attempt to define that position.' With this formal opinion Mr. Vaisey enclosed a personal note to Chilton, saying. . . . 'The interconnection between St. Peter's Hall, Hannington Hall, and the Advowson is decidedly difficult to define in legal terms, and the effect of the Church Patronage Trust decision may well be that none of the supposed Patrons has any title to the Advowson of St. Peter-le-Bailey.'

This opinion opened up various possibilities. On 8 March 1935 Chavasse and Chilton had a consultation with Mr. Vaisey in Lincoln's Inn, and it was agreed that Chancellor Errington should also be called in. On the following day Chavasse thanked Chilton for his help, and went on: 'Do you think you could put the matter to Mr. Ellington [sic] as follows?

(1) The Patrons of St. Peter-le-Bailey covenanted with us to found a Hall to commemorate the life and teaching of Bishop Chavasse.

(2) By the signing of the Covenant which precluded them from appointing as Rector of the Church and Master of the Hall a clergyman who subscribed to any other scriptural basis than that of the B.C.M.S., they made it impossible for themselves to appoint to the living and to the Hall the Founder of the Hall himself, if he had been alive.

'This, I think, puts the matter in a nutshell, and as clearly and strongly as it can be stated. It obviously reduces the whole thing to a farce, and means that tens of thousands of pounds have been subscribed to the Hall under false pretences as long as those Patrons retain the right of appointment.'

As it happened, Chancellor Errington was unable to help, because (as Chilton told Chavasse on 23 May 1935) 'he took the view that as he had settled St. Peter's Trust Deed and was also acting for the Martyrs Memorial Trust, he was not in a position to take sides. . . .[569] At Mr. Vaisey's request we have placed the matter before Mr. Humphrey King, who is Chancellor for the Diocese of Sheffield.' On 28 May a joint opinion was drawn up by Vaisey and King. They confirmed that the ownership of the advowson was highly dubious: '. . . the title to the advowson must be traced from the last survivor either of the five persons who presented in 1878[570] or of the five persons who presented in 1889 and again in 1893. . . .[571] There is nothing whatever to indicate that the advowson has ever been purchased since 1864. . . . That something should be done, and with as little delay as possible, seems to us to be obvious, because the difficulties of the position, as it now is, are likely to become even more formidable if the attempt to tackle them is postponed.'

Chilton sent Chavasse a copy of this opinion on 31 May 1935, with the remark: '. . . You will see from the Opinion that Counsel are inclined to believe that it may be necessary to find the heir either of the Rev. W. H. Barlow or of the Rev. H. E. Fox. . . .' On the following day Chavasse replied hopefully: 'I think that our procedure now is easy and straightforward. The heir of Dean Barlow is Sir Montague Barlow, who is very interested in St. Peter's Hall and will do anything he can for us. The heir of Prebendary H. E. Fox is the Rev. H. W. Fox . . . he was both a curate and a Rector of St. Peter-le-Bailey, and again would help the Hall in any way he was able. . . . Why not get them to sign deeds transferring the advowson to St. Peter's Hall?'

But there were still some difficulties ahead. For one thing, the resignation of Lord Gisborough from the Council had an awkward result: the Revd. H. B. Greene inevitably succeeded him on the Council.[572] Chavasse informed Greene of this on 27 May 1935, and sent him notice of a special meeting to be held on 12 June. On 28 May Greene replied: '. . . I must inform you that Lord Gisborough's resignation cannot take effect until the Deed of Resignation[573] has been signed by me. I don't purpose signing that document until I know who are to be appointed to fill the vacancies my signature would create. I have made my decision on this matter with the full concurrence of the Martyrs Memorial Trustees and their legal adviser. We feel that any vacancy occurring by the resignation, or decease, of any member of the Trust should be filled by that body. I should be much obliged if you would kindly let me have a copy of Chancellor Vaisey's opinion on the matter of Mrs. Rowcroft's Covenant.' Chavasse did not think it necessary to send such a copy.[574] On 7 June he told Pearman Smith about Greene's letter, and concluded: 'I would like to thank you for the help you have given us in threading our way through the tangle of the past two years. I hope that we shall soon be drawing to an end of our troubles.' Chavasse signed this letter 'Yours sincerely', for the first time in their correspondence. A week earlier[575] he had mentioned to Chilton that there was no longer any need for Pearman Smith to continue to act for the Trustees, now that Lord Gisborough had resigned; he may have hoped that Pearman Smith would take the hint and offer to withdraw.

In fact Pearman Smith was away when Chavasse's letter arrived. His firm wrote back[576] confirming that 'Lord Gisborough and Canon Foster Pegg have both signed an engrossment of a Deed by which they retire from their positions as Trustees of St. Peter's Hall and such engrossment is at present with Mr. Greene. We are afraid it is legally necessary that he should sign it[577] and we have by no means yet given up hope that we shall be able to persuade him to do so.' On 10 June Chavasse sent this letter on to Chilton, with the comment: 'Mr. Greene has simply become an obstructionist.' Chilton agreed:[578] 'It is difficult to understand the mentality of a man who apparently refuses to consent to what two of his friends wish to do.' But it remained true that Greene's signature was legally necessary.

Such was the background to the Special Meeting of the Council held on 12 June 1935.[579] This Council received and accepted the formal letters of resignation[580] from Gisborough and Foster Pegg, and authorised the Master to urge General Adair, while remaining a member of the Council, to resign from the Trusteeship of the Hall, in order to facilitate the preparation of the new Trust Deed. An important decision followed: 'after hearing the Master and Mr. Chilton, with regard to the position of those who had signed the Deed of Covenant dated 22 November 1930, to the effect that separate action was necessary in view of their double capacity (1) as Trustees of St. Peter's Hall and (2) as Patrons of St. Peter-le-Bailey Church, it was agreed to postpone discussion regarding the patronage of the Church, and that the following Resolution should be submitted to a Special Meeting of the Council to be summoned for June 28th: —

RESOLUTION

"It was resolved on the motion of Mr. J. G. Legge, seconded by the Principal of Wycliffe Hall, that, in the opinion of the Council, the Rev. H. B. Greene has ceased to be loyal to the Declaration contained in the Trust Deed of the Hall".'

This procedure was adopted under the terms of Cap. V, cl 9, of the Trust Deed:

If the Master or any Member of the Council shall in the opinion of the Council expressed in a resolution to that effect (passed by a two-thirds majority of the Council at a Meeting duly summoned for that purpose and held after not less than

fourteen days' notice and confirmed at a subsequent meeting
not less than thirty days thereafter) cease to be loyal to the
said Declaration he shall cease to be a Member of the
Council. . . . And if such Member of the Council be also a
Trustee he shall cease to be a Trustee and his place shall be
filled by the remaining Trustees as if a vacancy had occurred
by resignation.

It seemed to be an ideal way of getting rid of the obstructive
Mr. Greene.

It should be noted that General Adair found himself much
embarrassed: he had attended the meeting, and had not wished
to be awkward. On the following day he wrote to Bowdler, asking for it to be recorded in the minutes that he had left before
the resolution about Mr. Greene had been put. Since the resolution was not going to be put to the Council until 28 June,
Bowdler did not think it necessary to do this. In any case, on
15 June 1935 Chavasse was writing Adair a very polite letter:
'. . . in pressing you to resign your Trusteeship of the Hall, we are
asking you to surrender no power but simply . . . an act of helpfulness which will make the wheels of official procedure go
round the easier. May I add that we were all filled with respect
and admiration at your honourable behaviour in the very difficult
matter that came before us last Wednesday? I wish you could
have heard the tributes paid to you by your fellow-members as
they met at tea afterwards. . . .'[581] But Adair still felt embarrassed; on 17 June he replied: 'I have passed your letter to the
Secretary of the Martyrs Memorial and Church of England
Trust.[582] I hope to get a definite expression of opinion as to the
position before long. . . . I am truly sorry to give such a lot of
trouble! but I feel I must work with my colleagues who may
have some reason for wishing me to remain as a *Trustee to which*
no objection was made originally.'

Chavasse now asked Cumming to see what he could do. On
4 July Cumming wrote to Adair: 'I am sure you will give me
credit for understanding the feeling of honour which makes you
hesitate. But as Lord Gisborough and Canon Foster Pegg have
resigned, it seems to me that even your scruples should be satisfied. You will, I am sure, pardon me if I point out that you were
unable to prevent your co-Trustee Mr. Warrington from com-
mitting grave irregularities, and it is familiarity with business
transactions that is really required from our trustees – mainly
to keep me in order!' This rather neat transition from flattery to

gentle prodding had no effect. Three days later Adair replied:
'I have passed your letter . . . to the Secretary of the M.M.T.
who is, I believe, arranging with our Lawyer, for a thorough
investigation of the subject (Trusteeship of St. Peter's Hall).'

Three weeks later[583] Cumming tried again: 'I feel it my duty
to impress on you the embarrassing position you are placing us
in. Arrangements are practically completed for borrowing
£48,500 at a lower rate of interest to pay off our outstanding
mortgage.' This would entail the signing of various documents by
the Trustees; if Adair was resigning, there was no point in bringing him in. On the same day Chavasse also made another
appeal: [584] 'St. Peter's Hall is a public and prominent Society,
and its property has been given it in trust by numerous benefactors to whom we are responsible. It would not be right or
honourable to have as a Trustee one who had been intimately
concerned with the financial crash occasioned by the mis-
demeanours of the then Secretary of the M.M.T., which plunged
the Hall deeply into debt – especially as the scandal is widely
known. I know that in accepting the Trusteeship of the Hall
you did not realise that you were responsible for the guardianship
of its property. But the responsibility was there all the same . . .
and your position as Trustee is therefore discredited. If only you
could realise that your first duty is to the Hall and not to the
M.M.T., you would not hesitate as to the course which you would
be the first to recognise as the only possible one.' But it was no
good. In spite of subsequent telegrams, Adair left the matter
to the M.M.T. and would not resign.

7

If it was difficult to dislodge General Adair, who was friendly, it was even more difficult to dislodge Mr. Greene, who was the opposite of friendly. At the special meeting of the Council on 12 June 1935, the point had been raised that since Mr. Greene was now a member of the Council he might himself attend the next special meeting on 28 June and demand reasons for the proposal to expel him. On 21 June Chilton informed Chavasse that he had given considerable thought to this point: 'I confirm that if the resolution is duly passed, Mr. Greene can, if he so chooses, take proceedings against the Council to have the resolution rescinded, and I am of opinion that, in view of the possibility of such proceedings, it would be wise to give a reason if demand is made. I think that reason should be that, while a Trustee of St. Peter's Hall, Mr. Greene executed the covenant of November 1930. . . '585 At about the same time the M.M.T. solicitor, Mr. Robbins, had been writing to Chavasse, who asked Chilton586 to tell him 'that I could not answer his letter for two reasons — (1) I do not mind having personal communications with Mr. Greene himself, but I do not communicate with him through his solicitor; (2) the matter is not a personal one between me and Mr. Greene, but it is the Council of St. Peter's Hall who are proceeding in this matter, and they must be represented by their solicitor, not their Chairman, in dealing with the solicitor of either Mr. Greene or the M.M.T. . . .' He went on: 'If Mr. Greene threatens legal proceedings, the Council is perfectly ready to go into Court and to make public not only the fact of the document of Nov. 22, 1930, but the actual list of 70 livings implicated in that document.' It would appear from subsequent correspondence that Chilton thought it prudent not to put this threat into writing, but he may well have hinted at it in a telephone conversation which he had with Robbins on 27 June, and which he reported to the Council on the following day.

This was the special meeting held on 28 June 1935.587 Neither Adair nor Greene attended, and the resolution declaring that Greene had ceased to be loyal was carried unanimously. But the resolution would not take effect until confirmed by another special meeting to be held on 31 July. Meanwhile the Council authorized Chilton to assure Robbins that the resolution concerned the position of Mr. Greene *only* as a member of the Council and a Trustee of St. Peter's Hall. What was not minuted was that Chilton was privately authorized to tell Robbins that if Greene would now voluntarily resign from the Council and the Trusteeship, 'the steps contemplated by the Council against him will be stopped. . . .'[588] At this stage Robbins showed readiness to conciliate, but he would not go very far. On 3 July he thanked Chilton for his 'kind letter', but said 'Personally, I feel it is impossible to formulate anything against Mr. Greene to try and force his resignation. . . . I propose calling a meeting of the Martyrs Memorial Trustees at an early date to suggest the terms on which a friendly arrangement can be arrived at.' A week later he told Chilton: '. . . Mr. Greene will strongly resent any attempt to exclude him in any way from his position.'[589]

Chavasse himself did not believe for a moment that a friendly arrangement could be arrived at. On 5 July he told Chilton: 'I have learned to expect nothing from the M.M.C.E. Trust except twistings . . . the Council do not promise that they will not in the future take proceedings against Mr. Greene as a Trustee of St. Peter-le-Bailey Church. All that they assure him is that their present proceedings in casting him off the Council and Trusteeship of the Hall have no connection with his being Patron of the Church. . . .' Before long, the formal notices calling the special meeting for 31 July 1935 were sent out by Bowdler to all members of the Council, including Mr. Greene. Once more, confusion was revealed; on 24 July Greene wrote to Chavasse: 'I cannot possibly take my place on the Council of St. Peter's Hall until there is a vacancy. . . . May I remind you that no new Trust Deed can legally be drawn without the concurrence of the M.M.T. and Mrs. Rowcroft. Should your Council proceed to do so Mrs. Rowcroft will claim her £10,000. She is very decided in this matter. The Trustees of the M.M.T. will stand by their Covenant signatures.' Chavasse wrote back at once[590] to assure him that he was 'under a misapprehension', and that he was 'fully entitled to attend a Council Meeting of St. Peter's Hall of which you have been a member since June 12.' Whether Greene interpreted this as a hint that after all he might be retained on the Council is not clear, but on 29 July he wrote that he had sent Chavasse's letter to Mr. Robbins for his opinion, and that he was now going on holiday. So the Council met on 31 July without Mr. Greene[591] and confirmed the resolution. On the same day Bowdler informed Greene that the provisions of Cap. V of the Trust Deed had been complied with, 'and you have ceased to be a member of the Council of St. Peter's Hall and a Trustee of the Hall'.

A few minutes after the special meeting, the Council met in ordinary session. Chavasse was able to report progress in the matter of the advowson. On 16 July Chilton had told him that Chancellor King entirely agreed with the suggestion that transfers of the Advowson should be obtained both from the legal personal representatives of Dean Barlow and from those of the Revd. H. E. Fox. 'However, he did not think that these transfers should be made to you alone, as you are the Incumbent of the Living, but he saw no reason why the Advowson should not be transferred in each case to two or more persons who are now or who will be Trustees of the Hall.' Accordingly, Chavasse and Chilton had been in touch with Sir Montague Barlow, Bt., and the Revd. H. W. Fox, D.S.O., both of whom were quite willing to co-operate. As it happened, it proved possible to eliminate the Barlow family;[592] on 29 July Chilton informed Sir Montague that new documents showed that 'the outstanding legal interest in the Advowson of St. Peter-le-Bailey is vested in the representatives of the Rev. H. E. Fox.' Chavasse now reported to the Council that he and Chilton had interviewed H. W. Fox; 'and he speaking not only for himself but his co-representatives[593] had readily promised to do what was necessary to vest the advowson in Mr. J. G. Legge, the Principal of Wycliffe Hall and the Master, as Trustees of St. Peter's Hall.' The Council naturally approved, and on 23 August 1935 Chilton was able to tell Bowdler that the conveyance of the Advowson by the Fox representatives had been duly executed. To Chavasse this seemed to be at last the deliverance for which he had been yearning.

Meanwhile, Pearman Smith had continued to try to get Greene to sign Lord Gisborough's deed of resignation. On 26 July he had written to Chavasse: 'So far all my efforts to induce Mr. Greene to sign . . . have failed and now I am trying to see what can be done through Lord Gisborough . . . I can only suggest that we continue to be patient as I am convinced in the end he will be induced to sign.' It must have given Chavasse some satisfaction to be able to reply,[594] 'It is difficult when we are dealing with a person who does not seem to be quite sane, and I am sorry for all the trouble to which you have been put. With regard to Mr. Greene, the Council . . . are taking action by means of [the] disloyalty provision in the Trust Deed. . . . We therefore do not need his signature to the Deeds of Resignation. . . .[595] So let us count him out and allow him to retain the present Deeds if he wants to. Could you prepare two new Deeds and ask Lord Gisborough and Canon Foster Pegg to sign them again. . . . At the end of this month we are making big transfers in respect of the mortgage on St. Peter's Hall, and it is essential for us to prove who are the present Trustees. . . .'

There was an implied rebuke in Pearman Smith's reply: [596] 'We recognize that we are no longer Solicitors to the Trustees or to the Council[597] and doubtless you have taken or will take legal advice relative to your proposed course of action from your present Solicitors. In view of the fact that we are not now acting as Solicitors to the Trustees I would prefer any further documents should be prepared by the Solicitors who are now acting or will act for them.' Chavasse's own reply to this was in its way a masterpiece:[598] 'I was not surprised to receive your letter of July 29 requesting that the solicitors to the Council should take over your work as solicitor to the Trustees, as you had already informed me in conversation that when Lord Gisborough (for whom you had acted so long) ceased to be a Trustee of the Hall, it could not reasonably be expected that a firm of solicitors in Walsall could transact the business of a Society in Oxford without an unnecessary expenditure of time and trouble and money. I immediately got into communication with the Trustees of St. Peter's Hall, and I enclose the formal Request and Authority for your firm to hand over all documents and papers relating to the Hall to Mr. C. A. Chilton. . . . May I personally express my thanks to you for the way you have done your level best to help the Hall and straighten things out under most difficult circumstances. That there will remain one or two problems to solve is certainly none of your fault. I hope that as the Hall prospers and flourishes you will always cherish a feeling of satisfaction that you were personally concerned in the first stages of the enterprise.' Pearman Smith was sufficiently mollified to write back: [599] 'I thank you for your expression of appreciation of my past services and I should like to take this opportunity of conveying to you my cordial wishes for the future success of the Hall.'

On 16 August 1935 Chilton informed Bowdler: 'Mr. Pearman Smith has called here and handed to me the original Trust Deeds and Appointments of New Trustees of the Hall. He has not, of course, handed me any Deeds concerning the Advowson, and, in fact, told me that he had received instructions not to do so until he was specifically authorised to do so.' From whom Pearman Smith had received instructions is not clear; presumably from Lord Gisborough. By this time the Martyrs Memorial trustees were beginning to feel uneasy; they must have known from General Adair that Chavasse had something up his sleeve, but they were not sure exactly what it was. On 24 July 1935 their secretary, the Revd. R. R. Neill,[600] had tried to make a personal contact; he wrote to Chavasse that Adair had asked for advice, and suggested that 'it might be advantageous if you and I could have a chat some time soon. I can fully sympathise with you in desiring to get your new Trust Deed in order, and it seems to me that there ought not to be any insuperable difficulty or troublesome corners, except in one case,[601] and it is just possible that we *might* be able to help you a little in this, provided a wise approach can be made.' Chavasse replied stiffly:[602] '. . . I am afraid we must not have a personal meeting, for we should not be meeting for private reasons but as the Hon. Secretary of the Martyrs Memorial Trust and the Chairman of the Council of St. Peter's Hall. My Council absolutely and entirely repudiate any suggestion that St. Peter's Hall has any connection whatsoever with the Martyrs Memorial Trust. The Martyrs Memorial Trust was not one of the parties in the Trust Deed of the Hall.' Two days later Robbins appealed to Chilton: [603] 'I was so keen on Mr. Chavasse meeting Mr. Neill so that all outstanding questions might be at once arranged. Could you kindly arrange this at once?' Getting no help from Chilton, Robbins wrote once more to Chavasse.[604] 'Please, we must have an interview. . . .' The reply, by return of post, was curt: 'No useful purpose would be served by my meeting the M.M.T.'

After this there was an interval. But on 13 September 1935 Messrs. Robbins, Olivey and Lake wrote formally to Chavasse: 'Our attention has been called[605] to the fact that you are asking the Council of St. Peter's Hall to take the view that the Advowson of St. Peter-le-Bailey, Oxford, was never under the patronage of the Oxford Churches Trust, and that in consequence, the transfer of the Advowson to the Revd. D. J. Stather Hunt and others in 1928 was wholly void. We are at a loss to understand on what grounds you base this contention. . . .' Chavasse passed this on to Chilton, who took time to consider. On Wednesday, 23 October 1935 he informed Chavasse that he would be 'able to report to the meeting on Saturday Counsel's further advice as to opening the ball with Messrs. Robbins, Olivey and Lake.' He also mentioned that a question had arisen whether the heirs of Henry Linton might also have a claim to ownership of the Advowson. This worried Chavasse, who replied by return of post: '. . . Will you, please, on Saturday, talk to me privately about this "Canon Linton" business, and not refer to it at the Council Meeting? Brigadier General Adair will be present at the Council Meeting, and we must not allow any suggestion of a hitch to be mentioned in his presence.'

The Council duly met on Saturday, 26 October 1935.[606] Three of the minutes of this meeting may be quoted.

425. . . . the Master reported that the Rev. H. B. Greene had in his possession the deeds of resignation signed by Lord Gisborough and Canon Foster Pegg, as Trustees of St. Peter's Hall, but had refused to assent to these resignations or to return the documents: [607] and further, that he had refused to sign and retained in his possession mandates for the payment of interest to the Midland Bank which had been signed by all the other trustees.[608] The Council requested Mr. Chilton to prepare new deeds of resignation for signature by Lord Gisborough and Canon Foster Pegg, to which their existing co-trustees, with the exception of the Rev. H. B. Greene, who had now ceased to be a Trustee, would give their assent. The matter of taking action to enforce signature of the mandates was deferred to the next meeting.[609]

426. . . . Mr. Chilton stated the views of Counsel as to the Advowson of St. Peter-le-Bailey. He reported that, in accordance with these views, the personal representatives of the late Preb. Fox had executed a Conveyance of the Advowson to the Rev. C. M. Chavasse, the Rev. J. R. S. Taylor and Mr. J. G. Legge: and that Counsel had settled the terms of a letter to Messrs. Robbins, Olivey and Lake, setting out the position taken up by the Council with regard to the Advowson. Mr. Chilton produced the Conveyance for signature by the grantees, and read the letter aforesaid. The Council thereupon decided . . . that Mr. Chilton be authorised to send this letter to Messrs. Robbins, Olivey and Lake. Brig. General Adair expressed a wish to dissociate himself from this matter.

428. . . . The Master reported that he had written to Brig. General Adair, at the request of the Council, asking him if he could see his way to resign from the Trusteeship of the Hall. . . . [General Adair] then explained to the Council that, while he was willing to fall in with the views of the Council,

he felt bound to take into account the strongly-expressed wish of the Martyrs Memorial Trust that he should not resign. He requested that the Master should meet members of the Martyrs Memorial Trust, as already suggested by him: and after further discussion, it was resolved . . . that the Master and Mr. Chilton be empowered to arrange for an interview with the Trust, at which the position could be informally discussed.

On 28 October 1935 Chilton sent Chavasse a copy of the draft letter settled by Chancellor King for sending to Robbins, Olivey and Lake, setting out the position and ending: 'If after considera- tion your clients desire to dispute the title of our clients we shall be obliged if you would write to us fully explaining your views so as to avoid if possible any recourse to the Court.' On the following day Chavasse asked Chilton to wait: 'I think . . . that no letters should go out to Robbins or the other Trustees, regard- ing the Advowson . . . until this further matter of the Linton family has been put through. Would you please hold your hand till then?' By the same post Chavasse wrote to Bishop Martin Linton Smith,[610] explaining about the Rowcroft Deed and the legal question about the ownership of the advowson, and asking him to warn his cousin Capt. Henry Linton, M.C., to do nothing, if approached by anybody other than Linton Smith himself. He ended: 'The M.M.T. by now are aware that something is going on, though they do not know quite what it is. . . . The whole matter is rather interesting, and has its amusing side. I call it a crowning mercy, whereby without going to Court we sever all connection with the Martyrs Memorial Trust and become absolutely free!'

On the following day he[611] wrote to Mr. Neill, explaining that General Adair had begged the Council to allow an interview: 'When he made the same request in the summer, the Council refused leave. . . .[612] At our last meeting, however, they granted me leave to interview the M.M.T., on the understanding that the meeting was purely informal and one to clear away misunder- standing.' He added that he would bring a solicitor and a secretary, and suggested that General Adair should be present. On the same day Chavasse wrote a series of letters, hoping to get ammunition for use against the M.M.T. The first, marked private and confidential, was to E.W. Wykes: 'I am shortly to have an interview with the M.M.T. . . . and there is one fact about which you can inform me which would be useful to me. As you know, you cannot trust the Martyrs Memorial to tell the truth. I believe the Martyrs Memorial have still some, though infinitesimal, representation on the Governing Bodies of the various schools. . . .' He specially wanted to know whether there was any provision for *permanent* representation. The second letter was to Mr. Guy Johnson, of the National Church League, asking whether the M.M.T. had any official representation on the Governing Body of Clifton Theological College. The third was to the Revd. H. D. Hooper, Secretary for the African Missions of the C.M.S., asking whether the M.M.T. was officially represented in any way on the Council of a school in Kenya[613] which it had formerly supported; 'as you know, it is impossible to trust what you are told by the M.M.T. itself.'

The answers were not specially helpful. Wykes was able to state[614] that the M.M.T. had continuing representation (one out of fourteen) on the Central Committee of the Schools Trust and also (two out of twelve) on the Governing Bodies of the Schools, but his letter was cautious: 'I should not . . . wish it to be thought that I had in any way given you information in regard to the M.M.T. to assist you in any hostile action against them, because the relations between that Trust and myself are perfectly satisfactory, and from the time I carried through the complete reconstruction of the government and management of the Schools I have had practically no difficulty with the Memorial Trust. At the same time I am not in the slightest degree surprised . . . at the fact that you do not wish to have the Memorial Trust connected with St. Peter's Hall at all, and that Trust would not be in any way surprised to hear that said by me. Of course while one feels as one does about the M.M.T., the individual Members of that Trust were in fact entirely under the thumb and domination of Mr. Warrington and really knew nothing about his gigantic financial schemes.' The reply from Mr. Guy Johnson was perhaps of some negative use: [615] 'The M.M.T. has not now, nor during the last two years, had any connection with the [Clifton] College. When there were debts upon it they repudiated all responsibility for its affairs . . . when the crash came, I, in response to a request from Archdeacon Storr, Canon Mackean, Archdeacon Sharpe and others, set to work to see if I could do anything to save it from destruction. . . .' No answer arrived from Mr. Hooper until 12 November. He stated that he had no *direct* knowledge of Limuru School, but confirmed Chavasse's belief that the M.M.T. 'did nothing to save the School, but left it (like St. Peter's Hall) to its fate.'[616]

On 5 November Neill wrote suggesting 'a meal and a heart to

221

heart chat. . . . I fancy there has been a great deal of misunderstanding and that you have been affected by this both
towards the Trust and myself personally. . . .' It is certainly possible that Chavasse had suspected him of being in some kind of
league with Mr. Greene; and it was now that Chavasse instructed
Chilton to send the agreed letter to Robbins, Olivey and Lake,[617]
without further delay. A week earlier, Chavasse had sent Mrs.
Rowcroft a copy of the Seventh Annual Report, and had taken
the chance to write her another letter: [618] 'Now that we have
survived and appear to be in a fair way to becoming securely
established, the Martyrs Memorial Trust are using your name
to press that one of their number should be a Trustee of the
Hall. They affirm that your benefaction of £10,000, which was
so largely responsible for the inception of the Hall in its first
stages, entitles them to such representation; and they declare
that it is your wish that the Martyrs Memorial Trust should
thus represent your interests in safeguarding the money for the
use of the Hall. I write to know if it is *really* your wish that a
member of the Martyrs Memorial Trust, and one associated with
the financial transactions of Mr. Warrington, should be a
Trustee of the property of St. Peter's Hall? Such a Trustee would
cause us obvious embarrassment and difficulty. The names of
Mr. Warrington and the Martyrs Memorial Trust are so intimately connected and so deeply suspect in the public mind, that
it is impossible to make any large appeal on behalf of the Hall
so long as moneys donated to St. Peter's are entrusted to the
custody of anyone known to be an old associate of the former
and a member of the latter. In view of your letter to me of last
January, I find it difficult to believe that after your painful
experience you can wish either your own benefaction or the
whole property of the Hall to be under such guardianship.' He
added that he was shortly to meet the M.M.T. On 8 November
1935 Mrs. Rowcroft replied. The letter was typewritten, and had
probably been drafted by a solicitor. 'I am in receipt of your
letter of Oct. 29, and as the history of the Martyrs Memorial
Trust during the last few years has caused me to lose all confidence in it, I can understand your writing ["The names of Mr.
Warrington . . . member of the latter"]. Now, the motives which
influenced me in giving £10,000 to found St. Peter's Hall, and the
conditions on which that gift was made, are not in any wise
altered or invalidated by the untrustworthiness of those to whom
the money was entrusted. I was given definitely to understand
that St. Peter's Hall was to be a B.C.M.S. College and that the

Principal was to be an active member of the same. When I was informed that you were not a member of that Society, I was given various reasons for your selection, and my objections were over-ridden by a very emphatic promise that the next Principal would belong to that Society. These promises were given not only by an individual, but by the whole Trust, and were embodied in a Deed of Covenant, legally executed by all ten members of the Trust. As these promises have not been kept, I consider that the £10,000 should be refunded to me and my name should be taken off the Building.'

Chavasse made no reply to this until 20 November. He then wrote: [619] 'Thank you for . . . letting me know your mind so frankly. You will believe, I know, that none of us in Oxford had the slightest idea that your munificent benefaction was only given to the Hall on condition that St. Peter's was a B.C.M.S. College. Neither, I am certain, was Canon Stather Hunt (. . . a life governor and staunch supporter of the C.M.S.) . . . Certainly, when in the summer of 1927 (acting on the advice of Bishop Knox) he approached my Father to see if your benefaction could be utilised towards my Father's scheme . . . he made no mention whatsoever of there being a B.C.M.S. condition; or my father – being a strong supporter of the C.M.S. – would not have entertained the project for a single moment. The then Patrons of St. Peter-le-Bailey Church have told me that this condition was not even hinted at to them, when they agreed to transfer the living to the Trustees of St. Peter's Hall. Nor was it known to the Trustees of Hannington Hall (built with C.M.S. money) when they gave that fine hall to St. Peter's. Nor yet was I informed of it when as Rector of St. Peter-le-Bailey I agreed to sell the Rectory and Garden to the Trustees. . . .

'These facts will assure you that we in Oxford have acted in good faith from first to last; and we have been as deeply injured as yourself by the secret and dishonourable diplomacy of the Martyrs Memorial Trust. Consider the wrong done to me personally in their executing such a document,[620] and yet encouraging me to raise (up to the present) no less a sum than £65,000, chiefly from people who would not have given to a B.C.M.S. College; and in memory of my Father who would never have lent his name to such an undertaking. I am also horrified to find that – had the secret covenant taken effect – I should have obtained from the University of Oxford a licence for the Hall on false pretences; as it is most unlikely that Convocation would have given leave for a B.C.M.S. College. . . .

'I know it will be the wish of my Council – even as it is my own – that you should receive honourable treatment at our hands. Though, of course, there can be no legal obligation whatsoever on our part, you shall not have any cause to complain of us; as we both have reason to complain of the Martyrs Memorial Trust. I shall, therefore, bring your letter before the next meeting of the Council in February 1936. At the same time you will, I am sure, understand that we can do nothing in the matter while we are still loaded with a debt of £47,000, consequent upon the collapse of the M.M.T. – a debt we have reduced from the original figure of £97,000. When we are free of all liabilities and the Hall is safe, then – if it is still your wish – I can well believe that the Council of St. Peter's Hall will prefer to make every effort to refund to you this £10,000; even though it will mean that for a considerable period the Hall will have to forego that endowment of which it stands in such serious need.'

There can be no doubt that in writing on these lines Chavasse intended to take the wind out of the sails of the Revd. H. B. Greene and his supporters on the Martyrs Memorial Trust. At the same time, he almost certainly hoped that Mrs. Rowcroft would be moved to generosity; she might tell him to forget about the £10,000.[621] However that might be, he was now prepared to meet Mr. Neill, and he did so on 22 November 1935. What happened can be seen from a letter which he sent to Neill on the following day: 'I was very grateful to you for so kindly entertaining me to lunch yesterday at the National Club; and I think our talk together has cleared up misconceptions, and made the issue quite plain regarding the position of Brig. General Adair. . . . I enclose a copy of the letter received by me from Mrs. Rowcroft, and dated November 8th, 1935.

(1) The letter makes it quite clear that she does not desire a member of the M.M.T. to represent her interests . . . on the Trusteeship of the Hall; but that in this matter she will deal directly with the Council of the Hall. . . .

(2) The letter also makes it plain that if a member of the M.M.T. is honourably to discharge the covenanted obligations of that Trust to Mrs. Rowcroft, he must insist on the Hall being a B.C.M.S. College and the next Master an active member of the B.C.M.S. This means that we could never contemplate a member of the M.M.T., involved in this covenant, being a Patron of St. Peter-le-Bailey Church or a Trustee of the Hall. As you know, it has always been the intention that the two offices should be held together. Brig. General Adair is only a Trustee of the Hall, and

has no say in the appointment of the next Master; but we cannot get on with our revised Trust Deed, in which the Patrons of the Church and the Trustees of the Hall will be the same people, until Brig. General Adair has retired, as he wishes to do. I am quite willing for you to inform the M.M.T. that it is our intention to fill the vacancy caused by General Adair's resignation by asking Prebendary Hinde[622] not only to take his place as a Trustee, but to become a Patron of the Church.[623] Brig. General Adair is now the only representative of the M.M.T. on the Trusteeship of the Hall. We also believe that in the near future Lord Gisborough, Canon Foster Pegg and Mr. Greene will be declared in Court not to be the rightful Patrons of the Church. It is obvious to me, therefore, that the M.M.T. have nothing to lose in the substitution of Prebendary Hinde for Brig. General Adair as Trustee of the Hall, and his further appointment as Patron of the Church.'[624]

On 25 November 1935 Neill replied: 'I feel sure that [the M.M. Trustees] will be very pleased to know that you contemplate inviting Prebendary Hinde to be a Trustee and Patron. I am very pleased that we were able to have a chat at the National Club . . . and I earnestly trust that the result of it will be complete unanimity and harmony of action between all those concerned. . . .' So Neill was happy, and Prebendary Hinde was willing to help.[625] Chavasse too was happy, but not for precisely the same reasons as Mr. Neill. Three weeks earlier he had told Chilton: [626] 'Mr. Robbins . . . turned up in Oxford on Saturday, and paid Mr. Cumming and myself a visit. He was quite in a fog about the Advowson of St. Peter-le-Bailey, seeing that the Deeds supplied to him by Mr. Pearman Smith were inadequate to show the position. He was very frightened about litigation, and I believe he would do anything to keep the matter out of the Courts. When I pointed out to him that it was imperative that we went before a Judge . . . he practically promised that if the case were made plain to him he would get the nominal Trustees to sign a paper to present to the Judge saying that the nominal Trustees were quite satisfied.'[627] Now on 25 November he wrote to Chilton: '. . . after a talk I had with the Secretary of the M.M.T., I believe that they will come to terms if they are pushed. Once we institute proceedings I think you will have Mr. Robbins coming round and promising a settlement. . . .'

At this time Chavasse was hoping that in a very short time the revised Trust Deed could be settled. At the special meeting of the Council on 28 June 1935 copies of Chilton's draft had been

handed to the members, and at the ordinary meeting of 31 July
certain alterations were discussed and approved. Chilton was
thereupon authorised to submit the amended draft to Counsel.
Then at the meeting of 26 October he reported that he would
prepare, for submission to Counsel, a clause providing that the
Trustees of Hannington Hall and of St. Peter's Hall should be
the same persons. There was then no reason to think that this
would cause difficulty. Meanwhile Chavasse was impatient of
delay in putting pressure on the M.M.T. On 20 December 1935
he wrote to Chilton urging him to get on with it, and was not
too pleased when Chilton replied[628] 'I have been informed that
Messrs. Robbins are laying the whole case before their Counsel
for his opinion, and, in the circumstances. I think I ought not to
press them at once. . . .' One reason why he had become impatient was that on 17 December Neill had written a letter which
was not what he had expected: '. . . while the Trustees have
deep sympathy with you in the difficulties which you are so cour-
ageously facing, they have instructed me to write to Mrs. Rowcroft direct before taking the step which you have suggested. . . .'
It was not until 21 January 1936 that Neill informed him that
'Mrs. Rowcroft has not replied to my letter and I think we are
quite entitled to take this as implying that she has no objection
to General Adair's retirement.' Accordingly, Neill was prepared
to report to the Martyrs Memorial Trust at their next meeting on
12 Febuary that there was no barrier here.

On 1 February the Council of St. Peter's met[629] and passed the
following resolution: 'In the event of the retirement of Brig.
General Adair from the Trusteeship of the Hall, the Council
recommends the remaining Trustees of the Hall to appoint
Prebendary H. W. Hinde as one of the four Trustees of St. Peter's
Hall.' Chavasse sent a copy of this resolution to Neill, and on
10 February followed it up with a letter stressing that it was
vital to get through Adair's resignation very quickly: 'I was
dining with Dr. Norwood last night, and he told me that a writ
had been served upon Mr. Warrington, who is bringing, among
others, the M.M.T. into any proceedings in the Court that may
eventuate.[630] I have always dreaded lest this might happen. . . .'
Just what occurred at the M.M.T. meeting on 12 February 1936
is not quite clear; Adair himself thought 'the matter was dealt
with',[631] but Neill himself warned Chavasse[632] that the Martyrs
Memorial Trustees had been too busy to deal properly with the
resignation of General Adair. It is quite likely that the M.M.
Trustees had deliberately become awkward because their solicitor

had at last come under some pressure about the advowson. At the end of January[633] Chilton had told Chavasse 'Counsel now advises that Messrs. Robbins, Olivey and Lake's clients should be pressed to come into the open, and advises sending of the further letter' . . . of which he enclosed a copy. It ended: 'Unless you feel you can modify the position adopted in your letter to Rev. C. M. Chavasse dated 13 September 1935 . . . no alternative but to instruct Counsel to settle proceedings with a view to removing any question as to our clients' title.' Chilton had been authorised by the Council on 1 February to send this letter, and to prepare to start proceedings if a reply from Robbins were not received within a fortnight.

In these matters, the Council had done what Chavasse wanted. It had not been so willing to follow his lead in the matter of Mrs. Rowcroft's £10,000. He had reported her letter of 8 November 1935, and had read out his own reply. The Council considered that he had been quixotic in suggesting that the money might ever be refunded; moreover Judge Dowdall and Chilton held that to do so would be illegal. A resolution was passed in unambiguous terms: 'In as much as Mrs. Rowcroft's benefaction was offered to and accepted by the Council of St. Peter's Hall for the benefit of the Hall, without conditions, the Council are advised by their legal advisers that they are bound to retain the benefaction on the Trusts for which it was received.' It remained for Chavasse to break the news to Mrs. Rowcroft. This he did three days later: '. . . when I made known to them your wish that the £10,000 should be refunded to you, our legal members at once informed us that we had no power even to discuss such a proposition. They told us that your benefaction had become part of a Charitable Trust which we were bound to administer under the terms of the Trust Deed of the Hall . . . and that the Council would be guilty of a breach of trust if we paid away any part of that Trust money. Indeed, they affirmed that we had no more power to return your benefaction than to make a present of £10,000 to any member of the Council. Your lawyers will tell you the same; and assure you that – whatever our personal wishes may be – our duty as trustees of charitable property ties our hands completely in this matter.' He concluded with a final attempt to conciliate: 'I am glad to think that St. Peter's will continue to have one range of its buildings named "The Rowcroft Building"; and you will, I know, not think hardly of us for not being able to fall in with your wishes in a very difficult and most distressing matter. . . . Naturally, I am upset at the whole miserable business, and sympathise with your indignation.' His sympathy was wasted: Mrs. Rowcroft did not think it worth while to send any reply. She died in 1941, leaving £1,688,138 gross; net personalty £1,623,462. She left £12,000 to the B.C.M.S., but nothing to the Martyrs Memorial Trust or to St. Peter's Hall.

Meanwhile, there was the matter of the Linton interest in the advowson to be dealt with. On 11 February 1936 Chilton told Chavasse that Counsel 'states that if by any chance the Court should hold that some interest in the Advowson reverted to the estate of the late Canon Linton, it would not give the Trustees their costs of the proceedings unless, at the date of the Writ, every known interest was vested in them.' Luckily there was no difficulty here; Bishop Linton Smith saw to that. By the end of March Chilton was able to send a Conveyance, duly executed by the members of the Linton family,[634] for signature by Chavasse, Legge and Taylor, and this became effective on 3 April 1936. On that same day Chavasse, knowing that the way was now clear for legal action, wrote two letters. The first was to Chilton: 'Did I make the following quite clear – namely, that if, when you serve the writ on Mr. Robbins, he then wants to come to an agreement by which the Martyrs Memorial Trust will not contest their case, we shall agree to no such arrangements until we have in our hands the resignation from the Trusteeship of both Lord Gisborough and Brig. General Adair.'[635] The other letter was to Neill, protesting against the delay: 'I cannot believe that the M.M.T. are wilfully obstructing our efforts to get straight . . . but certainly the unaccountable delay in this matter is holding everything up at our end . . . I am beginning to feel like a man let down into a miry pit, and all the help I get from the Trust who let me down is to be pushed back at every effort I make to climb out.'[636]

On 30 April 1936 Chilton sent Chavasse a copy of 'the suggested endorsement of the Writ of Summons . . . as settled by Counsel.[637] I propose to issue the writ at an early date. . . . I think it would be wise at the same time to inform Messrs. Robbins, Olivey and Lake of the deed recently executed by the Linton family.' The writ was issued on 14 May 1936. On the previous day Chavasse had again written to Neill: 'The delay has taken a more serious turn owing to the publication in the papers of the heavy financial loss sustained by Lord Gisborough. . . . What do you consider will be the effect on the public, if, after reading that the Gisborough Estates Company has gone bankrupt, they are told[638] that Lord Gisborough is one of our Trustees?' Two days later

Chavasse thought it expedient to use a little butter on Mr. Robbins. After informing him that Chilton would be sending a deed of resignation to Adair, and asking him to send a similar deed to Lord Gisborough, he ended 'May I take this opportunity of thanking you for your good offices in this matter? I am sure I am right in seeing your guiding hand behind the freedom that St. Peter's Hall has now gained.' It would seem that when he wrote in these terms he had just heard[639] that on 13 May the Martyrs Memorial Trustees had at last approved Adair's resignation, though he received no formal notification of this until Neill sent it on 21 May. He now regarded Neill as a friend. On 22 May Chavasse wrote to him: '. . . I would thank you warmly for your help . . . and am glad that you and the Martyrs Memorial are not a party to a bewildering sequel which has certainly made an unpleasant impression upon us in Oxford. . . . The situation is becoming past bearing with these extraordinary procedures of unauthorised persons detaining and holding up Deeds of Resignation. Mr. Robbins is neither the solicitor of St. Peter's Hall Trustees, nor the solicitor of the principals with whom these deeds deal[640] – viz. Lord Gisborough, Canon Foster Pegg and Brig. General Adair.' He followed this up three days later by telling Robbins '. . . you have no legal right whatsoever to detain documents which do not belong to you or any of your clients.'[641]

Robbins at last began to give way. On 4 June 1936 his firm sent to Chilton's firm[642] a letter which deserves quotation in full:—

'We are enclosing herewith two Deeds of Retirement executed by our Clients, the Reverend Foster Pegg and General Adair, respectively, whereby they retire from the trusts of St. Peter's Hall, and we are obtaining the execution of Lord Gisborough to his Deed and will send you the same provided you do not ask for any costs against us in the proceedings you have commenced as we do not propose to enter any appearance thereto.

'At the same time we would point out that our Clients are only taking this course because the conduct of your clients has made it practically impossible for them to continue their trusteeship, and we desire to register the strongest possible protest on behalf of the Martyrs' Memorial and Church of England Trust with regard to the manner in which your clients are behaving and have behaved in this matter.

'As your Clients are well aware they have seised [sic] upon a legal technicality in order to obtain an advantage they were never intended to have and which is quite contrary to the wishes of the creator of the trust.

229

'We need perhaps scarcely point out that the Reverend Christopher Maude Chavasse was appointed to the Benefice of St. Peter-le-Bailey by persons whom [sic] he is now contending had no power to make any such appointment.

'With regard to the sum of £10,000 which our Clients the Martyrs' Memorial and Church of England Trust obtained from Mrs. Rowcroft and handed over to St. Peter's Hall it is now clear that the conditions subject to which such sum was obtained and handed over cannot be complied with, and we must ask that such sum should now be returned to our clients.'

On 6 June Chavasse wrote to Robbins that as soon as Lord Gisborough's deed of resignation had been received, Chilton 'will see you regarding the Advowson of the Church, and I am sure that a satisfactory arrangement can be arrived at.' It is by no means sure that Chilton himself would have approved this letter, for on 12 June he was writing to Chavasse: '. . . unless you receive Lord Gisborough's deeds of retirement this week I consider that I should write to Messrs. Robbins & Co. . . . and call upon them to return the Writ to us, and we will serve it on each defendant personally.[643] I do not believe that we shall get any satisfaction out of these people unless we show that we mean business, and I am quite sure that you have been put off long enough.' Chavasse at once told Chilton to go ahead, but there was still delay. On 24 June Chavasse wrote to him again: 'I phoned Mr. Robbins to know why the informal meeting between him and you, which I thought was arranged, had not come off. He says he thinks everything could be arranged in ten minutes, if he could see you. . . .' Two days later Chilton replied: 'Mr. Robbins, of course, has not made any attempt to see or talk to me, so today I rang him up and asked for the Deed of Retirement, and he stated again that he could only part with this if the matter of the Advowson was settled. I had a long talk with him, and eventually wrote him a letter.[644] He told me that if the question of the costs was not pressed in any way the three Defendants would not appear to the proceedings, and that the Order required could be obtained "in default of defence" and I agreed, but pointed out that the Defendants must either be served with the writ personally, or he, as a solicitor, must accept service on their behalf. As soon as Mr. Robbins found that we were prepared to let him off the question of costs of the action he started talking about Tarleton saying that he hoped there would be no trouble about this living being properly vested in the M.M.T., and I think his only intention can be to hold up the matter still further by dragging this in, and I have therefore told him that the offer to let them off the costs and general unpleasantness is only made on the understanding that no other matters are dragged in. I hope – though I rather doubt – that the Deed of Retirement may be in your hands by Monday, and I shall advise that if the terms offered to him now are not strictly complied with, you should not be put off any longer but, if necessary, proceed against him personally, as an official of the Court, for with-holding the Writ.'

On the same day, 26 June 1936, Robbins returned the original Writ to Chilton, but his firm's letter continued: 'One other point, we would mention the Advowson of Tarleton, and we enclose you a copy of a Deed of Covenant which our clients, as Trustees of St. Peter's Hall, entered into with our clients, the Trustees of the Martyrs Memorial Trust. We shall be glad to hear . . . that your clients, the present Trustees of St. Peter's Hall, will sign if necessary the document vesting the Advowson of Tarleton in our clients, the M.M.T. On receiving an undertaking from you on both these points [costs and Tarleton] we will immediately hand over the resignation of Lord Gisborough.'

To explain these references to Tarleton, it is necessary to go back to 19 February 1935. On that date Chavasse wrote to Mr. R. Clayton, Registrar of the Diocese of Blackburn: 'I am Master of St. Peter's Hall, and Chairman of its Council. I was surprised to read in the latest Crockford[645] that St. Peter's Hall were Patrons of the living of Tarleton, Preston, Lancs. I looked up an old Crockford and discovered that in 1927 the patrons were the Executors of the late Archdeacon Fletcher.' He asked for information, and discovered that St. Peter's Hall had been listed in Crockford as Patrons in 1933 and 1934. A complication was that under the provisions of the Benefices (Purchase of Rights of Patronage) Measure 1933, the Parochial Church Council of Tarleton was thinking of exercising its legal right to purchase the Advowson; alternatively, the Blackburn Diocesan Board would be very ready to take over the patronage. Prima facie, it seemed to Chavasse that there was no reason why St. Peter's Hall should not come to an amicable arrangement either with the parish or with the diocese, but on 25 February 1935 he had a letter from Archdeacon Fletcher's heir, Mr. M. H. R. Fletcher: 'If I may say so, I am rather perturbed to hear of the possibility of the transference of the advowson to the Diocesan Patronage Board. I must say that when the advowson was sold to St. Peter's Hall, I had hopes of a close connection between the Hall and the Parish . . . a direct and personal touch. It was not chance or price that guided me in the decision to sell the advowson to a benefactor[646] of St. Peter's Hall. I thought the religious outlook of the Trustees was in accord with the simple faith and leanings of the parishioners. . . .'

In the following months the Tarleton P.C.C., in spite of division of opinion among the parishioners, definitely decided to purchase the advowson, but it could do so only if it could raise the money, and in fact it failed to do so.[647] Meanwhile on 18 March 1935 Chilton informed Chavasse that he had discovered from Pearman Smith that 'The purchase money for this advowson was provided by the Martyrs Memorial Trust and the purchase took place in 1931. With the Deeds there is a Deed of Covenant entered into by the then Trustees of St. Peter's Hall with the whole of the Trustees of the M.M.T. whereby the Trustees of St. Peter's Hall covenanted to hold the said Advowson in Trust for the Martyrs Memorial Trustees and to present thereto the person nominated by them.'[648] On the following day Chavasse told Chilton 'What we really want to find out is whether the living of Tarleton (as we think) was transferred to the Trustees of St. Peter's Hall who happened to be certain gentlemen; or . . . to certain gentlemen who happened to be Trustees of St. Peter's Hall. I think that in view of Mr. Fletcher's letter the former is the case, and most certainly it was the intention of Mr. Fletcher to transfer the living to the Trustees of St. Peter's Hall. . . .'

That was still the position on 11 February 1936, when Mr. Neill wrote to Chavasse about Tarleton: 'In connection with its registration there is a letter from Mr. Warrington, declaring that the advowson really belonged to the Martyrs Memorial Trust notwithstanding its association with St. Peter's Hall, and that he adopted the course of putting it into the name of the . . . Trustees of St. Peter's Hall in accordance with the policy which he followed at that time of registering certain advowsons belonging to the Trust in the name of educational institutions which were controlled by the Trust.[649] The amount paid for the Advowson was £1,442 and the whole of this sum was paid by the Martyrs Memorial and Church of England Trust . . . we feel sure you will kindly help us to get this matter set right . . . I may add that the schools have acted along these lines with the Trust in every case and without hesitation. . . .'[650] He ended by stressing that no parish had yet been claimed as its own possession by any of the schools, and suggested that if St. Peter's Hall really wanted Tarleton it should pay for it.

Chavasse thought it politic to conceal from Neill how much he already knew about Tarleton. He replied[651] that he was 'in a fog about the whole matter. . . . As far as the position of the Council of St. Peter's Hall is concerned, you will readily understand they can do nothing until they have full information before them. The Council is composed of a body of men distinguished for their attainments, proberty [sic], and qualities of administration. They will, I know, take no step until (a) they know the full facts of the case; and (b) their legal advisers have assured them that any step they contemplate is in order. . . .' On the same day Chavasse wrote to Chilton: '. . . My view is that when we discover all the facts, we shall find (a) that the Trustees of St. Peter's Hall have no power to alienate trust property, even if the donors ask for it back again; and (b) that Mr. Fletcher . . . was under the impression that he was conveying the living to the Hall, *and not the M.M. Trust*; and that we cannot be parties to a fraud. I have not (as you will see) said these things to Mr. Neill.'

On 13 February 1936 Neill told Chavasse that he did not think the M.M. Trustees 'would mind in the slightest whether they had the Advowson or the cash, but the Capital A/c cannot be completed until this detail is agreed between us. . . .' Both of Neill's letters gave the impression that the matter needed to be settled quickly, and Chavasse was surprised to hear from Robbins, a week later,[652] that 'There is no urgency whatever in the matter, and nothing need be done, at any rate for the present. . . .' Moreover, five days later Robbins declared: 'There is no necessity for you to call a Meeting of your Council[653] for there is nothing further remaining to be done and you should not have been troubled in the matter. . . .' This change of front seemed suspicious; Chavasse jumped to the conclusion that the M.M.T., hearing that the Tarleton P.C.C. was likely to exercise its statutory power to buy the advowson back, were hoping, as being the real owners, to negotiate direct with the P.C.C.[654] There is no evidence that this suspicion was justified; it is much more likely that Robbins had already had the bright idea of bringing the advowson of Tarleton in with that of St. Peter-le-Bailey as part of the price which St. Peter's Hall would have to pay for a final settlement,[655] as he proposed in his letter of 26 June 1936.

To that letter Chilton replied immediately: [656] 'We will thank you . . . to hand over the Deed of Resignation of Lord Gisborough . . . as we cannot allow this to be made the subject of yet another bargain. Our clients are tired of the way they are being treated.' Three days later Robbins modified his position: '. . . we shall be prepared to hand over the Deed of Resignation and [not to defend the proceedings] in exchange for an assurance by you' about costs. Chilton sent Chavasse a copy of this letter, with a caution: 'I think it is necessary to word very carefully any . . . undertaking [about costs] because Mr. Greene, of course, may not be amenable and wish to fight the action. . . .' On 2 July 1936 Chavasse was able to write almost jubilantly to Chilton: 'I am glad to see that Mr. Robbins is climbing down.' The decisive point was that Chavasse himself had just been to Yorkshire to see Lord Gisborough: 'He had no idea that his resignation was being used as a bargain, and was horrified at the idea. He said "When I resign, I resign" . . . I am anxious that Lord Gisborough should not be caused any trouble or anxiety. He is nearly 80, and far from well. He is also extremely well disposed towards us. . . .'[657] On the following day Chilton sent Robbins a letter from Lord Gisborough, conveyed by Chavasse, and at last Robbins had no option but to hand over the Deed of Resignation.

The way was at last open for the appointment of the new Trustees whom Chavasse wanted. On 12 February 1936 he had written to Bishop Linton Smith about the Advowson of St. Peter-le-Bailey 'I am glad to say that we are almost ready to bring the matter to its final issue. This means that we can soon appoint our four proper Trustees,[658] and I believe (in confidence) that these will be yourself, Dr. Pickard-Cambridge, Sir Thomas Inskip and Prebendary Hinde. . . .' On 25 May 1936 he wrote to Hinde: '. . . we are very anxious to obtain [Sir Thomas Inskip's] consent to become one of our Trustees. I would like to add that it was the Bishop of Rochester's special request to me that you and Sir Thomas should be associated with him on the Trusteeship of the Hall. I have met Sir Thomas Inskip once, some years ago, when he dined in the Hall before addressing an Evangelical Meeting of undergraduates.[659] He knows about the Hall and is interested in it. But you know him far better than I do. [Please write to him.] You can assure him that we shall not expect him to attend meetings, and that the position will give him no trouble except when it comes to the appointment of a new Master.' Three days later Chavasse wrote direct to Inskip: '. . . if we possessed your name as one of our four Trustees, it would give great confidence in the country and encouragement to our friends. . . . I would once more emphasise the fact that our request will not involve you in any responsibility, financial or otherwise, save that you may be called upon some day to appoint a new Master to the Hall[660] and, of course, to fill a vacancy if one of your fellow Trustees resigned or died.'[661] On 3 June 1936 Inskip replied: 'At my time of life I am resigning positions which I hold as Trustee, but I feel you have made out a convincing case, and I shall be very happy to accept your invitation.'

So the position was as follows. At the end of 1934 there were eight Trustees (Chavasse, Adair, Gisborough, Greene, Foster Pegg, Legge, Pickard-Cambridge, Taylor). Greene had been got rid of in 1935; now in early July 1936 Adair, Foster Pegg and Gisborough had gone. That left four Trustees (Chavasse, Legge, Pickard-Cambridge, Taylor). In order to keep the number down to four and yet to bring in the new members, deeds were executed on 28 July 1936 by which Chavasse, Legge and Taylor gave up their Trusteeship and were succeeded by Bishop Linton Smith, Sir Thomas Inskip and Prebendary Hinde. By that time the whole financial outlook for the Hall had been changed, in a way not foreseen when the new members had been approached.

Here it is necessary to go back to the Annual Meeting of the Council held immediately after the Special Meeting on 28 June 1935.[662] These were the only Council meetings ever attended by Lord Nuffield. He had been more than satisfied with the arrangements made for the erection and unveiling of the Emily Morris Memorial,[663] and he soon showed an increasing interest in the Hall. On 15 June 1935 Chavasse wrote to Hobbs: 'Lord Nuffield told me he intended to consult you how best to help St. Peter's Hall. His most generous suggestion was that he should take on the mortgage on the Hall now held by the Legal and General Assurance Society, asking only the trifling interest of 2%. . . . His munificent offer is so timely and overwhelming. . . .' Hobbs seems to have advised against this particular proposal. Instead, Nuffield gave the Hall an outright present of £12,161 to pay off the debts on the Loan Account and the Playing Field Account; this of course in addition to his previous gift of £10,000. His idea was that an outright gift like this could and should be used as the basis for a new appeal; his taking over the mortgage would not have encouraged anybody else to subscribe. This was reported to the Council on 28 June; it was 'resolved with acclamation that the warmest thanks of the Council be accorded to Lord Nuffield for his most generous and timely benefactions . . . which have relieved them of the grave anxieties which have beset them during the past two years.' It was also reported that the Legal and General had refused to lower their rate of interest from $4\frac{1}{2}\%$ to 4%, so the Council decided to pay their mortgage off at the earliest possible moment, and instead to accept the offer of the Midland Bank to lend £50,000 on the security of the buildings of the Hall at bank rate minimum 4% maximum 5%.

In fact, Chavasse was able to do better than that. On 26 July he and Cumming were invited to have a talk with Mr. A. B. Gillett, the manager of Barclays Bank Cornmarket branch, who pointed out that, if asked to help, Barclays would have been willing to lend £50,000 at an even lower rate of interest. Gillett asked Chavasse to explain this to his Governing Body; moreover, having discovered that Nuffield, an old acquaintance of his was now on that Governing Body, Gillett took the trouble to write to him personally about the matter.[664] Chavasse reported all this to the Council on 31 July 1935, with the additional information that the Midland Bank were now prepared to reduce the minimum rate of interest to 3½%. After consideration, the Council decided to confirm their acceptance of the Midland Bank's offer, at the new minimum rate, but authorised Chavasse to write a polite letter to Gillett 'thanking him for the courtesy St. Peter's Hall had received at the hands of all connected with the Bank during the past seven years, and assuring him that it was special and fortuitous circumstances alone that have now necessitated the transfer of the banking account of the Hall.' On the following day, Chavasse told Hobbs what had happened: 'I purposely have not answered your letter about Barclays Bank till after the Council Meeting yesterday. . . . I regret more than I can say this attempt to bring personal relationships into the banking transactions of the Hall. . . . None of us cares a brass farthing whether we bank with X, Y or Z. . . . Our sole object is to secure the best terms possible for the Hall. . . . It was believed that 4% was the lowest interest that could be obtained from any bank; and we were not then aware that Banks had begun to undercut each other. If dog does eat dog, we were quite prepared to benefit by a chop. Mr. Gillett informed the Hon. Treasurer and myself, on July 26, that he knew we should communicate his suggestion of 3½% to the Midland Bank. We did so; and as the Midland Bank agreed to the reduced interest, there seemed no reason why the present arrangement already made with them should be altered.'

Hobbs replied at once:[665] 'Thus the whole matter is closed; but before it is forgotten, I would like to congratulate you very sincerely on your financial astuteness. I am supposed to know something about finance, but your success in obtaining an interest rate of 3½% minimum has rather undermined my self-confidence. My firm impression was that 4% was the lowest limit to which any Bank would go; and this impression, I know, is shared by everyone with whom I have discussed the point. You have shown us we were all wrong. . . .'

This episode can have done Chavasse no harm at all in his relations with Lord Nuffield; it may even have paved the way for what happened at the Encaenia Garden Party on 24 June 1936. It was a great day for Chavasse. On the previous day he had heard that he had been awarded the O.B.E. (Military Division) for his services as a Territorial Army Senior Chaplain; at the Encaenia his friend E. M. Walker[666] was given the honorary degree of D.Litt. In the afternoon a garden party was held in the grounds of St. John's, which was celebrating the third centenary of Laud's Canterbury Quadrangle, and it was a specially splendid occasion, replacing and outdoing the usual Vice-Chancellor's garden party. The weather was perfect, the gardens at their best. The band of the Irish Guards was cheerful, the strawberries and the ices were more than adequate. It was in these surroundings that Nuffield (resplendent in the robes of an Honorary D.C.L.) took Chavasse aside and told him that he was going to send him a cheque for £50,000. According to Cumming, all that Chavasse could do was to goggle at Nuffield and to stammer out 'B-b-but, can you afford it?' Chavasse's own account[667] was that since Nuffield had promised to send him the cheque on the next day, he went home in a daze and spent the night in prayer that Lord Nuffield might not die before morning.

Lord Nuffield did not die before morning, and his cheque went directly to the Midland Bank. Chavasse's own feelings can be judged from the letter which he dashed off to Nuffield: [668] 'My dear Lord Nuffield. If I lived 100 years I could never find words to express my thanks to you for founding St. Peter's Hall in Oxford – for that is what you have done; and if I wrote a letter every day I could never adequately put on paper what I feel like today or let you know in the least degree how full to bursting my heart is with gratitude. Such a burden has been lifted off me that I feel like a baloon [sic] with the ballast cast overboard. I go about on tip-toe, every now and then wondering what has happened to me – and then remembering. I can thank people quite prettily when they give me 5/- on my birthday; but this enormous sum! I cannot take it in; and you must take my dumbness as the real expression of what I feel; and so many more will feel when they know. You will hear from me again after our Council Meeting on Monday. I am giving out that you have offered to give pound for pound to St. Peter's Hall up to £50,000; and that you have set aside this sum already so that we can draw upon [it] as we raised equivalent amounts. I am not saying that the £50,000 is set aside in our own bank, and so has already cancelled the debt. This is I think what you would wish – and tomorrow I hope to get a start on asking some of our old supporters to come forward for the last time and help us to respond to your munificent offer. I am also about to begin to make tentative enquiries of the University on what conditions we can become a Public Hall or a New Foundation – so as to have all in readiness directly the necessary amount has been subscribed. Meanwhile, though we may only be small at present, as long as Oxford lasts your name will be perpetuated by the Hall. So many Colleges – such as Queens – have had a founder and a benefactor – in the case of Queens it was a Royal Chaplain who founded the College, and the Queen who was the benefactor who made it possible. With St. Peter's – it is my father who is founder and you are our benefactor; and I love to think of your two names commemorated together in this way for centuries to come. I do pray God that He will enable me to carry on the work here worthily as your steward; and that the day will not be far distant when even you with all your honours and the institutions named after you, will be proud to be the benefactor of Oxford's new College. May God bless and second you. Yours sincerely, C. M. Chavasse.'[669]

On 29 June 1936 the Annual Meeting of the Council took place.[670] After Chavasse had announced 'Lord Nuffield's wonderful munificence', the Council 'stood to recite the Doxology, as a thanksgiving to Almighty God'; and then passed with acclamation a resolution of thanks, ending: 'They trusted that Lord Nuffield would allow himself henceforth to be commemorated as the Benefactor of St. Peter's Hall even as Bishop Chavasse was known as its Founder; to which end they hoped, as soon as may be, to take the appropriate steps according to the precedents observed by Oxford Colleges.' The language was stilted, but the gratitude was genuine. Cumming was authorised to pay off the mortgage at once; for the first time it became possible to assure subscribers that their money would not have to be used to meet interest charges. A fortnight later[671] Chavasse asked Hobbs to tell Lord Nuffield 'that ever since June 24th I have felt a new creature, and hardly know myself. I had not realised what a strain the anxiety was until it was removed. It took me first in a very curious way – I never felt so tired in all my life. I suppose it is like a race: as long as you keep going all is well with you, but when you breast the tape you collapse.'

It was when he was in this mood that Chavasse entered into an exchange of letters with his father's old friend Bishop Knox, letters which throw light on the qualities of both the writers. On 5 July 1936 Bishop Knox wrote to congratulate him 'most heartily on Lord Nuffield's splendid offer. . . . I hope to send you a little contribution, but just now I am rather deeply pledged to the Manchester and Blackburn Dioceses. Forgive my suggesting it, but it would strengthen your Appeal to Evangelicals, if you sent a further letter to the *Record* showing how continuity of Evangelical teaching and worship is secured for St. Peter's. The Report[672] throws no light on this point, and Evangelicals having had some unhappy experiences are rather shy of educational contributions. Forgive the suggestion, and believe me to remain with kindest remembrances, Yours very affly [sic], E. A. Knox Bp.' On 7 July Chavasse replied: '. . . we can feel now that St. Peter's Hall is securely established, and the danger of its collapse is passed. I thank God with all my heart; and an enormous load is lifted off my mind. It was a real loss not being able to make mention of the Trustees and the Governing Body of St. Peter's Hall in my letter to the *Record*. Indeed, the fact that I have had to keep quiet about it up to the present has been a very serious difficulty in collecting money, and I think has lost us quite a few thousands – for which we have to thank the devious and inexplicable processes of the Martyrs Memorial Trust.' He explained about the Rowcroft Covenant, and asked 'What do you think would have been the effect if it had been publicly known that a subscriber to the C.M.S. could not be appointed Master of St. Peter's Hall? It has been almost as great a load lifted off me as the weight of debt by Lord Nuffield's benefaction that we have within the last few days secured the resignation of the Martyrs Memorial Trustees, and are now free to appoint our own Trustees. . . . These names will gain for us the respect and confidence of the public, instead of our being dogged by the suspicion and odium that the Martyrs Memorial Trust have earned. . . . For the past two years I have been obstructed and beset by a whole mass of shady work, such as secret documents, and deeds unlawfully withheld, and so forth. It was like living in a Dickens' novel; and I had not known that such practices were possible even among unChristian laymen. I had never come across what the Bishop of Durham described as the "Protestant underworld" till I touched the Martyrs Memorial Trust; and I still feel defiled, even though, thank God, we are now quit of them. . . . Meanwhile, I am only too glad to assure you that we are now respectable and not B.C.M.S.'

Bishop Knox made no reply till 14 July, but then he sent a long typed letter: [673] 'I have delayed replying to yours of the 7th partly to make enquiries about the alleged Secret Trust, but still more because the letter hurt me so much, that I feared being betrayed into expressions which I might afterwards regret. You probably forgot at the moment of dictating yours that my Ethel[674] is Secretary to the Secretary of the M.M. Trust and therefore in a measure implicated as an agent in the practices which you describe. I am sure that if you had thought of this you would have kept silence. . . . A word on the "secret Trust". It was not framed for St. Peter's Hall alone, but for all institutions or advowsons bought with Mrs. Rowcroft's money "as an assurance to her that it should be used only for Conservative Evangelical objects". I am assured that it was not designed to exclude from the Mastership all who subscribed to the C.M.S., but all who were not Conservative Evangelicals. Can it in fact be said that the C.M.S. has any *basis* to which its supporters are asked to subscribe? I never heard of it.

'. . . The original error was the acceptance of M.M. help with insufficient enquiry as to its character and methods. . . . Presently the Crash came which comes to so many building Societies. Enquiry threw light on the Secretary's methods[675] and he was dismissed. The Trust is painfully working towards solvency. Meanwhile under your Mastership the Hall became more and more unlike a Theological College on a B.C.M.S. basis, and friction arose, in the course of which you discovered a legal flaw in the Trust's hold of the Advowson of St. Peter's and so you were able to break the last link which bound the Mastership of the Hall to the M.M. Trust. It was not unnatural that friction should arise with this discovery and probably at this point came the Solicitor of the Trust's unwillingness to part with documents. In all this, unhappy and unpleasant as the story is, while the original Secretary of the Trust may have given some cause for such expressions as you used, I find the last Paragraph of your letter indefensible as regards the present Trust and "the last two years". The names of the Trustees are before me and, without definite evidence I find it impossible to accept the sweeping accusations which you make against them. Among the Trustees are Bishop Heywood, Lord Gisborough, Sir Charles King Harman, Sir Edgar Plummer and five Clergy. Do you seriously accuse them of "a whole mass of shady work". . . . If you can show this, as Ethel's father, I should feel it my duty to her to warn her against

240

such associations. If not I am sure that I need not point out to you your very obvious duty . . . Yours ever affectionately. . . .'

A month before, Chavasse might have been worried by this letter, but now he was 'on top of the world'. On 16 July he wrote to Bishop Knox: 'I had either forgotten or did not know that your daughter was secretary to Mr. Neill. I should not have thought that she was in any way implicated in Martyrs Memorial practices; though I am bound to say that I should be sorry if anyone I cared about had anything to do with them at all. I wish you were in Oxford and could see my files and correspondence with the Trust and various members of it, running back to 1928. I am sure you would feel you would want a bath after perusing them. [Oman, Dowdall, Walker, Legge] will tell you that the words I used to you were in no way too strong. Or you can ask the Manager of the Legal and General Assurance Society, and their Solicitor, Mr. Wykes. . . . Or best of all, you can ask the members of the Martyrs Memorial Trust themselves what they think of each other! . . . If you will cast your mind back to when Canon Stather Hunt consulted you with regard to the £10,000 with which Mrs. Rowcroft had presented him, and you advised him to go and talk to my father; you will remember that the idea of a B.C.M.S. college was not even mentioned. The idea came right afterwards, when the money had been spent, and was the result of suggestions by Dr. Bartlett[676] – hence the secret document. Certainly the C.M.S. have a basis, though there is no formal subscription to it. I thought you had some hand yourself in drawing it up, when the unhappy split came. Most assuredly the B.C.M.S. have a very precise basis, which you yourself describe most explicitly on p. 329 of your reminiscences.[677] There you define it as "verbal inspiration". My Council were horrified to discover that our Trustees had secretly agreed that my successor should be a verbal inspirationist. . . . But you are quite wrong when you say that the legal flaw was discovered during friction which had arisen because the Hall had become more and more unlike a theological college on a B.C.M.S. basis. It had never had such a basis, or my father would not have been Founder of the Hall, and I should not have been its first Master. . . . I can see quite clearly from your letter that you do not know the facts. I do know them; and I feel defiled. But thank God we are at last free. . . .'

Bishop Knox was accustomed to weighing documentary evidence,[678] and he did not find this letter convincing. On 18 July he replied: '. . . until you furnish me wtih definite proof, which yours of the 16th does not furnish, of their continuance of deliberate malpractices on their part under the new régime, I shall continue to believe that being a body of God-fearing men, they will behave accordingly. . . . There has come to me a message which I would pass on to you. Memory takes me back to the early days of my acquaintance with your father. I sit in his first little room in C.C.C. hotly denouncing some villain. He replies by reminding me of the words "There, but for the mercy of God goes John Bradford."[679] There is no one so bad, but that we owe it to the mercy of God that we are not equally bad. Now I want to put it to you that you have been placed by God's providence in such a position that you would justly be regarded as a typical Evangelical. It is right that you should regard with indignation what we may call for convenience shady transactions and should denounce them. But is it your duty to speak or write as you do of those whom you regard as the guilty parties? Let me suggest that they are not merely fellow Christians, but fellow Churchmen, fellow members of the Evangelical body whose cause it is your special care as Master of St. Peter's to present to the world in as favourable a light as possible. I fear that in your righteous indignation you are doing both yourself and the Evangelical cause grievous harm. The ordinary Churchman will not believe without convincing proof that there is not some other side to a question which seriously implicates the moral character of a body of men whom you charge indiscriminately with gross misconduct, deliberate and purposed. The ordinary citizen will say that you were allowing your annoyance to dominate your charity and your judgment. I cannot help thinking of Bishop Heywood. He was very very badly let down by the M.M. Trust over his Kenya schools. But instead of denouncing the M.M. Trust he made a splendid and successful effort to recover the situation and is now one of the Trustees. I do not for a moment suggest that you should do the same. But I do suggest that it is open to you to show a noble example of Christian charity by a different attitude to those whom you believe to have wronged you. In this connection one word on the B.C.M.S. I know something of gall of bitterness in that question, where again one man seems to be responsible for the trouble, as Warrington was. But I do pray you to remember that among them are God-fearing men and women, whose faith and self-sacrifice are an example to us. They are fellow Evangelicals. Why should they be treated and spoken of as Pariahs? The High Church party owes its success largely to its shielding its extremists, and never disowning them. I put it to you as an Evangelical leader today, have we not something to learn from the A.C.s here?[680] Forgive this long letter and its tone of admonition. Did I not love you for your own and your father's sake, did I not believe that God has a great work for you to do, I might have excused myself for keeping silence. I am sure you will take this letter in the spirit in which it is written, overlook its shortcomings, and prayerfully consider the possibility of a different attitude to the M.M.T. and the B.C.M.S.'

Chavasse kept no copy, not even a draft, of the letter which he sent back to the Bishop. Its tone can be deduced from that which he received from Bishop Knox, dated 31 July: 'Your very welcome letter for which I thank you with all my heart, relieved me from a great anxiety lest I had by mine done anything to impair the bond of affection which unites us. Thank God it is not so. . . .'[681] You ask about the M.M. Trust and Warrington. Unhappily he makes charitable relations difficult by writing extraordinarily defamatory letters against Neill – so bad and so widespread that they have had to take him into Court a *second* time. He received a very severe reprimand, and if he repeats the offence goes to prison without further proof. It is difficult to believe in his complete sanity.[682] I have been trying to make the M.M. Trust see your point of view, and consequently have seen more of theirs. Should it seem worth while with a view to a still better footing I may perhaps write you further on the subject. How they allowed themselves as you say to be "ciphers" to Warrington, it is hard to understand. He must have extraordinary gifts of persuasiveness. With warmest thanks for your patience with me I remain yours affectionately.'

Bishop Knox died in January 1937. Meanwhile Chavasse had been trying to tie up loose ends. General Adair, when he finally resigned his Trusteeship, had resigned also from the Council,[683] but had remained on friendly terms. On 15 May 1936 Chavasse had written to him: 'I am most thankful and glad that our personal friendship has survived it all, and that we sever our official association with mutual regard and esteem. If I may say so, I thought your letter was a model for a Christian and a gentleman. . . .'[684] The Revd. H. B. Greene was in another category. He was still holding up the transfer of investments to the new Trustees, and legal action became necessary to bring him to his senses. On 30 September 1936 Chilton's firm sent him a batch of transfer forms and asked him to sign them. They referred to his previous refusal to sign mandates, and went on '. . . we anticipate that you will take up the same attitude with regard to the

Transfers we now enclose. We have accordingly to inform you that in the event of your persisting in the attitude which you have adopted, and if we do not receive these Transfers back executed by Monday morning next at latest, our clients' instructions are such that there will be no alternative but to take proceedings to vest these securities in the names of the present Trustees, and we shall ask that you be ordered to pay costs of such proceedings. . . .' Greene still procrastinated, and on 9 November Chilton's firm informed Robbins, Olivey and Lake . . . 'We have been instructed to take proceedings against Mr. Greene and shall be glad to know whether you will accept service of Writ of Summons on his behalf.' On 17 November Robbins, Olivey and Lake wrote back: 'Herewith please find the transfers executed by the Rev. H. B. Greene.' So ended the obstruction campaign of the Vicar of Felixstowe.[685]

On that same day Chilton informed Chavasse that the undefended case of Chavasse, Taylor and Legge v. Gisborough, Pegg and Greene had 'come on again today before Mr. Justice Bennett and judgment was given that the Advowson [of St. Peter-le-Bailey] was not subject to any trust . . . and that the Defendants . . . have not, nor has any of them any estate or interest . . . in the said Advowson. Under the Rules of Court we were not able to obtain a decision that the Advowson is vested in you, Mr. Taylor and Mr. Legge . . . but of course we can do without that. . . . We did not ask for costs. . . . The next thing will be for you, Mr. Taylor and Mr. Legge to transfer the Advowson to the present Trustees of St. Peter's Hall'. There was no urgent hurry to execute this transfer. It was not till the Annual Meeting of the Council on 26 June 1937[686] that Chilton formally reported that a deed of conveyance had been signed on 4 March 1937 by which the Advowson was conveyed to Pickard-Cambridge, Linton Smith, Inskip and Hinde.

This, in the end, was simple enough. The Advowson of Tarleton gave more trouble. On 4 July 1936 Chavasse had written to Chilton: 'Now we have Lord Gisborough's Deed of Resignation, I want to re-open the question with Mr. Robbins of the living of Tarleton. I should like to get matters moving during the week or two that I remain a Trustee of the Hall, and before the Deed of Appointment of new Trustees has gone through. . . .' It was not in fact possible to move so quickly, but immediately the new Trustees had been appointed Chavasse began to urge Chilton[687] to take legal action to establish the ownership of the Advowson. Chilton, however, urged caution: [688] 'the endorsement of the Writ

244

setting out the claim is a matter that has to be very carefully considered as otherwise the proceedings might prove abortive and the Trustees become liable to costs.' The difficulty at this stage was to get hold of the relevant documents. The one thing that seemed certain was that the Fletcher family believed that they had conveyed the patronage to St. Peter's Hall[689], and that the then Trustees of the Hall had subsequently signed a covenant under which they purported to hold the living in trust for the M.M.T. It soon became clear too that the M.M.T. were prepared to fight any case that was brought to court.[690] In April 1937 Chilton put the legal difficulties to Mr. J. M. Gover, K.C. His opinion can be gathered from a letter written by Chavasse to Chilton on 7 May 1937: 'After your talk with me yesterday I do not see that we can do anything else save hold our hands for the moment and adopt Counsel's advice – namely, for the Trustees of St. Peter's Hall to present to the living of Tarleton immediately it is vacant, and thereby put the onus on the Martyrs Memorial Trust. . . .' After this there was some jockeying for position, on both sides. For instance, Linton Smith privately told the Bishop of Blackburn about the matter, and was able to get an assurance from him that St. Peter's should get early notice of any impending vacancy.[691] On the other hand, Mr. Robbins tried to convince the Solicitor to Queen Anne's Bounty that the M.M.T. were the real owners, and produced for his inspection a supplementary covenant dated 2 November 1936 executed by Lord Gisborough, Sir Charles King Harman, Canon Foster Pegg and Mr. Greene which purported to convey the advowson to the M.M.T.[692] A copy of this covenant, with other documents, was also sent to the Registrar of the Blackburn Diocese,[693] who found himself in an embarrassing position. He stood his ground, however, on the fact that the advowson had long been registered in the name of St. Peter's Hall. Meanwhile, the Fletcher family, indignant at the way they had been misled at the time of the sale, had had to be dissuaded from themselves taking legal action against the M.M.T.[694] Luckily, the living did not at this time fall vacant, and there was time for reflection. On 22 June 1938 Fletcher told Chavasse: 'I have been informed by Mr. Robbins of the Martyrs Memorial Trust, that their Trustees would be willing to hand over the Advowson if they were repaid the £1400 advanced out of their Trust funds for the purchase of the living.' To which Chavasse replied: [695] . . . 'there is no question about the Council considering finding the purchase money for the living and making a present of it to the Martyrs Memorial Trust. We are perfectly willing to receive livings; but we have no funds available whatsoever for the purchase of livings.' So the matter stood when war broke out in 1939 and made such things seem unimportant. The existing incumbent of Tarleton, the Revd. L. N. Forse, lived on. On 24 September 1949 he wrote to R. W. Howard 'I think it is now fairly well established that the Patronage is vested in St. Peter's Hall.' And so it was. There is no doubt that Chavasse himself took pleasure (gleeful at first, rueful as legal costs mounted up) in the thought that at Tarleton the M.M.T. had been hoist with their own petard. By their efforts to conceal from the sellers the true identity of the purchasers, they had succeeded only in making a present of the living to St. Peter's Hall.

The matter of Tarleton took a long time to settle. So did the execution of a new Trust Deed for the Hall. On 29 January 1936 Chilton wrote to Chavasse: 'After consideration of the draft of the new deed, Counsel has raised rather a big question. He finds great difficulty in respect of Hannington Hall. . . . It is Counsel's opinion . . . that it is open to very serious question whether the Trustees of Hannington Hall were justified in transferring Hannington Hall to the Trustees of St. Peter's Hall to be held on the trusts of the deed of 23 October 1928,[696] as they purported to do by the deed of 6 May 1929[697] . . . if the saving provisions [in the S.P.H. Trust Deed] are fully effective the inconvenient result is that in all matters affecting Hannington Hall reference must still be made to the original deed of 14 December 1897[698] and Hannington Hall cannot be treated for all purposes as part of St. Peter's Hall.' Counsel suggested applying to the Charity Commissioners for a new Scheme, which 'would have the advantage of clearing the ground for a petition for incorporation by Royal Charter. . . .' This letter brought it home to Chavasse that the present Trustees of Hannington Hall were still Lord Gisborough, King Harman and Warrington;[699] he had previously assumed that when they resigned trusteeship of St. Peter's Hall they automatically resigned also trusteeship of Hannington Hall. The matter was put to the Council on 1 February 1936, and Chilton was instructed to go ahead on the lines suggested by Counsel. On 23 June 1936 Chilton sent Chavasse 'a short report on the present position as to [the New Trust Deed] in order that the matter may be made clear to the Council.' He had interviewed the Charity Commissioners, who did not see how they could make a new scheme 'to bring the trusts of Hannington Hall within the terms of the trusts of St. Peter's Hall.' The Charity Commissioners thought 'that the purported transfer of Hannington Hall by the deed of 6 May 1929 to St. Peter's Hall was, in the circumstances, invalid, although that document may have transferred the legal interest in the property.[700] That being so, the subsequent appointment of new Trustees, while perfectly good as to St. Peter's Hall, did not pass any interest in Hannington Hall. . . . The Commissioners stated that in their opinion the obvious way out of the difficulty was for the Trustees of St. Peter's Hall to purchase Hannington Hall, and the purchase money could be schemed by them in such a way as to benefit both Hannington Hall and St. Peter's Hall . . . the income from the proceeds of the sale would have to be applied cy prés towards "forwarding the tenets and interests of the Church of England and more particularly to the promotion of foreign missions". . . . Such income could not properly be made available for the general support of St. Peter's Hall but under the trusts . . . it would be possible to provide a Bursary for an ordinand who was going to be a missionary . . . and grants could, of course, be made to Missionary Societies'. . . .

The Council which met on 29 June 1936 heard Chilton's report and instructed him to carry on with his negotiations with the Charity Commissioners. But in view of these negotiations and of the changed conditions brought about by the repayment of the mortgage debt and the possibility that St. Peter's Hall might thus, in the near future, be in a position to become a Public Hall in the University, the Council decided that no further steps be taken as yet with the revision of the Trust Deed. The next Council Meeting was on 31 October 1936.[701] Chilton reported that the Charity Commissioners were prepared to draw up a scheme for Hannington Hall, and the Council authorised Chavasse and Linton Smith, together with Chilton, to discuss the matter with the Commissioners. Further, Chavasse reported that he had already had an interview with the Vice-Chancellor about the possibility of St. Peter's becoming a Public Hall, and the Council now empowered the Master, Dr Walker, Sir Richard Livingstone and Mr. Legge to discuss with a committee of Hebdomadal Council the conditions upon which it would be willing to support such a proposal. The Master was also asked informally to interview the Registrar of the University 'as to what this step would involve with regard to the conveying of the St. Peter's Hall property to the University.'

It was lucky that Chavasse had this informal interview with Douglas Veale, the Registrar. It is worth while quoting the note which Chavasse sent out to members of the Council on 9

November 1936. 'On November 6th I had . . . a most helpful and illuminating conversation with the Registrar, who pointed out what struck us both as an insuperable objection to our petitioning to become a Public Hall; namely, that if the property of St. Peter's Hall was conveyed to the University, the University would become responsible for the Deeds of the Hall, and must therefore keep an inquisitive eye upon the accounts of the Hall and a control upon its expenditure. He asked why we did not petition to become a New Foundation. . . . He said that there would be no difference whatsoever as regards the government and administration of the Hall. As a New Foundation, we could remain as a Hall governed by a Council – that is, if Convocation gave leave in the same way as it would have to do if we petitioned to become a Public Hall. The real difference would be that as a New Foundation we should become incorporated by Royal Charter,[702] and manage our own affairs instead of being under the perpetual scrutiny of the University. The expense, he said, would be no greater, and our position infinitely more independent. He further pointed out that, as with Keble, if or when we thought good, we could, by Statute, proceed to the higher status of a College governed, as regards its internal administration, by its Fellows. . . . To all intents and purposes, by becoming a New Foundation, we should be a Public Hall with none of its drawbacks; and would be free to pass on to the status of a College if it was ever thought desirable.'

In view of this report, the Council which met on 30 January 1937[703] had no difficulty in deciding to postpone negotiations with Hebdomadal Council until the whole property of the Hall was vested in the Trustees. There was not only the difficulty about Hannington Hall; there was also the question of a disused church pathway, which originally ran from New Inn Hall Street along the south side of St. Peter-le-Bailey church[704] and out to Bulwarks Lane. The Rowcroft Building had been constructed right across this path. On 20 November 1936 Chavasse had written about this to Chilton in his capacity of Diocesan Registrar: . . .'when building operations were begun, with the foundation of St. Peter's Hall, the fact of this pathway had almost been forgotten, for there was a school behind Hannington Hall and its playground stretched behind the Church on to what had been the garden of the Rectory. . . .' Legally, this pathway was the property of the Ecclesiastical Commissioners. Luckily Linton Smith, as Bishop of Rochester, was one of the Commissioners, and he was able to give some help[705] in arranging a settlement, by which the Council was allowed to buy the built-over path for the nominal sum of £50, though the Commissioners insisted that the path adjoining the church should remain church property, for use in repairing and decorating in case a future Rector should not also be Master.[706] But it was not until the meeting on 13 November 1937[707] that Chavasse was able to report to the Council that the Deed of Conveyance had been received from the Ecclesiastical Commissioners.

Meanwhile Hannington Hall was causing headaches. On 14 December 1936 Chilton had suggested to Chavasse that the simplest thing would be to get Lord Gisborough, King Harman and Warrington to execute a deed of retirement from the trusts of Hannington Hall. 'If this could be done it would leave Mr. Talbot Rice and Bishop Knox as undoubted trustees of Hannington Hall, and they could at the first convenient opportunity appoint new Trustees . . . who could, of course, be the present Trustees of St. Peter's Hall.' Unfortunately Bishop Knox died shortly afterwards, and Percy Warrington once again had a chance to be awkward by refusing to execute any deed. Just at this time he was being threatened with bankruptcy proceedings,[708] and was ready to hit out at anybody; he would certainly not co-operate. This was specially frustrating, because Chavasse and Linton Smith had had a very satisfactory interview with the Charity Commissioners,[709] and no difficulties were expected on that side. Chilton was even compelled to ask the good offices of Mr. Robbins[710] in getting Warrington to sign the necessary documents, but to no effect. When the Council met on 29 January 1938,[711] Chilton had to report that Warrington had not budged. Prebendary Hinde offered to write to Warrington and the offer was gratefully accepted; but the Council also empowered Chilton to ask the Charity Commissioners to take steps to dispense with Warrington's signature if he continued to refuse to sign. The result of Hinde's approach was a lengthy reply from Warrington, so unbalanced in its arguments and so scurrilous in its language that on 25th June 1938 the Council[712] decided to send copies of it, through Chilton, to the Charity Commissioners, as evidence of the need to dispense with his signature. They found the evidence convincing. At its next meeting, on 12 November 1938, the Council[713] heard that the Commissioners were prepared to act without Warrington's signature, and on 2 May 1939 the Commissioners made an order approving a scheme for the administration of the Trusts of Hannington Hall, which would henceforth be known as 'The Bishop Hannington Memorial Fund.'[714] Finally, on 2 March 1942, at long last the purchase of Hannington Hall outright by the Council of St. Peter's Hall was completed, by the transfer to the Charity Commissioners of stock and cash totalling £6,843.

By that time, Julian Thornton-Duesbery had been Master for a year and a half. It only remains now to point out that there was one aspect of his appointment which revealed an unforeseen defect in the Trust Deed of the Hall, in its provisions to link up the Rectorship of St. Peter-le-Bailey with the Mastership of the Hall. Nobody had remembered that if a living became vacant by reason of its incumbent's having been made a diocesan Bishop, the right of presentation fell[715] to the Crown, and was exercised by the Lord Chancellor. In July 1939 it had been announced that Chavasse had been chosen to succeed Linton Smith as Bishop of Rochester. On 16 September 1939 Sir Thomas Inskip, who had just been made Lord Chancellor,[716] came to Oxford and informed C. E. Tinne that he had already appointed to the living of St. Peter-le-Bailey. Luckily, as he was himself a Trustee of the Hall, he knew the right man to appoint, Julian Thornton-Duesbery. But the question remained, what would have happened if an unfriendly Lord Chancellor had appointed the wrong man? It would have been very awkward, to say the least, even though it could have been held that the new Rector was not *ex officio* Master because he had not been appointed to the parish by the Patrons.[717]. With Thornton-Duesbery there was no difficulty; and on 18 September 1939 Pickard-Cambridge informed a special meeting of the Council[718] that the Trustees had appointed T-D to be Master.[719]

This volume has been concerned with the complicated relations between Chavasse and the Martyrs Memorial Trust, between the Council and the Trustees, and between all of them and the University. What would have happened to St. Peter's if the financial crash of 1933-34 had not loosened the hold of the M.M.T. is hard to imagine.

Luckily perhaps for their peace of mind, neither the tutors nor the undergraduates knew just what was going on.

SEQUENCE OF EVENTS

1884 November, birth of C. M. Chavasse.

1900 F. J. Chavasse Bishop of Liverpool.

1922 September, C. M. Chavasse Rector of St. Aldates.

1923 October, F. J. Chavasse resigned from Liverpool and went to live in St. Peter's House.

1926 January, Islington Conference: F.J.C. first mentioned scheme in public.

1927 Early (no date). P. Warrington given £10,000 by Mrs. Rowcroft.

21 May, Stather Hunt and Warrington met F. J. and C. M. Chavasse in Oxford.

Late May, M.M.T. decide to take up scheme.

June, C.M.C. tried to interest W. R. Morris.

23 September (probable date), Trustees of M.M.T. appointed C.M.C. to be Master of the proposed St. Peter's Hall.

1928 24 January, C.M.C. instituted to Rectory of St. Peter-le-Bailey.

11 March, F. J. Chavasse died.

16 and 23 March, C.M.C. advertised opening of Hostel for undergraduates in October 1928.

11 April, Trustees of St. P.-le-B. Schools agreed to hand over property to S.P.H.

19 April, application for licensing of Hostel.

31 May, first meeting of Provisional Council of St. Peter's Hall.

2 June, C.M.C. sent to Vice-Chancellor application for licensing of a Permanent Private Hall.

16 June, first public Appeal launched.

23 July, patronage of St. Peter-le-Bailey transferred to Trustees of M.M.T.

5 October, C.M.C. met M.M.T. in London; amendments to draft Trust Deed agreed.

8 October, Provisional Council accepted draft Trust Deed, as amended.

251

11 October, licence for St. Peter's House as Hostel received.

23 October, first Trust Deed signed and sealed.

4 December, Council approved draft Supplemental Deed to satisfy Hebdomadal Council.

1929   15 January, Supplemental Trust Deed signed and sealed.

29 January, debate in Convocation on decree empowering the Vice-Chancellor to license St. Peter's as a permanent private Hall.

6 May, Hannington Hall transferred to Trustees of S.P.H.

7 August, St. Peter's House sold to Trustees of S.P.H.

7 October, licence granted by Vice-Chancellor.

10 October, St. Peter's Hall opened: Staircases I, II, II in use.

6 December, Council took responsibility for building Staircase IV.

12 December, Coat of Arms granted to S.P.H.

15 December, death of Stather Hunt.

1930   2 May, Warrington makes charges against C.M.C.

3 October, first doubts about financial stability of M.M.T.

22 November, secret Deed of Covenant between Mrs. Rowcroft and M.M.T.

1931   5 February, Council put pressure on Warrington to produce a balance-sheet: Warrington threatened to resign.

7 May, M.M.T. Trustees passed resolution of no confidence against C.M.C.

7 November, Council recorded formal settlement of dispute. Warrington denied financial crisis but admitted financial difficulties.

1932   4 February, Warrington presented balance-sheet to Council.

5 November, Council decided to buy Wesleyan Hall on borrowed money, since Trustees could not pay.

1933   17 February, C.M.C. met new Central Finance Committee of M.M.T.; great financial strain; Warrington ill.

29 June. Council approved purchase of Annexe.

15 September, C.M.C. informed that Warrington had resigned from his functions in M.M.T.

4 November, Council informed that Warrington had resigned as Trustee both of the Hall and of the advowson; first steps taken to dissociate S.P.H. from M.M.T.

1934   26 January, meeting between representatives of S.P.H. and members of Schools Trust Finance Committee:

S.P.H. faced with necessity of taking over mortgages for £70,000.

11 May, emergency meeting of Trustees and Council to approve arrangements about mortgages; news that Nuffield had given £10,000. Revision of Trust Deed to be considered.

26 September, special meeting of Trustees and Council: settlement with Schools Trust.

1935   8 January, Emily Morris Memorial unveiled.

11 February, Counsel's opinion on Rowcroft covenant.

28 May, Counsel's opinion on patronage of St. Peter-le-Bailey.

28 June, Council informed that Nuffield had given £12,161 more.

1936   24 June, Nuffield gave £50,000.

28 July, new Trustees appointed.

31 October, Council informed that Charity Commissioners would draw up new scheme for Hannington Hall.

6 November, Veale suggested that S.P.H. might become not a Public Hall but a New Foundation.

1937   30 January, Council decided to postpone negotiations about a change of status.

1939   Retirement of C.M.C. Appointment of Thornton-Duesbury as second Master.

1940   Thornton-Duesbury takes up position of Master.

Notes

1 As late as 30 November 1957 the Revd. P. E. Warrington wrote to Canon R. W. Howard, formerly Master of St. Peter's Hall and then Rector of Westonbirt,
   'In due course Chavasse will have to answer Canon Foster Pegg's challenge, viz. – "How can a dead man found his own memorial?" Could you tell me whether there is any Tablet or Record displayed in the Hall recording the names of those men
   who founded St. Peter's Hall
   and appointed Chavasse the first Master. . . .'

2 *Victoria History of the County of Oxford*, Vol. 3, p. 335.

3 Under the provisions of the University's Statute for the dissolution of Halls (1881), on the death or retirement of its existing Principal, Dr. H. H. Cornish, New Inn Hall was to be united with Balliol. Dr. Cornish died in 1887.
   The Cramer Building had been erected by Principal Cramer at his own expense in 1833, to accommodate the undergraduates of New Inn Hall. It contained a dining-room and men's rooms on the ground floor, men's rooms on the first floor, attics beneath the roof and a kitchen in the basement.

4 In a letter to Prebendary Hinde, 22 June 1938, Warrington stated that on the day after Bishop Chavasse's Islington (1926) speech he (Warrington) wrote to the Bishop and offered to 'undertake' the 'Scheme he had outlined', and that on the same day he wrote to Canon Stather Hunt and 'gave him a full account of Bishop Chavasse's speech.' But it was certainly not till May 1927 that meetings took place in Oxford between leading members of the Martyrs Memorial Trust and the two Chavasses, father and son.

5 The Principals of St. Edmund Hall remained suspicious. On 17 January 1929, A. B. Emden, who had recently succeeded Dr. G. B. Allen as Principal, wrote to Chavasse:
   'As regards any question of conflict of interest between the St. Peter's House Scheme and St. Edmund Hall we should have appreciated your coming to us at an earlier stage in the development of your project with a view to discovering our attitude and of ascertaining whether the scheme upon which you had set your mind was calculated or not to impair existing efforts that were being made under University auspices to serve a similar purpose. . . .
   Frankly, I do not like your scheme – and my predecessors, the Bishop of Carlisle and the Bishop of Sherborne, are of the same opinion, and so was Mr. Cronshaw – , and the reasons for my view are based as much on general grounds of academic policy as on a consideration of the possible ill-effects upon our work here. . . .'

6 On this Dr. Kirk made a tart comment (12 May 1928) 'I feel certain that the Delegates will appreciate the disclaimer. . . . But I

venture to suggest that it would probably facilitate negotiations very much if you yourself were to publish such a disclaimer in the press and to secure for it as far as possible as much publicity as has been obtained by the announcements which, in your own words, "must have given rise to much misapprehension".'

Dr. Kirk's own use of words was always precise, orderly and lucid: he could not have failed to note the contradiction implicit in Chavasse's statement that the idea of a College 'never arose' and 'was relegated to the unknown future'.

7   This request was firmly refused. 16 May 1928, 'The Delegates are of opinion that so long as the house remains a Hostel under their supervision, confusion will be avoided if the word "Hall" is not used in its title.'

8   It was clearly intended at this stage that there would be five patrons of the Advowson and that all five would be members of the Council. In June/July 1928 it was decided to have only four patrons to start with, and Mr. Greene was omitted, apparently without consultation. On 5 February 1934 he wrote to Chavasse: 'My name was down on the first list of Members of the Council – a typed form of which I have somewhere. On enquiring about this later Mr. Warrington told me that my name had been left off at your request! I was surprised at this. . . .' No doubt Warrington preferred to put the blame on Chavasse for his own negligence.

9   Cp. 12 May 1928: Dr. Pember to C.M.C. 'The press certainly have been very troublesome about it; but I think everyone will understand that.'

Also on 12 May, Chavasse wrote to *The Times*, and on 15 May *The Times* replied that 'the Editor has taken steps which will, he hopes, prevent the title of "College" being applied to St. Peter's Hostel in *The Times* in future.'

10   Kirk to C.M.C., 21 May 1928.

11   20 June 1928, Kirk to C.M.C. 'The reprint of the Appeal seems to me quite satisfactory.'

12   The slip is perhaps of psychological interest, if compared with a similar slip on the second page of the first Annual Report, where October 1928 is printed by mistake for October 1929. Even if these mistakes were typist's or printer's errors, it is odd that Chavasse failed to notice and correct them in proof, in documents of some importance.

13   Council was not altogether satisfied with the Trust Deed of 23 October 1928, and insisted on certain additional provisions (e.g. a guarantee of the permanency of the Hall), which were embodied in a Supplementary Trust Deed executed on 15 January 1929.

14   In June 1928 *The Times*, *The Daily Telegraph*, *The Mirror*, *The Manchester Guardian* and *The Daily Sketch* all gave publicity to the Appeal.

15   Chavasse was sensitive to criticism on this score, even though it was not expressed publicly. He had taken a pass degree. His tutors had expected a second class, and nobody who knew him well in the nineteen-twenties believed that a 'pass' was his true standard.

16   Roxburgh's reply to Chavasse would have surprised and shocked Mr. Warrington: . . . .'Of course it is the fear of "verbal inspiration" that is behind the opposition – and of a chapel without a cross.

But so long as you are there, the fear is groundless. Good luck!. . . .'

17 Dr. F. B. Chavasse, Sidney Chavasse, Charles Chavasse, G. Foster Carter, C. S. Carter, Henry G. Willink.

18 The Revd. R. B. S. Gillman, in the parish magazine of Christ Church, Linnet Lane, Liverpool, October 1953.

19 This statement was strictly true, in the sense that a Roman Catholic or a Muslim would not be compelled to attend. But it was disingenuous, to say the least, in that Chavasse from the start had a chapel-attendance register, and 'warned' backsliders – a second warning could mean a fine.

20 It would have been more accurate to say 'have promised to provide'.

21 By now £10,000 had been received by the Hon. Treasurer of the Appeal and accounted for under 'General Fund', but it had not in fact been allocated to the endowment of teaching staff.

22 The Delegates of Lodgings (Kirk to C.M.C. 18 June 1928) had refused to allow the use of the term 'Tutor', because all men in the Hostel would be Non-Collegiate Students and their tuition would be provided by the Delegates of those Students.

23 It was probably thought necessary to stress arrangements for the provision of Tutors, because the story had been circulated in Senior Common Rooms that Chavasse had been so busy in planning buildings and raising money that he had quite forgotten the need for Tutors. The story may have originated from the then Principal of Brasenose, C. H. Sampson, who certainly told at least one of his colleagues, Dr. Stallybrass, that Chavasse had been taken aback when asked by the Principal what he proposed to do about tuition. (Stallybrass told this to E.H.F.S.)

24 In fact this was not a voluntary 'proposal', but a general requirement laid down by University Statute for residence in Permanent Private Halls, with very few exceptions allowed for married men and for those whose parents lived in Oxford.

25 It would have been more accurate to speak of bursaries, rather than scholarships and exhibitions, except as a distant hope.

26 This would seem to indicate that the signatories were aware that Chavasse was open to criticism as being inclined to 'jump the gun'. Some of them knew that he had already been rebuffed by the Delegates of Lodgings (16 May 1928) for suggesting that the name 'St. Peter's Hall' should be used for the Hostel.

27 C. S. Nye.

28 A prominent member of the Faculty of Oriental Studies.

29 26 January 1929. A. L. Poole of St. John's to C.M.C.: 'I am a strong supporter of St. Peter's and have already been urging friends to attend Convocation to vote for it. I am afraid the opposition is fairly powerful. The Anglo-Catholics, the Non-Collegiates etc. . . .'

28 January 1929. George Gordon, President of Magdalen, to C.M.C.: . . . .'I was surprised at the sudden opposition, and don't yet understand it fully. . . . My inclination is to approve of a movement with which your father and you are identified, but I suppose I must hear what the opposition has to say. . . .'

30 A matter concerning the Taylor Institution.

31 He probably meant Keble.

32 30 January 1929, Dr. E. M. Walker to C.M.C. . . . .'There was one feature in yesterday's proceedings that afforded me peculiar satisfac-

tion. It was the rally of those interested in Keble to the support of our Hall. No one can now say that St. Peter's Hall is meant as a challenge to Keble, and all that Keble stands for, or that it is intended to be worked in a narrow and aggressive spirit; and for this I am supremely thankful. . . .'

33 On 2 February 1929 Dr. Lock wrote to Chavasse: 'I spoke very willingly and from my heart. . . . My real regret is that I got flurried and did not say (what my first words showed that I intended to say) some words about your father. . . .'

34 14 October 1930, Hazel to C.M.C. 'My share in the effort to get it established is one of the things in my life I look back to with most satisfaction.'

35 29 January 1929, the President of Trinity, Dr. H. E. D. Blakiston, wrote to Chavasse: 'When I was V.C. I constantly exhorted benefactors to *provide a new residential college* if they wanted to do anything substantial (or help St. Edmund Hall); but they generally wanted Professorships.'

36 He died 28 February 1929.

37 He added: 'In spite of Cyril Bailey, I do not think that real Oxford opinion will think the less highly of it for that reason.'

38 30 January 1929, J. G. Legge to C.M.C. . . . . 'Your own splendid energy and courage have been an inspiration. Now we shall really go ahead, and I am sure that our modesty and good behaviour will soon win over the sympathy of those who were unfortunate enough to find themselves in the wrong lobby yesterday. . . .'

39 11 March 1929, Dr. P. S. Allen to C.M.C. . . . .'I know something of the bodies with which you have had to negotiate, so you must allow me to say that I doubt whether anyone else could have found his way through all the difficulties that have surrounded you.'

40 In 1922 the Revd. C. E. Douglas was moving heaven and earth (or at any rate the Bishop of Oxford and the Archbishop of Canterbury) to hear a charge of heresy against the Principal of Ripon Hall, Oxford, Dr. Major, a leader of 'modernist' thought.

41 Later known as Tyndal Hall, but then as the B.C.M.S. College.

42 A phrase used by Hensley Henson, Bishop of Durham.

43 It was formed by the amalgamation of the Church of England Trust Society (of which Canon D. J. Stather Hunt was the chairman) and the Martyrs Memorial Trust Society (of which the Revd. P. E. Warrington was the honorary secretary).

44 . . . .'Church Patronage, by means of which those adhering to the Conservative Evangelical position may be assured of preferment in due course' (Report, p. 6).

45 In a letter to the editor of the *Church Times*, answering an attack upon Patronage Trusts, in which it had been said that the M.M.T. owned more than 200 advowsons.

46 In appearance he was not remarkable. I remember him as short and solid, with a red face, rather like Mr. Pickwick but devoid of Pickwickian geniality. E.H.F.S.

47 Monkton Combe School was an Evangelical foundation, but it was quite independent of Warrington and the M.M.T.

48 It is not clear to whom this refers. In any case, such accusations by Warrington need to be treated with reserve.

49 'If I had had a Committee to dog my steps', he told the reporter,

'you may take it from me that there would have been no Stowe, Canford or Westonbirt today. I did the work, got the schools going, and formed the committees afterwards.'

50 According to Mrs. Stather Hunt (writing to C.M.C. 4 June 1930 and referring to entries in her diary), Canon Stather Hunt had first talked to Bishop Knox at Beckenham about Bishop Chavasse's scheme on 13 April 1927, and had gone to see Bishop Chavasse at Oxford on 4 May. Mr. Warrington had not been present on either occasion.

51 14 July 1936.

52 22 June 1938.

53 Attended by Lord Gisborough, Sir Charles King Harman, Canon Foster Pegg, the Revd. H. B. Greene and one or two others.

54 The Revd. H. B. Greene, however, told a different story. Writing to Chavasse on 5 February 1934 about things which had happened in 1927-28, he said: . . . .'I had only met you once, when we went down to Oxford to interview your father. I on that occasion suggested that you should be first Master if the scheme matured. I spoke to your father about it and he assured me that nothing would give him more pleasure. I then broached the matter to the members of the M.M.T. through Warrington with the result we all know.'

55 Christopher Chavasse was five years older than Percy Warrington.

56 'Broad' would not have pleased Warrington, but there is no reason to suppose that he saw or knew of this document.

57 In fact the City of Oxford School remained in George Street until, many years later (1966) it was amalgamated with another Secondary School in East Oxford as Oxford School; the site long reserved for it in Summertown, on Marston Ferry Road, was then used for another school.

58 This must be a mistake for 'Southern'.

59 Here too there is confusion between northern and southern. Actually the Canal Basin site lay from S.E. to N.W.

60 22 June 1927.

61 8 June 1928.

62 4 June 1930, Mrs. Stather Hunt to C.M.C., quoting diary.

63 5 January 1937, C.M.C. informed C. A. Chilton: 'As regards St. Peter's Hall,. . . . it was founded through negotiations with the Martyrs Memorial Trust itself from the beginning, and not with Mr. Warrington personally, though he was undoubtedly the driving force of the team.'

64 Two of them, Mr. J. F. W. Deacon and the Revd. H. H. Gibbon, were very old friends and associates of the Bishop.

65 The Revd. H. H. Gibbon had recently died and his place as a Trustee had been filled by the Revd. H. Drown.

66 In April 1928 the application to open a Hostel had given the name of the Revd. H. B. Greene as a fifth patron, and it seems clear that the original intention had been to replace the five Trustees of the Oxford Churches Trust by five Trustees of the Martyrs Memorial Trust.

67 30 January 1935. Gislingham is in Suffolk. The transaction remains obscure. The Oxford Churches Trust would not normally have been interested in an East Anglian parish, and at a later date Gislingham was recorded in Crockford (as it still was in 1973) as being in the gift of the Martyrs Memorial Trust.

68 Church of England Zenana Missionary Society.

69 'The primary object of this Trust is to devote the said site premises and buildings. . . . in perpetuity to forwarding the tenets and interests of the Church of England and more particularly to the promotion of Foreign Missions with which the work of the late Bishop Hannington was identified and no use shall ever be made of Hannington Hall which is inconsistent with the primary object here mentioned.'

70 These clauses were embodied in a schedule forming part of the proposed conveyance of Hannington Hall.

71 Including Bishop Knox.

72 'As a permanent and fitting recognition of their great service the Dynevor Arms borne by Mr. Talbot Rice, the Senior Trustee, are emblazoned upon one of the windows of the dining hall.'

73 In general, the 'constitution' described resembles that set out in the application (19 April 1928) for the licensing of a hostel. But the application lists five patrons of the advowson, who will all be members of the Council, whereas the 'constitution' gives the patrons only four representatives on the Council. This suggests that the paper was not earlier than June 1928.

74 St. Edmund Hall later became entirely independent, and its statutes were used as a model for the original Statutes of St. Peter's College.
    'The University itself' presumably means 'The Vice-Chancellor unofficially'.

75 The two 'appointed by the Hall' were at first to be appointed by the Trustees.

76 Sic – but 'Members of the Council' must be intended.

77 The Revd. G. F. Graham Brown, a close friend of Chavasse's.

78 Dr. P. S. Allen. Bishop F. J. Chavasse was an Honorary Fellow of Corpus.

79 Dr. E. M. Walker.

80 M.P. for Oxford University; Chichele Professor of Modern History and Fellow of all Souls.

81 31 March 1928, Dr. Hetherington to C.M.C. '. . . .although we agreed there was nothing in our Charter to prevent our appointing representatives to the Council. . . . it was felt that such an action might give rise to difficulties here. . . . you will, I am sure, understand that this attitude. . . . does not imply in the very faintest degree a want of sympathy with the objects of the new Foundation, or anything but the keenest desire to join in doing honour to your father's memory.'

82 3 April 1928, C.M.C. to Lord Derby 'If you would most kindly consent, we should like Dr. Hetherington above all others. . . . as for other names, Mr. J. G. Legge (late Director of Education in Liverpool) lives now in Oxford and is deeply interested in the Hall and is helping the scheme with all his power. So is Judge Dowdall who also lives in Oxford, and Professor J. L. Myres who was at Liverpool University is now Professor of Ancient History at Oxford. All of these were great friends of my Father.'

83 The place was still vacant on 19 April when the application for a Hostel was made.

84 As Chancellor of the Duchy of Lancaster. In September 1928 he was Acting Foreign Secretary.

85 The postal service was so good at this period that a letter posted in Somerset in the afternoon would be sure of delivery in Oxford by the first post on the next day.

86 Under the heading 'ST. PETER'S COLLEGE.'

87 In June 1927 Chavasse had told Morris that the Trust was 'to begin operations with £20,000'. By June 1929 (First Annual Report), the Trustees 'had pledged themselves to an expenditure of £60,000'. It is not clear what sum Warrington here envisages.

88 Chavasse's solicitor, and a member of the congregation of St. Aldate's.

89 Of 7 Lathbury Road, Oxford; retired Indian Civil Servant; another member of the congregation at St. Aldate's. He had in fact been acting as Hon. Treasurer for some time past.

90 On 18 May 1928 Chavasse had written to Houghton. . . . 'I should like to invite you definitely to join me on the staff of the proposed St. Peter's Hall . . . . My invitation is of course dependant [sic] upon the sanction of the Council. . . .'

The term 'Assistant Tutor', used also in the first Appeal, implied that the Master was ex officio the chief Tutor.

91 President of the M.M.T.

92 Both Warrington and Chavasse used the tactical device of attributing to their Trustees or Council views which were essentially their own.

93 Chavasse was quite unaware at this time of the part played by mortgages in the financial operations of the M.M.T.

94 Messrs. S. Pearman Smith and Sons of Walsall (Senior Partner, W. J. Pearman Smith).

95 It was not till 7 August 1929 that the conveyance was signed by which Chavasse, as Rector, with the approval of the patrons and with the consent of the Archbishop of Canterbury and the Bishop of Oxford, sold the property to the Trustees of St. Peter's Hall for a sum of £4,000 paid to Queen Anne's Bounty.

96 i.e. of St. Aldate's. On 18 May the *Church of England Newspaper* had announced that Chavasse proposed to resign the living, but he continued to live in St. Aldate's Rectory throughout the summer of 1928.

97 i.e. between Warrington and Chavasse. Words underlined were inserted by C.M.C. in his own writing.

98 This did not in fact happen: the sale was to the Trustees of St. Peter's Hall.

99 This was obscure: it presumably meant that the Trust Society would undertake to hand over the property if and when it was conveyed to the Trust.

100 29 June 1928, P. E. Warrington to C.M.C.

101 Probably that of Chancellor Errington, who normally acted for the M.M.T.

102 A statement which can hardly be accepted without evidence.

103 Writing from Tetsworth Vicarage, where he was doing holiday duty.

104 23 August 1928, Warrington to C.M.C. 'I have before me a letter from our solicitors informing me that they must advise the Trustees not to proceed with the purchase of St. Peter's Rectory'. . . . [because they cannot be the real owners].

25 August 1928, C.M.C. to Warrington. Suggests immediate conference in Oxford between themselves, Mr. Pearman Smith and the Diocesan Registrar. 'It is Mr. Rose (the Diocesan Registrar)

who suggests this for he says we can arrange matters together in five minutes while correspondence may take weeks . . . the difficulty is simply one of phraseology.'

105 Four or five pages follow of detailed comment on the amendments desired by Chavasse. One comment deserves notice: 'Mr. Chavasse would ask the Trust to make the position of Master as honourable as possible and to bring it into line with that of other heads of Colleges [sic] in Oxford.'

106 Present: Chavasse (chairman), Allen, Graham Brown, King Harman. Legge, Oman, Stather Hunt, Walker, Warrington.

107 W. J. Pearman Smith witnessed the signatures of the Trustees, C. L. Teal that of Chavasse.

108 i.e. Trustees of the Hall.

109 Both in the interests of the M.M.T.

110 There were only four Patrons at the time, but it would have been quite legal for the Patrons to increase their own number, if the M.M.T. thought fit.

111 This referred primarily to future appointments. Chavasse himself was in a peculiar position: he had not been appointed to the Parish by the Patrons referred to, but he had been appointed Master by the same persons (for all practical purposes) in their capacity of Trustees of the M.M.T.

112 To be nominated by Hebdomadal Council.

113 To be nominated by the Chancellor of that University.

114 Though the Council might by a two-thirds majority extend his office for 'a period not exceeding five years'.

115 By a two-thirds majority at a special meeting.

116 According to a letter from Chavasse to the Vice-Chancellor, 22 December 1928, these three clauses were taken practically verbatim from the Statutes of Lady Margaret Hall.

117 Though not the sole Trustees of the Trust Society, they were the dominant Trustees.

118 10 October 1933, W. J. Pearman Smith to C.M.C.: '. . . . you will remember that at the outset when the Hall was formed the Trustees thereof were appointed from the Martyrs Memorial Trust on the understanding that whenever new Trustees were necessary they should appoint them from the same body. The same remarks of course also apply to the Advowson of St. Peter-le-Bailey. . . .'

119 27 February 1934, Pearman Smith to R. H. Bowdler: . . . 'So far as we are aware the Trustees have not kept Minutes since the foundation of the Hall. We ourselves started a Minute Book commencing with the Meeting held on Wed. 15 November 1933 which has been regularly kept since.'

120 Present, Chavasse (chairman), Allen, King Harman, Legge, Walker, Warrington.

121 Canon Stather Hunt.

122 The Provisional Council on 8 October 1928 had decided that £6000 (from the £8556 so far received in the Appeal Fund) should be invested to provide an endowment for the first tutorship.

123 15 December 1929.

124 16 July 1936.

125 19 June 1931, E.H.F.S., diary: 'Chavasse submitted for comment today his annual report . . . he uses most fulsome language about

the Trustees and about Warrington in particular; yet he is often complaining of the Trustees letting the Hall down, and this evening in hall he calmly referred to the possibility of getting Joynson Hicks' firm to act for him if a threat of libel action proved necessary to make Warrington withdraw certain recent statements.'

126 18 September 1928, J. A. Cumming to Warrington.
127 21 September 1928, Warrington to Cumming.
128 25 September 1928, Warrington to Cumming.
129 Chavasse was still waiting to be repaid for this piano in August 1929. Finally (19 October 1929) he repaid himself, all but £2-3-9, from a payment by Queen Anne's Bounty, really due to the Trustees. He told Warrington : 'If the Trustees like to refund me the balance . . . I should be glad to receive it, otherwise I shall count it as another of these donations to the Hall which one in my position is always being called upon to make.'
130 29 September 1928, Cumming to Warrington.
131 Chavasse had now left St. Aldate's Rectory and had rented No. 27 Norham Road. During term he himself had to live in St. Peter's House, rejoining his wife and family in vacation. Mrs. Chavasse acted from the start of the Hostel as an unpaid assistant domestic bursar. She never forgot the crisis in October 1928 when the first men were due to arrive : their beds and bedding were not delivered till the very last moment, the woman engaged to look after them collapsed in hysterics, and Mrs. Chavasse herself had to make all the beds.
132 Present : Chavasse, Allen, King Harman, Legge, Walker, Warrington.
133 'The Master stated that claims had been received from Sir Herbert Baker for £226 and from Mr. R. F. Dodd for £400 for professional services in preparing the general layout and plans of St. Peter's Hall. He had engaged these Architects on the advice of the late Bishop Chavasse . . . It was resolved that these claims should be paid from the Appeal Fund. . . .' (Council Minutes)
134 17 December 1928, Warrington to Cumming : 'My Trustees wish me to say they are of opinion, that as they are paying the rent on the Master's house the Council should pay the rates from the General Fund.'
      22 December 1928, Cumming to Warrington : 'I really cannot understand the Trustees objecting to pay Mr. Chavasse's rates, when they have covenanted with him to pay "Such allowance for rates and taxes as may be agreed upon" . . . To make *no* allowance is a breach of that covenant and is certainly not agreed to by Mr. Chavasse. Do you really suggest that this charge should be met from the Appeal Fund? That seems to be an improper use of the fund. . . .'
135 This letter was dictated while he was in bed ill.
136 The point was that he assumed that the complaint about delay referred to the furnishing bills, about which he had a sensitive conscience. Cumming spotted that the minute had not been explicit. and thought it proper to explain: on 8 March he wrote to Warrington—
      'I should like to let you know how deeply I regret the typist's error in the Minutes . . . which has caused you such indignation . . . . I am particularly vexed that it should have reached you and worried

you when you were ill.

The payments on capital account, e.g. furnishing St. Peter's House, were not considered by the Committee. I may say that I was specially desirous that you should be present at the meeting so that on behalf of the Trustees you could get any information you wished about the running expenses of St. Peter's.'

137 This refers to an overdraft. On 8 January Cumming had written to Warrington: 'I have informed Mr. Chavasse of our conversation of yesterday, and am writing to say we depend on you asking Barclays to let us have (if required) an over-draft on St. Peter's House Account at their Cornmarket Street Branch.'

138 An early example of Warrington's dislike of any enquiry into his financial transactions.

139 C.M.C. to Warrington, 7 March 1929, starting (exceptionally) 'My dear Mr. Warrington'.

140 The rent of 27 Norham Road, the Master's salary, bursaries etc.

141 Chavasse did not mention that he had received the following letter from W. Talbot Rice, dated 25 January 1929:

'My dear Christopher, I heartily rejoice with you over the new bit of work done towards the new Hall. The dear old Church has been transformed wonderfully . . . It is a joy to behold it and the Reredos is a beautiful and most appropriate addition and a lovely memorial to your beloved Mother – a mother to us all . . . . the Rectory transformation has been extraordinarily well done . . . The Hannington Hall will be a dream when complete; the Conference in March will be breathless over it all!

'I enclose cards of Smith Williamson [sic], the Chartered Accountants. Mervyn is to be taken into partnership almost at once. He was seven years with Price Waterhouse and was in Oxford for them a little while back auditing the University accounts . . . It will be a delightful link if he and his firm become the Chartered Accountants to the new Hall.

Yours affectionately, W. Talbot Rice.'

142 9 March 1929, Burn to Chavasse.

143 Present: Chavasse, Graham Brown, King Harman, Legge, Oman.

144 Apart from the quite minimal concession that Bursaries should be paid seven days before the end of each term (8 May 1929, Burn to Cumming).

145 27 May 1929, Warrington to Cumming.

146 6 July 1929, Cumming to Warrington. He wanted Thompson to come for preliminary discussions, but could not find his name in the lists of the Institute of Chartered Accountants.

8 July 1929, Warrington to Cumming. Dodged the implied question whether Thompson was a Chartered Accountant. . . . 'I see no reason why Thompson should not audit the Accounts of the Appeal Fund.'

147 26 July 1930, Cumming to Warrington.

148 Cape and Co., Ltd., who had supplied the furniture for St. Peter's House.

149 8 May 1929, Chavasse sent Warrington a letter from one of the partners of Capes, reminding him that bills sent in on 26 November 1928, 8 February 1929 and 24 April 1929 had so far been disregarded.

150 11 July 1929, C.M.C. to Warrington: 'I am so glad you were able to assure me on Saturday that Cape's bill would be paid this week. . . .'

151 13 August 1929, Warrington to Minty Ltd., Oxford.

152 The accounts had been sent to Warrington as under:—

26	Nov.	1928	£163- 7-2
8	Feb.	1929	35-12-6
24	April	„	1-18-0
7	June	„	1-13-5

202-11-1

The bills were for a great number (nearly 250) of small items, ranging from garden tools and carpet-sweepers to tea-pots and trays.

153 10 October 1929, Warrington to Cumming.

154 26 June 1929. Cumming to Warrington.

155 On which No. IV Staircase was later built.

156 Work had been held up by frosty weather, and Chavasse feared that the building would not be ready for occupation in October. He wrote: 'I feel so strongly on the subject that I would be willing to pay £100 out of my own pocket rather than face the anxiety and the terrible rush that may otherwise be my lot' (1 May 1929).

157 29 April 1929, Warrington to C.M.C.

158 He added: 'I might inform you that when Parnells built the Boarding House at Stowe for 70 boys, plus Housemaster's Quarters, they dug the foundations in February and finished the work in September, when the House was ready for occupation.'

159 Previously a bleak room, with iron ties spanning the space beneath the roof. It was used as a gymnasium by the girls of the Central School next door.

160 This was long before the introduction of striplighting with neon tubes.

161 29 April 1929, C.M.C. to Warrington.

162 29 July 1929, Warrington to C.M.C. He said that St. Peter's House 'is too plain, and even with the proposed alterations it is unworthy of St. Peter's, and of him whose Memorial it is to be.'

163 This involved building a wall linking St. Peter's House with St. Peter-le-Bailey Church (so blocking the previous side-entry), and demolishing an exterior corridor on the southern half of the east frontage.

164 9 August 1929, Warrington to C.M.C.

165 12 August 1929, C.M.C. to Warrington.

166 12 September 1929, C.M.C. to Warrington. The letter refers to correspondence in the previous February:

13 February, Warrington to C.M.C., 'With reference to the Furniture, I do not see the necessity for any orders to be placed now. When Stowe was opened, and Canford, the orders for the Furniture for both schools were not placed until two months beforehand' . . . 14 February, C.M.C. to Warrington: . . 'As regards furniture, I will, if you don't mind, begin at once to make enquiries . . . Furnishing schools is a little different from furnishing men's studies.'

167 Warrington has assumed that fitted wardrobes and shelves would make dressing-tables unnecessary. Later (28 October 1929) Chavasse reminded him that 'if we had no dressing-tables we should have had

to provide some kind of table for each room on which a man might keep his bible and prayer-book and what not.'

168 18 September 1929, C.M.C. to Warrington.

169 Ideally, 20 freshmen, 20 second year, 20 third year.

170 30 May 1929, C.M.C. to Warrington: 'I am very glad that you will consider most carefully the matter of future building. And you may be sure that if you think I can co-operate in any way in gathering the necessary funds I will work for you heart and soul.'

171 Ramsay MacDonald took office in June 1929 for the second time. The previous occasion had been in January 1924.

172 8 June 1929, C.M.C. to Warrington.

173 The original Wesleyan chapel.

174 20 July 1929, C.M.C. to Brown. During the cold winter of 1928-29 it had been necessary to buy oil-stoves 'so that the inspector of schools should not interfere.'

175 23 July 1929, C.M.C. to Warrington. 'I have had terrible trouble with the St. Aldate's Schools, and was afraid, at one time that building might be stopped . . . but all is well now.'

176 The Rowcroft Building ended abruptly with a blank wall immediately to the south of the imaginary archway shown in the picture.

177 Chavasse may well have made this particular point because he knew that Warrington had not been keen on calling in Sir H. Baker as a consultant in the first place.

178 27 August 1929, Warrington to Chavasse.

179 In fact the stone of the Wesleyan Hall would have needed total refacing if refaced at all, and the expense was prohibitive.

180 i.e. Block 1 and the alterations to Hannington Hall and St. Peter's House.

181 23 October 1929, C.M.C. to Warrington.

182 24 October 1929, Warrington to C.M.C.

183 Present: Chavasse, Allen, King Harman, Legge, Walker, Warrington.

184 It seems that the Council was hedging on the vital question whether to adapt or to replace, but Chavasse remained optimistic.
    8 November 1929, E.H.F.S., Diary: '. . . to bed late, for Chavasse came in and kept me talking about plans for new building on site of Wesleyan Schools.'

185 4 December 1928, the Council had decided to invest £6000 in $3\frac{1}{2}\%$ Conversion Loan in the name of the Trustees, through Barclays Bank at Wellington, Shropshire.
    11 March 1929, the Council decided to invest £1500 in $4\frac{1}{2}\%$ Conversion Loan in the name of the Trustees, for further endowment of the first Tutorship, bringing the total sum up to £7,500. In November 1929 the total sum invested was brought up to £10,000. Barclays Bank at Wellington had been used by Warrington when he took over the Wrekin School near by, and he kept Trust funds there.

186 Present: Chavasse, Allen, Cushendun, Graham Brown, King Harman, Legge, Walker, Warrington.
    According to Warrington (16 January 1931, Warrington to C.M.C.), Lord Cushendun 'strongly urged that all the money should be found before we did any building.' The statement must refer to this particular meeting of the Council. Lord Cushendun attended only two meetings.

187 11 December 1929, Parnells wrote to Dodd that they were willing to

undertake Block 2 on the same terms as Block 1, and referred to an 'interview with you and the Revd. Father [sic] Chavasse, on Monday last.'

188 Present: Chavasse, Allen, Lord Cushendun, Graham Brown, King Harman, Legge, Warrington.

189 Present: Chavasse, Allen, Dowdall, King Harman, Legge, Oman, Warrington.

190 30 November 1928.

191 20 February 1930, P. G. Green to C.M.C.

192 21 February 1930, C.M.C. to Burn.

193 7 April 1930, Cumming to Warrington. Sends cheque for £1,500 for Parnells, who will soon need £2,500 more. 'I am afraid we cannot help you to meet this further payment as the cheque I now send you reduces the Appeal Fund to a rather low figure. However, as you can get about £10,000 from Barclays Bank on our securities you should have no difficulty. . . .'

194 3 January 1930, Burn to Cumming: 'The Trust has already advanced a very considerable sum to St. Peter's and Mr. Warrington has no intention of straining the Trust Funds any further.'
'. . . 15 January 1930, Burn to Cumming: '. . . at the end of last term it was quite impossible to use the Funds of the Trust for the payment of the St. Peter's Hall Accounts. The Schools had the prior claim on our Funds. . . .'

195 25 November 1929, Cumming to Warrington: 'I appreciate your remarks regarding extended credit [letter of 10 October] as a sound business principle, but these people had no reason to suppose they would have to wait for their money when their estimates were asked for.' 14 January 1930, Cumming to Warrington: 'I was shocked to receive this letter from Dobson and Bing yesterday. It is the first time an Oxford tradesman has been able to charge me with breach of promise, and I hope it will be the last. . . .'

196 Total £683-4-3.

197 3 June 1930, Burn to Cumming.

198 11 June 1930, Cumming to Warrington.

199 It had been needed; the account was overdrawn in December 1928, March, June, July, August and September 1929, though there had been no need to overdraw since October 1929.

200 The Management Committee (Chavasse, Graham Brown, Legge) met on 18 June and 'recommended that the Trustees be asked to raise the guaranteed overdraft to £1000 and to pay the interest thereon, to ensure that bills during the long vacation may be met.'

201 20 June 1930, Cumming to Warrington: 'It was a great score meeting you yesterday as we can do more in a quarter of an hour's talk than in a month of writing. This was a point Curzon impressed on me in India and I always found it useful there.'

202 25 June 1930, Green to Cumming.

203 26 June 1930, Burn to Chavasse.

204 11 November 1929, Warrington to C.M.C.

205 26 November 1929, C.M.C. to Warrington: 'I was more surprised than I can say to receive your letter about Mr. Bryan Green. . . .'

206 15 February 1930, Warrington to C.M.C.

207 19 February 1930, C.M.C. to Warrington.

208 Of which the Principal was Sidney Carter, brother of Foster Carter

who was Chavasse's brother-in-law. The 'young fellow' became in the course of time a well known Evangelical clergyman.

209   19 March 1930, Warrington to C.M.C.

210   The Conference of Evangelical Clergy and Laymen, which changed its name in 1930 from the 'Cheltenham Conference' to the 'Oxford Conference', and continued to meet annually in St. Peter's.

211   Not really convincing to Warrington, who was always quick to detect the forked tongue of Satan.

212   Incautiously expressed: he was *not* here referring to 'young Cooper', but it could have been taken to refer to him.

213   20 May 1930, Warrington to C.M.C.

214   i.e. the Trustees of the M.M.T. It is not clear whether at this time he was thinking of resigning from the Council while remaining a Trustee of the Hall; presumably so.

215   24 April 1930, C.M.C. to King Harman.

216   3 May 1930, C.M.C. to Mrs. E. M. Rowcroft, Pilmuir, Torquay. She was a member of the wealthy Wills family of Bristol.

217   8 May 1930, C.M.C. to Mrs. Rowcroft.

218   That he disliked the phrase 'staunch conservative' in this context was not really reassuring to Mrs. Rowcroft.

219   Mrs. Rowcroft's sister.

220   Bishop of Birmingham, a leading 'Modernist.'

221   Mrs. Rowcroft might have thought 'qui s'excuse, s'accuse'.

222   8 May 1930, C.M.C. to Warrington.

223   8 August 1930, Warrington to C.M.C.

224   29 May 1933, C.M.C. to the Revd. T. H. Thurland, vicar of Edwardstone, Colchester, who had complained that his family vault had disappeared and was not mollified when told that the vault must now lie beneath at least four feet of gravel drive. In January 1934 his solicitors, faced with 'cynical indifference' on the part of 'the Wesleyan Authorities' and by a refusal to take action on the part of St. Peter's Hall, threatened to 'invoke the assistance of the Court or the Home Office', and in the following October renewed their threat to start legal proceedings both against St. Peter's Hall and the Wesleyan Trustees. On 7 November 1934 R. H. Bowdler informed Mr. Thurland that the Council had asked Chavasse, Legge and himself to meet Mr. Thurland and discuss the matter. After many postponements, Mr. Thurland finally came to lunch with Chavasse and Legge on 6 November 1935. The lunch was sufficient to satisfy Mr. Thurland's misgivings, and the file was closed. No trace of the vault was discovered when the Matthews and Latner Buildings were under construction.

225   24 May 1933, C.M.C. to Thurland: . . . 'the Council of St. Peter's Hall offered to place at the disposal of the Wesleyan Trustees all gravestones which they wished to preserve . . . We have been assured by the Trustees . . . that there was no desire on the part of anyone that any gravestone should be preserved, save that of Mr. Richardson, a late Headmaster of the school. . . .'

A Thurland headstone, and a marble Thurland memorial from a wall of the old chapel, were later handed over to the Wesleyan Trustees (2 June 1933, C.M.C. to Thurland).

226   12 May 1930, C.M.C. to Warrington: 'I have just heard with dismay from Mr. Cumming that you will be unable to attend the Building

Committee.'

227 20 May 1930, C.M.C. to Warrington.

228 Cp. 12 March 1929, Cumming to King Harman: . . 'We are grateful to the Trustees for guaranteeing an overdraft if required. But I suggest it is not good business that we should pay the bank interest on an overdraft when money is due to us by those who have guaranteed the overdraft.'

229 20 May 1930, Cumming to Warrington.

230 Warrington took these words seriously; 22 May 1930, he wrote to Cumming 'As for a bill of sale on the furniture which the Trustees have paid for, they will not allow it for one moment.' Cumming had to explain, 23 May, . . . 'Pardon my reference to a possible bill of sale. It was by way of a joke, but Scotch jokes are often somewhat dull. . . .'

231 Present: Chavasse, Allen, Foster Pegg, Gisborough, Graham Brown, King Harman, Legge, Oman, Walker, Warrington.

232 On 7 January 1930 Chavasse had told Warrington that Prebendary Hinde would be willing to become a Trustee if asked, but Warrington had replied at once that he thought Canon Foster Pegg should succeed Canon Stather Hunt.

233 29 May 1930, C.M.C. to Foster Pegg: 'I particularly want to have you and no one else this year, both because you are a Trustee of the Hall and a member of our Council, and also for the great respect I bear you. . . .'

234 Tutors were invited to the lunch. E.H.F.S., Diary, 30 June 1930: 'The man who surprised me was Warrington, who turns out to be a little, youngish man with a red face and a conical head.'

235 30 [?31] July 1930, King Harman to C.M.C.

236 On 3 July 1930 Cumming wrote to Messrs. Smith and Williamson, asking to have the St. Peter's Hall accounts audited by Mr. M. G. Talbot Rice, who was now a partner in the firm.

237 3 July 1930, Warrington to Cumming.

238 26 July 1930, Cumming to Warrington, on Cumming's return from holiday.

239 17 October 1930, Cumming to Talbot Rice: 'I hope you have not found me a nuisance in connection with this audit. It is exactly such an audit as I have been pressing for since St. Peter's Hall was started, as I myself, though not a trained accountant, had to draw up the necessary accounts. I am most appreciative of the real assistance you have given me.'

240 8 August 1930, Warrington to Cumming.

241 It was perhaps a good thing that Warrington did not know what Cumming later told Talbot Rice (16 October 1930): 'I was informed by the University Chest that they do not care what accounts we keep or whether we keep any.' A permanent private hall had only to satisfy the Vice-Chancellor as to its financial stability before it was licensed.

242 23 October 1929, C.M.C. to Warrington.
    24   „   „   Warrington to C.M.C.
    28   „   „   C.M.C. to Warrington.

243 'I happen to know that Dr. Norwood, when referring to St. Peter's, said to an acquaintance of mine: "This is what we have been waiting for for years".'

244 21 May 1930, Warrington to C.M.C.

245 Cp. 13 June 1929, C.M.C. to Warrington: . . . 'I do not wish to offend Canon Stather Hunt, and he has always spoken to me about the original £10,000 as if he was personally interested in it. . . .'

246 23 May 1930, C.M.C. to Warrington, 'private and confidential'.

247 24 May 1930, Warrington to C.M.C.

248 30 July 1930, King Harman to C.M.C.

249 2 September 1930, Warrington to C.M.C.

250 6 September 1930, C.M.C. to Warrington.

251 'As it is Canon Stather Hunt's memorial we cannot mention other names such as yours. And in any case, the Canon was chairman of the Trust when you were doing your mighty works, and in many letters and conversations you have testified to his wisdom in this capacity.'

252 8 September 1930, Warrington to C.M.C.

253 Presumably Chavasse meant that a Stather Hunt memorial appeal might have been organised by the M.M.T. for the benefit of its schools.

254 11 September 1930, Warrington to C.M.C.

255 12 September 1930, Warrington to Cumming.

256 Messrs. Parnell had become restive and were demanding some payment to go on with.

257 11 October 1930, Warrington to Cumming.

258 That may have been all; but it was an indication that Barclays Bank at Wellington took it for granted that St. Peter's Hall was the property of the Trustees of the Martyrs Memorial Trust and that the Trustees of St. Peter's Hall were only nominees.

259 23 October 1930, Warrington to C.M.C.

260 Bishop of Warrington.

261 There may have been genuine misunderstanding here, Chavasse assuming that Warrington had taken in all that he had been told.

262 For some years Chavasse was Hon. Secretary of the Simeon Trustees, an evangelical Patronage Trust whose members happened to support the C.M.S. St. Aldates was one of their churches.

263 Isle of Man.

264 He countered the charge of enmity to B.C.M.S. by mentioning that Dr. S. Carter of B.C.M.S. College had just applied for entrance to St. Peter's for his son.

265 Present: Chavasse, Allen, Graham Brown, King Harman, Legge, Warrington.

266 31 October 1931, Warrington to Chavasse: '. . . it is quite out of the question for the Trustees, even when the Mortgage has been raised, to release the £10,000 Endowment . . . I am afraid you and others have been labouring under the impression that the Martyrs Memorial Trust can pour out money like water . . . I have other liabilities on my hands in addition to St. Peter's. I have saved the Jersey Ladies' College from closing down: also the Felixstowe Ladies College. . . .'

267 14 January 1931, C.M.C. to Warrington.

268 He must have known that this was not at all what Warrington meant.

269 14 January 1931.

270 16 January 1931, Warrington to C.M.C.

271 It is a nice thought that Warrington was so staunch a supporter of B.C.M.S., whose Constitution stated 'The Society deprecates the

use of worldly methods for raising funds and shall not knowingly incur debt.'

272 21 January 1931, C.M.C. to Warrington.
273 These figures were given in an enclosure:

'No. 2 Block' Estimate		Already paid	4,500
for building	17,787	In hand and expected	1,500
Walls and quad	1,743	shortly	
Architect's fees (say)	976	Loan on hypothecated	9,500
		securities (10,000) (say)	
		STILL REQUIRED	5,000
	£20,506		£20,500

N.B. The whole furnishing etc. of No. 2 Block has been paid for.'
274 30 January 1931, Warrington to C.M.C.
275 30 January 1931, C.M.C. to Warrington. The quotation is from a manuscript draft of a letter sent in Chavasse's own handwriting.
276 31 January 1931, Warrington to C.M.C.
277 Present: Chavasse, Allen, Judge Dowdall, Graham Brown, King Harman, Legge, Warrington.
278 5 February 1931, E.H.F.S., Diary.
There was an additional comment: 'It's curious how Chavasse has sobered down in financial matters lately.'
279 On 7 November 1930 Warrington had put an advertisement in *The Record*, asking support for an appeal for £10,000 (11 November 1930, C.M.C. to Warrington).
280 4 February 1931, Warrington to C.M.C.
281 On or about 17 November 1930 Warrington had sent out a large number of copies of the Annual Report, with a personal letter from himself inviting subscriptions. It included the statement: 'To meet the payments due to Contractors we have yet to raise £10,000 by the end of the present year.'
282 23 January 1931, C.M.C. to Warrington.
283 23 January 1931, Warrington to C.M.C.
284 Cp. 28 May 1931, Warrington to the Council: . . . 'during the past ten years I have worked very amicably with the Headmaster of Stowe, and the other Heads of our Schools . . . The Trust has received from them loyalty. . . .'
285 Present: Chavasse, Graham Brown, Legge. These also constituted the Management Committee on 23 January 1931.
286 29 October 1930, Warrington to C.M.C.
287 30 October 1930, C.M.C. to Warrington.
288 29 January 1931, Warrington to C.M.C.
289 30 January 1931, C.M.C. to Warrington, MS draft.
290 31 January 1931, Warrington to C.M.C.
291 There is no direct evidence to support this story, and Warrington was capable of distorting facts and of telling outright lies, as will be proved later. But Chavasse never actually contradicted it, though Warrington repeated it more than once. In any case, Chavasse's relations with Canon Stather Hunt remained entirely friendly.
292 10 February 1931, Chavasse mentioned to King Harman 'the frivolous and ridiculous charge he brought against me at our last Council meeting and which was almost an insult to be called upon to deny.'

293 11 March 1931, Burn to C.M.C.

294 9 February 1931, C.M.C. to Warrington.

295 10 February 1931, C.M.C. to Warrington.

296 But cp. 14 February 1931, Warrington to C.M.C.: . . . 'If the Trustees decide that these people's donations must be used to pay you, then I shall be left with no option but to send a letter to every supporter of the Trust giving my reasons for declining to go on with the work.'

297 11 February 1931, C.M.C. to H. Hogan, 'strictly confidential'.

298 16 February 1931, Hogan to C.M.C.

299 This must refer to December 1928, when St. Peter's was still a hostel.

300 13 February 1931, C.M.C. to King Harman.

301 14 February 1931, King Harman to C.M.C.

302 17 February 1931, C.M.C. to King Harman.

303 18 February 1931, King Harman to C.M.C. (handwritten).

304 Trust Deed Cap. VIII
18. The Trustees shall have power from time to time to make and revoke or alter any regulations as to the amount and mode of payment of the salary or other remuneration of the Master guaranteed by them as hereinafter mentioned and they shall make a report to the Council in regard thereto.

305 He was referring to people like the Revd. J. Montagu Harris. Cp. 11 February 1931, C.M.C. to Warrington: 'As you probably know Mr. Harris has been a very good friend to me, and it was he and his brother who gave my Father the first £1000 towards the St. Peter's scheme.'

306 24 February 1931, Warrington to C.M.C.

307 25 February 1931, C.M.C. to Warrington.

308 Warrington had already, 27 February 1931, told C.M.C. that this article had 'closed MANY purses.'

309 3 March 1931, C.M.C. to King Harman.

310 This was a rather flimsy cross of gilded wood, added as an after-thought in 1929, and removed in the early nineteen seventies.

311 A gentle hit at the M.M.T. members who did. The passage ran: 'There are Catholic students – so a resident informs us – who seem happy enough at St. Peter's Hall.'

312 Another passage in this letter throws light on Chavasse's outlook: . . . 'From the first I have made up my mind that I would never introduce controversy into my sermons at Chapel Services which were compulsory . . . When anything controversial is required to be emphasized I resolved, either at St. Peter's, or through St. Aldate's, to arrange a meeting to which men could be invited to attend.'

313 6 March 1931, King Harman to C.M.C.

314 On 12 March 1931 Parnells sent Cumming a bill for £422 dated 15 December 1930 for work on boundary walls; Warrington had told them that the Master of St. Peter's should pay. Cumming referred the matter to Warrington, and no action was taken.

315 20 March 1931, C.M.C. to King Harman.

316 21 April 1931, C.M.C. to Warrington.

317 The Revd. H. B. Greene had been co-opted as an additional Trustee of St. Peter's Hall on 11 April 1930.

318 Enclosing copies of the recent correspondence with Warrington.

319 There is no reason to doubt the sincerity of a resolution passed by

the Council on 28 May 1931: 'The Council of St. Peter's Hall wish to place on record their sense of real personal loss in the resignation of Sir Charles King Harman . . . they had come to feel for him a regard which amounted to affection . . . they had learned to rely on the wisdom and high ideals he brought to their discussions. . . .'

320 Ouse Manor, Sharnbrook.

321 22 June 1931, C.M.C. to Pearman Smith.

322 16 July 1936, C.M.C. to Bishop Knox: 'As I then had much the same opinion of [the M.M.T.] as I have now, I did not fall into the trap; but took some honourable men down with me from Oxford; and the whole thing exploded.' J. G. Legge was one of the 'honourable men.'

323 Presumably Chavasse was told verbally of the resolution on 13 May but did not receive a written copy till 20 May.

324 What these new points were remains unknown.

325 7 May 1931, Cumming to X.

326 11 May 1931, X to Cumming.

327 16 May 1931, Cumming to Pearman Smith. The letter ended: 'I would again impress on you that these notes make no charges against anyone, but simply ask for information.'

328 Presumably the 'theological' charges against Chavasse.

329 Cumming had asked Pearman Smith about this gift: 'It does not appear under "Donations" and the only other head it can be included in is "Advances made by the M.M. and C.E. Society". If it is so included, is it expected to be repaid to that Society?'

330 He brings up again the 'foal of an ass' and the 'Chancellor Errington' stories.

331 Present: Chavasse, Allen, Dowdall, Graham Brown, Foster Pegg, Legge, Oman, Walker.

332 The actual telegram read: 'Impossible for me to take Mr. Warrington's place on the Council could not do his work nor serve under existing conditions. Greene.' This telegram, sent from Felixstowe, arrived at 3.45 p.m. At 1.0 p.m. a telegram, sent from Monkton Combe, purporting to be from Greene, had reached Foster Pegg, asking him to see that Chavasse, as Chairman, read out the telegram from Greene to the Chairman. Chavasse suspected that Foster Pegg believed for the moment that he had suppressed this telegram. All very odd, and never explained.

333 This refers to the meeting of 30 June 1930. On 11 August 1930 Cumming had pointed out to Warrington that 'The appointment of another auditor was not sprung on the Council without notice. It came up as a recommendation of the Management Committee which was circulated to all members of Council before the meeting.' It has already been shown that on 6 March 1929 Warrington had specifically noted that 'the Management Committee considers that Messrs. Smith and Williamson . . . should be employed to audit the Accounts.'

334 This is rich, when one remembers that on 7 March 1929 Chavasse himself had told Warrington that the Auditor sent would be 'Mervyn Talbot Rice, son of Talbot Rice of Onslow Square'.

335 If there had been a libel action, it might well have been Teal v. Warrington.

336 This was perhaps the occasion when Stather Hunt and Chavasse met Chancellor Errington.

337 A favourite phrase of Warrington's, introducing a nasty allegation.

338 17 January 1935, C.M.C. to Foster Pegg.

339 Cumming mentioned that this was because 'When the date of completion arrived the Trustees could not find the money.' This stung Warrington into making the revealing comment (8 June 1931, Burn to Cumming): 'The Trustees could have found the money, but it meant using money which the Trustees wanted for the development of their Schools.'

340 10 June 1931, Cumming to Warrington: . . . 'I have paid £2250 in part discharge of Mr. Chavasse's loan.'

341 23 June 1931, Pearman Smith to C.M.C.

342 24 June 1931, C.M.C. to Gisborough.

343 26 June 1931, Gisborough to C.M.C., in his own handwriting.

344 13 June 1931, C.M.C. to Cushendun.

345 Dictated to and written out by Lady Cushendun.

346 Present: Chavasse, Allen, Foster Pegg, Graham Brown, Legge, Oman, Walker.

347 E.H.F.S., Diary: 'Sermon by Foster Pegg, who was not good. Seemed to think he was addressing children at times. He gave a good summary of Bishop Chavasse's character, however.'

348 At its previous meeting on 28 May 1931 the Council had warmly thanked Mrs. Chavasse for her services in the past two years in the domestic arrangements and furnishing of the Hall.

349 No date.

350 Present: Chavasse, Allen, Foster Pegg, Graham Brown, Legge, Oman, Walker, Warrington.

351 21 May 1931, Cumming to Pearman Smith, who would certainly have shown the letter to Warrington.

352 2 October 1931, Cumming to Warrington.

353 Chavasse's insistence on bringing in Sir Herbert Baker as consultant architect had caused heart-burnings long before this. In October 1928 R. F. Dodd had complained that the *Oxford Magazine* had mentioned only Baker's name, and Chavasse had tried to reassure him (23 October 1928) . . 'If I were you I would not raise this point with anyone. You will quite understand that Sir Herbert Baker's name gives confidence to those who might subscribe to our building scheme, and when the buildings go up you will have all the publicity and the glory that you may desire and which you will certainly deserve.' In fact, Chavasse was able to get Baker himself to write a generous letter of explanation to the *Oxford Magazine*. Yet in January 1929 Dodd found it necessary to inform the editor of the *University Gazette*: 'I am responsible for the design and carrying out of this building while Sir Herbert Baker is the Consultant Architect. I think a repetition of a misleading description of a professional character such as this needs to be corrected.' This was because Chavasse had allowed the letter from Allen, Legge, Oman and Walker to state that the additional block had been designed by Sir Herbert Baker and Mr. Dodd.

354 25 August 1931, Warrington to C.M.C.

355 Present: E. M. Walker (in the chair), Allen, Legge, Warrington.

On 17 August 1931 Pearman Smith and Sons had notified Teal that the Trustees wished a Council to be summoned to receive notice of the appointment of Trustees.

356 This point was not made clear till the Council Meeting of 7
November, when Warrington reported that the Trustees had
appointed Adair to the Council. On 12 November Adair sent a
postcard to the Bursar asking for a prospectus, and on 15 November
wrote to Chavasse: . . . 'I really cannot express to you, how proud
I am to have been permitted to associate myself with such a
wonderful enterprise – such a glorious memorial! . . . I am afraid
I am a terribly rabid Protestant! but, coming from an Ulster world,
I know what the other side means!. . . .'

357 Present: Chavasse, Allen, Foster Pegg, Graham Brown, Legge,
Oman, Walker, Warrington.

358 Another ambiguity: had the meeting been with the Trustees of the
Hall or with the Trustees of the M.M.T.?

359 That is to say, Warrington had effected this mortgage in spite of the
Council's resolution of 5 February 1931.

360 'This redemption policy' is ambiguous, but the words were taken to
cover the full amount of £7,000 a year.

361 No such special Meeting was called; the subcommittee reported to
the usual meeting of the Council in February 1932.

362 24 October 1931, Burn to Teal: 'the Auditor is preparing the Trustees
Accounts and we hope they will be ready in a few days.'

363 Even though on the previous day, 6 November 1931, Burn had
told Teal (when sending the copies of the accounts) that 'the
Accountant regrets owing to great pressure of business, he will not
be able to be present. . . .'

364 15 January 1932, Cumming to X.

365 18 January 1932, X to Cumming, 'private and confidential'.

366 On 4 February 1932.

367 Always discreet, Cumming added 'Please destroy this', and received
word that his friend had done so. But Cumming omitted to tell his
own secretary to remove the carbon copy from the files.

368 Present: Chavasse, Adair, Allen, Foster Pegg, Gisborough, Legge,
Warrington.

369 E.H.F.S. Diary, 27 September 1931: 'Chavasse had breakfast with
[the Tutors] . . and afterwards was in great form with a crop of
new building schemes. He's a wonderful man for those!'

370 A building containing a large hall and some smaller rooms, plus
caretaker's quarters, occupying the site of a group of cottages to the
north-west of the Wesley Memorial Church and extending to New
Inn Hall Street.

371 Viz., the old Methodist chapel.

372 On 18 November 1931 Chavasse had asked Warrington to fix a date
for this sub-committee to meet, but Warrington had then been ill;
and on 15 January 1932 Warrington had told Cumming that he had
been too busy to attend to St. Peter's affairs because the headmistress
of Westonbirt had suddenly resigned and the Trust had had to find
an immediate successor.

373 Present: Chavasse, Adair, Dowdall, Foster Pegg, Gisborough, Legge,
Walker, Warrington.

P. S. Allen had only once before missed a Council Meeting, but
he was now ill, and never attended again. Graham Brown, now
consecrated as 'Bishop in Jerusalem', attended the Commemoration
service in the afternoon but not the Council Meeting in the morning.

374 Fourth Annual Report, p. 20: 'If, as now seems certain, the approaching Fourth Centenary of the Reformation is nationally celebrated, that great thanksgiving will trace its origin to a series of informal conferences held in an Oxford Hall . . . which did not exist four years ago.'

375 As against £724 a month in the first year, £668 in the second, and £492 in the third.

376 The Wesleyans had started work on their new building, and their solicitors had stated that formal notice might soon be given, under the original contract, to require completion.

377 Early in February 1932 Convocation had allowed his house, 29 Beaumont Street, to be licensed as an annexe of the Hall, which meant that for the first time since October 1928 he was able to sleep at home during term. But this was not satisfactory as a permanent arrangement.

378 Though Chavasse may well have suspected that he had instigated Foster Pegg's question [see p. 13] whether Bishop Chavasse was rightly described on his memorial as the "Founder" of the Hall.

379 A retired Surrey rector.

380 He went on to quote *The Record* on the needs of St. Peter's Hall in particular.

381 On 6 November 1931.

382 One cannot help wondering whether Warrington was impelled by megalomania or by an insane desire to acquire yet more property on which mortgages might be raised.

383 Presumably at the meeting of the sub-committee to deal with the joint appeal.

384 The surroundings of the Wimpole Hall estate were entirely rural.

385 The B.C.M.S. College, of which Sydney Carter had been Principal, was not for graduate students.

386 The first brochure, issued in March 1932, stated that it had been 'founded in May [sic] 1932 through the efforts and generosity of the Rev. P. E. Warrington . . . as a memorial to the late Rev. R. Weston, Vicar of Burntwood, near Lichfield.' The College was described as 'a stately building in the Renaissance style', standing in 'well-timbered grounds of about 15 acres.'

387 In January 1937, in answer to questions put to him by solicitors in the case of Ashford v. Warrington and others.

388 There is no evidence that Chavasse attended the opening, even though Sydney Carter was a family connection, but it is known that Warrington invited Cumming to attend (letter of 23 April 1932).

389 Chavasse may have had in mind this advice to go for the wealthy when he told Warrington (2 July 1932) 'I am sorry that you could not stay for our Commemoration Service on Wednesday, as both the numbers and the importance of those who attended would have rejoiced your heart.'

390 Written on paper headed St. Mary's Rectory, Weymouth, but sent from Little Leighs Rectory, Chelmsford.

391 26 September 1933, Adair to C.M.C.

392 It was in fact declared legally null in 1938, shortly before his death.

393 19 June 1936, C.M.C. to the Rev. Wilson Cash, general secretary of C.M.S.

394 21 May 1931, W. F. Scott, H.M.S. Erebus, Devonport, to C.M.C.

395 Children's Special Service Mission, a strictly conservative Evangelical body.
396 23 May 1931, C.M.C. to Scott.
397 29 June 1932.
398 Present: Chavasse, Adair, Dowdall, Foster Pegg, Legge, Oman, Warrington and J. R. S. Taylor, who had succeeded Graham Brown as Principal of Wycliffe.
399 Foster Pegg, always cautious and reluctant to commit himself, objected that the paragraph dealt not with facts but with opinions.
400 Teal had written both to Pearman Smith and to Warrington on 20 August 1932.
401 Who had written on the previous day that he had only just heard from Pearman Smith that the Wesleyans needed £6000 in a hurry.
402 The final sentence was added in Warrington's own writing.
403 The argument is obscure: the £7,200 was certainly not for 'maintenance'.
404 29 October 1932, C.M.C. to Warrington.
405 A curious arrangement, perhaps interesting as illustrating Warrington's liking for a multiplicity of accounts.
406 Until now it had been taken for granted that undergraduates should have 'sets', i.e. two rooms each.
407 Chavasse, Legge, Walker, Warrington, plus Tinne as Bursar.
408 Present: Chavasse, Adair, Legge, Taylor.
409 The lowest tender (by £90) was from Coles Brothers of Bath, who had been recommended by Warrington. It was agreed to accept this tender (£2,200), provided that on 23 February the Council should decide to go ahead with the conversion. Tenders were also received from seven other firms.
410 11 February 1933, Green to C.M.C.
411 This was the first intimation that Warrington was losing his absolute control over the M.M.T.
412 Mr. D. Neal, 106 Edmund Street, Birmingham, chartered accountant.
413 Vice-Chancellor of Sheffield University.
414 Present: Chavasse, Adair, Legge, Walker.
415 11 July 1933, Warrington to C.M.C. . . 'May I congratulate you on your most excellent Report, which is a pleasure to read, and I hope it will make a strong appeal to a wide circle of St. Peter's friends.'
12 July 1933, C.M.C. to Warrington: 'I am indeed grateful for the kind words you say about it.'
416 St. Peter's House, the Old Rectory, had come to be called Linton House in the course of Michaelmas Term 1930. On 1 December 1930 the arms of Canon Linton, carved in stone, had been fixed above the door leading from the house into the quadrangle, which also came to be called the Linton Quad.
417 The Vice-Chancellor agreed at once to transfer the licence for an Annexe from Beaumont Street to New Inn Hall Street.
418 Present: Chavasse, Legge, Oman, Walker.
419 30 September 1933, S. Pearman Smith & Sons to C.M.C.
420 No. V Staircase.
421 Presumably in place of Greene, whose resignation was still supposed to be effective. Warrington himself had not yet resigned.
422 3 October 1933, Gisborough to C.M.C.
423 This letter was typical of Brigadier-General Adair's style of writing.

A retired officer of the Royal Artillery, living at Chatham, he looked like Mr. Punch and was very much an Army man of a former generation. But he was straightforward and honest and everybody liked him.

424 Dictated on 3 October 1933.

425 An optimistic statement.

426 Solicitor for the Legal and General Assurance Society, whose officers were the driving force behind the enquiry into the affairs of the M.M.T.

427 This was so; but the Trustees of the Hall did not appoint Trustees of the Advowson, who were ex-officio Trustees of the Hall. Obscurity was the right word!

428 11 October 1933, C.M.C. to Pearman Smith. But Chavasse was not at all happy about the proposal to appoint Mr. Neill. A little later (27 October 1933) he wrote to Mr. E. W. Wykes (of Lawrence, Graham & Co., Lincoln's Inn), solicitor to the Legal and General Society: . . . 'if the Council are to be given that full opportunity which is essential for the immense effort demanded of them, and if their appeal is to survive the many and damaging rumours consequent upon Mr. Warrington's resignation; they must be able to point to a new Trustee in his place—
(1) who will bring distinction to the Hall in the eyes of a critical and enquiring University;
(2) whose name will encourage parents and schoolmasters to send young men to the Hall, *and give assurance that the Hall will not close during their three years University course*;
(3) and whose connection with St. Peter's will gain the backing of leading Evangelicals and find favour with the general public.

Quite definitely the association of the Hall with the Martyrs Memorial Trust has not assisted the cause of St. Peter's . . . The appointment as Trustee of the new Secretary of the M.M.T. would in no way meet the requirements outlined above, and must prove fatal. . . .

I believe that the Legal and General Assurance Society are proposing to reconstitute the Governing Bodies of the Schools. I would ask that (at the moment) they require the present Trustees of St. Peter's Hall to appoint Dr. Pickard-Cambridge to fill the vacancy. . . .'

429 So they were, in so far as they had guaranteed the loan, interest etc. But Pearman Smith had not yet revealed this.

430 11 October 1933. S. Pearman Smith and Sons to C.M.C. This letter also stated, wrongly, that General Adair was a Trustee of the Advowson – an example of the 'obscurity' of which C.M.C. complained. He was a Trustee of the Hall but not of the Advowson.

431 12 October 1933, C.M.C. to Pearman Smith.

432 That very day he had received notification from a Mr. C. E. Corney, Acting Secretary, that the office of the Schools Trust had been moved from Monkton Combe Vicarage to 25/27 Charles Street, Haymarket, London.

433 27 October 1933, C.M.C. to Wykes: 'I am grateful for the time you gave me yesterday to discuss the position of St. Peter's Hall . . . the situation with which the Hall is confronted, as it emerged from our conversation [is] so serious that the appointment of a Trustee in Mr. Warrington's place becomes a matter of vital importance.'

27 Oct. 1933, C.M.C. to Bowdler: 'I had a very successful time with the Legal and General, who are prepared to back me to the uttermost.'

434 Present: Chavasse, Adair, Dowdall, Gisborough, Legge, Oman, Taylor.

435 No doubt Chavasse thought at the time that this was the end of Mr. Greene. But even if the Council could have enforced his resignation as a Trustee of the Hall in this way, it could not have removed him from the patronage of St. Peter-le-Bailey.

436 Legally, the resignation from both offices took effect on 15 November 1933.

437 Gisborough and Foster Pegg. But this was on the false assumption that Greene had resigned from the Advowson.

438 It is by no means clear that it was an oversight; v. p. 143-4. Warrington probably had a reason of his own for the arrangement.

439 8 November 1933, Gisborough to C.M.C.

440 10 November 1933, C.M.C. to Gisborough.

441 6 November 1933, S. Pearman Smith & Sons to C.M.C.

'In our own justification we have confidence that you will give the enclosed copy letter the same amount of publicity as your statement and we request that the receipt of the same be recorded in the Minutes of the Council.'

442 7 November 1933, C.M.C. to Pearman Smith.

'I would point out that this letter [of 30 Sept.] is not to *notify* me of Mr. Greene's withdrawal of his resignation, but to inform me of a fact I should never otherwise have learned unless I myself had instituted enquiries at your office . . . You informed our Council on Nov. 4th that you had heard that Mr. Greene had withdrawn his resignation at a meeting of the Martyrs Memorial Trust held on August 25 . . . I do not consider that information which I elicited by chance by enquiry of your office, more than a month after the meeting of the M.M.T. was held, to be that information to which I am entitled as Chairman of the Council of St. Peter's Hall.'

443 11 November 1933, C.M.C. to Pearman Smith.

444 27 February 1934, Pearman Smith to Bowdler: 'So far as we are aware the Trustees have not kept Minutes since the foundation of the Hall. We ourselves started a Minute Book commencing with the Meeting held on Wed. 15 November 1933 which has been kept regularly since.'

445 Proposed by Gisborough, seconded by Greene.

446 The tax had been quite properly deducted but improperly retained.

447 18 November 1933, S. Pearman Smith & Sons to Tinne.

448 20 November 1933, Tinne to Pearman Smith & Sons.

449 C. E. Corney, Acting Secretary, Schools Trust. A few days earlier Chavasse had tried to find out from him about investments of the Hall, hypothecated by the Trustees, a matter 'in which the finances of the Hall have been interlocked with those of the Schools Trust.'

450 23 November 1933, Pearman Smith & Sons to Tinne.

451 Secretary, Mr. D. Neal.

452 19 December 1933, C.M.C. to Pearman Smith.

Cp. 23 December 1933, C.M.C. to Wykes: 'As the matter of the Trustees has not been settled, the members of St. Peter's Hall

Council will not be in a position to discuss with the Central Finance Committee ways and means regarding the liabilities on the Hall undertaken by the M.M.T. . . If the Trustees of St. Peter's Hall are not in a position to carry out the obligations they have contracted to fulfil and it is desired that the Council of the Hall should share the responsibility with them, then the first necessity is for the Council to have the five Trustees they asked for at their Council Meeting on November 4. . . .'

453   27 December 1933, Gisborough to C.M.C.

454   A phrase which shows that Lord Gisborough was still confused: the vacancy was for a Trustee of the Hall, not for a patron of the Advowson.

455   Chavasse, Legge and Taylor attended, together with Bowdler and Cumming.

456   12 January 1934, Pearman Smith had sent Cumming a copy of the Trustees' balance-sheet as at 1 October 1933, prepared by Price Waterhouse & Co. This contained an item '£15,400 suspense account – Council of St. Peter's Hall' which worried Cumming, and another puzzling item: 'Suspense account. Amounts charged in the books of St. Peter's Hall of which the source of payment has not been traced £2,266.' 23 January 1934, Pearman Smith sent Cumming a copy of a letter from Price Waterhouse about the second item: . . . 'The position is that a Balance Sheet was prepared as at 31 August 1929 by a Mr. Seale [sic], a Bristol accountant . . . and the books of The Trustees of St. Peter's Hall were opened on the basis of Mr. Scale's figures. Details are not, however, available of the firms and individuals to whom payments making up the Balance Sheet figures were made. We have been able to identify that many payments were made by the Martyrs Memorial Trust and by the various Schools within the Schools Trust on account of St. Peter's Hall, but after dealing with these items we were left with differences . . which we could only credit to Suspense Account . . Our opinion is that in all probability payments making up that figure [£2,266] have been made by one or other of the Schools, and we are afraid that at this stage it is rather unlikely that they can be identified.'

457   29 January 1934, E.H.F.S., Diary: 'Chavasse told us that Martyrs Memorial Trust have now given up all connection with us, as they've practically been 'dispossessed' by their creditors, the Legal and General Insurance people. Means St. Peter's is saddled with whole liability for about £90,000.'

458   In his book *The Chavasse Twins* Selwyn Gummer tells the following story:
'The morning the letter arrived with its shattering news the Master walked into the Bursar's office and said to his friend Toby Tinne: "I can gather from all sources about £10,000. Can you find a similar amount?" A little breathlessly Tinne said he could and would. "Well now", said Chavasse as casually as could be, "I can go back and finish my letters".'
This story is told as if the incident occurred in January 1934, but it would appear to be based on a dramatised and compressed version of events which had occurred in October 1930 and February/June 1933.

459   General Manager, Legal and General.

460 The effect of these elections was: —
    (1) Patrons of the Advowson: Adair, Foster Pegg, Gisborough, Greene, Taylor (five).
    (2) Trustees of the Hall: Adair, Chavasse, Foster Pegg, Gisborough, Greene, Taylor (six).
    (3) Patrons upon the Council: Adair, Foster Pegg, Gisborough, Taylor (four).

461 Presumably he was thinking of claiming the right to be the fourth Trustee on the Council, instead of Taylor, who had a place ex officio.

462 The meetings were held in the Charing Cross Hotel. Pearman Smith attended. On 6 February 1934 Chavasse asked him to 'have in readiness deeds of resignation, as it may be that we may still persuade Mr. Greene to sign such deeds, tho' I express myself doubtful on the point.'

463 24 March 1934, C.M.C. to Pickard-Cambridge: 'You will remember that at the meeting we both attended in London last autumn to be informed of the crisis which had overtaken the Martyrs Memorial Trust, you very kindly told me that you would be willing to become a Trustee and a member of Council of St. Peter's Hall in place of Mr. Warrington.'

27 October 1933 Chavasse had written to Wykes: 'The obvious person to be appointed as the new Trustee is Dr. A. W. Pickard-Cambridge, Vice-Chancellor of Sheffield University, and already a member of the Schools Trust. . . His appointment would silence all rumour in the University; and would undoubtedly influence Sir Richard Livingstone to take the place of the late Dr. P. S. Allen upon the Council. Sir Richard, who is Vice-Chancellor of Belfast University, succeeds Dr. Allen as President of Corpus Christi College. Both these gentlemen are Evangelicals . . . Dr. Pickard-Cambridge . . so far possesses the confidence of the Martyrs Memorial Trust that he has been made a member of the Central Finance Committee of its Schools.'

464 Trust Deed, Cap. III, s. 4.

465 The position now was: —
    (1) Patrons of the Advowson: Chavasse, Foster Pegg, Gisborough, Greene, Taylor (five).
    (2) Trustees of the Hall: Adair, Chavasse, Foster-Pegg, Gisborough, Greene, Legge, Pickard-Cambridge, Taylor (eight).
    (3) Patrons upon the Council: Chavasse, Foster-Pegg, Gisborough, Taylor (four).

466 Back in October 1929 Chavasse had asked Warrington whether the Trustees could help 'towards the £100 I need to provide a curate for St. Peter-le-Bailey' (19 October 1929, C.M.C. to Warrington). Warrington refused: (22 October 1929) . . 'I do not think there is any possibility of . . . a Grant towards the maintenance of a Curate . . . if they did so, they would be acting contrary to the terms of their Trust Deed, which does not provide for the payment of Curates' salaries. [Chavasse had been helped to have a curate at St. Aldate's while he was getting St. Peter's going, but] I provided that money, not the Trust.'

467 Investments made from the Appeal Fund.

468 These were the investments which the Council on 8 February

resolved to sell. The first use to be made of the proceeds was to pay off the £3250 loan referred to in (4).

469 It seems that Pearman Smith and Sons had ceased to be the M.M.T. solicitors shortly before this time, though they continued to act for the Trustees of St. Peter's Hall because they also acted for Lord Gisborough. Robbins Olivey and Lake were a London firm.

470 Senior partner of Robbins Olivey and Lake.

471 13 February 1934, Adams to Cumming: 'Both of us have been put in a false position and it is really a question of how to deal with the situation to our mutual advantage in the friendliest way possible as we both obviously have to suffer. . . .'
Cumming had had a talk with Adams in London on 8 February.

472 15 February 1934, Cumming to Adams.

473 2 July 1934, Cumming to Adams: . . . 'When you interviewed the Inspector of Taxes here, you gave me to understand that you had arranged to pay the arrears of Income Tax by instalments and that it was improbable that we should be called on to meet this. . . .'

474 23 March 1934, Cumming to Adams: refers to meeting on the previous day, and adds 'I have never before faced the Martyrs Memorial [sic].'

475 Cp. 26 September 1932, C.M.C. to Talbot Rice: 'My dear Mervyn . . . I cannot tell you what a help it is to have a friend and adviser like yourself pilotting [sic] us through these first difficult years.'

476 28 February 1934, Pearman Smith had sent Cumming particulars of the five persons on whose lives the policies had been taken out. They were three clerks, one accountant, an assistant bursar at Wrekin College, and Warrington himself.

477 24 March 1934, C.M.C. to Pearman Smith: asks for 'a copy of the document that the Trustees of St. Peter's Hall were asked to sign last Thursday . . . I do not understand the Trustees . . being summoned by their own solicitors to a meeting at 2 p.m. to sign, at a moment's notice, a document which they had been given no opportunity of even reading.'
26 March 1934, Pearman Smith to C.M.C. '. . . as Solicitors to the Trustees we were prepared at the meeting . . . to explain fully the purport of the Deed of Substituted Charge and we should have thought you could have relied on us as such Solicitors to have fully protected the interests of the Trustees. We wrote each of the Trustees (yourself included) on the 8th inst. informing them of the details of the proposal and it would have been an unusual course indeed for us to have sent to each of the Trustees a copy of the proposed Deed of Substituted Charge.'

478 28 March 1934, C.M.C. to Gisborough, private.

479 Dr. Pickard-Cambridge was a man of gracious appearance, who spoke with an air of benign authority which could sometimes be deceptive. The story was told that on one occasion as a Senior Fellow of Balliol he had scotched a proposal that certain iron railings should be removed by pointing out that, as he well remembered, they had been firmly fixed in concrete foundations; afterwards two Junior Fellows pulled up the railings with the utmost ease finding them innocent of all foundations.

480 29 March 1934, C.M.C. to Pickard-Cambridge.

481 31 March 1934, C.M.C. to Talbot Rice. No copy in the files.

482   27 February 1934, Pearman Smith to Bowdler: 'There has never
been any actual connection in a legal sense between St. Peter's Hall
and the Schools. The property of the seven School Companies,
namely, Stowe School Ltd., Wrekin College Wellington Company
Ltd., The Schools Trust Ltd., Felixstowe School Ltd., Harrogate
College Ltd., Canford School Ltd., and Westonbirt School Ltd.
have been mortgaged to secure the £50,000 Mortgage advanced to
St. Peter's Hall by the Legal and General but not to secure the
£20,000 Mortgage advanced by the Clerical Medical and General'
. . . 'Hannington Hall was mortgaged with other property to the
Legal and General to secure the £50,000.'
10 April 1934, Pearman Smith to Cumming: . . . 'The Legal and
General would only lend this £50,000 in consideration of guarantees
being given by the School Companies . . . under these Guarantees
these School Companies make themselves liable for the £50,000 and
for the interest and also for the premiums on the life policies. These
guarantees are in the form of Debentures.'

483   26 September 1929, C.M.C. to Hobbs . . 'I am very anxious to keep
him interested in the St. Peter's Scheme . . . I really hope that
some day he may find himself able to give a great push forward to
a work which must appeal to him.' Mr. Morris was by then Sir
William Morris.

484   21 November 1930, C.M.C. to Morris, enclosed in a letter to Hobbs,
to make sure that it reached him.

485   This was the second time that Chavasse drew Morris' attention to
the site which he later purchased for Nuffield College.

486   The Wingfield Hospital, later called the Wingfield-Morris Hospital
and finally the Nuffield Orthopaedic Centre.

487   28 November 1930, C.M.C. to Hobbs.

488   By Canon J. B. Lancelot, published 1929.

489   He regarded it as the working of Providence.

490   No letters have been preserved. On 11 May 1934 the Council
'expressed their keen appreciation of the signal services which Mr.
J. G. Legge had rendered in bringing the financial position of St.
Peter's Hall to Lord Nuffield's notice.'

491   E.H.F.S., Diary, 27 April 1934: 'Heard news that Lord Nuffield has
today given Chavasse £10,000 for the Hall . . . It's come just at the
critical moment, when Chavasse was getting really worried about
finance. Not that it will go very far, but at least it's a good start.'

492   30 April 1934, Pearman Smith to C.M.C., in his own hand-writing,
from his house, Park Hall, Walsall.

493   1. That the interest on the Mortgage shall be 5% for the present.
A lower rate of interest may be considered when the principal
has substantially been reduced, say to £45,000.

2. That the £5,000 surrender value of the policies taken out with
the Legal & General shall be used towards paying off the
Mortgage of £20,000 with the Clerical and Medical Assurance
Society, and that the title deeds thus released be deposited with
the Legal and General Assurance Society, who will then become
the sole mortgagee of the Hall.

3. That the Legal & General Assurance Society will receive at any
time any sum for the reduction of the Mortgage; but that the
Hall shall find on an average £1,000 per annum for this purpose.

4. This involves a payment of £3,500 for the first year, decreasing by £50 each year for 50 years. If more than £1,000 is found in any year the interest will be further decreased to a proportionate extent.

5. The Schools Trust can give no help for at least 2 years, but they are still pledged to give what help they can, and may do so hereafter.

6. The Council as well as the Trustees of the Hall to become parties to this agreement, which involves no personal liability.

494 Present: Chavasse, Adair, Foster Pegg, Gisborough, Greene, Legge, Oman, Taylor, Walker together with Pearman Smith.

495 No. IV Staircase, henceforth officially 'The Emily Ann Morris Building'.

496 The sale of which had already been recommended by the Council on 8 February 1934.

497 10 May 1934, Robbins Olivey & Lake to S. Pearman Smith & Sons:
. . . 'our clients the Martyrs Memorial & Church of England Trust, are prepared to release the two life policies of £10,000 each [with the Clerical, Medical & General Society] to the Trustees of St. Peter's Hall, provided they are released from the covenants contained in the mortgage and from all liability . . . In releasing these policies, we wish to place on record that our clients, the M.M.C.E. Trust, are not in any way giving up any claim they may have against St. Peter's Hall in connection with any other matter or transaction.'

The particulars of this mortgage with the Clerical & Medical were: —

Interest on mortgage of £20,000	£1100-0-0
Premiums on policies on two lives of £10,000 each to produce £20,000 by the year 1951	£834-3-4
Total annual payment	£1934-3-4

498 Present: Chavasse, Adair, Dowdall, Legge, Oman, Pickard-Cambridge.

499 16 May 1934, Cumming to Pearman Smith.

500 13 March 1929, C.M.C. to Warrington: 'Mr. Pearman Smith quite defeats me . . . Of course it is difficult for a solicitor outside Oxford to grasp the situation.'

501 3 August 1934, C.M.C. to Pearman Smith.

502 8 August 1934, Pearman Smith to 'C. A. Chilton Esq., Solicitor, 88 St. Aldates.'
Copy to Cumming for information.

503 11 August 1934, Cumming to Pearman Smith: . . . 'it is useless calling a meeting of the Council and Trustees this month as comparatively few will attend.'
13 August 1934, Pearman Smith to Cumming: 'I have all along appreciated the difficulties which would arise during the month of August and have done my utmost to avoid them.'

504 14 August 1934, Cumming to Pearman Smith.

505 15 August 1934, Pearman Smith to Cumming, who replied on 17 August: 'I find it difficult to reconcile your letter dated 15th August with your previous letters.'

506 The office of the Schools Trust had now been shifted to Thames House, Millbank.

507 29 June 1934, K. H. Adams to Cumming.

508 3 July 1934, Adams to Cumming: 'I am sorry if my letter gave you a nasty shock.'

509 The Council had wished Pearman Smith to attend, but he was unable to do so.

30 June 1934, Bowdler to Pearman Smith: [The Council] 'very much wished that you should be present, as they believed that you have a knowledge of the situation possessed by no one else.'

510 14 May 1934, C.M.C. to Gisborough: '. . . one name certainly we ought to consider [for the Council, in place of Cushendun], that of Dr. Norwood, who will be taking up residence in Oxford as President of St. John's College this October.'

511 E.H.F.S., Diary, 3 November 1934. 'Heard [from C.M.C.] that Warrington has let Hall in for £3000 income-tax claim. Very strange stories now about Warrington. Seems as if he is bound to get into very hot water.'

512 15 May 1934, C.M.C. to Pickard-Cambridge: 'I am sure you will rejoice with me that the last link has now been severed between the Hall and the Martyrs Memorial Trust; and that we are now free to go forward uncrippled by our unhappy and unsavoury past. I would only thank you most warmly for joining us in a desperate hour, and helping us on our way to stability and self-respect.'

513 For the sake of clarity, it may be useful to set out the position in June 1934.

Patrons of St. Peter-le-Bailey

* Lord Gisborough	* Revd. J. R. S. Taylor
* Canon Foster Pegg	* Revd. C. M. Chavasse
* Revd. H. B. Greene	

Council of St. Peter's Hall

* Revd. C. M. Chavasse ⎫
* Lord Gisborough   ⎬ ex officio as Patrons of St.
* Canon Foster Pegg ⎪ Peter-le-Bailey (4 only out of 5
* Revd. J. R. S. Taylor ⎭ Patrons were entitled to be
                              members of the Council)

* General Adair   ⎫ additional members appointed by
* Dr. A. W. Pickard-Cambridge ⎬ the Trustees under Cap. III, s. 4.

Judge Dowdall ⎫ appointed by Lord Derby
* J. G. Legge   ⎭

Dr. E. M. Walker ⎫ appointed by Hebdomadal Council
Sir R. Livingstone ⎭ (Livingstone from 1 Oct. 1934)

Lord Cushendun ⎫
Sir Charles Oman ⎭ appointed by the Trustees under Cap. III s. 3c.

* Trustee of the Hall.

N.B. Chavasse was also Chairman of the Council ex officio as Rector of St. Peter-le-Bailey.

Taylor was also member of the Council ex officio as Principal of Wycliffe Hall.

514 2 July 1934, C.M.C. to Chilton: 'The Council of St. Peter's Hall have appointed a sub-committee to alter their Trust Deed, and they would like to employ you as the Solicitor for this purpose . . . I do not think it will be a big matter. . . .'

515 Present: Chavasse, Legge, Pickard-Cambridge, Taylor.

516 27 September 1934, C.M.C. to W. J. Robbins (of Robbins, Olivey and Lake, 218 Strand): asked him to take action in these matters.

517 14 September 1934, Cumming to Adams.

518 15 September 1934, Adams to Cumming.

519 26 October 1934, Gisborough to C.M.C.

520 27 October 1934, C.M.C. to Gisborough. The copy in the files is dated 29th but this is a mistake.

521 Lord Cushendun had been an invalid for some time. The last service done by him to the Hall was on 6 January 1934, when he sent Chavasse a manuscript letter of introduction to the then Prime Minister, Stanley Baldwin. This letter was in fact never used, and remains in the files. It reads: 'My dear Baldwin. As a member of the Council of St. Peter's Hall, Oxford, I have been asked by the Master, the Rev. C. M. Chavasse, to give him a personal introduction to you as he wants to consult you on some point connected with the finances of the Hall. I am therefore sending him this letter for him to forward to you when asking for an appointment, which I hope you will be kind enough to give him. With best wishes, yours sincerely, Cushendun.'

522 Cp. 14 September 1934, Cumming to Pearman Smith: 'Isn't it rather late for the Trustees to want to be satisfied as to the correctness of the demand for income-tax, seeing that for four years they neglected to give any information to the Inland Revenue authorities? Especially as you now admit they have no means of checking it.'

523 25 October 1934, C.M.C. to Nuffield.

524 29 October 1934, Nuffield to C.M.C.: willing to serve, but cannot undertake to attend meetings.

525 Miss Anstey.

526 Chavasse was always apt to speak and write with a vehemence which made him seem dictatorial even when he was anxious to conciliate.

527 1 November 1934, Gisborough to C.M.C., 'private and confidential'.

528 He explained that at his age he found train journeys more and more trying.

529 31 October 1934.

530 2 November 1934, Pearman Smith to C.M.C.: . . . 'I cannot, at the moment, refer to the Minute Book, but whether there is a Minute or not as to Lord Gisborough being chairman, I can say that he has always been recognised as such, even by yourself.'

531 Present: Chavasse, Adair, Dowdall, Legge, Pickard-Cambridge, Taylor, Walker.

532 Chavasse also suggested that it might be best in future if Bowdler acted as secretary for the Trustees as well as for the Council.

533 19 December 1934, C.M.C. to Gisborough.

534 12 December 1934.

535 9 January 1935, C.M.C.to Foster Pegg: . . . 'I am glad to think that with your resignation one of your many anxieties and responsibilities will be removed from your shoulders. It is tragic that you have to bear so heavy a burden after your retirement from long and distinguished service in the Church.'

536 This in fact never happened.

537 14 January 1935, C.M.C. to Adair.

538 21 January 1935, C.M.C. to Adair, who replied by postcard (23

January): 'All clear – many thanks. On we go. HRA.'

539   21 January 1935, C.M.C. to Foster Pegg 'He has expressed his willingness to resign the Trusteeship, for, as he told the Council, he had come on the Governing Body of the Hall to help to guide its traditions and had not realised that he was responsible for keeping a watchful eye on its finances.'

      Foster Pegg had heard from Pearman Smith that there was 'a possibility' that General Adair might go, and had asked Chavasse for an explanation (Foster Pegg to C.M.C., 18 January 1935).

540   4 January 1935, Greene to C.M.C.

541   A date which rebutted his statement in the letter of 31 December 1934 that the covenant had been made 'when she gave' the £10,000.

542   5 January 1935, Robbins to C.M.C.

543   17 January 1935.

544   Chavasse was writing in a hurry and had not checked his facts: Lord Gisborough had said nothing of the sort, though it had been hoped that he would.

545   26 January 1935, C.M.C. to Pearman Smith.

546   28 January 1935, Pearman Smith to C.M.C.

547   28 January 1935, Gisborough to C.M.C.

548   It is interesting that Gisborough thought that the advowson had been obtained by purchase and not by exchange.

549   Chilton had prepared a draft of a remodelled Trust Deed, but on 11 January 1935 Bowdler had warned him that serious delay might be caused by Greene's refusal to resign.

550   There was an element of bluff here, for at this date Chavasse did not possess a copy of any 'Advowson Deed of the Church'. On 17 January 1935 he had asked Pearman Smith to send him 'the Patronage Deed of St. Peter-le-Bailey'.

551   26 January 1935, C.M.C. to Gisborough. 'I have received this morning a letter from Mr. Pearman Smith which has worried me. He tells me that you are resigning from the Trusteeship of St. Peter's Hall . . . but not from the advowson of St. Peter-le-Bailey. . . .'

552   The letter, marked 'private and confidential', started 'Dear Chavasse'. All his previous letters had started 'Dear Mr. Chavasse'.

553   A remarkable confession, showing how easy it had been for Warrington to dominate his colleagues.

554   Pearman Smith would hardly have relished this statement.

555   9 February 1935, Greene to C.M.C.

556   It is not clear when this happened.

557   It is curious that Chavasse did not at once refute the statement that the living had been bought. Presumably he was as much in the dark as Lord Gisborough, since Warrington had handled everything himself; but he certainly knew that there had been an exchange of livings, not a purchase.

558   28 January 1935, Mrs. Rowcroft to C.M.C.

559   Cp. 19 February 1934, C.M.C. to Adair: 'I had a talk with Mr. Greene and promised him that I would add the words "the Thirty Nine Articles" in any official description of the aim and purposes of the Hall . . . [but] it is a little unsafe today to play on the 39 Article pitch, as Modernists such as Professor Streeter and Dr. Major have asserted in the *Times* that Modernists find no difficulty in signing the 39 Articles. . . .'

560 31 January 1935, C.M.C. to Mrs. Rowcroft. Knowing that she objected to typewritten letters, he wrote in his own hand, but left a draft in the file which is here quoted.

561 Chavasse was clearly thinking of advice he had received from Chilton (dated 14 July 1934): 'I have considered the two Trust Deeds . . . it seems clear that under Cap. XV the Trustees . . . can, by a further Deed, revoke or vary the administrative provisions . . . but not the primary objects and principles as set out therein.'

562 Present: Chavasse, Legge, Taylor.

563 On 8 January 1935 Nuffield had unveiled the Emily Ann Morris Memorial, a bronze bust by the sculptor Alec Miller, in a niche designed by Dodd, in the entrance lobby of No. IV Staircase. The Latin inscription incised beneath the bronze had been composed by Cyril Bailey, who was then Public Orator.

564 Pearman Smith had reported on 13 February that Gisborough had signed a deed of retirement, and Foster Pegg had telephoned on 15 February that he also had signed the deed.

565 This was the result of conversations between Chavasse and the local manager of the Midland Bank, which had been so helpful in 1933.

56S No wonder Pearman Smith a month earlier had not been able to send Chavasse 'the Patronage Deed'.

567 Sent to Chilton by Bowdler on 4 February 1935. By a deed of 5 April 1864 Lord Chancellor Westbury, acting under powers given by the Lord Chancellor's Augmentation Act, had sold for £1000 to Henry Linton the advowson of St. Peter-le-Bailey, of which he was already Rector. By the deed of 20 April 1864 Henry Linton transferred the Advowson to five Trustees, providing that all future Trustees should be 'well known to be zealously attached to the great Evangelical principles of the Reformed Faith'.

568 The grantees were
   (1) W. W. Champneys, Rector of St. Pancras (later Dean of Lichfield; died 1875).
   (2) E. Auriol, Rector of St. Dunstan's in the West (died 1880).
   (3) Henry Linton himself (died 1878).
   (4) J. C. Colqhoun, of Chartwell, Westerham (died 1870).
   (5) E. P. Hathaway, of Lincoln's Inn (died 1897).

569 Chilton added that Vaisey was much disappointed.

570 29 January 1878, F. J. Chavasse was presented by the Rev. E. Auriol, Canon H. Linton, the Rev. E. P. Hathaway, the Rev. H. Wright, and the Rev. W. H. Barlow, who later became Dean of Peterborough.

571 28 October 1889, H. C. Squires was presented by the Rev. E. P. Hathaway, the Rev. W. H. Barlow, the Rev. H. E. Fox, the Earl of Harrowby, and J. Deacon.
   3 October 1893. W. Talbot Rice presented by the same five.

572 Because four of the five patrons were ex-officio members of the Council.

573 Greene was pardonably confused. The deed of Resignation dealt with Trusteeship, not membership of the Council, which was technically different. For that reason the Council of 16 February 1935 had asked for formal letters from Gisborough and Foster Pegg resigning from the Council; they both complied.

574 On 13 February 1935 Pearman Smith and Sons had informed

Bowdler that they had received a letter from Messrs. Robbins, Olivey and Lake stating that they had been called upon to advise the M.M. Trustees in the matter of the Advowson of St. Peter-le-Bailey and requesting copies of all relevant documents.

575 1 June 1935, C.M.C. to Chilton.
576 8 June 1935 Pearman Smith and Sons to C.M.C.
577 i.e. as a co-Trustee.
578 11 June 1935, Chilton to C.M.C.
579 Present: Chavasse, Adair, Legge, Livingstone, Taylor, Walker.
580 i.e. from the Council.
581 It was always Chavasse's belief that if you were going to use flattery, you should lay it on with a trowel; but here he was quite sincere. He might well have applied to General Adair some words of R. L. Stevenson: 'I judged him a man of a childlike nature – with that sort of innocence and courtesy that, I think, is only to be found in old soldiers or old priests.'
582 The Revd. R. R. Neill.
583 25 July 1935, Cumming to Adair.
584 Neill had asked Chavasse to meet him and discuss Adair's position, but Chavasse had quite properly refused.
585 It was always easy to be confused about Mr. Greene. In this case, Chavasse objected that Chilton's wording would not do because Greene had signed the covenant *before* he became a Trustee of the Hall: '. . . it is not so much a case of Mr. Greene having "ceased to be loyal" . . . but that he has never been loyal and his disloyalty has been found out.' In fact, as Chilton was able to point out (24 June 1935), Greene had become a Trustee of the Hall by deed dated 11 April 1930, so there was no difficulty.
586 22 June 1935, C.M.C. to Chilton.
587 Present: Chavasse, Dowdall, Legge, Livingstone, Nuffield, Oman, Pickard-Cambridge, Taylor, Walker.
588 1 July 1935, Chilton to Robbins.
589 10 July 1935, Robbins to Chilton.
590 25 July 1935, C.M.C. to Greene.
591 Present: Chavasse, Dowdall, Legge, Pickard-Cambridge.
592 Chilton had obtained some missing documents (deeds of 1875, 1882 and 1889) from the Oxford Churches Trust, to which the purported Trustees of St. Peter-le-Bailey had belonged in 1928. That Trust also owned the advowsons of St. Clement and St. Ebbe in Oxford.
593 His mother, Effie Fox, widow.
594 27 July 1935, C.M.C. to Pearman Smith.
595 Because after 31 July 1935 he would no longer be a Trustee.
596 29 July 1935, Pearman Smith to C.M.C.
597 There is no trace in the files of any letter informing Pearman Smith that he was no longer solicitor to the Trustees, and there was no reference in the Council minutes.
598 2 August 1935, C.M.C. to Pearman Smith.
599 9 August 1935, Pearman Smith to C.M.C.
600 Then vicar of a church in West London.
601 Presumably that of Mr. Greene.
602 25 July 1935, C.M.C. to Neill.
603 27 July 1935, Robbins to Chilton. The letter started: 'I tried to get you on the telephone to confer with you yesterday.' Chilton made

a note in pencil here: 'I was in the office all day.' The letter ended 'With kind regards', a form of words not then usual in business correspondence except between personal friends. Chilton did not regard Robbins in that light.

604 1 August 1935, Robbins to C.M.C.

605 Possibly by General Adair, on receipt of his copy of the minutes of the Council Meeting of 31 July 1935.

606 Present: Chavasse, Adair, Dowdall, Legge, Livingstone, Pickard-Cambridge, Walker.

607 On 8 August and 16 August 1935 Chilton had written to Greene asking for the documents to be sent to him, as he had taken over from Pearman Smith, and telling him that his signature was not now required.

608 On 27 September and 2 October 1935 Cumming had sent Greene mandates for paying interest on investments to the Midland Bank instead of to Barclays. On 15 October Greene had informed the manager of the Midland Bank that he did not intend to sign them. On 24 October the Midland Bank informed Cumming that a legal opinion had been obtained 'and it appears that the matter can be dealt with under an Order of Court . . . and it is suggested that you should put the matter in the hands of your Solicitor. . . .'

609 On 13 November 1935 Greene wrote to the Midland Bank: 'Should any suggestion be made to you to the effect that I am no longer a member of the Council of St. Peter's Hall and one of its Trustees I wish to state that I hold myself so to be, and warn you that until the matter is settled by the Courts you will be well advised to disregard any suggestion for handing over any moneys you may hold without my signature as well as those of Lord Gisborough, General Adair and Canon Foster Pegg.'

610 Bishop of Rochester, an old friend. On 22 July 1935, Linton Smith had written to Chavasse: 'My dear Chris, I have been thinking over your very kind suggestion that I should be one of the Trustees of St. Peter's Hall. Nothing would give me greater personal pleasure for many reasons. But I am writing to question the proposal in the interests of the Hall. My name does not inspire confidence in a very large number of those whose support you need; as I have had occasion to say to you before, I unfortunately rouse mistrust, and it seems to me that in the best interests of the Hall personal considerations should be put on one side, and you should get someone whose name has not these unpleasant associations in the minds of a good many of the stricter Evangelicals!'

611 30 October 1935. Three days earlier Judge Dowdall had made a personal appeal to General Adair: 'We all of us only want to do what is right . . . What I have called the B.C.M. deed [i.e. the Rowcroft covenant] though not widely known is widely suspected, and as a member of the National Church Assembly I for one became aware of the widespread aversion to it especially among Evangelicals of the Bishop Chavasse type . . . Some of your colleagues of the Martyrs Memorial . . . have thought that it is the "right and proper thing" to resign their trust in favour of those on whose shoulders not only the welfare but the very existence of the Hall now rests. And who am I to say they are wrong?' On 29 October 1935 Adair had replied to Dowdall . . . 'I am confident that if representatives

of the Council of St. Peter's Hall and of the Martyrs Memorial Trust get together, and hear each other's case quietly stated, without any ill feeling, a just settlement will be arrived at. We have – or think we have – all, been badly let down – well, let us come together – and surely we can agree. . . .'

612 This was not strictly true. There was certainly no such refusal recorded in the Council minutes.

613 Chavasse called this 'the Mombasa School'. Actually the school was at Limaru, not far from Nairobi, though it was in the Anglican diocese of Mombasa.

614 31 October 1935, Wykes to C.M.C., private and confidential.

615 31 October 1935, Johnson to C.M.C., private and confidential.

616 It was saved at his own expense, by the Bishop of Mombasa.

617 5 November 1935, Chilton to C.M.C.: 'I am of opinion that before I have any kind of talk with Mr. Robbins, Counsel's letter should be sent to his firm. It is imperative that an Order of Court should be obtained . . . and it would not do to let Mr. Robbins think that there was any weakening on this point . . .'
6 November 1935, C.M.C. to Chilton: 'Please send Counsel's letter to Mr. Robbins, together with a private letter from yourself offering to let him see documents. . . .'

618 29 October 1935, C.M.C. to Mrs. Rowcroft. A pencil draft only, as before.

619 This time, typescript.

620 The deed of covenant of 22 Nov. 1930, 'kept secret from the Governing Body of the Hall and (as I learn) from certain members of the M.M.T. themselves.'

621 In any case, she was old and frail; she might well die before the question of repayment became pressing.

622 Principal of Oak Hill College, Southgate, a conservative Evangelical.

623 To make this possible, Chavasse himself was willing to resign from the patronage.

624 The letter ended: 'The fact is, St. Peter's Hall cannot carry on its back a debt of £47,000 and the Martyrs Memorial Trust.'

625 28 November 1935, Hinde to C.M.C. . . . 'I am at your service, but I would like to say that unless you are fully determined to remain there for the rest of your days, you ought to be one of the four trustees, and I should be sorry if I took your place on it, I feel this rather strongly. . . .'
29 November 1935, C.M.C. to Hinde: . . . 'I am overjoyed . . . As regards myself, I am a younger man; and I hope that if ever I had to move from St. Peter's – which is, to me, an unthinkable and distressing prospect – I might be co-opted some day to fill a vacancy on the Trusteeship of the Hall. But at the moment I am not going to give anyone any grounds for saying that I wrenched the power over St. Peter's Hall out of the hands of the M.M.T. in order to hold it myself. As long as I remain Master, I wish to be the humble servant of the Trustees and Council of the Hall.'

626 4 November 1935, C.M.C. to Chilton.

627 Robbins was perhaps perturbed by the thought that if the M.M.T. title to the advowson of St. Peter-le-Bailey were proved defective, questions might be raised about the title to some of their other advowsons.

628 23 December 1935, Chilton to C.M.C.
Cp. 25 December 1935, C.M.C. to Chilton: 'You will find the Martyrs [sic] will delay and waste our time – that is their policy . . . They have to be pushed and pushed hard – then they crumple.'

629 Present: Chavasse, Adair, Dowdall, Legge, Livingstone, Oman, Pickard-Cambridge, Taylor, Walker.

630 This was presumably the case of Ashford v. Warrington, in its earliest stages.

631 17 February 1936, Adair to C.M.C. He added: 'How extraordinarily slowly things move sometimes!'

632 13 February 1936, Neill to C.M.C.

633 30 January 1936, Chilton to C.M.C.

634 Captain Henry Linton (the surviving executor of Canon Linton), Miss P. M. Linton, Mrs. L. L. Maude-Roxby, Mrs. O. H. Montgomery, Miss I. S. Linton.

635 Chavasse and Chilton were becoming wary in their relations with Mr. Robbins. On 7 March 1936, in a private note, Chilton had told Chavasse: 'I have had a talk with Robbins . . . I don't rely on him a bit.'

636 6 April 1936, Neill to C.M.C.: 'I am doing my best . . . I am sure that you realise that my position is not an easy one.'

637 Chancery Division. Between C. M. Chavasse, J. R. S. Taylor and J. G. Legge, Plaintiffs and Lord Gisborough, H. Foster Pegg & H. B. Greene, Defendants. Plaintiffs claim a declaration that the advowson is not subject to any trusts created or declared by the various indentures and instruments.

638 i.e. in an Appeal. Gisborough Estates Ltd., a private company formed in 1922 to relieve Lord Gisborough of tax, had just been compulsorily wound up, at the instance of the Income Tax authorities. The Gisborough iron-mines had closed as a result of the slump about 1930, and Lord Gisborough's income from debentures had dried up.

639 14 May 1936, Adair to C.M.C.: 'We had a Martyrs Memorial Trust Meeting yesterday. The Council dealt with the question of my resignation of Trusteeship. They definitely accepted it and Mr. Robbins was directed to take the necessary legal steps . . . I resign that Trusteeship with a clear conscience.'

640 It would have been more accurate to say that Robbins represented them only in their capacity of Trustees of the M.M.T.

641 On 22 May 1936 Chavasse had complained to Adair about Robbins' holding up the deed of resignation . . . 'I have a letter waiting to go to Prebendary Hinde, asking him to become a Trustee in your place, as we promised. We will certainly fulfil our agreement, and Prebendary Hinde is waiting to come on our Governing Body. . . .'

642 Robbins, Olivey and Lake to Markby, Stewart and Wadesons.

643 Robbins and Co. had so far declined to accept service of the writ on behalf of their clients.

644 26 June 1936, Markby, Stewart and Wadesons to Robbins, Olivey and Lake . . . 'The position is that our clients must have an Order of Court to the effect that the Advowson is vested in them . . . but if they are not put to unnecessary expense by the action of any of the defendants they will not ask for any costs. We maintain our contention that you have no right to retain the Deed of Retirement

by Lord Gisborough . . . such deed having nothing whatever to do with the proceedings in the above-mentioned action. . . .'

645 He had looked up Crockford because Pearman Smith had sent in a bill for the resignation of Warrington from the Trusteeship of Tarleton (C.M.C. to Neill, 12 February 1936).

646 ? Lord Gisborough.

647 27 December 1936, Fletcher to C.M.C.
10 February 1937, R. Clayton to Markby, Stewart and Wadesons.

648 16 March 1935, S. Pearman Smith and Sons to Markby, Stewart and Wadesons.

649 The only purpose of this policy must have been to conceal that the advowsons were controlled by the M.M.T. Cp. C.M.C. to Bishop Knox (19 July 1936): . . . 'I do not think that you, as a Bishop, would ever have countenanced their habitual practice of buying livings on false pretences – a practice which, as you know, became such a scandal that it led to special legislation in the National Assembly.'

650 Cp. 24 February 1936, Pickard-Cambridge to C.M.C.: 'The arrangement which is being made by the Schools who hold Livings . . . is that [those] who were mainly paid for by the M.M.T. shall be re-conveyed to the Trust. . . .'

651 12 February 1936, C.M.C. to Neill.

652 20 February 1936, Robbins to C.M.C.

653 Chavasse had told Neill that there was no ordinary meeting of the Council until 29 June, but offered to call a special one if necessary.

654 26 February 1936, C.M.C. to Chilton: . . . 'Mr. Robbins' last letter . . . makes me wonder whether the sale of Tarleton is going through, and that the Martyrs Memorial hope quietly to pouch the money.'

655 The living of Tarleton was not in itself a desirable one, by worldly standards. Robbins would see no reason why St. Peter's should be anxious to retain it. He probably underestimated the tenacity of Chavasse.

656 26 June 1936, Markby, Stewart and Wadesons to Robbins, Olivey and Lake.

657 Lord Gisborough died on 23 January 1938, aged 81. He left unsettled estate of gross value £2,369, net personalty nil.

658 The plan being that there would in future be only four Trustees of the Hall, and these four would also be the patrons of St. Peter-le-Bailey.

659 Inskip had been Solicitor-General 1922-23, 1924-28, 1931-32; Attorney-General 1928-29, 1932-36. From 1936 to 1939 he was Minister for Co-ordination of Defence. In 1928 he had been one of the chief opponents of the proposed new Prayer Book. In 1936 he was aged 60.

660 Here Chavasse spoke more truly than he knew.

661 Yet while trying to get the former Trustees to resign, Chavasse had stressed that it was essential to have Trustees who could spend time and trouble on the affairs of the Hall, and had pointed out that they were personally liable for debts; this would not be so under the revised Trust Deed, but that had not yet been executed.

662 Present: Chavasse, Dowdall, Legge, Livingstone, Nuffield, Oman, Pickard-Cambridge, Taylor, Walker.

663 Several members of the Morris family had been invited – Mr. & Mrs. Yockney, Mr. & Mrs. Rawlence, Miss Anstey, Mrs. J. H.

Hawes. The occasion was marked by a judicious blending of the stately academic and the homely personal.

664 Nuffield instructed Hobbs to send on Gillett's letter in confidence to Chavasse. There was nothing at all improper in the letter (he described Chavasse as 'a first rate fellow'), but Hobbs remarked: 'Personally, I cannot help thinking that Gillett shows rather doubtful taste in approaching Lord Nuffield on such a subject . . . but these Bankers are strange people and their ways are often odd.' (Hobbs to C.M.C. 30 July 1935).

665 2 August 1935, Hobbs to C.M.C., in his own handwriting.

666 Honorary degrees were also conferred on Cardinal Seredi, Anthony Eden, Field-Marshal Chetwode, Professor Adrian, Gilbert Murray and E. V. Lucas. But E. M. Walker 'got the warmest cheer of all' (E.H.F.S., Diary).

667 Often given in private to his friends, and repeated publicly in his speech at the first St. Peter's Gaudy on 26 June 1947.

668 C.M.C. to Nuffield, 25 June 1936. In his own handwriting, and no copy kept in the files. Original found among Nuffield's papers, and photostat copy communicated to Sir Alec Cairncross by the Warden of Nuffield College.

669 He could not have foreseen that a year later Nuffield would give the University the site between St. Peter's and New Road, with a sum of £900,000 for the building and endowment of Nuffield College.

670 Present: Chavasse, Legge, Livingstone, Oman, Walker.

671 15 July 1936, C.M.C. to Hobbs.

672 This would be the Seventh Annual Report, 1934-35. The Eighth Report was not ready for distribution till the autumn of 1936.

673 His other letters were in his own writing. He used the old style of writing 's' as 'f' in words like message (mefsage).

674 One of his two daughters.

675 During Bishop Knox's lifetime, 1847-1937, building societies had not been so carefully regulated as they were afterwards, and he knew about certain smashes. With these in mind, he stated that Warrington 'ran the Trust on the most reckless building society principles.'

676 A well known Evangelical theologian.

677 *Reminiscences of an Octogenarian*, published 1935.

678 He had demonstrated this in his study of *The Tractarian Movement, 1833-1845*, published 1933.

679 John Bradford 1510-55. On seeing some felons led to execution.

680 A.C. = Anglo-Catholic.

681 It was probably about this time that Chavasse mentioned to E.H.F.S. that the thing which impressed him most about Bishop Knox, that fervent adversary of Rome and the Romish, was that he retained the constant affection of his sons Ronald and Wilfred, though Ronald became a Roman Catholic Monsignor and Wilfred a distinguished Anglo-Catholic priest.

682 On 6 November 1937 Warrington sent to J. G. Legge a copy of a 26 page duplicated letter addressed to 'All Members of the Martyrs Memorial and Church of England Trust.' In this letter Warrington made fantastic charges against Neill and most of his old colleagues. He even claimed that in 1932 one member of his own staff had been

'approached by two Secret Agents' and offered £1,000 if he would make a false charge against his employer.

683   14 May 1936, Adair to C.M.C. 'I wish to thank you one and all for your kindness to me . . . My few years have been very happy in the precincts of St. Peter's Hall. . . .'

684   Adair's last letter to C.M.C. as Master was on 19 February 1937, about a proposal to procure a portrait of Lord Nuffield 'If he would add to his benefactions by a substantial gift to the Martyrs Memorial Trust, I should have pleasure in subscribing . . . but as matters are at present, I fear I must refuse.'

Adair died in November 1946, aged 83.

685   On 9 October 1936 Chilton had forwarded to C.M.C. a letter from Robbins suggesting that the Hall should give up any claim to the Tarleton Advowson in return for Mr. Greene's signature to the transfers. Chilton commented: 'You will see that they are playing the same game as they tried in the case of the Trusteeship of the Hall and of the Advowson of St. Peter-le-Bailey, and I think we may take their letter, therefore, as a sign of weakness.'

686   Present: Chavasse, Dowdall, Hinde, Legge, Linton Smith, Livingstone, Oman, Taylor, Walker.

687   29 July 1936, C.M.C. to Chilton; 30 July, R. H. Bowdler to Chilton.

688   30 July 1936, Chilton to C.M.C.

689   13 July 1937, Chilton sent C.M.C. copies of letters supplied by Mr. H. Fletcher. These letters, dated between 23 April 1930 and 4 July 1930, were from W. Pearman Smith and Sons to H. Fletcher; they made it quite clear that Fletcher was being asked to convey the Advowson to St. Peter's Hall.

690   12 February 1937, Chilton to C.M.C. . . . 'Messrs. Robbins, Olivey and Lake are adopting a rather high tone to the effect that the Trustees [of S.P.H.] can take any action they think fit.'

691   27 November 1937, Linton Smith to C.M.C.

692   29 March 1938, Chilton to C.M.C.

693   21 April 1938, Clayton to Markby, Stewart and Wadesons.

      28 April 1938, Chilton to C.M.C.

694   28 May 1937, H. Fletcher to Markby, Stewart and Wadesons.

      13 July 1937, Chilton to C.M.C.

      2 December 1937, H. Fletcher to C.M.C.

695   29 June 1938, C.M.C. to H. Fletcher.

696   The original Trust Deed of St. Peter's Hall.

697   The deed by which the Trustees of Hannington Hall (W. Talbot Rice, Bishop Knox and T. W. Ketchlee, formerly rector of St. Aldates) conveyed Hannington Hall to Stather Hunt, Gisborough, King Harman and Warrington.

698   On 13 December 1897 there was an Indenture made between W. Talbot Rice and F. J. Chavasse (who had purchased Hannington Hall from Balliol on 27 January 1896) and themselves plus Sir John Kennaway, Canon Christopher, R. B. Girdlestone and Bishop Knox. On 14 December 1897 these same six persons made a Deed Poll, here referred to.

699   30 January 1936, C.M.C. to Chilton: . . . 'Whatever else we do, it will be necessary to remedy this state of things immediately.'

700   Mr. Humphrey King had given an opinion that 'the transfer . . . though a breach of trust, was effective to pass the legal estate.'

701 Present: Chavasse, Dowdall, Hinde, Legge, Linton Smith, Oman, Pickard-Cambridge, Taylor, Walker.

702 In fact it proved that no Royal Charter was needed for the transition from Hall to New Foundation.

703 Present: Chavasse, Dowdall, Hinde, Legge, Linton Smith, Livingstone, Pickard-Cambridge, Taylor.

704 The main entry to the church, until 1928, was on the south side, from this path.

705 12 March 1937, Linton Smith to C.M.C.

706 5 April 1937, Chilton to C.M.C.

6 April 1937, C.M.C. to Chilton: . . . 'There will be no difficulty with the University Authorities. St. Peter-le-Bailey Church bites into the property of St. Peter's Hall, and it does not matter whether this bite is confined to the Church building or also includes the path along the south side of the Church.'

707 Present: Chavase, Legge, Linton Smith, Livingstone, Oman, Walker.

708 28 May 1937, Chilton to C.M.C. Wykes had told Chilton 'that he was not in a position now to exercise any kind of influence upon Warrington . . . he had acted in the recent proceedings of Ashford v. Warrington, for the third parties, and that Mr. Warrington's counter-claim against the Martyrs Memorial had been knocked out and judgement went against Warrington. Mr. Wykes also told me that Warrington had managed to pay this judgement off, or at least to pay sufficient to stave off bankruptcy . . . he knew of other proceedings being threatened. . . .'

709 Reported to the Council, 30 January 1937.

710 31 May 1937, C.M.C. to Chilton, agreeing that Robbins should be approached.

711 Present: Chavasse, Dowdall, Hinde, Linton Smith, Livingstone, Oman, Pickard-Cambridge, Taylor, Walker.

712 Present: Chavasse, Legge, Oman, Walker.

713 Present: Chavasse, Hinde, Legge, Linton Smith, Livingstone, Oman, Taylor, Walker.

714 The Fund was to be administered by the Rector of St. Peter-le-Bailey and the Principal of Wycliffe Hall, both ex officio, plus four representative trustees appointed from time to time by the Council of St. Peter's Hall.

715 Pro hac vice, i.e. on that particular occasion only, not permanently.

716 He was accordingly raised to the peerage as Viscount Caldecote. He held office as Lord Chancellor for only a few months. In 1940 he became Lord Chief Justice. He retired in 1946, and died in 1947, at the age of 71.

717 Trust Deed Cap. III, s. 3(b).

718 Present: C. E. Tinne (Acting Master), Legge, Livingstone, Oman, Pickard-Cambridge, Taylor, Walker. Chavasse was in hospital in Northern Ireland at this time.

719 T. D. was held up in Jerusalem for a year, and did not in fact become Master until October 1940.

Index

Note: the newspaper Index is to be found on page 301.